DEDICATION

For Rachelle, Simon, and Adrienne.

—KS

ACKNOWLEDGMENTS

This project could not have been completed without the assistance, support, guidance, mentorship, and friendship of many people. First, I would like to thank Drs. Thomas Ingram and Raymond Laforge for their initial support and faith in me as I embarked on this project. I would also like to thank my research assistant, Katie Guiney. Your hard work and dedication allowed this project to succeed, and for that, I thank you. I also wish to thank Darragh McManamon. Your advice and legal expertise helped with several chapters of the text. A big thank-you also goes to Suzanne Simpson Millar for keeping me on track every step of the way. Dawn Hunter also deserves a special note of thanks for her superb editing. A special note of appreciation is also extended to Nelson Education Inc., and especially to Amie Plourde and Imoinda Romain for their dedication to the project. And thank you to Dr. Alan Bush, whose ongoing support has guided me through my career. Finally, for her unwavering support and invaluable advice, I thank my wife, best friend, and research partner, Dr. Rachelle Shannahan.

—KS

BRIEF CONTENTS

FOR STUDENTS

Over the past four years we have spent time in classrooms across Canada, speaking to students just like you.

We've asked what you want to see in a textbook, how you learn, how many hours a week you spend online, and what you find most valuable when preparing for a test. Based on your feedback, we've developed a new hybrid learning solution—*SELL*. Your textbook, the Chapter Review cards, Continuing Case cards, and the online resources found at **www.sell.nelson.com** present a new, exciting, and fresh approach to learning. Check out the website for great tools like:

- Interactive quizzing
- Interactive e-book
- Flashcards
- Games
- Glossary
- PowerPoint notes
- Role-play videos
- **And more!**

NELSON EDUCATION

SELL, First Canadian Edition

by Thomas N. Ingram; Raymond W. LaForge; Ramon A. Avila; Charles H. Schwepker, Jr.; Michael R. Williams; and Kirby L. J. Shannahan

Vice President, Editorial Higher Education:
Anne Williams

Executive Editor:
Amie Plourde

Marketing Manager:
David Stratton

Developmental Editor:
Suzanne Simpson Millar

Photo Researcher/ Permissions Coordinator:
Carrie McGregor

Senior Content Production Manager:
Imoinda Romain

Production Service:
MPS Limited, a Macmillan Company

Copy Editor:
Dawn Hunter

Proofreader:
Jennifer A. McIntyre

Indexer:
Edwin Durbin

Manufacturing Manager:
Joanne McNeil

Design Director:
Ken Phipps

Managing Designer:
Franca Amore

Interior Design:
Joe Devine, Red Hangar Design

Cover Design:
Johanna Liburd

Cover Image:
Debbie Yea/Nelson Education Ltd.

Compositor:
MPS Limited, a Macmillan Company

Printer:
R.R. Donnelley

Library and Archives Canada Cataloguing in Publication

SELL / Thomas N. Ingram . . . [et al.].—1st Canadian ed.

Includes bibliographical references and index.
ISBN 978-0-17-650436-6

1. Selling—Textbooks. 2. Sales management—Textbooks. I. Ingram, Thomas N

HF5438.25.S44 2012   658.85
C2011-905732-8

ISBN 13: 978-0-17-650436-6
ISBN 10: 0-17-650436-2

CONTENTS

1 Overview of Personal Selling 2

© SAMI SARKIS/PHOTOGRAPHER'S CHOICE/GETTY IMAGES

2 Building Trust and Sales Ethics 32

3 Understanding Buyers 56

© VAL DODGE

4 Communication Skills 92

© MIKE KEMP/JUPITERIMAGES

5 Strategic Prospecting and Preparing for Sales Dialogue 118

6 Planning Sales Dialogues and Presentations 136

© MM PRODUCTIONS/CORBIS/JUPITERIMAGES

7 Sales Dialogue: Creating and Communicating Value 160

8 Addressing Concerns and Earning Commitment 184

9 Expanding Customer Relationships 204

10 Adding Value: Self-Leadership and Teamwork 226

11 Sales Management and Sales 2.0 252

To succeed in sales,

talk *with* the customer, not *at* the customer

what do you think?

Successful salespeople must be very aggressive in their attempts to convince buyers to make purchases.

1 2 3 4 5 6 7

strongly disagree   strongly agree

I

Overview of Personal Selling

After completing this chapter, you should be able to

LO1 Define personal selling and describe its unique characteristics as a marketing communications tool.

LO2 Distinguish between transaction-focused traditional selling and trust-based relationship selling, with the latter focusing on customer value and sales dialogue.

LO3 Describe the evolution of personal selling from ancient times to the modern era.

LO4 Explain the contributions of personal selling to society, business firms, and customers.

LO5 Discuss five alternative approaches to personal selling.

LO6 Understand the sales process as a series of interrelated steps.

Introduction

In recent years there has been a profound evolutionary shift in the way goods and services are sold. Today, customers are far more educated and sophisticated, with access to more information than ever before. And we all operate in an expanding global economy, facing intensified competition in almost every industry and sector. Therefore, historic approaches to sales are no longer effective.

Until recently, we all believed that the fundamental role of sales representatives was to get people to buy your product or service. But today, we finally realize that the single biggest key to sales success is to actually stop selling altogether. In today's marketplace, people (at home and in business) don't want to be "sold." In fact, they resist it strongly. Instead, customers want to "buy" independently, or work with business "partners." In order to succeed, we must break the historical push-pull dance that happens between salespeople and customers (sales tries to convince, and customers try to resist).

Today, professional selling requires a completely different approach than historically employed. It involves shifting focus away from what *you* want (the sale) and instead becoming entirely focused on the *customer*. Sales professionals must now adopt a truly value-based approach, whereby their mission is to add as much value as possible to the customer's bottom-line.

The Canadian Professional Sales Association (CPSA) is one of the oldest associations in Canada. It was officially incorporated as a fraternal benefits society known as the Commercial Travellers Association by a special act of Parliament in 1874. In 1991 the association changed its name to the Canadian Professional Sales Association and updated its mission "to be the leader in developing and serving sales professionals."

Today the CPSA boasts a membership of 30,000 across Canada and has four key areas of focus: (1) developing salespeople through its comprehensive suite of offline and online sales training and coaching programs; (2) certifying sales people through Canada's only government-endorsed designation: CSP, Certified Sales Professional; (3) providing extensive sales resources for members through its online Knowledge Centre; and (4) offering a comprehensive member benefit cost-saving program, the hallmark of which is its business travel cost saving program for hotel stays, car rentals, and other related travel services.

—Harvey Copeman, President and CEO of CPSA

LO1
Personal Selling Defined

the successful professional salesperson is likely a better listener than a talker; is oriented more toward developing long-term relationships with customers than using high-pressure, short-term sales techniques; and has the skills and patience to endure lengthy, complex sales processes. Today's salesperson strives to deliver relevant presentations based on unique customer needs, and meeting those needs requires teamwork between salespeople and others in the organization.

Personal selling, an important part of marketing, relies heavily on interpersonal interactions between buyers and sellers to initiate, develop, and enhance customer relationships. The interpersonal communications dimension sets personal selling apart from other marketing communications, such as advertising and sales promotion, which are directed at mass markets. Personal selling is also distinguished from direct marketing and electronic marketing in that salespeople are talking with buyers before, during, and after the sale. This contact allows for a high degree of immediate customer feedback, which becomes a strong advantage of personal selling over most other forms of marketing communications.

Although advertising is a far more visible activity, personal selling is the most important part of marketing communications for most businesses. This is particularly true in business-to-business marketing, in which more is spent on personal selling than on advertising, sales promotion, publicity, or public relations. In this book, we typically describe personal selling in this business-to-business context, in which a salesperson or sales team interacts with one or more individuals from another organization.

> **personal selling** An important part of marketing that relies heavily on interpersonal interactions between buyers and sellers to initiate, develop, and enhance customer relationships.
>
> **trust-based relationship selling** A form of personal selling that requires that salespeople earn customer trust and that their selling strategy meets customer needs and contributes to the creation, communication, and delivery of customer value.
>
> **customer value** The customers' perception of what they get for what they have to give up, for example, benefits from buying a product in exchange for money paid.

LO2
Trust-Based Relationship Selling

trust-based relationship selling (a form of personal selling) requires that salespeople earn customer trust and that their selling strategy meets customer needs and contributes to the creation, communication, and delivery of customer value. As illustrated in Exhibit 1.1, trust-based relationship selling is quite different from traditional selling. Rather than trying to maximize sales in the short run (also called a transaction focus), trust-based relationship selling focuses on solving customer problems, providing opportunities, and adding value to the customer's business over an extended period. Chapter 2 will provide detailed coverage of how salespeople can earn buyers' trust.

IMPORTANCE OF CUSTOMER VALUE

As personal selling continues to evolve, it is more important than ever that salespeople focus on delivering customer value while initiating, developing, and enhancing customer relationships. What constitutes value will likely vary from one customer to the next depending on the customer's situation, needs, and priorities, but **customer value** will always be determined by customers' perception of what they get in exchange for what they have to give up. In the simplest situations, customers buy a product in exchange for money. In most situations, however, customers define value in a more complex manner, by addressing such questions as these:

- Does the salesperson do a good job in helping me make or save money?
- Is this salesperson dependable?
- Does this salesperson help me achieve my strategic priorities?
- Is the salesperson's company easy to work with, that is, hassle-free?
- Does the salesperson enlist others in his or her organization when needed to create value for me?
- Does the sales representative understand my business and my industry?

Personal selling also recognizes that customers would like to be heard when expressing what they

EXHIBIT 1.1

Comparison of Transaction-Focused Traditional Selling with Trust-Based Relationship Selling

	Transaction-Focused Traditional Selling	Trust-Based Relationship Selling
Typical skills required	Selling skills, e.g., finding prospects, making sales presentations	Selling skills Information gathering Listening and questioning Strategic problem solving Creating and demonstrating unique, value-added solutions Teambuilding and teamwork
Primary focus	The salesperson and the selling firm	The customer and the customer's customers
Desired outcomes	Closed sales, order volume	Trust, joint planning, mutual benefits, enhanced profits
Role of salesperson	Make calls and close sales	Business consultant and long-term ally Key player in the customer's business
Nature of communications with customers	One-way, from salesperson to customer Pushing products	Two-way and collaborative Strive for dialogue with the customer
Degree of salesperson's involvement in customer's decision-making process	Isolated from customer's decision-making process	Actively involved in customer's decision-making process
Knowledge required	Product knowledge Competitive knowledge Identifying opportunities Account strategies	Product knowledge Selling company resources Competitive knowledge Identifying opportunities General business and industry knowledge and insight Customer's products, competition, and customers Account strategies Costs
Postsale follow-up	Little or none: move on to conquer next customer	Continued follow-through to • ensure customer satisfaction • keep customer informed • add customer value • manage opportunities

Successful salespeople must be able to make sales presentations, but they must also be able to engage customers in sales dialogue, or business conversations that build customer relationships.

© JANET KIMBER/GETTY IMAGES

a productive dialogue with customers than in simply pitching products that customers may or may not want or need. In our highly competitive world, professional buyers have little tolerance for aggressive, pushy salespeople.

IMPORTANCE OF SALES DIALOGUE

Sales dialogue refers to the series of conversations between buyers and sellers that take place over time in an attempt to build relationships. These conversations have several purposes:

- To determine whether a prospective customer should be targeted for further sales attention
- To clarify the prospective customer's situation and buying processes
- To discover the prospective customer's unique needs and requirements
- To determine the prospective customer's strategic priorities
- To communicate how the sales organization can create and deliver customer value
- To negotiate a business deal and earn a commitment from the customer
- To make the customer aware of additional opportunities to increase the value received
- To assess sales organization and salesperson performance so that customer value is continually improved

As you can see, sales dialogue is far more than idle chitchat. The business conversations that constitute the dialogue are customer-focused and have a clear purpose; otherwise, there would be a high probability of wasting both the customer's and the salesperson's time, which no one can afford in today's business environment.

Whether the sales dialogue features a question-and-answer format, a conversation dominated by the buyer conveying information and requirements, or a formal sales presentation in which the salesperson responds to buyer feedback throughout, the key idea is that both parties participate in and benefit from the process.

Throughout this course, you will learn about new technologies and techniques that have contributed to the evolution of the practice of personal selling. This chapter provides an overview of personal selling,

Customers want to be heard loud and clear when expressing what they want from suppliers and salespeople.

want suppliers and salespeople to provide for them. In days gone by, personal selling often consisted of delivering a message or making a pitch. That approach was typically associated with a "product push" strategy in which customers were pressured to buy without much appreciation for their real needs. Today, sales organizations are far more interested in establishing

sales dialogue Business conversations between buyers and sellers that occur as salespeople attempt to initiate, develop, and enhance customer relationships. Sales dialogue should be customer focused and have a clear purpose.

affording insight into the operating rationale of today's salespeople and sales managers. It also describes different approaches to personal selling and presents the sales process as a series of interrelated steps. The appendix at the end of the chapter discusses several important aspects of sales careers, including types of selling jobs and characteristics and skills needed for sales success. In the highly competitive, complex international business community, personal selling and sales management have never played more critical roles.

LO3
Evolution of Personal Selling

ancient Greek history documents selling as an exchange activity, and the term *salesman* appears in the writings of Plato.[1] However, true salespeople—those who earned a living only by selling—did not exist in any sizable number until the Industrial Revolution in England, from the mid-eighteenth century to the mid-nineteenth century. Before this time, traders, merchants, and artisans filled the selling function. These predecessors of contemporary marketers were generally viewed with contempt because deception was often used in the sale of goods.[2]

In the later phase of the Middle Ages, the first door-to-door salesperson appeared in the form of the peddler. Peddlers collected produce from local farmers, sold it to townspeople, and, in turn, bought manufactured goods in town for subsequent sale in rural areas.[3] Like many other early salespeople, they performed other important marketing functions, too—in this case, purchasing, assembling, sorting, and redistributing goods.

INDUSTRIAL REVOLUTION ERA

With the onset of the Industrial Revolution in the middle of the eighteenth century, the economic justification for salespeople gained momentum. Local economies were no longer self sufficient, and as intercity and international trade began to flourish, economies of scale in production spurred the growth of mass markets in geographically dispersed areas. The continual need to reach new customers in these dispersed markets called for an increasing number of salespeople.

POST-INDUSTRIAL REVOLUTION ERA

By the early nineteenth century, personal selling was well established in England but just beginning to develop in North America.[4] This situation changed noticeably after 1850, and by the later part of the century, salespeople were a well-established part of business practice.

At the dawning of the twentieth century, an exciting time in the economic history of North America, it became apparent that marketing, especially advertising and personal selling, would play a crucial role in the rapid transition of the economy from an agrarian base to one of mass production and efficient transportation.

Glimpses of the lives of salespeople in the early 1900s, gained from the literature of that period, reveal an adventuresome, aggressive, and valuable group of employees often working on the frontier of new markets. Already, however, the independent maverick salespeople who had blazed the early trails to new markets were beginning to disappear. One clear indication that selling was becoming a more structured activity was the development of a **canned sales presentation** by John H. Patterson, of the National Cash Register Company (NCR). This presentation, a script to guide NCR salespeople on how to sell cash registers, was based on the premise that salespeople are not "born, but rather they are made."[5]

WAR AND DEPRESSION ERA

The 30 years from 1915 to 1945 were marked by three overwhelming events: two world wars and the Great Depression. Because economic activity concentrated on the war efforts, new sales methods did not develop quickly. During the Great Depression, however, business firms, starved for sales volume, often employed aggressive salespeople to produce badly needed revenue. Then, with renewed prosperity in the post–World War II era, salespeople emerged as important employees for an increasing number of firms that were beginning to realize the benefits of research-based integrated marketing programs.

PROFESSIONALISM: THE MODERN ERA

In the middle of the 1940s, personal selling became more professional. Not only did buyers begin to demand more, but they also grew

canned sales presentation Sales presentations that include scripted sales calls, memorized presentations, and automated presentations.

Sales is becoming more professional as indicated by a growing knowledge base with publications and training material available from academics, corporate trainers and sales executives, and professional organizations.

intolerant of high-pressure, fast-talking salespeople, preferring instead a well-informed, customer-oriented salesperson.

An emphasis on **sales professionalism** is the keynote of the current era. The term has varied meanings, but in this context we use it to mean a customer-oriented approach that uses truthful, nonmanipulative tactics to satisfy the long-term needs of both the customer and the selling firm. The effective salesperson of today is no longer a mere presenter of information and now must stand equipped to respond to a variety of customer needs before, during, and after the sale. In addition, salespeople must be able to work effectively with others in their organizations to meet or exceed customer expectations.

Although many business-to-business salespeople have considerable decision-making autonomy, others have

sales professionalism A customer-oriented approach that uses truthful, nonmanipulative tactics to satisfy the long-term needs of both the customer and the selling firm.

very little. Public trust could be improved by a widely accepted certification program similar to the CA or CMA designations for accountants. At present, however, very few salespeople have professional certification credentials, and public trust in certification programs is modest. Thus, the results are mixed as to whether the sales profession meets this professional criterion.

The final area in which sales needs to improve is in adherence to a uniform ethical code. Although many companies have ethical codes and some professional organizations have ethical codes for salespeople, there is no universal code of ethics with a mechanism for dealing with violators. Until such a code is developed and widely accepted in business, some members of society will not view sales as a true profession.

Whether or not sales is viewed as a true profession, comparable to law and medicine, salespeople can benefit tremendously from embracing high ethical standards, participating in professional organizations, and working from a continually evolving knowledge base. In so doing, they will not only be more effective but will also help advance sales as a true profession.

Evolution is inevitable as tomorrow's professional salesperson responds to a more complex, dynamic environment. And the increased sophistication of buyers and of new technologies will demand more from the next generation of salespeople. Exhibit 1.1 summarizes some of the likely events of the future.*,[6]

LO4
Contributions of Personal Selling

as mentioned earlier in this chapter, more money is spent on personal selling than on any other form of marketing communications. Salespeople are usually well compensated, and salesforces of major companies often number in the thousands. For example, Microsoft has 16,000 salespeople, American Express has 23,000, and Pepsico has 36,000.[7]

We now take a look at how this investment is justified by reviewing the contributions of personal selling to society in general, to the employing firm, and to customers.

---

*Page 7–8: From INGRAM/LAFORGE/AVILA/SCHWEPKER. *Professional Selling*, 4E. © 2008 South-Western, a part of Cengage Learning. Reproduced by permission. www.cengage.com/permissions.

EXHIBIT 1.2
Continued Evolution of Personal Selling

Change	Salesforce Response
Intensified competition	More emphasis on developing and maintaining trust-based, long-term customer relationships
	More focus on creating and delivering customer value
More emphasis on improving sales productivity	Increased use of technology (e.g., laptop computers, electronic mail, databases, customer relationship management software)
	Increased use of lower-cost-per-contact methods (e.g., telemarketing for some customers)
	More emphasis on profitability (e.g., gross margin) objectives
Fragmentation of traditional customer bases	Sales specialists for specific customer types
	Multiple sales channels (e.g., major accounts programs, telemarketing, electronic networks)
	Globalization of sales efforts
Customers dictating quality standards and inventory/shipping procedures to be met by vendors	Team selling
	Salesforce compensation sometimes based on customer satisfaction and team performance
	More emphasis on sales dialogues rather than on sales pitches
Demand for in-depth, specialized knowledge as an input to purchase decisions	Team selling
	More emphasis on customer-oriented sales training

SALESPEOPLE AND SOCIETY

Salespeople contribute to their nations' economic growth in two basic ways: They act as stimuli for economic transactions, and they further the diffusion of innovation.

Salespeople as Economic Stimuli

Salespeople are expected to stimulate action in the business world—hence the term **economic stimuli**. In a fluctuating economy, salespeople make valuable contributions by assisting in recovery cycles and helping to sustain periods of relative prosperity. As the world economic system deals with such issues as increased globalization of business, more emphasis on customer satisfaction, and building competitiveness through quality improvement programs, it is expected that salespeople will be recognized as a key force in executing the appropriate strategies and tactics necessary for survival and growth.

Salespeople and Diffusion of Innovation

Salespeople play a critical role in the **diffusion of innovation**, the process whereby new products, services, and ideas are distributed to the members of society. Consumers who are likely to be early adopters of an innovation often rely on salespeople as a primary source of information. Frequently, well-informed, specialized salespeople provide useful information to potential consumers who then purchase from a lower-cost outlet. The role of salespeople in the diffusion of industrial products and services is particularly crucial. Imagine trying to purchase a companywide computer system without the assistance of a competent salesperson or sales team!

While acting as an agent of innovation, the salesperson invariably encounters a strong resistance to change in the later stages of the diffusion process. The status quo seems to be extremely satisfactory to many parties, even though, in the long run, change is necessary for continued progress or survival. By encouraging the adoption of innovative products and services, salespeople may indeed be making a positive contribution to society.

economic stimuli Something that stimulates or incites activity in the economy.

diffusion of innovation The process whereby new products, services, and ideas are distributed to the members of society.

SALESPEOPLE AND THE EMPLOYING FIRM

Because salespeople are in direct contact with the all-important customer, they can make valuable contributions to their employers. Salespeople contribute to their firms as revenue producers, as sources of market research and feedback, and as candidates for management positions.

Salespeople as Revenue Producers

Salespeople occupy the somewhat unique role of **revenue producers** in their firms. Consequently, they usually feel the brunt of that pressure along with the managers in the firm. Although accountants and financial staff are concerned with profitability in bottom-line terms, salespeople are constantly reminded of their responsibility to achieve a healthy "top line" on the profit and loss statement. This should not suggest that salespeople are concerned only with sales revenue and not with overall profitability. Indeed, salespeople are increasingly responsible for improving profitability, not only by producing sales revenues but also by improving the productivity of their actions.

Market Research and Feedback

Because salespeople spend so much time in direct contact with their customers, it is only logical that they would play an important role in market research and in providing feedback to their firms. For example, entertainment and home products retailer Best Buy relies heavily on feedback from its sales associates in what it calls a customer-centricity initiative, which places the customer at the centre of its marketing strategy. Feedback from sales associates helps Best Buy offer tailored products to specific customer segments, design appealing in-store merchandising formats, increase sales volume for in-home services, and improve the effectiveness of customer-support call centre. Results of the customer-centricity program have been so positive that Best Buy is rapidly increasing the number of participating stores as it tries to fend off Wal-Mart and other major competitors.[8]

> Along with the management of a firm, salespeople occupy the somewhat unique role of revenue producers in their firms.

revenue producers A role fulfilled by salespeople that brings in revenue or income to a firm or company.

Some would argue that salespeople are not trained as market researchers, or that salespeople's time could be better used than in research and feedback activities. Many firms, however, refute this argument by finding numerous ways to capitalize on the salesforce as a reservoir of ideas. It is not an exaggeration to say that many firms have concluded they cannot afford to operate in the absence of salesforce feedback and research.

Salespeople as Future Managers

In recent years, marketing and sales personnel have been in strong demand for upper management positions. Recognizing the need for a top management trained in sales, many firms use the sales job as an entry-level position that provides a foundation for future assignments. As progressive firms continue to emphasize customer orientation as a basic operating concept, it is only

© HILL STREET STUDIOS/JUPITER IMAGES

natural that salespeople who have learned how to meet customer needs will be good candidates for management jobs.

SALESPEOPLE AND THE CUSTOMER

Given the increasing importance of building trust with customers and an emphasis on establishing and maintaining long-term relationships, it is imperative that salespeople are honest and candid with customers. Salespeople must also be able to demonstrate knowledge of their products and services, especially as they compare competitive offerings. Customers also expect salespeople to be knowledgeable about market opportunities and relevant business trends that may affect a customer's business. There has been a long-standing expectation that salespeople need to be the key contact for the buyer, who expects that they will coordinate activities within the selling firm to deliver maximum value to the customer.

The overall conclusion is that buyers expect salespeople to contribute to the success of the buyer's firm. Buyers value the information furnished by salespeople, and they expect salespeople to act in a highly professional manner.[9] (See "An Ethical Dilemma" for a scenario in which the salesperson must think about where to draw the line in sharing information with customers.)

As salespeople serve their customers, they simultaneously serve their employers and society. When the interests of these two groups conflict, the salesperson can be caught in the middle. By learning to resolve these conflicts as a routine part of their jobs, salespeople further

An Ethical Dilemma

Terry Kelly, sales representative for the computer software company EFAX, has just finished a sales call with Landnet, one of her distributors. During the call, purchasing agent Linda Meyer mentioned that Don Hawkes, Landnet's top salesperson, had suddenly resigned and moved out of the province. Meyer said that this unexpected resignation could not have come at a worse time, as several key customer contracts were pending renewal, and Landnet had no candidates to replace Hawkes. On the way to her next sales call with Netserve, her largest distributor, Kelly debated whether or not to share the news of Hawkes's resignation. After all, the buyer at Netserve viewed Kelly as a great source of market information, and Kelly figured that the Netserve buyer would hear the news anyway before the day was over. What should Kelly do?

© HIDESY/ISTOCKPHOTO

contribute to developing a business system based on progress through problem solving. Sales ethics will be discussed in detail in Chapter 2.

As salespeople serve their customers, they simultaneously serve their employers and society.

LO5
Alternative Personal Selling Approaches

In this section, we take a closer look at alternative approaches to personal selling that professionals may choose from to best interact with their customers. Some of these approaches are simple; others are more sophisticated and require that the salesperson play a strategic role to use them successfully. More than four decades ago, four basic approaches to personal selling were identified: stimulus response, mental states, need satisfaction, and problem solving.[10] Since that time, another approach to personal selling, termed consultative selling, has gained popularity. All five approaches to selling are practised today. Furthermore, many salespeople use elements of more than one approach in their own hybrids of personal selling.

Recall from earlier in the chapter that personal selling differs from other forms of marketing communications because it is personal communication delivered by employees or agents of the sales organization. Because the personal element is present, salespeople have the opportunity to alter their sales messages and behaviours during a sales presentation or as they encounter unique situations and customers. This method is referred to as **adaptive selling**. Because salespeople often encounter buyers with different personalities, communications styles, needs, and goals, adaptive selling is an important concept. Adaptive selling is prevalent with the need satisfaction, problem-solving, and consultative approaches. It is less prevalent with mental states selling and essentially nonexistent with stimulus-response selling.

Adaptive selling requires that salespeople alter their sales messages and behaviours during sales presentations or as they encounter unique sales situations or customers. Selling at a trade show is quite different from selling in a customer's office.

adaptive selling The ability of salespeople to alter their sales messages and behaviours during a sales presentation or as they encounter different sales situations and different customers.

stimulus-response selling An approach to selling in which the key idea is that various stimuli can elicit predictable responses from customers. Salespeople furnish the stimuli from a repertoire of words and actions designed to produce the desired response.

continued affirmation An example of stimulus-response selling in which a series of questions or statements furnished by the salesperson is designed to condition the prospective buyer to answering "yes" time after time, until, it is hoped, he or she will be inclined to say "yes" to the entire sales proposition.

STIMULUS-RESPONSE SELLING

Of the five views of personal selling, **stimulus-response selling** is the simplest. The theoretical background for this approach originated in early experiments with animal behaviour. The key idea is that various stimuli can elicit predictable responses. Salespeople furnish the stimuli from a repertoire of words and actions designed to produce the desired response. This approach to selling is illustrated in Figure 1.1.

An example of the stimulus response view of selling would be **continued affirmation**, a method in which a series of questions or statements furnished by the salesperson is designed to condition the prospective buyer to answering "yes" time after time, until, it is hoped, he or she will be inclined to say "yes" to the entire sales proposition. This method is often used by telemarketing personnel, who rely on comprehensive sales scripts read or delivered from memory.

Stimulus-response sales strategies, particularly when implemented with a canned sales presentation, have some advantages for the seller. The sales message can be structured in a logical order. Questions and objections from the buyer can usually be anticipated and addressed before they are magnified during buyer-seller interaction. Inexperienced salespeople can rely on stimulus-response sales methods in some settings, and this may eventually contribute to sales expertise.

The limitations of stimulus-response methods, however, can be severe, especially if the salesperson is dealing with a professional buyer. Most buyers like to take an active role in sales dialogue, and the stimulus-response approach calls for the salesperson to dominate the flow of conversation. The lack of flexibility in this approach is also a disadvantage, as buyer responses and unforeseen interruptions may neutralize or damage the effectiveness of the stimuli.

FIGURE 1.1
Stimulus-Response Approach to Selling

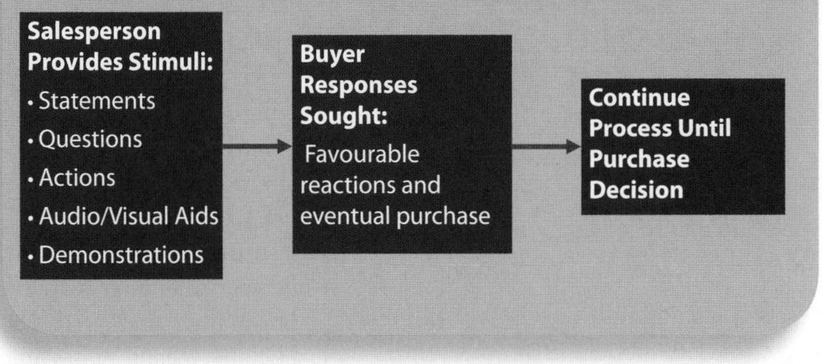

Salesperson Provides Stimuli:
- Statements
- Questions
- Actions
- Audio/Visual Aids
- Demonstrations

→ **Buyer Responses Sought:** Favourable reactions and eventual purchase

→ **Continue Process Until Purchase Decision**

The salesperson attempts to gain favourable responses from the customer by providing stimuli, or cues, to influence the buyer. After the customer has been properly conditioned, the salesperson tries to secure a positive purchase decision.

Considering the net effects of this method's advantages and disadvantages, it appears most suitable for relatively unimportant purchase decisions, when time is severely constrained and when professional buyers are not the prospects. As consumers in general become more sophisticated, this approach will become more problematic.

MENTAL STATES SELLING

Mental states selling, or the *formula approach* to personal selling, assumes that the buying process for most buyers is essentially identical and that buyers can be led through certain mental states, or steps, in the buying process. These mental states are typically referred to as **AIDA** (attention, interest, desire, and action). Appropriate sales messages provide a transition from one mental state to the next. The mental states method is illustrated in Exhibit 1.3.[11] Note that this version includes "conviction" as an intermediate stage between interest and desire. Such minor variations are commonplace in different renditions of this approach to selling.

As with stimulus-response selling, the mental states approach relies on a highly structured sales presentation. The salesperson does most of the talking, as feedback from the prospect could be disruptive to the flow of the presentation.

A positive feature of this method is that it forces the salesperson to plan the sales presentation before calling on the customer. It also helps the salesperson recognize that timing is an important element in the purchase decision process and that careful listening is necessary to determine which stage the buyer is in at any given point.

EXHIBIT 1.3
Mental States View of Selling

Mental State	Sales Step	Critical Sales Task
Attention	Curiosity	Get prospects excited, and then you get them to like you.
Interest	Interest	Interview: needs and wants
Conviction	Conviction	"What's in it for me?" Product—"Will it do what I want it to do?" Price—"Is it worth it?" "The hassle of change" "Cheaper elsewhere" Peers—"What will others think of it?" Priority—"Do I need it now?" (sense of urgency)
Desire	Desire	Overcome their stall.
Action	Close	Alternative choice close: which, not if!

mental states selling
An approach to personal selling that assumes that the buying process for most buyers is essentially identical and that buyers can be led through certain mental states, or steps, in the buying process; also called the formula approach.

AIDA An acronym for the various mental states salespeople must lead their customers through when using mental states selling: attention, interest, desire, and action.

An Ethical Dilemma

Rachel Duke sells advertising for her university newspaper. One of her potential clients is contemplating buying an ad for an upcoming special issue featuring bars and restaurants. Over the past two weeks, Duke has tried unsuccessfully to get a commitment from the restaurant owner to place an ad. Her sales manager has suggested that Rachel call the prospect and tell him that there is only one remaining ad space in the special issue and that she must have an immediate answer to ensure that the prospect's ad will appear in the special issue. The sales manager said, "Rachel, this guy is stalling. You've got to move him to action, and this technique will do the trick." Duke was troubled by her manager's advice because the special issue had plenty of ad space remaining. If you were Duke, would you follow her sales manager's advice? Why or why not?

© ROB BYRON/SHUTTERSTOCK

Need satisfaction selling is based on the notion that the customer is buying to satisfy a particular need or set of needs. This approach is shown in Figure 1.2. It is the salesperson's task to identify the need to be met and then help the buyer meet that need. Unlike the mental states and stimulus-response methods, this method focuses on the customer rather than on the salesperson. The salesperson uses a questioning, probing tactic to uncover important buyer needs. Customer responses dominate the early portion of the sales interaction, and only after relevant needs have been established does the salesperson begin to relate how his or her offering can satisfy these needs.

A problem with the mental states method is that it is difficult to determine which state a prospect is in. Sometimes a prospect is spanning two mental states or moving back and forth between two states during the sales presentation. Consequently, the heavy guidance structure the salesperson implements may be inappropriate, confusing, and even counterproductive to sales effectiveness. We should also note that this method is not customer oriented. Although the salesperson tailors the presentation to each customer somewhat, this is done by noting customer mental states rather than needs. (See "An Ethical Dilemma" for a situation in which the salesperson is contemplating the movement of the prospect into the "action" stage.)

Customers seem to appreciate this selling method and are often willing to spend considerable time in preliminary meetings to define needs before a sales presentation or written sales proposal. Also, this method avoids the defensiveness that arises in some prospects when a salesperson rushes to the persuasive part of the sales message without adequate attention to the buyer's needs.

need satisfaction selling An approach to selling based on the notion that the customer is buying to satisfy a particular need or set of needs.

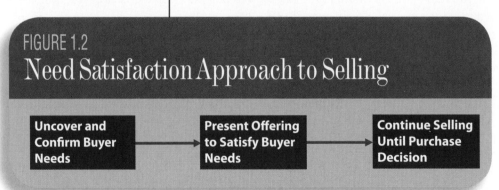

FIGURE 1.2
Need Satisfaction Approach to Selling

Uncover and Confirm Buyer Needs → Present Offering to Satisfy Buyer Needs → Continue Selling Until Purchase Decision

The salesperson attempts to uncover customer needs that are related to the product or service her or she is offering. This may require extensive questioning in the early stages of the sales process. After confirming the buyer's needs, the salesperson proceeds with a presentation based on how the offering can meet those needs.

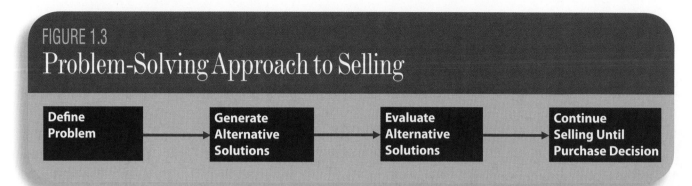

FIGURE 1.3

Problem-Solving Approach to Selling

| Define Problem | → | Generate Alternative Solutions | → | Evaluate Alternative Solutions | → | Continue Selling Until Purchase Decision |

The salesperson defines a customer problem that may be solved by various alternatives. Then an offering is made that represents at least one of these alternatives. All alternatives are carefully evaluated before a purchase decision is made.

PROBLEM-SOLVING SELLING

Problem-solving selling is an extension of need satisfaction selling. It goes beyond identifying needs to developing alternative solutions for satisfying these needs. The problem-solving approach to selling is depicted in Figure 1.3. Sometimes even competitors' offerings are included as alternatives in the purchase decision.

The problem-solving approach typically requires educating the customer about the full impact of the existing problem and clearly communicating how the solution delivers significant customer value. This is true in cases where the customer does not perceive a problem or even when the solution seems to be an obviously beneficial course of action for the buyer.

Jody Kinmon, a sales coach for Miami-based Carnival Cruise Lines, says, "Sometimes people feel safer not doing anything, especially if there is not an immediate need or crisis. As a salesperson, your job is to open their eyes. If customers knew what they wanted, they wouldn't need salespeople."[12] To be successful in problem-solution selling, salespeople must be able to get the buyer to agree that a problem exists and that solving it is worth the time and effort required.

The problem-solving approach to selling can take a lot of time. In some cases, the selling company cannot afford this much time with each prospective customer. In other cases, the customers may be unwilling to spend the time. Insurance salespeople, for example, report this customer response. The problem-solving approach appears to be most successful in technical industrial sales situations, in which the parties involved are usually oriented toward scientific reasoning and processes and thus find this approach to sales amenable.

CONSULTATIVE SELLING

Consultative selling is the process of helping customers reach their strategic goals by using the products, services, and expertise of the sales organization.[13] This approach is shown in Figure 1.4. Notice that this method focuses on achieving strategic goals of customers, not just meeting needs or solving problems. Salespeople confirm their customers' strategic goals and then work collaboratively with customers to achieve those goals.

In consultative selling, salespeople fulfill three primary roles: strategic orchestrator, business consultant, and long-term ally. As a **strategic orchestrator**, the salesperson arranges the use of the sales organization's resources in an effort to satisfy the customer. This usually calls for involving other individuals in the sales organization. For example, the salesperson may need expert advice from production or logistics personnel to address a customer problem or opportunity fully. In the **business consultant** role, the

problem-solving selling An extension of need satisfaction selling that goes beyond identifying needs to developing alternative solutions for satisfying these needs.

consultative selling The process of helping customers reach their strategic goals by using the products, services, and expertise of the sales organization.

strategic orchestrator A role the salesperson plays in consultative selling in which he or she arranges the use of the sales organization's resources in an effort to satisfy the customer.

business consultant A role the salesperson plays in consultative selling in which he or she uses internal and external (outside the sales organization) sources to become an expert on the customer's business. This role also involves educating customers on the sales firm's products and how these products compare with competitive offerings.

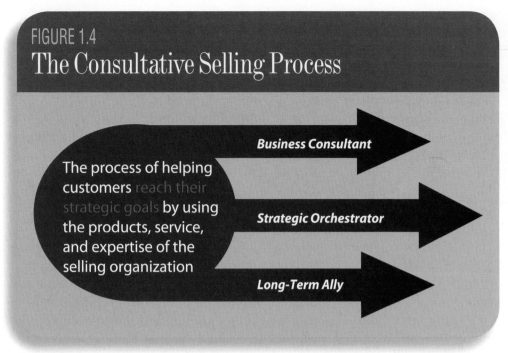

FIGURE 1.4

The Consultative Selling Process

The process of helping customers reach their strategic goals by using the products, service, and expertise of the selling organization

Business Consultant

Strategic Orchestrator

Long-Term Ally

The salesperson helps customers reach their strategic goals by fulfilling three roles with customers.

YPG incorporates these topics into its sales training program.[14]

LO6

The Trust-Based Sales Process

The nonselling activities on which most salespeople spend a majority of their time are essential for the successful execution of the most important part of the salesperson's job: the **sales process**. The sales process has traditionally been described as a series of interrelated steps beginning with locating qualified prospective customers. From there, the salesperson plans the sales presentation, makes an appointment to see the customer, completes the sale, and performs postsale activities.

As you should recall from the earlier discussion of the continued evolution of personal selling (refer to Exhibit 1.2), the sales process is increasingly being viewed as a relationship management process, as depicted in Figure 1.5.

In this conceptualization of the sales process, salespeople strive to attain lasting relationships with their customers. The basis for such relationships may vary, but the element of trust between the customer and the salesperson is an essential part of enduring relationships. To earn the trust of customers, salespeople should be customer oriented, honest, and dependable. They must also be competent and able to display an appropriate level of expertise to their customers. Finally, the trust-building process is facilitated if salespeople are compatible with their customers—that is, if they get along with and work well with each other.[15]

Another important element of achieving sound relationships with customers is to recognize that individual customers and their particular needs must be addressed with the appropriate selling strategies and tactics. In selling, we discuss strategy at four levels: corporate, business unit, marketing department, and

salesperson uses internal and external (outside the sales organization) sources to become an expert on the customer's business. This role also includes an educational element—that is, salespeople educate their customers on products they offer and how these products compare with competitive offerings. As a **long-term ally**, the salesperson supports the customer, even when an immediate sale is not expected.

Yellow Pages Group (YPG), Canada's leading local commercial search provider and largest directory publisher, uses consultative selling to satisfy the needs of a wide variety of small businesses. Nearly all of YPG's revenues are derived from the sale of Yellow Pages directory advertising to businesses, mostly small- and medium-sized enterprises (SME). To be successful, YPG salespeople must be able to understand and explain the value of their products in the context of the customer's overall business strategy and be able to provide details of the expected and actual return on investment. Accordingly,

long-term ally A role the salesperson plays in consultative selling in which he or she supports the customer, even when an immediate sale is not expected.

sales process A series of interrelated steps beginning with locating qualified prospective customers. From there, the salesperson plans the sales presentation, makes an appointment to see the customer, completes the sale, and performs postsale activities.

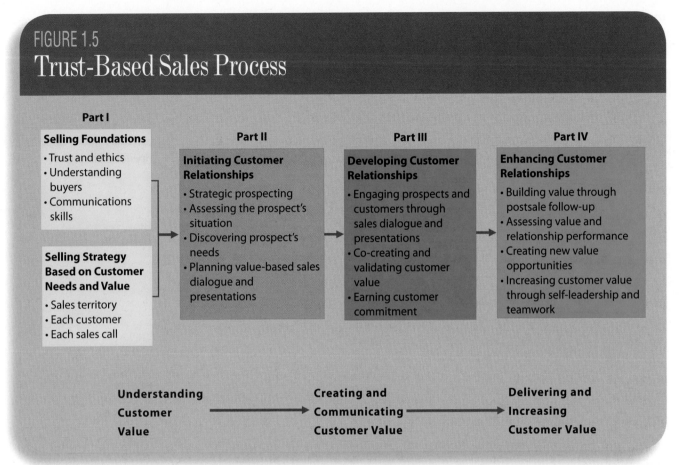

FIGURE 1.5
Trust-Based Sales Process

Part I

Selling Foundations
- Trust and ethics
- Understanding buyers
- Communications skills

Selling Strategy Based on Customer Needs and Value
- Sales territory
- Each customer
- Each sales call

Part II

Initiating Customer Relationships
- Strategic prospecting
- Assessing the prospect's situation
- Discovering prospect's needs
- Planning value-based sales dialogue and presentations

Part III

Developing Customer Relationships
- Engaging prospects and customers through sales dialogue and presentations
- Co-creating and validating customer value
- Earning customer commitment

Part IV

Enhancing Customer Relationships
- Building value through postsale follow-up
- Assessing value and relationship performance
- Creating new value opportunities
- Increasing customer value through self-leadership and teamwork

Understanding Customer Value → **Creating and Communicating Customer Value** → **Delivering and Increasing Customer Value**

The three major phases of the sales process are initiating, developing, and enhancing customer relationships. Salespeople must possess certain attributes to earn the trust of their customers and be able to adapt their selling strategies to different situations. Throughout the sales process, salespeople should focus on customer value, first by understanding what it is and then by working with customers to create value, communicate value, and continually increase customer value.

the overall sales function. An individual salesperson is strongly guided by strategy at these higher levels in the organization but must also develop selling strategies and tactics to fit the sales territory, each customer, and, ultimately, each sales call. Our coverage in this text focuses on developing sales strategies for individual customers and specific sales calls.

When studying the sales process, we should note that there are countless versions of the process in terms of number of and names of steps. If, however, you were to examine popular trade books on selling and training manuals used by corporations, you would find that the various depictions of the sales process are actually more alike than different. The sales process shown in Figure 1.5 is comparable to most versions of the sales process, with the exception of those versions that advocate high-pressure methods focusing on getting the customer to "say yes" rather than focusing on meeting the customer's true needs. Our version of the sales process suggests that salespeople must have certain

attributes to inspire trust in their customers and that salespeople should adapt their selling strategy to fit the situation.

Another point that should be stressed is that the sales process is broken into steps to facilitate discussion and sales training, not to suggest discrete lines between the steps. The steps are actually highly interrelated and, in some instances, may overlap. Further, the stepwise flow of Figure 1.5 does not imply a strict sequence of events. Salespeople may move back and forth in the process with a given customer, sometimes shifting from step to step several times in the same sales encounter. Finally, claiming a new customer typically will require multiple sales calls.

The remainder of this book explores the sales process shown in Figure 1.5. Chapters 2–4 comprise the foundations of personal selling. Chapter 2 discusses the important topics of building trust and sales ethics. Chapter 3 provides in-depth coverage of buyer behaviour, and Chapter 4 focuses on the communications skills necessary for sales success. Chapters 5 and 6 are about initiating customer relationships, starting with strategic prospecting in Chapter 5. Chapter 6 covers planning value-based sales dialogue and presentations as well as initiating contact with the customer. Developing customer relationships is next, with Chapter 7 discussing issues that arise during sales dialogues and presentations, and Chapter 8 discussing how salespeople can validate customer value and earn customer commitment. Enhancing customer relationships is presented in Chapters 9 and 10, and focuses on how salespeople add customer value through follow-up (Chapter 9) and through self-leadership and teamwork (Chapter 10). Chapter 11 concentrates on the techniques to develop and implement sales strategies, understanding and evaluating employees' performance while creating value to the customer through technology. To learn more about careers in professional selling, please see Appendix Chapter 1.

 Visit **sell.nelson.com** to find the resources you need today!

Located at the back of the textbook are rip-out Chapter Review cards. Make sure you also go online to check out other tools that SELL offers to help you successfully pass your course.

- Flashcards
- Glossary
- PowerPoint Notes

- Role-Play Videos
- Games
- Interactive Quizzing

Sales Careers

This appendix is designed to give an in-depth look at sales careers. We first discuss characteristics of sales careers and then describe several different types of personal selling jobs. The appendix concludes with a discussion of the skills and qualifications necessary for success in sales careers.

Characteristics of Sales Careers

Although individual opinions will vary, the ideal career for most individuals offers a bright future, including good opportunities for financial rewards and job advancement. As you read the following sections on the characteristics of sales careers, you might think about what you expect from a career and whether your expectations could be met in a sales career. The following characteristics are discussed:

- Job security
- Advancement opportunities
- Immediate feedback
- Prestige
- Job variety
- Independence
- Compensation

JOB SECURITY

Salespeople are revenue producers and thus enjoy relatively good job security compared with other occupational groups. Certainly, individual job security depends on individual performance, but in general, salespeople are usually the last group to be negatively affected by personnel cutbacks.

Competent salespeople also have some degree of job security based on the universality of their basic sales skills. In many cases, salespeople are able to move successfully to another employer, maybe even change industries, because sales skills are largely transferable. For salespeople working in declining or stagnant industries, this is heartening news.

ADVANCEMENT OPPORTUNITIES

As the business world continues to become more competitive, the advancement opportunities for salespeople will continue to be an attractive dimension of sales careers. In highly competitive markets, individuals and companies that are successful in determining and meeting customer needs will be rewarded with opportunities for advancement. One reason that many successful salespeople ultimately find their way into top management is that they display some of the key attributes required for success in executive positions. Top executives must have highly developed personal skills, be able to communicate clearly and persuasively, and have high levels of self-confidence, motivation, business judgment, and determination.

IMMEDIATE FEEDBACK

Salespeople receive constant, immediate feedback on their job performance. Usually, the results of their efforts can be plainly observed by both salespeople and their sales managers—a source of motivation and job satisfaction. On a daily basis, salespeople receive direct feedback from their customers, and this can be stimulating, challenging, and productive. The opportunity to react immediately to customer feedback during sales presentations is a strong benefit of adaptive selling, and it distinguishes selling from other forms of marketing communications, such as advertising and public relations. The spontaneity and creativity involved in reacting to immediate feedback is one dimension of selling that makes it such an interesting job.

PRESTIGE

Traditionally, sales has not been a prestigious occupation in the eyes of the general public. There is some evidence that as the general public learns more about the activities and qualifications of professional salespeople, the image of salespeople, and thus the prestige of selling, is improving. An analysis of the popular press (excluding business publications) reveals that there are more positive than negative mentions of news-making salespeople. In a positive light, salespeople are frequently seen as knowledgeable, well-trained, educated, and capable of solving customer problems. The negative aspects of salespeople's image often center on deception and high-pressure techniques.[1]

Another study indicates that salespeople historically have been depicted in movies and television programs more often than not in a negative light.[2] Even so, the struggling, down-and-out huckster as depicted by Willy Loman in Arthur Miller's 1949 classic *Death of a Salesman* is hardly typical of the professional salesperson of today and the future. Professional salespeople destroy such unfavourable stereotypes, and they would not jeopardize customer relationships by using high-pressure sales techniques to force a premature sale.[3] These perceptions are especially true in the business world, where encounters with professional salespeople are commonplace.

© DEAN TURNER/ISTOCKPHOTO

JOB VARIETY

Salespeople rarely suffer from boredom. Their jobs are multifaceted and dynamic. For a person seeking the comfort of a well-established routine, sales might not be a good career choice. In sales, day-to-day variation on the job is the norm. Customers change, new products and services are developed, and competition introduces new elements at a rapid pace. In addition to interacting with customers, many salespeople spend a considerable amount of time on such activities as training, attending trade shows, working with other salespeople at the distributor and retail levels to stimulate demand, and completing administrative tasks.

INDEPENDENCE

Sales jobs often allow independence of action. This independence is frequently a byproduct of decentralized sales operations in which salespeople live and work away from headquarters, therefore working from their homes and making their own plans for extensive travel.

Independence of action and freedom to make decisions are usually presented as advantages that sales positions have over tightly supervised jobs. Despite its appeal, however, independence does present some problems. New recruits working from their homes may find the lack of a company office somewhat disorienting. They may need an office environment to relate to, especially if their past work experience provided regular contact in an office environment.

The independence of action traditionally enjoyed by salespeople is being scrutinized by sales managers more heavily now than in the past. The emphasis on sales productivity, accomplished in part through cost containment, is encouraging sales managers to take a more active role in dictating travel plans and sales call schedules.

COMPENSATION

Compensation is generally thought to be a strong advantage of sales careers. Pay is closely tied to performance, especially if commissions and bonuses are part of the pay package.

Starting salaries for inexperienced salespeople with a university degree typically average $45,000, with opportunities to earn more through bonuses and commissions. Between the extremes of the highly experienced salesperson and the inexperienced recruit, an average salesperson earns approximately $60,000–$70,000 per year. More experienced salespeople, including those who deal with large customers, often earn in the $85,000–$135,000 range. Top salespeople can earn hundreds of thousands of dollars annually, with some exceeding a million dollars in annual earnings.

Classification of Personal Selling Jobs

because there are so many unique sales jobs, the term *salesperson* is not by itself very descriptive. A salesperson could be a flower vendor at a busy downtown intersection or the sales executive negotiating the sale of Boeing aircraft to a major airline.

We briefly discuss six types of personal selling jobs:

- Sales support
- New business
- Existing business
- Inside sales (nonretail)
- Direct-to-consumer sales
- Combination sales jobs

SALES SUPPORT

Sales support personnel are not usually involved in the direct solicitation of purchase orders. Rather, their primary responsibility is dissemination of information and performance of other activities designed to stimulate sales. They might concentrate at the end-user level or another level in the channel of distribution to support the overall sales effort. They may report to another salesperson who is responsible for direct handling of purchase orders, or to the sales manager. There are two well-known categories of support salespeople: missionary or detail salespeople and technical support salespeople.

Missionary salespeople usually work for a manufacturer but may also work for brokers and manufacturing representatives, especially in the grocery industry. There are strong similarities between sales missionaries and religious missionaries. As with their counterparts, sales missionaries are expected to "spread the word" with the purpose of conversion—to customer status. Once converted, the customer receives reinforcing messages, new information, and the benefit of the missionary's activities to strengthen the relationship between buyer and seller.

In the pharmaceutical industry, the **detailer** is a fixture. Detailers working at the physician level furnish valuable information regarding the capabilities and limitations of medications in an attempt to get the physician to prescribe their product. Another sales representative from the same pharmaceutical company will sell the medication to the wholesaler or pharmacist, but it is the detailer's job to support the direct sales effort by calling on physicians.

Technical specialists are sometimes considered to be sales support personnel. These **technical support salespeople** may assist in design and specification processes, installation of equipment, training of the customer's employees, and follow-up service of a technical nature. They are sometimes part of a sales team that includes another salesperson who specializes in identifying and satisfying customer needs by recommending the appropriate product or service.

NEW BUSINESS

New business is generated for the selling firm by adding new customers or introducing new products to the marketplace. Two types of new-business salespeople are pioneers and order-getters.

---

sales support personnel A firm's personnel whose primary responsibility is dissemination of information and performance of other activities designed to stimulate sales.

missionary salespeople Salespeople who usually work for a manufacturer but may also be found working for brokers and manufacturing representatives. Sales missionaries are expected to "spread the word" to convert noncustomers to customers.

detailer A salesperson in the pharmaceutical industry working at the physician level to furnish valuable information regarding the capabilities and limitations of medications in an attempt to get the physician to prescribe their product.

technical support salespeople Technical specialist who may assist in design and specification processes, installation of equipment, training of the customer's employees, and follow-up service of a technical nature.

pioneers Salespeople who are constantly involved with either new products, new customers, or both. Their task requires creative selling and the ability to counter the resistance to change that will likely be present in prospective customers.

order-getters Salespeople who actively seek orders, usually in a highly competitive environment.

order-takers Salespeople who specialize in maintaining existing business.

inside sales Nonretail salespeople who remain in their employer's place of business while dealing with customers.

Pioneers, as the term suggests, are constantly involved with new products, new customers, or both. Their task requires creative selling and the ability to counter the resistance to change that will likely be present in prospective customers. Pioneers are well represented in the sale of business franchises, in which the sales representatives travel from city to city seeking new franchisees.

Order-getters are salespeople who actively seek orders, usually in a highly competitive environment. Although all pioneers are also order-getters, the reverse is not true. An order-getter may serve existing customers on an ongoing basis, whereas the pioneer moves on to new customers as soon as possible. Order-getters may seek new business by selling an existing customer additional items from the product line. A well-known tactic is to establish a relationship with a customer by selling a single product from the line, then to follow up with subsequent sales calls for other items from the product line.

Most corporations emphasize sales growth, and salespeople operating as pioneers and order-getters are at the heart of sales growth objectives. The pressure to perform in these roles is fairly intense; the results are highly visible. For these reasons, the new-business salesperson is often among the elite in any company's salesforce.

EXISTING BUSINESS

In direct contrast to new-business salespeople, other salespeople's primary responsibility is to maintain relationships with existing customers. Salespeople who specialize in maintaining existing business include **order-takers**. These salespeople frequently work for wholesalers and, as the term *order-taker* implies, they are not too involved in creative selling. Route salespeople who work an established customer base, taking routine reorders of stock items, are order-takers. They sometimes follow a pioneer salesperson and take over the account after the pioneer has made the initial sale.

These salespeople are no less valuable to their firms than the new-business salespeople, but creative selling skills are less important to this category of sales personnel. Their strengths tend to be reliability and competence in ensuring customer convenience. Customers grow to depend on the services provided by this type of salesperson. As most markets are becoming more competitive, the role of existing-business salespeople is sometimes critical to prevent erosion of the customer base.

Many firms, believing that it is easier to protect and maintain profitable customers than it is to find replacement customers, are reinforcing sales efforts to existing customers. For example, Frito-Lay uses 18,000 route service salespeople to call on retail customers at least three times weekly. Larger customers see their Frito-Lay representative on a daily basis. These salespeople spend a lot of their time educating customers about the profitability of Frito-Lay's snack foods, which leads to increased sales both for the retailer and for Frito-Lay.

INSIDE SALES

In this text, **inside sales** refers to nonretail salespeople who remain in their employer's place of business while dealing with customers. The inside-sales operation has received considerable attention in recent years not only as a supplementary sales tactic but also as an alternative to field selling.

Inside sales can be conducted on an active or a passive sales basis. Active inside sales include the solicitation of entire orders, either as part of a telemarketing operation or when customers walk into the seller's facilities. Passive inside sales imply the acceptance, rather than solicitation, of customer orders, although it is common practice for these transactions to include add-on sales attempts. We should note that customer service personnel sometimes function as inside-sales personnel as an ongoing part of their jobs.

DIRECT-TO-CONSUMER SALES

Direct-to-consumer salespeople are the most numerous types of salespeople. There are approximately 1.6 million retail salespeople in Canada, with another 570,000 selling real estate, insurance, and securities. Not included in these numbers are the many sales representatives selling directly to the consumer for such companies as AVON, Mary Kay, and Tupperware.

This diverse category of salespeople ranges from the part-time, often temporary salesperson in a retail store to the highly educated, professionally trained stockbroker on Bay Street. As a general statement, the more challenging direct-to-consumer sales positions are those involving the sale of intangible services, such as insurance and financial services.

COMBINATION SALES JOBS

Now that we have reviewed some of the basic types of sales jobs, let us consider the salesperson who performs multiple types of sales jobs within the framework of a single position. We use the case of the territory manager's position with GlaxoSmithKline Consumer Healthcare (GSK) to illustrate the **combination sales job** concept. GSK, whose products include Aqua-Fresh toothpaste, markets a wide range of consumer healthcare goods to food, drug, variety, and mass merchandisers. The territory manager's job blends responsibilities for developing new business, maintaining and stimulating existing business, and performing sales support activities.

During a typical day in the field, the GSK territory manager is involved in sales support activities, such as merchandising and in-store promotion at the individual retail store level. Maintaining contact and goodwill with store personnel is another routine sales support activity. The territory manager also makes sales calls on chain headquarters personnel to handle existing business and to seek new business. And it is the territory manager who introduces new GSK products in the marketplace.

Qualifications and Skills Required for Success by Salespeople

because there are so many different types of jobs in sales, it is rather difficult to generalize about the qualifications and skills needed for success. This list would have to vary according to the details of a given job. Even then, it is reasonable to believe that for any given job, different people with different skills could be successful. These conclusions have been reached after decades of research that has tried to correlate sales performance with physical traits, mental abilities, personality characteristics, and the experience and background of the salesperson.

Success in sales is increasingly being thought of in terms of a strategic team effort, rather than the characteristics of individual salespersons. For example, three studies of more than 200 companies that employ 25,000 salespeople found that being customer oriented and cooperating as team players were critical to salespeople's success.[4]

Being careful not to suggest that sales success is solely a function of individual traits, let us consider some of the skills and qualifications that are thought to be especially critical for success in most sales jobs. Five factors that seem to be particularly important for success in sales are empathy, ego drive, ego strength, verbal communication skills, and enthusiasm. These factors have been selected after reviewing three primary sources of information:

- A study of more than 750,000 salespeople in 15,000 companies[5]
- Two reviews of four decades of research on factors related to sales success[6]
- Surveys of sales executives[7]

EMPATHY

In a sales context, empathy (the ability to see things as others would see them) includes being able to read cues furnished by the customer to better determine the customer's viewpoint. According to Spiro and Weitz, empathy is crucial for successful interaction between a buyer and a seller.[8] An empathetic salesperson is presumably in a better position to tailor the sales presentation to the customer during the planning stages. More important, empathetic salespeople can adjust to feedback during the presentation.

The research of Greenberg and Greenberg found empathy to be a significant predictor of sales success. This finding was partially supported in the review by Comer and Dubinsky, who found empathy to be an important factor in consumer and insurance sales but not in retail or industrial sales. Supporting the importance of empathy in sales success is a multi-industry study of 215 sales managers by Marshall, Goebel,

combination sales job A sales job in which the salesperson performs multiple types of sales jobs within the framework of a single position.

empathy The ability to see things as others would see them; salespeople with empathy are better able to adapt to various sales situations and adjust to customer feedback.

and Moncrief.[9] These researchers found empathy to be among the top 25 percent of skills and personal attributes thought to be important determinants of sales success. Even though some studies do not find direct links between salesperson empathy and success, empathy is generally accepted as an important trait for successful salespeople. As relationship selling grows in importance, empathy logically will become even more important for sales success.

EGO DRIVE

In a sales context, **ego drive** (an indication of the degree of determination a person has to achieve goals and overcome obstacles in striving for success) is manifested as an inner need to persuade others in order to achieve personal gratification. Greenberg and Greenberg point out the complementary relationship between empathy and ego drive that is necessary for sales success. The salesperson who is extremely empathetic but lacks ego drive may have problems in taking active steps to confirm a sale. However, a salesperson with more ego drive than empathy may ignore the customer's viewpoint in an ill-advised, overly anxious attempt to gain commitment from the customer.

EGO STRENGTH

The degree to which a person is able to achieve an approximation of inner drives is **ego strength**. Salespeople with high levels of ego strength are likely to be self-assured and self-accepting. Salespeople with healthy egos are better equipped to deal with the possibility of rejection throughout the sales process. They are probably less likely to experience sales call reluctance and are resilient enough to overcome the disappointment of inevitable lost sales.

Salespeople with strong ego drives who are well-equipped to do their jobs will likely be high in **self-efficacy**; that is, they will strongly believe that they can

be successful on the job. In situations in which their initial efforts meet resistance, rejection, or failure, salespeople high in self-efficacy are likely to persist in pursuing their goals. In complex sales involving large dollar amounts and a long sales cycle (the time from first customer contact to eventual sale), it is crucial to continue working toward a distant goal despite the very real possibility of setbacks along the way. For example, airplane manufacturers hoping to land contracts with the airlines typically pursue such contracts for several years before a buying decision is made. For those who persevere, however, the payoff can be well worth the extended effort.

INTERPERSONAL COMMUNICATION SKILLS

Interpersonal communication skills, including listening and questioning, are essential for sales success. An in-depth study of 300 sales executives, salespeople, and customers of 24 major sales companies in North America, Europe, and Japan found that effective salespeople are constantly seeking ways to improve communication skills that enable them to develop, explain, and implement customer solutions. The companies in the study are some of the best in the world at professional selling: Sony, Xerox, American Airlines, Fuji, and Scott paper.[10]

Another major study across several industries found that three communications skills in particular were among the top 10 percent of success factors for professional salespeople.[11] The highest-rated success factor in this study was listening skills, with ability to adapt presentations according to the situation and verbal communications skills following close behind.

To meet customer needs, salespeople must be able to solicit opinions, listen effectively, and confirm customer needs and concerns. They must be capable of probing customer expectations with open- and closed-ended questions and responding in a flexible manner to individual personalities and different business cultures in ways that demonstrate respect for differences.[12] This requires adaptable, socially intelligent salespeople, especially when dealing with multicultural customers.[13]

The importance of communication skills has been recognized by sales managers, recruiters, and sales researchers. These skills can be continually refined throughout a sales career, a positive factor from both a personal and a career development perspective.

ENTHUSIASM

When sales executives and recruiters discuss qualifications for sales positions, they invariably include **enthusiasm**. They are usually referring to dual dimensions of enthusiasm—an enthusiastic attitude in a general sense and a special enthusiasm for selling. On-campus recruiters have mentioned that they seek students who are well beyond "interested in sales" to the point of truly being enthusiastic about career opportunities in sales. Recruiters are somewhat weary of "selling sales" as a viable career, and they welcome the job applicant who displays genuine enthusiasm for the field.

COMMENTS ON QUALIFICATIONS AND SKILLS

The qualifications and skills needed for sales success are different today from those required for success two decades ago. As the popularity of relationship selling grows, the skills necessary for sales success will evolve to meet the needs of the marketplace. For example, Greenberg and Greenberg's research has identified what they call an "emerging factor" for sales success, a strong motivation to provide service to the customer. They contrast this **service motivation** with ego drive by noting that although ego drive relates to persuading others, service motivation comes from desiring the approval of others. For example, a salesperson may be extremely gratified to please a customer through superior post-sale service. Greenberg and Greenberg conclude that most salespeople will need both service motivation and ego drive to succeed, although they note that extremely high levels of both attributes are not likely to exist in the same individual. Nonetheless, there is a growing interest in bringing service concepts and practices into the world of professional selling. Whereas it may be difficult to recruit salespeople who are high on the service dimension, it is certainly feasible to provide appropriate training and to reinforce the desired service behaviours through sales management practices. Without significant emphasis on servicing existing customers, a company is not truly practising relationship selling.[14]

Our discussion of factors related to sales success is necessarily brief, as a fully descriptive treatment of the topic must be tied to a given sales position. Veteran sales managers and recruiters can often specify with amazing precision what qualifications and skills are needed to succeed in a given sales job. These assessments are usually based on a mixture of objective and subjective judgments.

Professional selling offers virtually unlimited career opportunities for the right person. Many of the skills and qualifications necessary for success in selling are also important for success as an entrepreneur or as a leader in a corporate setting. For those interested in learning more about sales careers, consult these sources: *Sales & Marketing Management* magazine at http://salesandmarketing.com; *Selling Power* magazine at http://sellingpower.com; and Sales and Marketing Executives International, a professional organization, at http://www.smei.org.

enthusiasm A strong feeling of excitement. Salespeople should have an enthusiastic attitude in a general sense and a specific enthusiasm for selling.

service motivation A strong desire to provide service to the customer. Service motivation comes from desiring the approval of others.

PLIABLE PLASTICS

Background

Pliable Plastics, Inc., located in Toronto, is a manufacturer of plastic components. The company is noted for producing high-quality products. Its salesforce calls on large accounts, such as refrigerator manufacturers that might need large quantities of custom-made products, such as door liners. Increases in new-home sales over the past several years have fuelled refrigerator sales and, subsequently, sales at Pliable Plastics. Moreover, federal regulations requiring that dishwasher liners be made of plastic, rather than porcelain, have enhanced Pliable Plastic's sales.

Current Situation

Adrienne Frost had recently been assigned to the Alberta territory. Although this was her first sales job, she felt confident and was eager to begin. She had taken a sales course in university and had just completed the company's training program. The company stressed the use of an organized sales presentation in which the salesperson organizes the key points into a planned sequence that allows for adaptive behaviour by the salesperson as the presentation progresses. She was familiar with this approach because she had studied it in her university sales course.

Frost's first call was at a small refrigerator manufacturer in Calgary. She had called the day before to set up an appointment with materials purchasing manager David Kline at 9:00 a.m. On the morning of her meeting, Frost was running behind schedule because of an alarm clock malfunction. As a result, she ended up in traffic she did not anticipate and did not arrive for her appointment until 9:10 a.m. When she informed the receptionist she had an appointment with Kline, she was told he was in another meeting. He did agree, however, to see Frost when his meeting was finished, which would be about 9:45 a.m. Frost was upset Kline would not wait 10 minutes for her and let the receptionist know it.

At 9:50 a.m. Frost was introducing herself to Kline. She noticed his office was filled with University of Alberta memorabilia. She remembered from her training that the first thing to do was build rapport with the prospect. Thus, she asked Kline if he went to the University of Alberta. This got the ball rolling quickly. Kline had graduated from Alberta and was a big fan of the basketball and hockey teams. He was more than happy to talk about them. Frost was excited; she knew this would help her build rapport. After about 25 minutes of hockey and basketball chitchat, Frost figured it was time to get down to business.

After finally getting Kline off the subject of sports, Frost began to discuss the benefits of her product. She figured if she did not control the conversation, Kline would revert to discussing sports. She went on and on about the material compounds composing Pliable Plastics plastics, as well as the processes used to develop plastic liners. She explained the customizing process, the product's durability, Pliable Plastics' ability to provide door liners in any colour, and her company's return and credit policies. After nearly 25 minutes, she finally asked Kline if he had any questions.

Kline asked her if she had any product samples with her. Frost had to apologize—in all the confusion this morning she ran off and left the samples at home. Then Kline asked her about the company's turnaround time from order to delivery. Knowing quick turnaround was important to Kline, and feeling this prospect may be slipping away, she told him it was about four weeks, although she knew it was really closer to five. However, she thought, if Kline ordered from them and it took a little longer, she could always blame it on production. When the issue of price emerged, Frost was not able to justify clearly in Kline's mind why Pliable Plastics was slightly higher than the competition. She thought that she had clearly explained the benefits of the product and that it should be obvious that Pliable Plastics is a better choice.

Finally, Kline told Frost he would have to excuse himself. He had a meeting to attend on the other side of town. He thanked her for coming by and told her he would consider her offer. Frost thanked Kline for his time and departed. As she reflected on her first call, she wondered where she went wrong. She thought she would jot down some notes about her call to discuss with her sales manager later.

Questions

1. What problems do you see with Frost's first sales call?
2. If you were Frost's sales manager, what would you recommend she do to improve her chances of succeeding?

Role Play

Characters: Adrienne Frost, Pliable Plastics sales representative.

Scene:

Location—Pliable Plastics' Alberta office during a weekly sales meeting shortly after her sales call with David Kline.

Action—Frost reviews her sales call with Kline with other Pliable Plastics sales representatives and their sales manager. This is a regular feature of the weekly meetings, with the idea being that all sales representatives can learn from the experiences of others. Frost has decided to compare her call with Kline with some of the material from her sales training with Pliable Plastics. This material, which contrasts transaction-focused selling with trust-based relationship selling, is shown in Exhibit 1.2. Her review will analyze whether she did or did not practise trust-based relationship selling during her call with Kline.

Upon completion the role play, address the following questions:
1. Is Frost's review of her sales call accurate?
2. What steps should Frost take to begin to develop a strong relationship with Kline?

Didactic Designers, Inc.

Background

Didactic Designers, Inc., an Ottawa-based manufacturer of educational models of the human body, has been in business since the mid-1960s. The company's products, sold primarily to elementary schools in Canada, are available in plastic or as computer images. Accompanying products include lesson plans for teachers and workbooks and computer programs for students. Didactic Designers has enjoyed healthy sales increases in recent years, as schools increasingly integrate computer-assisted instruction into their curricula. Five years ago, Didactic Designers began selling consumer versions of its models through selected specialty educational toy stores and recently began selling on its own website. In addition, Didactic Designers is also selling on the Web through educational-online.com and Ed-Toys. Further, Didactic Designers has had discussions with Toys "R" Us, and the giant retailer seems eager to stock Didactic Designers products.

Didactic Designers has employed Zack Wilson, a recent graduate of Dalhousie University, for the past six months. He has become familiar with all aspects of marketing the Didactic Designers product line and is now the sales representative for electronic retailing accounts. Wilson is truly excited about his job, as he sees the explosive growth potential for selling Didactic Designers products on the Internet. His first big success came when he convinced educational-online.com to sell Didactic Designers products. After all, Educational-Online has the reputation in most circles as the premier product retailer. Thirty days after his initial sales to Educational-Online, Wilson was thrilled to land Ed-Toys as his second electronic retailer.

No doubt about it, Zack Wilson was on a roll. Securing commitments from Educational-Online and Ed-Toys within a month was almost too good to be true. In fact, there was only one problem facing Wilson. Educational-Online had begun discounting the Didactic Designers product line as much as 20 percent off suggested retail, and Ed-Toys was unhappy with the intense price competition. The following conversation had just taken place between Wilson and Ed-Toys buyer Andrea Haughton:

Haughton: Zack, your line looked really promising to us at suggested retail prices, but meeting Educational-Online's pricing sucks the profit right out of the equation. Are you selling to Educational-Online at a lower price than to us?

Wilson: Absolutely not! Educational-Online just decided to promote our line with the discounts.

Haughton: So the discounts are just a temporary promotion? When will Educational-Online stop discounting?

Wilson: Well, I don't really know. What I mean by that is that Educational-Online often discounts, but in the case of the Didactic Designers line, I've got to believe it's just a temporary thing.

Haughton: Why do you think so?

Wilson: Because they haven't asked me for a lower price. Like you, they can't be making much of a profit after the discounts.

Haughton: Well, Zack, we need to stop the bleeding! I can't go on meeting their prices. If they're not making money either, maybe it's time you get them to stop the discounting. Can you talk with them about getting up to suggested retail?

Wilson: Andrea, you know I can't dictate retail selling prices to them any more than I could to you.

Haughton: Nor am I suggesting you try to dictate prices. I am simply suggesting that you let them know that if they choose to go back to suggested retail, we will surely follow. If we can't sell at suggested retail, we will have little choice but to stop selling the Didactic line. I'm sure you can appreciate the fact that we have profit expectations for every line we sell. At 20 percent off, Zack, the Didactic Designers line just doesn't cut it for us.

Wilson: O.K., I will see what I can do.

Later in the day, Wilson checked his email and found a disturbing message from Barbara Moore, a Didactic Designers sales representative for the retail store division. Moore's message informed Wilson that one of her key retailers had visited the Educational-Online website and was extremely upset to see the heavy discounting on the Didactic Designers line. Moore claimed that she was in danger of losing her account and that she feared a widespread outcry from other specialty stores as word of the Educational-Online discounting would quickly spread. Moore strongly urged Wilson to do what he could to get Educational-Online back to suggested retail. Wilson noted that Moore had copied both her sales manager and Rebecca Stanley, Wilson's sales manager, with her email message.

The following day, Wilson called on Warren Bryant, Educational-Online's buyer for the Didactic Designers line. He conveyed to Bryant that Ed-Toys and some of the store retailers were upset with the discounting. Bryant shrugged off the news, commenting only that "it's a dog-eat-dog world" and that price competition was part of the game. Wilson asked Bryant if he was happy with the profit margins on the Didactic Designers line, and Bryant responded that he was more concerned with growing Educational-Online's market share than with profit margins. He told Wilson, "Our game plan is grab a dominant share, then worry about margins." At this point, Bryant gave Wilson something else to think about:

Bryant: Hey, Zack, I noticed you guys are selling the same products on your own website as the ones we're selling on ours.

Wilson: True, what's the problem?

Bryant: Well, I just read in the trade press where Home Depot told their vendors that they don't buy from their (Home Depot's) competitors and that they view vendor websites as competitors to their retail business. Maybe we feel the same way. We sell on the Web, and if you do too, then you're really a competitor for us.

Wilson: Warren, you know that we only do a little volume on the Web. Our site is really more of an information site.

Bryant: But you do offer an alternative to other electronic retailers and us by selling on your own site. And by the way, don't your store retailers oppose your selling on the Web?

Wilson: At this point, most of them are small retailers, and frankly speaking, they view you as more of a threat than us selling on our own site. Besides, our store division salesforce is working on a software package that will enable our store retailers to easily set up their own websites over the next six months or so.

Bryant: Unbelievable! What you're saying is that another division in your company is creating even more Web-based competition for me! I thought we had a real future together, but I've got to do some heavy-duty thinking on that. Thanks, Zack, but I'm really busy and need to move on to some other priorities this afternoon. Call me if you have any new thoughts on where we go from here.

Wilson left Educational-Online and began the hour-long drive back to the office. "Good thing I've a little time to think about this situation," he thought as he drove along. "I need to talk with Rebecca Stanley just as soon as I get to the office."

Role Play

Characters: Zack Wilson, Didactic Designers sales representative; Rebecca Stanley, Didactic Designers sales manager

Scene 1: *Location*—Stanley's office
Action—Wilson explains to Stanley what has occurred with the Ed-Toys and Educational-Online accounts. Rather than telling Wilson how to deal with Educational-Online and Ed-Toys from this point forward, Stanley directs Wilson to devise his own strategy. Rebecca then tells Wilson that she would like to visit both accounts with him within a week, and that she would like to review his strategy for Educational-Online and Ed-Toys within 48 hours.

After completing the role play, address the following questions:
1. Is Stanley justified in telling Wilson to devise his own strategy rather than giving him specific direction at this time? What are the advantages and disadvantages of her approach?
2. How could this situation have been prevented?

Scene 2: *Location*—Stanley's office.
Action—Wilson presents his strategy to Stanley.

After completing the role play, address the following questions:
1. What are the strengths and weaknesses of Wilson's interaction with Ed-Toys and Educational-Online?
2. What further suggestions can you make for dealing with Educational-Online and Ed-Toys?

71% The percentage of students who go online to study for a class.

LOG IN!

SELL was designed for students just like you: busy people who want choices, flexibility, and multiple learning options.

SELL delivers concise, electronic resources, such as role-play videos, crossword puzzles, flashcards, interactive quizzing, PowerPoint notes, and more!

At **www.sell.nelson.com**, you'll find electronic resources, such as **flashcards, PowerPoint notes, games, interactive quizzing,** and **role-play videos** to test your knowledge of key concepts. These resources will help supplement your understanding of core **sales** concepts in a format that fits your busy lifestyle.

"I really like how you use students' opinions on how to study and made a website that encompasses everything we find useful. Seeing this website makes me excited to study!"

—Abby Boston, Fanshawe College

Visit **www.sell.nelson.com** to find the resources you need today!

what do you think?

Salespeople are perceived by their buyers to be trustworthy.

1 2 3 4 5 6 7

strongly disagree   strongly agree

Successful salespeople

have to understand the lifeline of an organization today
is repeat business. This can only be done by building
trust and long-term relationships with customers.

2

Building Trust and Sales Ethics
Developing Trust and Mutual Respect with Clients

After completing this chapter, you should be able to

LO1 Explain what trust is, explain why it is important, and understand how to earn trust.

LO2 Know how knowledge bases help build trust and relationships.

LO3 Understand the importance of sales ethics and its legal implications.

Introduction

rick Spence, a writer, consultant, and speaker suggests that business owners tap into a secret weapon that most entrepreneurs don't realize exists. This secret weapon can help to boost sales, speed up transactions, build more solid client relationships, and even increase employee motivation.

"It's not sold in any store, so if you decide to unsheath this secret weapon, competitors will find it hard to copy you. But reaping the benefits won't be easy. You'll have to do things most other businesses wouldn't. You'll have to take more chances."

The secret weapon Spence is referring to is trust. "Imagine asking your best friend to lend you $100 till next month. He or she wouldn't say, 'Are you a customer here?' or 'Do you have three pieces of ID?' They'd open up their wallet, because they trust you."

Spence continues: "Business is rarely so simple. Many companies don't really know their customers; many stores and restaurants never even learn their names. You can't lend money to people you don't know. Except that we do, every day. What are credit cards but a token of accountability? Both parties derive huge benefits from this trust network: consumers feel safer, because they don't have to carry around big wads of cash. Merchants enjoy bigger-ticket sales and more 'impulse' purchases because customers aren't restricted to spending only the money they have with them.

"Sadly, other aspects of the trust transaction don't benefit from confidence-building formal structures—so customers tend to shoulder most transaction risks. Can your products really do what you say they can? If I buy from you, will I get my money's worth? Can I count on you to perform the services I'm paying for? Customers must usually take vendors' propositions on faith.

"Yet customers get burned every day. I think of my mobile device that sometimes fails to work for no discernible reason, the hotel that charged me an undisclosed resort fee (even though it was no resort), the grocer that wouldn't consider a return without a receipt, or the retailer who told me my extended warranty wasn't actually a guarantee. Fear of similar experiences clings to consumers like morning fog. In lieu of trust, they are told caveat emptor: unwary buyers deserve what they get.

"Changing this paradigm could give you a competitive advantage. Customers will go out of their way to deal with trustworthy businesses. They buy more from people they trust. And they'll buy even more if you can offer sound advice to help them accomplish their goals.

"A few years ago, I bought a URL for a website I intended to build. To motivate me to develop the site quickly, I also bought a monthly hosting plan. But the months passed, and I never got around to it. A year later, when I called the domain-registration company about a separate problem, the customer rep looked at my account and noticed I had never used the hosting service I was paying for. Then he asked me the last question I never expected to hear: 'Since you haven't used that service, would you like me to refund the fees you've paid?'

"After picking up my jaw from the floor, I transferred other domains I had bought from other companies to this one. I still bring all my online projects to them because they've proved I can trust them to put my needs ahead of theirs."

Spence suggests that trust can be the factor to help set you apart you from the competitors.

Source: Rick Spence. "The Power of Trust." *The Financial Post*, May 16, 2011. Reprinted with permission.

trust reflects the extent of the buyer's confidence in the salesperson's integrity, but trust can mean different things to different people. According to John Newman,[1] vice president of Integrated Supply Chains Segment at A. T. Kearney, trust is defined in many ways. Buyers define trust with such terms as **openness**, dependability, candour, **honesty, confidentiality, security, reliability, fairness**, and predictability.[2] For example, in a Kearney study, one manufacturer related trust to credibility: "What trust boils down to, in a nutshell, is credibility, and when you say you are going to do something, you do it, and the whole organization has to be behind that decision."

Another manufacturer related trust to confidentiality in that "they were afraid that the sales guys were going around and telling account B what account A is doing," which was identified as a violation of trust. Another company related trust to openness, claiming "we have to share information that traditionally is not shared." One president told how his engineers were sharing manufacturing secrets with their suppliers that would have cost the engineers their jobs five years earlier.[3]

trust The extent of the buyer's confidence that he or she can rely on the salesperson's integrity.

openness Completely free from concealment; exposed to general view or knowledge.

honesty Fairness and straightforward conduct.

confidentiality A salesperson is entrusted with information from a buyer that cannot be shared.

security The quality of being free from danger.

reliability Consistency over time of doing what is right.

fairness Impartiality and honesty.

FIGURE 2.1
Trust Builders

Trust means different things to different people. Trust can be developed by using any of the trust builders. It is the salesperson's job, through questioning, to determine what trust attributes are critical to relationship building for a specific buyer.

Research reveals that little is known about what ongoing behaviours (i.e., service behaviours) salespeople can employ to satisfy and build trust with customers.[4] A salesperson has to determine what trust means to each of his or her buyers, as shown in Figure 2.1. If it is confidentiality, then the salesperson must demonstrate how his or her company handles sensitive information. If credibility is the concern, then the salesperson must demonstrate that all promises will be kept. Therefore, the buyer defines trust; it is the salesperson's job through questioning to determine what trust attributes are critical to relationship building for a specific buyer.

In this chapter, we first discuss the meaning of trust in the sales context. Next, we explore the importance of trust to salespeople. This is followed by a discussion of how to earn trust and what knowledge bases a salesperson can use to build trust in buyer-seller relationships. Finally, we review the importance of sales ethics in building trust.

LO1
What Is Trust?

trust occurs when an industrial buyer believes that he or she can rely on what the salesperson says or promises to do in a situation where the buyer is dependent on the salesperson's honesty and reliability.[5] One of the keys to a long-term relationship with any client is to create a basis of trust between the sales representative and the client organization.[6]

Thus, gaining trust is essential to being seen as a reliable salesperson. Long-term sales success in any industry will generally be built on the concept of referral, in which trust plays an important role. Others argue that truthfulness is valuable for its own sake and instrumental to other goals, such as improved long-term relationships.[7] Clients obviously seek a salesperson they can trust. The problem is, depending on the industry and the situation; they may be influenced by previous bad experiences that make them wary of future partners. "*An Ethical Dilemma*" illustrates how easy it is for a salesperson to lose the trust of a buyer even when the salesperson has the backing of his or her company to meet the customer's delivery requirements. Consultative salespeople are in a unique position to capitalize on building credibility with customers who place a high value on trust. Customers are looking for trustworthy business partners but may have difficulty trusting most salespeople; the salesperson should recognize this as an opportunity.

The "trust" described here is beyond the typical transaction-oriented trust schema. Many issues—Will the product arrive as promised? Will the right product actually be in stock and be shipped on time? Will the invoice contain the agreed-on price? Can the salesperson be found if something goes wrong?—are only preliminary concerns. In relationship selling, trust is based on a larger set of factors because of the expanded intimacy and long-term nature of the relationship. The intimacy of this relationship will result in both parties sharing information that could be damaging if leaked or used against the other partner.

Trust answers these questions:

1. Do you know what you are talking about?—competence; expertise

An Ethical Dilemma

Scott Chow, account manager for a large computer firm, was in the running for a larger order. One of the key criteria was a critical delivery date deadline. Chow talked to his branch manager, Wes Johnson, who in turn talked to the district manager as well as to headquarters about whether the deadline could be met. The district manager assured Chow that the deadline would be met. Chow submitted his proposal and a few weeks later he was pleased to learn his company had won the bid. Today, Chow received a phone call from his branch manager saying that the system was going to be ten days late. What did Chow do wrong? How would you handle this situation?

© FENG YU/SHUTTERSTOCK

2. Will you recommend what is best for me?—customer orientation

3. Are you truthful?—honesty; candour

4. Can you and your company back up your promises?—dependability

5. Will you safeguard confidential information that I share with you?—customer orientation; dependability

Trust is an integral part of the relationship between customers and suppliers and results in increased long-term revenues and profits.[8]

Good salespeople will anticipate their buyers' concerns.

WHY IS TRUST IMPORTANT?

In today's increasingly competitive marketplace, buyers typically find themselves inundated with choices regarding both products and suppliers. In this buyers' market, traditional selling methods that focused on closing the sale have been inefficient and often counterproductive to the organization's larger, longer-term marketing strategy. In this new competitive environment, buyers are demanding unique solutions to their problems—product solutions that are customized on the basis of their particular problems and needs. Additionally, the adversarial, win-lose characteristics so customary in traditional selling are fading fast. In their place, long-term buyer-seller relationships are evolving as the preferred form of doing business. Although buyers are finding it more effective and efficient to do *more* business with *fewer* suppliers, sellers are finding it more effective to develop a continuing stream of business from the right customers. Such long-term relationships develop mutually beneficial outcomes and are characterized by trust, open communication, common goals, commitment to mutual gain, and organizational support.[9]

This shift toward relationship selling has altered both the roles salespeople play and the activities and skills they exercise in carrying out these roles—the selling process itself. Today's more contemporary selling process is embedded within the relationship marketing paradigm. As such, it emphasizes the initiation and nurturing of long-term buyer–seller relationships based on mutual trust and value-added benefits. The level of problem-solving activity common to relationship selling requires deliberate and purposeful collaboration between both parties. These joint efforts are directed at creating unique solutions based on an enhanced knowledge and understanding of the customer's needs and the supplier's capabilities so that both parties derive mutual benefits. The nature of this integrative, win-win, and collaborative negotiation relies on augmented communication and interpersonal skills that nurture and sustain the reciprocal trust that allows all parties to share information fully and work together as a strategic problem-solving team.

The skills and activities inherent to relationship selling can be classified according to their purpose as (1) initiation of the relationship (Chapters 5 and 6), (2) development of the relationship (Chapters 7 and 8), and (3) enhancement of the relationship (Chapters 9 and 10). As the activities composing the selling process have changed, so too have the relative importance and degree of selling effort devoted to each stage of the process.

HOW TO EARN TRUST

Trust is important to any relationship. Several critical variables help salespeople earn a buyer's trust, such as **expertise**, dependability, candour, customer orientation, and compatibility. The importance of each is briefly discussed.

Expertise

Inexperience is a difficult thing for a young salesperson to overcome. Most recent university graduates will not have the expertise to be immediately successful, especially in industrial sales. Companies spend billions of dollars to train new recruits in the hope of speeding up the expertise variable. Training to gain knowledge on company products and programs, industry, competition, and general market conditions are typical subjects covered in most sales training programs. Young salespeople can shadow more experienced salespeople to learn what it takes to be successful. They must also go the extra distance to prove to their customers their dedication to service. For example, Missy Rust, of GlaxoSmithKline, had recently spent a few minutes with an anesthesiologist discussing a new product, a neuromuscular blocker. A few days later, the physician called her at 1 p.m. to discuss a patient whom he thought was a good candidate for this drug. He was unsure of the correct dosage and needed Rust's expertise in this matter. Rust immediately drove to the hospital and was in the operating room for more than four hours observing the surgery and answering the doctor's questions about this new drug.[10]

Another factor to consider is that many organizations have recently been downsized, thus dramatically

> A salesperson can build trust by demonstrating dependability by assisting in an order delivery.

© PNC/JUPITER IMAGES

cutting the purchasing area in terms of both personnel and support resources. As a result, buyers have to do more with less and, as such, are thirsty for expertise, be it insights into their own operations, financial situation, industry trends, or tactical skills in effectively identifying emerging cost-cutting and revenue opportunities in their business. Of course, expertise will be even more critical with certain buyers who are technical, detail-driven, or just uninformed in a certain area.

Salespeople should strive to help clients meet their goals. As an example, individuals or business owners can go online and trade stocks for themselves, but if they think a financial planner or securities company is more knowledgeable and brings more expertise to the table, then they will employ one.

Today's buyers will respond positively to any attempts to assist them in their efforts to reach bottom-line objectives, be it revenue growth, profitability, or financial or strategic objectives. Thus, expertise will take on an even more important role in the customer's assessment of the seller's credibility. For some buyers, especially those with economic or financial responsibilities (e.g., CFO, treasurer, owner-manager), a representative's ability to contribute to the bottom line will dominate the perception of a seller's credibility. This is a very important consideration for salespeople, given their pivotal strategy of penetrating accounts at the economic buyer level. Salespeople are seeking to convince clients that they are (1) actively dedicated to the task of positively influencing their bottom-line objectives and (2) capable of providing assistance, counsel, and advice that will positively affect the ability to reach objectives.[11] This is easier said than done because salespeople frequently do not understand the long-term financial objectives of their clients.[12]

Buyers today want recommendations and solutions, not just options. Salespeople must be prepared to help their clients meet their goals by adding value.

Buyers are continually asking themselves whether or not the salesperson has the ability, knowledge, and resources to meet his or her prospective customers' expectations. Salespeople are selling not only their knowledge but also the entire organization and the support that they bring to the buyer. Does the salesperson display a technical command of products and applications (i.e., is he or she accurate, complete, objective)? During one sales call, a buyer asked about a specific new product that the company was promoting in its advertising. The salesperson responded that the product was launched before he was trained on it. This response cast doubt not only on the salesperson's ability but also on the company for failing to train the salesperson.

Expertise also deals with the salesperson's skill, knowledge, time, and resources to do what is promised and what the buyer wants. Small customers must think that they are being treated as well as larger customers and have access to the same resources.

Salespeople must exhibit knowledge generally exceeding that of their customer, not just in terms of the products and services they are selling but in terms of the full scope of the customer's financial and business operations (e.g., products, programs, competitors, customers, vendors). They must bring skills to the table, be it discovery, problem solving, program and systems development, financial management, or planning. These skills must complement those of the customer and offer insight into the best practices in the customer's industry. It is not enough to be an expert. This expertise must translate into observable results and **contributions** for the buyer.

Dependability

Dependability hinges on the **predictability** of the salesperson's actions. Buyers have been heard to say, "I can always depend on her. She always does what she says she is going to do." Salespeople must remember the promises they make to a customer or prospect. Once a promise is made, the buyer expects that promise to be honoured. The buyer should not have to call the salesperson to remind him or her of the promise. The salesperson should take notes during all sales calls for later review. It is harder to forget to do something if it is written down. A salesperson is trying to establish that his or her actions fit a pattern of prior dependable behaviour. That is, the salesperson refuses to promise what he or she cannot deliver. The salesperson must also demonstrate an ability to handle confidential information. Buyers and sellers depend on each other to guard secrets carefully and keep confidential information confidential.

Candour

Candour deals with the honesty of the spoken word. A sales manager was overheard telling his salesforce

contributions Something given to better a situation or state for a buyer.

dependability The predictability of a person's actions.

predictability A salesperson's behaviour that can be foretold on the basis of observation or experience by a buyer.

candour Honesty of the spoken word.

"whatever it takes to get the order." One of the salespeople replied, "Are you telling us to stretch the truth if it helps us get the order?" The manager replied, "Of course!" The trustworthy salesperson understands doing "anything to get an order" will ultimately damage the buyer-seller relationship.

Salespeople have more than words to win over the support of the buyer; they have other sales aids, such as testimonials, third-party endorsements, trade publications, and consumer reports. The salesperson must be just as careful to guarantee that the proof is credible. It takes only one misleading event to lose all credibility. "An Ethical Dilemma" demonstrates what some unethical sales managers and salespeople will do to secure an order.

Customer Orientation

Customer orientation means placing as much emphasis on the customer's interests as on your own. An important facet of customer orientation is that salespeople work to satisfy the long-term needs of their customers rather than their own short-term goals.

A salesperson who has a customer orientation gives fair and balanced presentations. This includes covering both the pros and the cons of the recommended product. The pharmaceutical industry has done a good job understanding this principle, as many firms require their salespeople to describe at least one side effect of their drug for each benefit given. This is done not only because of the legal consideration but also to demonstrate expertise and trustworthiness to the physician. Traditional salespeople often ignored negative aspects of a product, which can turn off many buyers. A customer orientation should also

include clear statements of benefits and not overpower the buyer with information overload.

Salespeople with a customer orientation really turn into advisers; that is, they advise rather than sell. It is critical not to push a product that the buyer does not need to meet a short-term goal. Kim Davenport of Shering-Plough (see "Professional Selling in the 21st Century: The Importance of Information Gathering") states, "It is critically important to have a customer-orientation, as customer-oriented salespeople are good information gatherers."[13]

Salespeople must truly care about the partnership, and they must be willing to go to bat for the client when the need arises. A warehouse fire left one company without any space to store inventory. The salesperson worked out same-day delivery until the warehouse was rebuilt. This left a lasting impression on the buyer. They knew that if they ever needed any help, their salesperson would come through for them.

Salespeople must be fully committed to representing the customer's interests. Although most salespeople are quick to talk the talk about their absolute allegiance to their customer's interests, when it comes to walking the walk for their customer on such issues as pricing, production flexibility, and design changes,

An Ethical Dilemma

Lawrence Nakamura, a sales representative for a large restaurant supply company, just heard from his sales manager, Betty Oldenburg, that the first quarter was not going well. In fact, some heads were going to roll if orders did not pick up. Oldenburg gave every rep a new quota for the last month of the quarter and told her reps she did not care how they got the orders as long as they got them! At the next sales meeting, the reps asked Oldenburg for some advice on how to accomplish their goals. An exasperated Oldenburg waved her arms and shouted, "Tell them our special pricing we've had on for the past several months is going off at the end of the quarter. If they don't buy now they won't be able to get these deals again." What do you think will happen if these tactics are used? How would you handle this situation?

many lack the commitment or skills necessary to support the interests of their clients.

To be an effective salesperson and gain access to a customer's business at a partnership level, the client must feel comfortable with the idea that the salesperson is motivated and capable of representing his or her interests. Exhibit 2.1 looks at some of the questions salespeople need to answer satisfactorily to gain the buyer's trust and confidence.

Compatibility/ Likeability

Customers generally like to deal with sales representatives whom they know and like, and with whom they can feel a bond.

Some salespeople are too quick to minimize the importance of rapport building in this era of the economic buyer. It also may be true that today's buyers are not as prone to spending time discussing personal issues in sales calls as they might have been 10 or 15 years ago. Salespeople today have to be more creative and resourceful when attempting to build rapport. It is not unusual for a pharmaceutical salesperson to take a lunch for the entire staff into a physician's office. These lunches can be for as many as 20 to 40 people. The salesperson now has time to discuss his or her products over lunch with a captive audience.

PROFESSIONAL SELLING IN THE 21ST CENTURY

The Importance of Information Gathering

Kim Davenport, a district manager with Schering-Plough Pharmaceutical Company, talks about the importance of trust-building relationships. It is critically important that his field reps have the ability to build trust and transform this trust into long-term partnerships. His salespeople call on physicians, hospitals, and pharmacies with the ultimate goal of building not only trust but also long-term relationships.

I've been in this business for over 30 years now, first as a salesperson and now district manager. I've literally worked with hundreds of salespeople, and I know from experience the best sales reps are the best information gatherers. We discuss at each of our sales meetings what information we need from our doctors to give them our best advice. In fact, my best sales reps are viewed by their doctors as "trusted advisers." The only way we can give good advice is to thoroughly know our doctors' business and what they are up against. Only then will they be open to our sales presentations.

EXHIBIT 2.1
Questions That Salespeople Need to Answer Satisfactorily to Gain a Buyer's Trust

Expertise: Does the salesperson know what he or she needs to know? Does the salesperson and his or her company have the ability and resources to get the job done right?

Dependability: Can I rely on the salesperson? Does the salesperson keep promises?

Candour: Is the salesperson honest in his or her spoken word? Is the salesperson's presentation fair and balanced?

Customer orientation: Does the salesperson truly care about the partnership? Will the salesperson go to bat for the customer (e.g., wrong order, late delivery)?

Compatibility: Will the buyer like doing business with the salesperson? Will the buyer like doing business with the salesperson's company?

> Good salespeople are never in a hurry to earn commitment!

Salespeople have to be aware that their buyers are under considerable time pressure and that some will find it difficult to dedicate time to issues outside of the business. However, remember that buyers are human and do value compatibility, some more, some less.

Compatibility and likeability are important to establishing a relationship with key gatekeepers (e.g., receptionists and secretaries). First impressions are important, and a salesperson's ability to find commonalities with these individuals can go a long way in creating much-needed allies within the buying organization. Likeability is admittedly an emotional factor that is difficult to pin down, yet it is a powerful force in some buyer–seller relationships.

If a salesperson has done a good job of demonstrating the other trust-building characteristics, then compatibility can be used to enhance trust building. Buyers do not necessarily trust everyone they like; however, it is difficult for them to trust someone they do not like.

compatibility and likeability A salesperson's commonalities with other individuals.

LO2
Knowledge Bases Help Build Trust and Relationships

the more the salesperson knows, the easier it is to build trust and gain the confidence of the buyer. Buyers have certain expectations of the salesperson and the knowledge that he or she brings to the table. As outlined in Figure 2.2, salespeople may draw from several knowledge bases. Most knowledge is gained from the sales training program and on-the-job training.

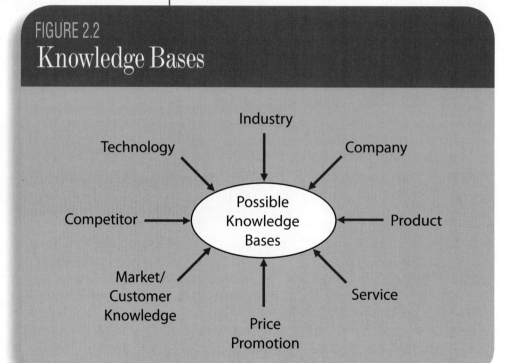

FIGURE 2.2
Knowledge Bases

The more the salesperson knows, the easier it is to build trust and gain the confidence of the buyer. Buyers have certain expectations of the salesperson and the knowledge that he or she brings to the table. Most knowledge is gained from the sales training programs and on-the-job training.

Sales training will generally concentrate on knowledge of the industry and company history, company policies, products, promotion, prices, market knowledge of customers, **competitor knowledge**, and basic selling techniques. Exhibit 2.2 summarizes topics generally covered during initial sales training programs.

INDUSTRY AND COMPANY KNOWLEDGE

Salespeople may be asked what they know about their company and industry. Every industry and company has a history. The personal computer industry has a short history of 30 years; fax technology, even shorter. Other industries have been around for centuries. Some industries change so quickly, such as the pharmaceutical industry through multiple mergers, that it is critical for the salesperson to know his or her industry to keep physicians informed on new companies, drugs, and procedures. Many buyers are too busy to stay informed and count on their salespeople to help them make sound decisions.

Salespeople should be familiar with their own company's operation and policies. Buyers may ask the salesperson such questions as, How long has your company been in the market? How many people does the company employ? Does the company have a local, a regional, a national, or an international customer base? Who started the company? Who is the president? CEO? What is the company's market share? What is the market share on this particular product? Salespeople who could not answer such questions would not inspire the trust of the buyer.

Each company initiates policies to ensure consistent decisions are made throughout the organization. An organization implements policies to control such factors as price, guarantees, warranties, and how much to spend per week taking clients out to lunch. Knowing the company's policies prevents a misunderstanding.

For example, if a representative says a customer can return goods 60 days after receipt when company policy is 30 days, the shipping department might refuse to accept the returned merchandise. The salesperson looks incompetent to both sales management

competitor knowledge
Knowledge of a competitor's strengths and weaknesses in the market.

Companies provide extensive training to be sure they send knowledgeable sales representatives into the field.

© ERIC AUDRAS/JUPITER IMAGES

product knowledge Detailed information on the manufacture of a product and knowing whether the company has up-to-date production methods.

service issues Concerns of the buyer that the salesperson should address.

and the customer. If the customer is not allowed to return the goods to the factory, the angry customer probably will never buy from the salesperson again.

Salespeople must understand their company policies. This includes being familiar with the company's formal structure and key personnel. It is important to work as a team with all company personnel. This helps build team spirit and a willingness to cooperate when a salesperson needs help in meeting a customer's need. It is difficult to provide outstanding service when the sales department is not on good terms with shipping and delivery, for instance.

PRODUCT KNOWLEDGE

Product knowledge includes detailed information on the manufacture of a product and knowing whether the company has up-to-date production methods. What materials are used when making the products? What quality control procedures are involved? Who are the design engineers?

Salespeople representing their company are expected to be experts on the products they sell. The fastest way to win the respect of a buyer is to be perceived as an expert. If the buyer truly feels the salesperson knows what he or she is talking about, then the buyer will be more willing to discuss the salesperson's solution to the buyer's problems or opportunities.

© STEVE HELBER/AP IMAGES

Buyers expect their salespeople to be experts on the products they sell.

The salesperson must know what his or her product can and cannot do. Just knowing product features is insufficient.

SERVICE

The effective salesperson must be ready to address such **service issues** as these:

- Does the company service its products or does the company send them to a third party?
- Does the company service its products locally or send them off to another city for service?
- Does the price include service or will there be a service charge when service is needed?
- What does the service agreement include? Shipping? Labour? Or neither of these?
- How long does the service generally take? Same day? Within a week? Will a loaner be provided until the product is fixed?
- Are there any conditions that make service not available? After five years? Damage from flood? Fire?

Buyers need to be comfortable answering these questions, and a good salesperson will make sure they are answered appropriately.

John Smith from ADZ Systems in Regina spends considerable time talking with his prospects about the service aspects of his company. ADZ systems sells collection software (i.e., receivables) that requires support from his field engineers. ADZ Systems also has a support group that takes calls 24 hours a day, seven days a week. Why is this important to Smith? One of his major competitors also has a support group, but only 8–5, Monday through Friday. Smith knows that he has service superiority. Salespeople who can offer the better service have an advantage for generating new business and taking away business from the competition. The salesperson's service mission is to provide added value for the customer. It is important for the salesperson to understand what service dimensions concern the buyer.

For instance, delivery, installation, training, field maintenance, and investing are all issues that a salesperson may be prepared to talk about. Buyers, however, may be concerned only with inventory because their present supplier runs out of stock frequently.

Exhibit 2.3 reviews service dimensions in which a salesperson could demonstrate service superiority. Additions may be made depending on specific customer demands.

EXHIBIT 2.3
Service Superiority

Dimension	Potential Superiority
1. Delivery	Can our company demonstrate speed? Deliver more often?
2. Inventory	Can we meet the demands of our customers at all times?
3. Training	Do we offer training? At our site? At our customer's?
4. Field maintenance	Do we go to the field to fix our products? Do our customers have to bring their equipment to us to fix?
5. Credit and financial consideration	Do we grant credit? Do we help finance?
6. Installation	Do we send a team to our customer's site for start-up?
7. Guarantees and warranties	What are our guarantees? How long? What do we cover?
8. Others	Do we offer anything unique that our competition does not?

PROMOTION AND PRICE

Promotion and **price knowledge** are other knowledge tools that the salesperson must understand. The ability to use this knowledge often makes the difference between a well-informed buyer who is ready to make a decision and another buyer who is reluctant to move the sales process forward. Hershey Foods Corporation supports its retailers with heavy promotions during Halloween, Christmas, and Easter. The promotional programs must be explained properly so the buyer can place the correct order size during the promotion. How many dollars are to be spent? Is it a national program? Is this a co-op program? What will it cost the buyer? If these questions are answered properly, the buyer will be more at ease and ready to make a purchase.

Price can be another area that makes a buyer hesitant if not properly explained. Knowledge of pricing policies is important because the salesperson often is responsible for quoting price and offering discounts. As a representative of the selling firm, the salesperson's quotes legally bind a company to their completion.

Salespeople need complete understanding of their companies' pricing policies. Does the company sell its products for a set price or can the salesperson negotiate? Can the salesperson give additional discounts to get a potential client whom the company has been after for years? Does the company allow trade-ins?

MARKET AND CUSTOMER KNOWLEDGE

Market knowledge and **customer knowledge** are critical to a salesperson's success. Some companies today, because of their size, send their salesforce out to call on all customer types. Larger companies typically break their customers into distinct markets. Computer manufacturers may break out their customer types by markets (i.e., salespeople sell to a particular line of business). For instance, the salesperson may sell only to manufacturers, wholesalers, financial institutions, government, education, or medical companies. This specialization allows the salesperson to become an expert in a line of business. For a salesperson to be effective, the salesperson must learn what the client needs, what benefits the client is seeking, and how the salesperson's products satisfy the buyer's specific needs. Buyers are not interested in factual knowledge unless it relates to fulfilling their specific needs. Having the salesforce learn one line of business well allows the salesperson to concentrate on the needs

promotion knowledge A knowledge tool salespeople must have to explain promotional programs their firms have.

price knowledge A knowledge tool salespeople must have about pricing policies to quote prices and offer discounts on products.

market knowledge A knowledge tool salespeople must have if larger companies break their customers into distinct markets; salespeople must be familiar with these markets to tailor their sales presentations.

customer knowledge Information about customers that is gathered over time and from very different sources that helps the salesperson determine what needs those customers have to better serve them.

of a specific market. The salesperson can become an expert in one line of business more quickly than if he or she has to know how the entire marketplace uses the salesperson's products.

Information about customers is gathered over time and from very different sources. A salesperson can use trade associations, credit agencies, trade magazines, trade directories, newspapers, and the World Wide Web as valuable resources. Canada 411, owned by Yellow Pages Group, has directories on people, businesses, and websites. Using the web to do an initial search on a company can tell a salesperson about what products a company makes, what markets they serve, and so on. A salesperson must use his or her time wisely when gathering information. Jon Young, national account manager for Ontario Systems Corporation, (see "Professional Selling in the 21st Century: Do What You Say You Are Going to Do")

PROFESSIONAL SELLING IN THE 21ST CENTURY

Do What You Say You Are Going to Do

Jon Young, national account manager for Ontario Systems Corporation, discusses his philosophy on why buyers buy from whom they do.

I've been in the sales business for over 25 years now, and I know what my buyers want. They want me to do what I say I am going to do! I have learned to measure my words carefully. It is easy to agree with the prospect or buyer when they ask for something, just to get an order signed. The trouble comes in when it is time to make it happen, and we can't. Then my company and I look bad. It can cost us the order down the road or, at the very least, a lot of ill will that takes a long time to make right.

The cornerstone of my selling philosophy is trust and expertise. I have to know what I am talking about—but, equally important, my customers and prospects have to trust what I am saying. Sometimes it is better to give up business to a competitor than to over-promise and under-deliver. Clients and prospects talk to their friends when you do a good job for them. They also tell their friends when you screw up and don't keep your promises. As I said before, I measure my words carefully. I want to be able to keep every promise I make during the time frame the customer expects the promise to come true. I live by this golden rule of keeping promises, and it does pay huge dividends in the long run.

states, "I have to know what I am talking about—but, equally important, my customers and prospects have to trust what I am saying."

COMPETITOR KNOWLEDGE

Salespeople will probably be asked how their product stands up against the competition. The buyer may ask, Who are your competitors in our marketplace? How big are you compared with your competitors? How do your company's prices compare with others in your industry? How does your product quality compare with the industry norm? These are important questions that every salesperson must be prepared to answer. Salespeople must have knowledge of their competitor's strengths and weaknesses to better understand their own products' position when comparing. A good salesperson must adjust his or her selling strategy depending on whom he or she is selling against.

Salespeople must be able to deliver complete comparative product information in a sales presentation. Comparisons of competitors' products for a customer's decision are critical, especially when your features and benefits are superior to those of the competition.

It is important that salespeople distinguish their products from the competition. The ultimate question a buyer asks is, Why should I use your product over the one I am presently using? A salesperson must have competitive knowledge to answer this question. What are the competitor's relative strengths and weaknesses? What weaknesses make this competitor vulnerable? Once the salesperson can determine the competitor's limitations, the salesperson can demonstrate the superiority of his or her product. A salesperson must answer these questions: How are you different from the competition? How are you better than the competition? A salesperson must be able to determine his or her differential competitive advantage.

TECHNOLOGY KNOWLEDGE

Salespeople must use technology to their advantage. Twenty years ago, salespeople had to know where a reliable pay phone was located in each city they visited. Many opportunities were missed because salespeople could not reach prospects while they were in the field. Today's salesperson has the luxury of cell phones, facsimile technology, the World Wide Web, voice mail, and email. Salespeople should communicate in the manner their prospects and clients prefer. Some clients use email extensively and want to use email over phone conversations. Some buyers like to fax orders in and would rather not meet the salesperson face to face. A good salesperson must recognize these preferences and act accordingly. Each of these can either be a bridge to the customer or an obstacle. Salespeople should be building bridges to all their prospects and customers by using technology appropriately (see Exhibit 2.4). If a buyer likes to email requests to a salesperson, then the salesperson must not use email to screen buyers. Likewise, if a facsimile number is given to prospects, then the fax machine

> Salespeople must be well versed in technology tools and how to use them effectively to build a bridge to the buyer.

must be turned on at all times and working properly.

Probably the most oversold form of technology is voice mail. Many companies have gone to this method of communication hoping to free up secretaries and make it easier to leave messages for the salesperson. The difficulty arises when a customer wants to talk to a salesperson and can only get a recording. Sometimes, the voice mail is

technology knowledge A knowledge tool salespeople must have about the latest technology.

EXHIBIT 2.4
Using Technology to Build Bridges to Customers

Technology	Bridge
World Wide Web	Price updates can be placed on the Web for customers to access. New product information can be made available to customers and prospects.
Email	Buyer and salesperson can communicate 24 hours a day. Mass communications can be sent out to all customers and prospects.
Facsimile	Nonelectronic documents can be transmitted 24 hours a day. Fax on demand.
Cell phones	Buyer and seller have immediate access to each other.
Voice mail	Salesperson and buyer can leave messages for each other and save time and effort.

full and it is impossible to leave a message. It is also possible to use voice mail to screen calls, and many buyers and salespeople complain that it is virtually impossible to make contact when their counterpart refuses to return their call.

Technology can be a friend or a foe of a salesperson. If used properly, technology can build bridges to prospects and clients and develop relationships. If technology is not used properly, a salesperson can find himself or herself alienating customers and turn a potential resource into a reason for a prospect not to do business with the salesperson.

LO3
SALES ETHICS AND LEGAL IMPLICATIONS

Ethics refers to right and wrong conduct of individuals and the institutions of which they are a part. Personal ethics and formal codes of conduct provide a basis for deciding what is right or wrong in a given situation. Ethical standards for a profession are based on society's standards, and most industries have developed a code of behaviours that are compatible with society's standards. Many professions in North America owe much of their public regard to standards of conduct established by professional organizations. Reflecting this, the American Marketing Association has adopted a code of ethics, which is available in the book companion website.[14]

Salespeople are constantly involved with ethical issues. In fact, salespeople are exposed to greater ethical pressures than individuals in many other occupations.[15] A sales manager might encourage his or her salesforce to pad their expense account in lieu of a raise. A salesperson might sell a product or service to a customer that the buyer does not need. A salesperson might exaggerate the benefits of a product to get a sale. The list can go on and on.

Recall that sales professionalism requires a truthful, customer-oriented approach. Customers are increasingly intolerant of nonprofessional, unethical practices. Sales ethics is closely related to trust. Deceptive practices, illegal activities, and noncustomer-oriented behaviour have to be attempted only once for a buyer to lose trust in his or her salesperson. Research has identified some of the sales practices deemed unethical as shown in Exhibit 2.5.[16]

Image of Salespeople and Sales Executives

Sales and Marketing Executives International (SMEI) has been concerned with the image of salespeople since the 1880s. Over the years SMEI has developed a code of ethics as a set of principles that outline the minimum requirements for professional conduct. Through its certification process SMEI declares that a salesperson will support and preserve the highest standards of professional conduct in all areas of sales and in all relationships in the sales process. Exhibit 2.6[17] is the SMEI Code

---

EXHIBIT 2.5
What Types of Sales Behaviours Are Unethical?

According to a survey of 327 customers, salespeople are acting unethically if they do any of the following:

1. Show concern for their own interest, not their clients'
2. Pass the blame for something they did wrong
3. Take advantage of poor or uneducated buyers
4. Accept favours from customers so the seller feels obliged to bend policies
5. Sell products/services that people do not need
6. Give answers when they do not really know answers
7. Pose as a market researcher when doing phone sales
8. Sell dangerous or hazardous products
9. Withhold information
10. Exaggerate benefits of product
11. Lie about product availability to make sale
12. Lie to competitors
13. Falsify product testimonials

EXHIBIT 2.6
SMEI Certified Professional Salesperson Code of Ethics

The SMEI Certified Professional Salesperson (SCPS) Code of Ethics is a set of principles that outline minimum requirements for professional conduct. Those who attain SCPS status should consider these principles as more than just rules to follow. They are guiding standards above which the salesperson should rise.

An SCPS shall support and preserve the highest standards of professional conduct in all areas of sales and in all relationships in the sales process. Toward this end an SCPS pledges and commits to these standards in all activities under this code.

As an SCPS I pledge to the following individuals and parties:

I. With respect to **The Customer, I** will:

Maintain honesty and integrity in my relationship with all customers and prospective customers.

Accurately represent my product or service in order to place the customer or prospective customer in a position to make a decision consistent with the principle of mutuality of benefit and profit to the buyer and seller.

Continually keep abreast and increase the knowledge of my product(s), service(s), and industry in which I work. This is necessary to better serve those who place their trust in me.

II. With respect to **The Company** and other parties whom I represent, I will:

Use their resources that are at my disposal and will be utilized only for legitimate business purposes.

Respect and protect proprietary and confidential information entrusted to me by my company.

Not engage in any activities that will either jeopardize or conflict with the interests of my company. Activities that may be or which may appear to be illegal or unethical will be strictly avoided. To this effect I will not participate in activities that are illegal or unethical.

III. With respect to **The Competition**, regarding those organizations and individuals that I compete with in the marketplace, I will:

Only obtain competitive information through legal and ethical methods.

Only portray my competitors, and their products and services in a manner which is honest, truthful, and based on accurate information that can or has been substantiated.

IV. With respect to **The Community** and society which provide me with my livelihood, I will:

Engage in business and selling practices which contribute to a positive relationship with the communities in which I and my company have presence.

Support public policy objectives consistent with maintaining and protecting the environment and community.

Participate in community activities and associations which provide for the betterment of the community and society.

I AM COMMITTED to the letter and spirit of this code. The reputation of salespeople depends upon me as well as others who engage in the profession of selling. My adherence to these standards will strengthen the reputation and integrity for which we strive as professional salespeople.

I understand that failure to consistently act according to the above standards and principles could result in the forfeiture of the privilege of using the SCPS designation.

Candidate's Name (Please Print) _____

Signature _____

Date _____

Today's professional salesperson is a trusted adviser to his or her buyers and receives a great level of respect for the services he or she provides to customers.

of Ethics that pledges a salesperson will adhere to these standards. Like SMEI, the Canadian Professional Sales Association (CPSA) has a professional development program that allows individuals to become a Certified Sales Professional. Once certified a salesperson must abide by the CPSA code of ethics as outlined in Exhibit 2.7.

A sales professional deserves and receives a high level of respect on the job. Buyers who do not interact with professional salespeople on a regular basis may believe in the negative stereotype of the salesperson as pushy, shifty, and untrustworthy. Where does this stereotype come from? Some salespeople are not professional in their approach and contribute to the negative stereotype. In the past, television programs, movies, and theatre productions have fostered the negative image of salespeople. During the 1960s and 1970s, the popular press also contributed to this negative image. A study of how salespeople are portrayed in the popular press found that salespeople are often associated with deceptive, illegal, and noncustomer-

price fixing Agreements between sellers to prevent or unduly lessen competition or to unreasonably enhance the price of a product by selling at a fixed price.

bid rigging An agreement in which competitors agree in advance who will win a bid based on the tenders submitted.

price discrimination Knowingly and systematically selling the same goods or services at different prices to different buyers.

predatory pricing A firm or an individual deliberately sets prices to incur losses for a long time to eliminate a competitor or to inhibit competition in the expectation that the firm or individual will later be able to recoup its losses by charging prices above competitive levels.

oriented behaviour.[18] Dilemmas exist also for sales executives implementing strategic account relationships regarding such issues as information sharing, trust, and hidden incentives for unethical behaviours.[19] Three of the more important areas of unethical behaviour, deceptive practices, illegal activities, and noncustomer-oriented behaviour, are discussed.

Deceptive Practices

Buyers have been known to be turned off by all salespeople because a few salespeople are unscrupulous and are even scam artists. This is unfortunate because all salespeople (good and bad) pay the price for this behaviour. Unfortunately, some salespeople do use quota pressure as an excuse to be deceptive. The salesperson has the choice to either ignore the trust-building approach and persuade the customer to buy or go to the next sales meeting and face the wrath of his or her sales manager for being under quota. Salespeople giving answers when they do not know, exaggerating product benefits, and withholding information may appear only to shade the truth, but when it causes harm to the buyer, the salesperson has jeopardized future dealings with the buyer.

NONCUSTOMER-ORIENTED BEHAVIOUR

Most of today's sales organizations emphasize trust-building behaviours and are customer oriented. Unfortunately, there are a few salespeople and companies today that concentrate on short-term goals and allow outmoded sales tactics to be practised. Most buyers will not buy from salespeople who are pushy and practise the hard sell. Too much is at stake to fall for the fast-talking, high-pressure salesperson. Buyers have been through their own training, and they understand the importance of developing a long-term relationship with their suppliers. Exhibit 2.8 summarizes these practices.

LEGAL IMPLICATIONS

When considering the legal implications involved in professional selling, it is important to consider the provincial, territorial, and federal legislation that is in place to regulate these activities.

The Competition Act is the major federal legislation in Canada that defines illegal practices, including **price fixing**, **bid rigging**, **price discrimination**, **predatory pricing**, **bait and switch selling**, and **pyramid selling**.

EXHIBIT 2.7
CPSA Sales Institute Code of Ethics

Canadian Professional
Sales Association

L'association canadienne
des professionnels
de la vente

Since/Depuis 1874

SELL MORE. SELL SMARTER.

CPSA
ACPV

VENDEZ PLUS. VENDEZ MIEUX.

Member since/membre depuis

The CPSA Sales Institute Code of Ethics is the set of principles and standards that a certified sales professional will strive to adhere to with customers, organizations, competitors, communities, and colleagues.

The Certified Sales Professional pledges and commits to uphold these standards in all activities:

I will:

1. Maintain honesty and integrity in all relationships with customers, prospective customers, and colleagues and continually work to earn their trust and respect.

2. Accurately represent my products or services to the best of my ability in a manner that places my customer or prospective customer and my company in a position that benefits both.

3. Respect and protect the proprietary and confidential information entrusted to me by my company and my customers and not engage in activities that may conflict with the best interest of my customers or my company.

4. Continually upgrade my knowledge of my products/services, skills and my industry.

5. Use the time and resources available to me only for legitimate business purposes. I will only participate in activities that are ethical and legal, and when in doubt, I will seek counsel.

6. Respect my competitors and their products and services by representing them in a manner which is honest, truthful and based on accurate information that has been substantiated.

7. Endeavour to engage in business and selling practices which contribute to a positive relationship with the community.

8. Assist and counsel my fellow sales professionals where possible in the performance of their duties.

9. Abide by and encourage others to adhere to this Code of Ethics.

As a certified sales professional, I understand that the reputation and professionalism of all salespeople depends on me as well as others engaged in the sales profession, and I will adhere to these standards to strengthen the reputation and integrity for which we will strive. I understand that failure to consistently act according to this Code of Ethics may result in the loss of the privilege of using my professional sales designation.

bait and switch selling
Firms or individuals advertise products at bargain prices that they do not have available in reasonable quantities and try to sell more expensive products instead.

pyramid selling Fees or commissions paid not on the basis of product sales but on the recruitment of others to make sales.

express warranty
A way a salesperson can create product liabilities by giving a product warranty or guarantee that obligates the selling organization even if the salesperson does not intend to honour the warranty.

misrepresentation
Making a false claim about a product

negligence A way a salesperson can create product liability by making a claim about a product without exercising reasonable care to see that this claim is accurate.

All Canadian provinces and territories have established a *cooling off* period during which the consumer may void a contract to purchase goods or services. These cooling off laws vary across jurisdictions, but their primary purpose is to give customers an opportunity to reconsider a buying decision made under a salesperson's persuasive influence. In most places, this legislation is referred to as The Direct Sellers Act or The Consumer Protection Act. For more information about the legislation involved with professional selling, please visit the Competition Bureau's website at http://www.competitionbureau.gc.ca.

It is also important to remember that sales representatives often have to engage in a contract with an individual or a firm to secure the sale. A *contract* is a promise or promises that the courts can enforce. Oral contracts are enforceable, but written contracts

are preferable as they reduce the possibility of disagreement. Courts give written contracts greater weight in a lawsuit. A written contract may consist of a sales slip, a notation on a cheque, or any other writing that offers evidence of the promises the party made.

When a salesperson is hired, he or she may be asked to sign an employment contract. Most of these agreements include a *noncompete clause*. This prohibits salespeople from working for a competing firm for a set time (often a year) after they leave the position. Most clauses are legally binding even when an employee's position is cut.

Illegal Activities

Misuse of company assets has been a long-standing problem for many sales organizations. Using the company car for personal use, charging expenses that did not occur, and selling samples for income are examples of misusing company assets. Some of these violations of company property also constitute violations of the Canada Revenue Agency (CRA) law and are offences that could lead to jail or heavy fines.

Bribery is another area that causes some salespeople to run afoul of the law. A competitor may be offering bribes; this, in turn, puts pressure on the salesperson's company to respond with bribes of its own. It is difficult for a salesperson to see potential sales going to the competition. Salespeople offering bribes on their own can be punished. Companies that engage in bribery may find themselves being prosecuted and fined. In some cultures, giving bribes is perceived to be acceptable business practice. However, bribes or payoffs may violate federal government legislation. Canada has the Corruption of Foreign Public Officials Act and for Canadian salespeople working with U.S. companies, the U.S. Foreign Corrupt Practices Act (FCPA) exists.

Another area of legal concern that involves the salesforce is product liability. Salespeople can create product liabilities for a company in three ways: **express warranty**, **misrepresentation**, and **negligence**. A salesperson can create a product

FROM INGRAM. SELL, 2E (BOOK ONLY), 2E. © SOUTH-WESTERN, A PART OF CENGAGE LEARNING, INC. REPRODUCED BY PERMISSION. WWW.CENGAGE.COM/PERMISSIONS.

EXHIBIT 2.8
Areas of Unethical Behaviour

Deceptive Practices	Illegal Activities
Deceive	Defraud
Hustle	Con
Scam	Misuse company assets
Exaggerate	
Withhold information/bluff	

Noncustomer-Oriented Behaviour
Pushy

Hard sell

Fast talking

High pressure

warranty or guarantee that obligates the selling organization even if they do not intend to give the warranty. Express warranties are created by any affirmation of fact or promise, any description, or any sample or model that a salesperson uses, which is made part of the basis of the bargain.

Basis of the bargain is taken to mean that the buyer relied on the seller's statements in making the purchase decision. If a salesperson tells a prospect that a machine will turn out 50 units per hour, a legal obligation has been created for the firm to supply a machine that will accomplish this. A salesperson's misrepresentation can also lead to product liability even if the salesperson makes a false claim thinking it is true. The burden of accuracy is on the seller. Salespeople are required by law to exercise reasonable care in formulating claims. If a salesperson asserts that a given drug is safe without exercising reasonable care to see that this claim is accurate, the salesperson has been negligent. Negligence is a basis for product liability on the part of the seller.

Although these tactics may increase sales in the short run, salespeople ultimately ruin their trust relationship with their customer and company. Given the legal restrictions that relate to selling practices, a salesperson, as well as the selling organization, should exercise care in developing sales presentations.

HOW ARE COMPANIES DEALING WITH SALES ETHICS?

Many companies spend time covering ethics in their training programs. These programs should cover such topics as the appropriateness of gift giving, the use of expense accounts, and dealing with a prospect's unethical demands. Each company will have its own policies on gift giving. John Huff of Shering-Plough states, "Just a few years ago, I could spend my expense account on Indiana Pacers tickets or a golf outing with doctors. That is not the case today. There is a lot of grey area concerning gift giving by salespeople to their business clients and prospects. The pharmaceutical industry has policed itself so now gift giving has all but been eliminated. I must know the rules of my company and industry."[20]

Receiving holiday gifts is another area that must be explained during training. Some buyers are not allowed to accept gifts from salespeople.

Another important training area is the use of expense accounts. Salespeople should be trained in how to fill out the expense account form and what is acceptable for submission. Some companies allow personal kilometrage to be included; others do not. If guidelines are established, there is less chance for salesperson misunderstanding.

Sometimes unethical behaviour is not initiated by the salesperson but by the buyer. Salespeople must be trained in dealing with prospects who make unethical demands. Buyers can be under pressure from their company to stay within budget or to move up the timetable on an order. A buyer may ask a salesperson to move him or her up on the order list in exchange for more business down the road. One pharmacist set up a deal with a salesperson to buy samples illegally. The trust-based salesperson has to shut down any short-term gain for long-term success. A salesperson's career is over if the word circulates that he or she cannot be trusted.

A salesperson must also be concerned with our legal system and that of other countries. It cannot be an excuse for today's well-trained salesperson to say he or she did not know that a law was being broken. When in doubt, the salesperson must check out all provincial, territorial, and local laws. In addition, there are industry-specific rules and regulations to be considered. Exhibit 2.9 covers a number of legal reminders.

A salesperson has his or her reputation to tarnish only once. In this day and age of mass communication (phone, email, websites), it is easy for a buyer to get the word out that a salesperson is acting unethically and end that salesperson's career.

basis of the bargain A term used when a buyer relies on the seller's statements in making a purchase decision.

EXHIBIT 2.9
Legal Reminders

For salespeople

1. Use factual data rather than general statements of praise during the sales presentation. Avoid misrepresentation.

2. Thoroughly educate customers before the sale on the product's specifications, capabilities, and limitations.

3. Do not overstep your authority, as the salesperson's actions can be binding to the selling firm.

4. Avoid discussing these topics with competitors: prices, profit margins, discounts, terms of sale, bids or intent to bid, sales territories or markets to be served, rejection or termination of customers.

5. Do not use one product as bait for selling another product.

6. Do not try to force the customer to buy only from your organization.

7. Offer the same price and support to buyers who purchase under the same set of circumstances.

8. Do not tamper with a competitor's product.

9. Do not disparage a competitor's product without specific evidence of your contentions.

10. Avoid promises that will be difficult or impossible to honour.

For the sales organization

1. Review sales presentations and claims for possible legal problems.

2. Make the salesforce aware of potential conflicts with the law.

3. Carefully screen any independent sales agents the organization uses.

4. With technical products and services make sure the sales presentation fully explains the capabilities and dangers of products and service.

Visit **sell.nelson.com** to find the resources you need today!

Located at the back of the textbook are rip-out Chapter Review cards. Make sure you also go online to check out other tools that SELL offers to help you successfully pass your course.

- Flashcards
- Glossary
- PowerPoint Notes
- Role-Play Videos
- Games
- Interactive Quizzing

CABOT BUSINESS STATIONERY

Background

Congratulations! As a new salesperson for Cabot Business Stationery, you have just completed training and have been assigned the southwest territory. Cabot Business Stationery designs and manufactures a full line of stock and customized forms for use in all types of business. Operating throughout Canada, Cabot is recognized as one of the three leaders in the industry.

Current Situation

Aceso General Hospital was once a major account in your territory. Over this past year, the hospital's forms business has been switched from Cabot to one of your main competitors. Because of the large volume and many types of forms used, Aceso has placed the purchasing responsibility for all forms in the hands of Jim Adams in the purchasing department. An experienced professional purchasing agent, Adams has been in this position for several years and has purchased significant volumes of forms from Cabot in the past. While calling on Adams at his office in the hospital, you have learned that Aceso's dropping Cabot as a forms source did not happen overnight. Although the loss of this account was not related to any single problem, you have learned that the switch to your competitor was basically due to a combination of events that resulted in a loss of trust in Cabot. Several shipments did not arrive as promised, causing major problems for both billing and admissions. Even though the final proof copies were correct, a newly designed, multipart computer form was found to be short one of its pages. This required

emergency room staff to take the time to use a copier (located one floor up) until the forms could be rerun and delivered two weeks later. The final straw concerned an admissions form that Cabot had been supplying the hospital for more than three years. For some reason, a new shipment of the admissions forms was the wrong size and would not fit into patient files without being folded. In each event, the prior salesperson worked with Adams to get the problems resolved and the correct forms delivered. Discounts were also given to help offset the inconvenience incurred. Nevertheless, Cabot has lost the account, the previous salesperson has quit the company, and you have inherited the challenge of winning back Adams and Aceso General Hospital.

Questions

1. Put yourself in the role of the salesperson for Cabot Business Stationery in the selling situation just described and review the *trust-building behaviours* presented in this chapter. Using the following as a guide, discuss and give examples of how you might use each of the *trust builders* to reestablish a relationship with Jim Adams and win back the Aceso General Hospital account.

Trust Builders

1. Expertise: _____

2. Dependability: _____

3. Candour: _____

4. Customer Orientation: _____

5. Compatibility: _____

Birch Electronics

Background

Birch Electronics specializes in manufacturing home appliances. Birch is a new company trying to break into the market. They have had trouble breaking into the larger accounts (Lowes, Sears, Home Depot). As an account development specialist for Birch, you are making an initial sales call to Mary Miller, director of purchasing for Lowes. The purpose of the initial call is to assess Lowes' current needs and to determine why Lowes has not opted to carry Birch at this time. According to the initial information you gained from a short conversation with Miller, she appears to have erroneous information that Birch regularly misses delivery deadlines and that their quality is average at best.

At first Miller was hesitant about keeping her appointment with you. She has decided to keep your appointment but the tone of her voice has you concerned. You are also unsure of where she heard the erroneous information. During your conversation with Miller, she alluded to the fact that one of your competitors passed on this information to her.

Role Play

Location: Mary Miller's office

Action: Role play the questions you will ask about Miller's concerns. Then role play how you will begin to earn Miller's trust. You should be prepared to use the trust builders.

TEST COMING UP? NOW WHAT?

With **SELL**, you have a multitude of study aids at your fingertips. After reading the chapters, check out these ideas for further help:

Chapter Review cards include a chapter summary of the learning objectives, definitions, and any key visuals for that chapter.

Continuing Case cards let you go further into the sales industry with a case involving each chapter's key concepts as well as discussion questions and space for notes.

Other great ways to help you study include **games, role-play videos, interactive quizzing,** and **flashcards**.

"I like the flashcards, the videos, and the quizzes. Great format! I love the cards in the back of the book!"

—Asha Thtodort, Algonquin College

Visit **www.sell.nelson.com** to find the resources you need today!

© Anderson Ross/Getty Images

Understanding buyers

provides a foundation for building customer value.

3

Understanding Buyers

After completing this chapter, you should be able to

LO1 Categorize the primary types of buyers, and discuss the distinguishing characteristics of business markets.

LO2 List the steps in the business-to-business buying process.

LO3 Discuss the different types of buyer needs.

LO4 Describe how buyers evaluate suppliers and alternative sales offerings by using the multiattribute model of evaluation.

LO5 Explain the two-factor model that buyers use to evaluate the performance of sales offerings and develop satisfaction.

LO6 Explain the different types of purchasing decisions.

LO7 Describe the four communication styles and how salespeople must adapt their own styles to maximize communication.

LO8 Explain the concept of buying teams and specify the different member roles.

Introduction

fred Boss, sales manager at Ticona Engineering Polymers, a manufacturer of high-performance plastics found in everything from laptop computers to washing machines, says his organization faces three key challenges today.

The first is globalization: As Ticona's customers expand into every corner of the globe, Boss's team is dealing with complexities that didn't exist even five years ago. One of the biggest challenges is successfully navigating the cultural differences in other countries. Boss recently launched a multicultural training initiative to help his sales team understand and respect the myriad differences. His salespeople have learned how to handle everything from email and first meetings to relationship building and problem solving—without committing a deal-breaking faux pas.

The second challenge that Boss identifies is value creation. As the pace of business increases, Boss says keeping his team focused on value creation is a growing challenge. "We want our account managers to be as close to customers as possible, but you can't do that for everyone," he observes. Helping his team understand where to spend time and how to create value for key customers comes down to understanding customers' businesses and how Ticona can help them achieve their strategic goals, says Boss. This, in turn, leads to sustainable, long-term business.

A third challenge for Ticona is talent development. Finding salespeople who are business savvy, can think strategically, are able to navigate the cultural intricacies of a global marketplace—and who can top all that off with a solid background in chemical engineering or science—is no small task. That's why retaining his team and helping each team member meet the changing needs of Ticona's customers are top priorities for Boss. He accomplishes these goals by using a strength-based management philosophy: Rather than focus on where people need to shore up weaknesses, he invests in developing their strengths and matching those strengths to the sales role.

Boss expects these trends to continue accelerating. Relationships, he says, will consequently take on greater importance, keeping sales teams grounded as the pace of business shifts into warp speed. Already, Ticona account managers who once relied on close connections at a single site are finding they must build relationships with their contacts' extended networks throughout the world.

"No matter what you know about one technology or another, I continually stress to my team that you need to be relatable," says Boss. "I invest a lot of my time—and I encourage my team to do the same—in learning how to better interact with people. You need to be a great listener and have great people skills, whether you're talking to someone on the shop floor or the top floor."

Source: Heather Baldwin. "Chemical Reaction: How to Keep Pace in a Business World Explosive with Change." *Selling Power*. http://www.sellingpower.com/magazine/article. php?i=1333&ia=9214.

this chapter focuses on preparing you to better understand buyers. Following a discussion on different types of buyers, this chapter develops a model of the buying process and the corresponding roles of the salesperson. Buyer activities characteristic of each step of the purchase decision process are explained and related to salesperson activities for effectively interacting with buyers. This is followed by an explanation of different types of purchasing decisions to which salespeople must respond. The influence of individual communication styles on selling effectiveness is also discussed. The growing incidence of multiple buying influences and buying teams is then demonstrated, along with their impact on selling strategy. Finally, emergent trends, such as relationship strategies, supply-chain management, target pricing, and the growing importance of information and technology, are discussed from the perspective of the salesperson.

LO1
Types of Buyers

Salespeople work and interact with many different types of buyers. These buyer types range from heavy industry and manufacturing operations to consumers making a purchase for their own use. These variants of customer types arise out of the unique buying situations they occupy. As a result, one type of buyer will have needs, motivations, and buying behaviour that are very different from another type of buyer. Consider the different buying situations and the resulting needs of a corporate buyer for Foot Locker compared with the athletic equipment buyer for a major university or Joe

consumer markets A market in which consumers purchase goods and services for their use or consumption.

business markets A market composed of firms, institutions, and governments that acquire goods and services to use as inputs into their own manufacturing process, for use in their day-to-day operations, or for resale to their own customers.

derived demand Demand in business markets that is closely associated with the demand for consumer goods.

Smith, attorney at law and weekend warrior in the local YMCA's basketball league. As illustrated in Exhibit 3.1, each of these buyers may be looking for athletic shoes, but their buying needs are very different. To maximize selling effectiveness, salespeople must understand the type of buyer with whom they are working and respond to their specific needs, wants, and expectations.

The most common categorization of buyers splits them into either (1) **consumer markets** or (2) **business markets**. Consumers purchase goods and services for their own use or consumption and are highly influenced by peer group behaviour, aesthetics, and personal taste. Business markets are composed of firms, institutions, and governments. These members of the business market acquire goods and services to use as inputs into their own manufacturing process (e.g., raw materials, component parts, and capital equipment), for use in their day-to-day operations (e.g., office supplies, professional services, insurance), or for resale to their own customers. Business customers tend to stress overall value as the cornerstone for purchase decisions.

DISTINGUISHING CHARACTERISTICS OF BUSINESS MARKETS

Although there are similarities between consumer and business buying behaviours, business markets tend to be much more complex and possess several characteristics that are in sharp contrast to those of the consumer market. These distinguishing characteristics are described in the following sections.

Concentrated Demand

Business markets typically exhibit high levels of concentration in which a small number of large buyers account for most of the purchases. The fact that business buyers tend to be larger in size but fewer in numbers can greatly affect a salesperson's selling plans and performance. For example, a salesperson selling grade industrial silicon for use in manufacturing computer chips will find that his or her fate rests on acquiring and nurturing the business of one or more of the four or five dominant chip makers around the world.

Derived Demand

Derived demand denotes that the demand in business markets is closely associated with the demand for consumer goods. When the consumer demand for new cars and trucks increases, the demand for rolled steel

EXHIBIT 3.1
Different Needs of Different Athletic Shoe Buyers

	Buyer for Foot Locker Shoe Stores	University Athletic Equipment Buyer	Joe Smith—YMCA Weekend Warrior
Functional needs	• Has the features customers want • Well constructed—minimizes returns • Offers point-of-sale displays for store use • Competitive pricing	• Individualized sole texture for different player performance needs • Perfect fit and size for each team member • Custom match with university colours • Size of supplier's payment to coach and school for using their shoes	• Cutting-edge shoe features • Prominent brand logo • Highest-priced shoes in the store
Situational needs	• Can supply stores across North America • Ability to ship to individual stores on a just-in-time basis • Offers 90-day trade credit	• Ability to deliver on time • Provide supplier personnel for team fittings • Make contract payments to university and coach at beginning of season	• Right size in stock, ready to carry out • Takes Visa and MasterCard
Social needs	• Invitation for buying team to attend trade show and supplier-sponsored reception	• Sponsor and distribute shoes at annual team shoe night to build enthusiasm • Include team and athletes in supplier brand promotions	• Offers user-group newsletter to upscale customers • Periodic mailings for new products and incentives to purchase
Psychological needs	• Assurance that shoes will sell at retail • Brand name with strong market appeal • Option to return unsold goods for credit	• Brand name consistent with players' self-images • The entire team will accept and be enthusiastic toward product decision • Belief that the overall contract is best for the university, team, and coaches	• Reinforces customer's self-image as an innovator • Product will deliver the promised performance • Customer wants to be one of only a few people purchasing this style of shoe
Knowledge needs	• Level of quality—how the shoe is constructed • How the new features affect performance • What makes the shoe unique and superior to competitive offerings • Product training and materials for sales staff	• What makes the shoe unique and superior to competitive offerings • Supporting information and assurance that the contracted payments to university and coaches are superior to competitive offerings	• What makes the shoe unique and superior to competitive offerings • Assurance that everybody on the court will not be wearing the same shoe

also goes up. Of course, when the demand for consumer products goes down, so goes the related demand in business markets. The most effective salespeople identify and monitor the consumer markets that are related to their business customers so they can better anticipate shifts in demand and assist their buyers in staying ahead of the demand shifts rather than being caught with too much, too little, or even the wrong inventory. Republic Gypsum's salespeople accurately forecasted a boom in residential construction and the pressure it would put on the supply of sheetrock wallboard. Working closely with their key customers, order quantities and shipping dates were revised to prevent those customers from being caught with inadequate inventories to supply the expanded demand. This gave those customers a significant advantage over their competitors, who were surprised and suddenly out of stock.

Higher Levels of Demand Fluctuation

Closely related to the derived demand characteristic, the demand for goods and services in the business market is more volatile than that of the consumer market. In economics, this is referred to as the **acceleration principle**. As demand increases (or decreases) in the consumer

---

PROFESSIONAL SELLING IN THE 21ST CENTURY

Salespeople Have Become Sources of Advantage for the Customer

John Sullivan is the senior management consultant for Prime Resource Group, where he works with a list of global accounts in improving sales performance. Sullivan has an extensive background in sales and sales management and offers his reflections on the evolution of personal selling.

The salesperson's role in Era 1 would best be described as that of a persuader. Training was focused exclusively on three areas: presenting, handling objections, and closing. The agenda was to get the customer to do what the salesperson wanted the customer to do. Era 1 was replaced with an emphasis on a new set of skills and a more enlightened win-win perspective of the salesperson's role. This was Era 2 and emphasized questioning, listening, and building a relationship with the customer. Communication was directed toward developing an understanding of the customer's needs. The salesperson's role was that of a problem solver—to understand the customer's needs and close the gap with his or her product as the solution. Era 2 has continued to evolve and today, more than ever before, salespeople have become a source of business advantage for the customer. One point of view regarding this business advantage is that salespeople become consultants to the customer, applying their business acumen and understanding of the customer's business situation to create a solution that the customer truly values. Often, this is a solution that the customer has never experienced and would never think of asking for.

---

market, the business market reacts by accelerating the buildup (or reduction) of inventories and increasing (or decreasing) plant capacity. A good example would be the rapidly growing demand for tri-mode wireless phones with advanced capabilities, such as voice-activated dialling and vision-enabled access to the Internet and Web with enhanced full-colour screens. In response to higher consumer demand, wholesalers and retailers are increasing their inventories of these advanced phones while decreasing the number of single-mode voice-only devices they carry. In response, manufacturers have shifted their production away from the voice-only wireless phones to increase their production of the more advanced Internet-capable models. Salespeople are the source of valuable information and knowledge, enabling their customers to anticipate these fluctuations and assisting them in developing more effective marketing strategies. As a result, both the buying and selling organizations realize mutual positive benefits.

Purchasing Professionals

Buyers in the business markets are trained as purchasing agents. The process of identifying suppliers and sourcing goods and services is their job. This results in a more professional and rational approach to purchasing. As a result, salespeople must possess increased levels of knowledge and expertise to provide customers with a richer and more detailed assortment of application, performance, and technical data.

Multiple Buying Influences

Reflecting the increased complexity of many business purchases, groups of individuals within the buying firm often work together as a buying team or centre. As a result, salespeople often work simultaneously with several individuals during a sales call and even different sets of buyers during different sales calls. Buying team members come from different areas of expertise and play different roles in the purchasing process. To be effective, the salesperson must first identify, and then understand and respond to, the role and key buying motives of each member.

Close Buyer–Seller Relationships

The smaller customer base and increased usage of supply chain management, characterized by buyers becoming highly involved in organizing and administering logistical processes and actively managing a reduced set of suppliers, has resulted in buyers and sellers becoming much more interdependent than ever before. This increased interdependence and desire to reduce risk of the unknown has led to an emphasis on developing long-term buyer–seller relationships characterized by increased levels of buyer–seller interaction and higher levels of service expectations by buyers. "Professional Selling in the 21st Century: Salespeople Have Become Sources of Advantage for the Customer"[1] describes the shift in selling models to that of a consultant serving

© NYUL/ISTOCKPHOTO

Salespeople in business markets work closely with buyers to satisfy various needs aimed at improving their business performance.

as a source of business advantage for the customer. This shift requires salespeople to change their focus from quickly selling the buyer and closing the current transaction, to adapting a longer-term perspective emphasizing continuing multiple exchanges into the future. This perspective often includes making multiple sales calls to develop a better understanding of the buyer's needs and then responding to those needs with a sales offering that solves the buyer's needs and enhances the buyer–seller relationship in favour of future interactions.

LO2
The Buying Process

lthough not always the case in the consumer marketplace, buyers in the business marketplace typically undergo a conscious and logical process in making purchase decisions. As depicted in Figure 3.1, the sequential and interrelated phases of the business buyers's purchase process has eight phases: (1) recognition of the problem or need, (2) determination of the characteristics of the item and the quantity needed, (3) description of the characteristics of the item and quantity needed, (4) search for and qualification of potential sources, (5) acquisition and analysis of proposals, (6) evaluation of proposals and selection of suppliers, (7) selection of an order routine, and (8) performance feedback and evaluation.

Depending on the nature of the buying organization and the buying situation, the buying process may

FIGURE 3.1

Comparison of Buying Decision Process Phases and Corresponding Steps in the Selling Process

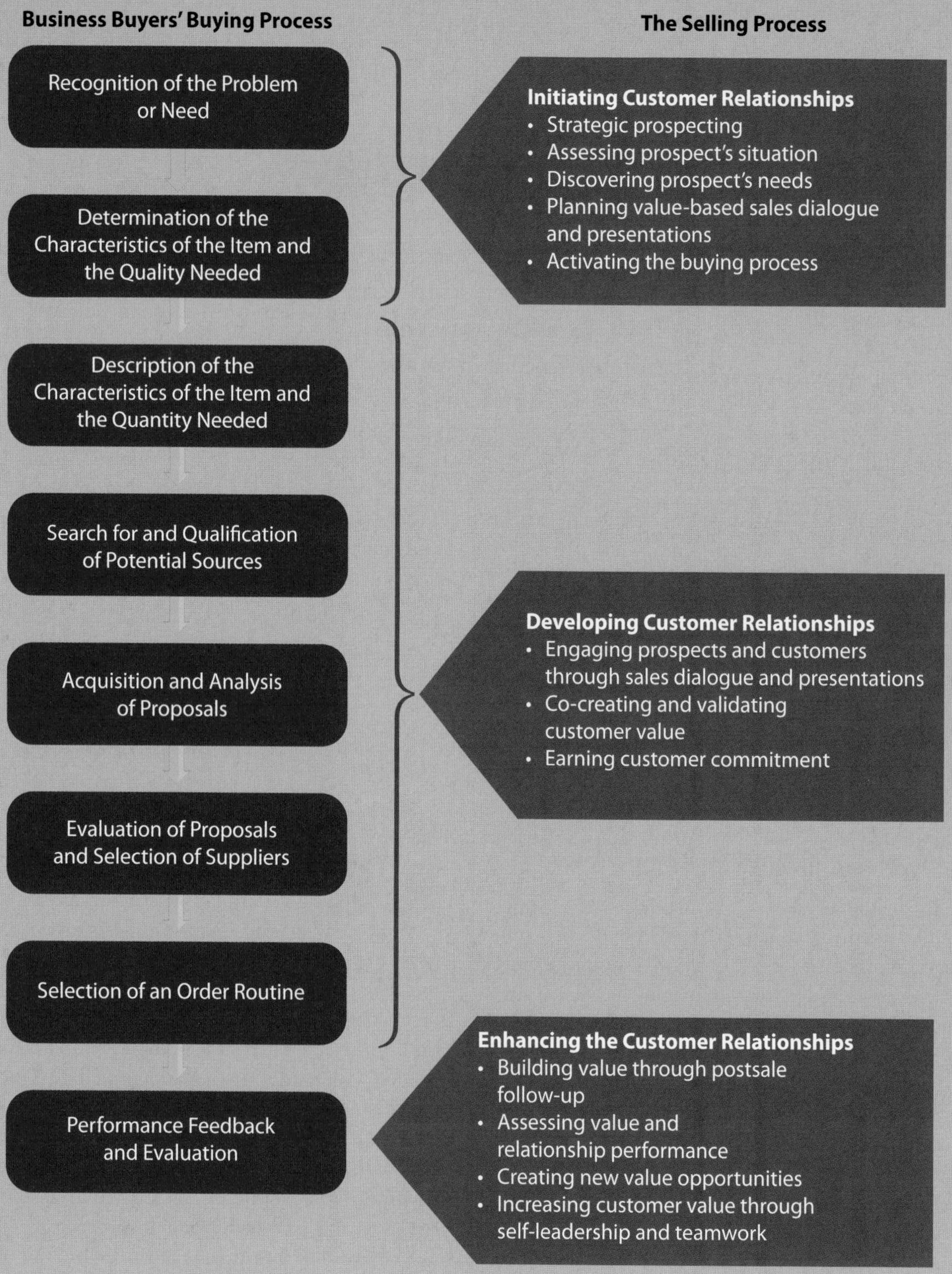

Business Buyers' Buying Process

The Selling Process

- Recognition of the Problem or Need

- Determination of the Characteristics of the Item and the Quality Needed

Initiating Customer Relationships
- Strategic prospecting
- Assessing prospect's situation
- Discovering prospect's needs
- Planning value-based sales dialogue and presentations
- Activating the buying process

- Description of the Characteristics of the Item and the Quantity Needed

- Search for and Qualification of Potential Sources

- Acquisition and Analysis of Proposals

Developing Customer Relationships
- Engaging prospects and customers through sales dialogue and presentations
- Co-creating and validating customer value
- Earning customer commitment

- Evaluation of Proposals and Selection of Suppliers

- Selection of an Order Routine

Enhancing the Customer Relationships
- Building value through postsale follow-up
- Assessing value and relationship performance
- Creating new value opportunities
- Increasing customer value through self-leadership and teamwork

- Performance Feedback and Evaluation

be highly formalized or simply a rough approximation of what actually occurs. The decision process General Motors employs for the acquisition of a new organization-wide computer system will be highly formalized and purposefully reflect each of the previously described decision phases. Compared with General Motors, the decision process of Bloomington Bookkeeping, a single office and four-person operation, could be expected to consist of be less formalized. In the decision to replenish stock office supplies, both of the organizations are likely to use a much less formalized routine—but still, the routine will reflect the different decision phases.

As Figure 3.1 further illustrates, there is a close correspondence between the phases of the buyer's decision process and the selling activities of the salesperson. It is important that salespeople understand and make use of the interrelationships between the phases of the buying process and selling activities. Effective use of these interrelationships offers salespeople numerous opportunities to interact with buyers in a way that shapes product specifications and the selection of sources while facilitating the purchase decision.

PHASE ONE—RECOGNITION OF THE PROBLEM OR NEED: THE NEEDS GAP

Needs are the result of a gap between buyers' **desired states** and their **actual states**. Consequently, need recognition results from an individual cognitively and emotionally processing information relevant to his or her actual state of being and comparing it with the desired state of being. As illustrated in Figure 3.2, any perceived difference, or **needs gap**, between these two states activates the motivation or drive to fill the gap and reach the desired state. For example, the SnowRunner Company's daily production capacity is limited to 1000 moulded skimobile body housings. Their research indicates that increasing capacity to 1250 units per day would result in significant reductions in per-unit costs and allow them to enter

additional geographic markets—both moves that would have significant and positive impacts on financial performance. The perceived need to expand production activates a corresponding motivation to search for information regarding alternative solutions and acquire the capability to increase production by 250 units.

desired states A state of being based on what the buyer desires.

actual states A buyer's actual state of being.

needs gap A perceived difference between a buyer's desired and actual state of being.

Business buyers typically undergo a conscious and logical process in making purchase decisions.

However, if there is no gap, then there is no need and no active buying motive. It is common for salespeople to find themselves working with buyers who, for one reason or another, do not perceive a needs gap to be present. It is possible that they do not have the right information or lack a full understanding of the situation and the existence of options better than their current state. It is also possible that their understanding of the actual state might be incomplete or mistaken. For example, SnowRunner's buyers might not understand the

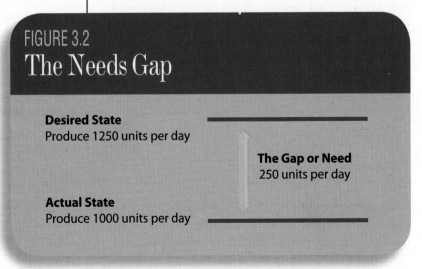

FIGURE 3.2
The Needs Gap

Desired State
Produce 1250 units per day

The Gap or Need
250 units per day

Actual State
Produce 1000 units per day

The needs gap is the difference between the buyer's perceived desired state and the buyer's perceived actual state.

cost reduction possibilities and increased market potential that could result from increased capacity. As a result, they perceive no need to increase production—the desired state is the same as their actual state. Similarly, the buyers might be functioning with incomplete information regarding the company's actual state of reduced production capacity because of SnowRunner's existing moulding machines requiring increased downtime for maintenance. Properly realized, this lowering of the actual state would result in a needs gap. Successful salespeople position themselves to assist buyers in identifying and understanding needs as a result of their broader expertise and knowledge regarding product use and application. Salespeople can also use sales conversations to present buyers with information and opportunities that effectively raise the desired state, generate a need, and trigger the purchase decision process. Topperforming salespeople understand the importance of assisting their buyers in forming realistic perceptions of the actual state and the desired state. In this manner, the salesperson can continue to serve as a nonmanipulative consultant to the buyer while affecting buying motives that yield mutual benefits to all parties. However, it should be noted that the persuasive power of assisting the buyer in determining and comparing desired and actual states can also be misused and lead to unethical and manipulative selling behaviours, such as those exhibited in "An Ethical Dilemma."

LO3
Types of Buyer Needs

The total number of potential customer needs is infinite and sometimes difficult for salespeople to grasp and understand on a customer-by-customer basis. Consequently, many salespeople find it helpful to group customer needs into one of five basic types or categories that focus on the buying situation and the benefits to be provided by the product or service being chosen.[2]

These five general types of buyer needs are described as follows:

- **Situational needs** are the specific needs that are contingent on, and often a result of, conditions related to the specific environment, time, and place (e.g., emergency car repair while travelling out of town, a piece of customized production equipment to fulfill a customer's specific situational requirements, or providing for quick initial shipment to meet a buyer's out-of-stock status).

- **Functional needs** represent the need for a specific core task or function to be performed—the functional purpose of a specific product or service. The need for a sales offering to do what it is supposed to do (e.g., alcohol disinfects, switches open and close to control some flow, the flow control valve is accurate and reliable).

- **Social needs** comprise the need for acceptance from and association with others—a desire to belong to some reference group. For example, a product or service might be associated with some specific and desired affinity group or segment (e.g., Polo clothing is associated with upper-income, successful people; ISO 9000 Certification is associated with high-quality vendors; leading e-commerce websites include discussion groups to build a sense of community).

- **Psychological needs** reflect the desire for feelings of assurance and risk reduction, as well as positive emotions and feelings, such as success, joy, excitement, and stimulation (e.g., a Mont Blanc pen generates a feeling of success; effective training programs create a sense of self-control and determination; selection and use of well-known, high-quality brands provides assurance to buyers and organizations alike).

- **Knowledge needs** represent the desire for personal development, information, and knowledge to increase thought and understanding as to how and why things happen (e.g., product information, newsletters, brochures, along with training and user support group meetings or conferences, provide current information on products and topics of interest).

Categorizing buyer needs by type can assist the salesperson in bringing order to what could otherwise be a confusing and endless mix of needs and expectations. Organizing the buyer's different needs into their basic types can help salespeople in several ways. First, as Exhibit 3.1 (discussed earlier on page 58) and the example worksheet in Exhibit 3.2 illustrate, the basic types can serve as a checklist or worksheet to ensure that no significant problems or needs have been overlooked in the process of needs discovery. Organizing what at first might appear

EXHIBIT 3.2

Example Worksheet for Organizing Buyer Needs and Benefit-Based Solutions

Primary Buyer: **Bart Waits**
Buying Organization: **SouthWest Metal Stampings**
Primary Industry: **Stamped Metal Parts and Subcomponents**

Basic Type of Need	Buyer's Specific Needs
Buyer's situational needs	• Requires an 18 percent increase in production to meet increased sales • On-hand inventory will not meet production/delivery schedule • Tight cash flow pending initial deliveries and receipt of payment
Buyer's functional needs	• Equipment to provide effective and efficient increase in production • Expedited delivery and installation in six weeks or less • Equipment financing extending payments beyond initial receipts
Buyer's social needs	• Expansion in production transforms them into Top 10 in Industry • Belonging to user group of companies using this equipment • Feeling that they are an important customer of the supplier
Buyer's psychological needs	• Confidence that selected equipment will meet needs and do the job • Assurance that seller can complete installation in six weeks • Saving face—to believe borrowing for equipment is common
Buyer's knowledge needs	• Evidence that this is the right choice • Understanding new technology featured in the selected equipment • Training program for production employees and maintenance staff

to be different needs and problems into their common types also helps the salesperson to better understand the nature of the buyer's needs along with the interrelationships and commonalities between them. In turn, this enhanced understanding and the framework of basic types combine to serve as a guide for salespeople in generating and then demonstrating value-added solutions in response to the specific needs of the buyer.

As previously discussed, the specific circumstances or types of solution benefits that a buyer is seeking should determine a salesperson's strategy for working with that buyer. Consequently, it should be noted that the needs of business buyers tend to be more complex than consumers' needs. As with

DAN BARNES/ISTOCKPHOTO

> The ship-building company commissioned to build this ocean freightliner had specialized functional needs when it came to the boat's massive propeller.

consumers, organizational buyers are influenced by the same functional, social, psychological, knowledge, and situational experiences and forces that affect and shape individual needs. However, in addition to those individual needs, organizational buyers must also satisfy the needs and requirements of the organization for which they work. As Figure 3.3 depicts, these organizational needs overlay and interact with the needs of the individual. To maximize selling effectiveness in the organizational or business-to-business market, salespeople must generate solutions addressing both the individual and organizational needs of business buyers.

FIGURE 3.3
Complex Mix of Business Buyer Needs

Organizational Needs

- Social
- Psychological
- Situational
- Knowledge
- Functional

Individual Needs

- Situational
- Social
- Psychological
- Knowledge
- Functional

Business buyers' needs are a combination of the buyers' individual needs and the organization's needs.

PHASE TWO— DETERMINATION OF THE CHARACTERISTICS OF THE ITEM AND THE QUANTITY NEEDED

Coincident to recognizing a need or problem is the motivation and drive to resolve it by undertaking a search for additional information leading to possible solutions. This particular phase of the buying process involves the consideration and study of the overall situation to understand what is required in the form of a preferred solution. This begins to establish the general characteristics and quantities necessary to resolve the need or problem. Through effective sales conversations, salespeople use their knowledge and expertise at this point to assist the buyer in analyzing and interpreting the problem situation and needs. Salespeople offer valuable knowledge of problem situations and solution options that buyers typically perceive as beneficial.

> Buyers sometimes attend trade shows to find qualified suppliers.

PHASE THREE— DESCRIPTION OF THE CHARACTERISTICS OF THE ITEM AND THE QUANTITY NEEDED

Using the desired characteristics and quantities developed in the previous phase as a starting point, buyers translate that general information into detailed specifications describing exactly what is expected and required. The determination of detailed specifications serves several purposes. First, detailed specifications guide supplier firms in developing their proposals. Second, these specifications give the buyer a framework for evaluating, comparing, and choosing among the proposed solutions. Postpurchase specifications serve as a standard for evaluation to ensure that the buying firm receives the required product features and quantities. Trust-based buyer-seller relationships allow salespeople to work closely with buyers and collaboratively assist them in establishing the detailed specifications of the preferred solutions.

© ETHAN MILLER/GETTY IMAGES

PHASE FOUR—SEARCH FOR AND QUALIFICATION OF POTENTIAL SOURCES

Next, buyers must locate and qualify potential suppliers capable of providing the preferred solution. Although buyers certainly use information provided by salespeople to identify qualified suppliers, an abundance of information is available from other sources, such as trade associations, product source directories, trade shows, the Internet, advertising, and word of mouth. Once identified, potential suppliers are qualified on their ability to perform and deliver consistently at the level of quality and quantity required. Because of the large number of information sources available to buyers researching potential suppliers, one of the most important tasks in personal selling is to win the position of one of those information sources and keep buyers informed about the salesperson's company, its new products, and solution capabilities.

PHASE FIVE—ACQUISITION AND ANALYSIS OF PROPOSALS

Based on the detailed specifications, **requests for proposals** (known in the trade as an **RFP**) are developed and distributed to the qualified potential suppliers. Based on the RFP, qualified suppliers develop and submit proposals to provide the products as specified. Salespeople play a critical and influential role in this stage of the buying process by developing and presenting the proposed solution to the buyers. In this role, the salesperson is responsible for presenting the proposed features and benefits in such a manner that the proposed solution is evaluated as providing higher levels of benefits and value to the buyer than other competing proposals. Consequently, it is imperative that salespeople understand the basic evaluation procedures used by buyers in comparing alternative and competitive proposals so they can be more proficient in demonstrating the superiority of their solution over the competition.

Procedures for Evaluating Suppliers and Products

Purchase decisions are based on buyers' comparative evaluations of suppliers and the products and services they propose for satisfying buyers' needs. Some buyers may look for the sales offering that receives the highest rating on the one characteristic they perceive as being most important. Others may prefer the sales offering that achieves some acceptable assessment score across each and every attribute desired by the buyer. However, research into how purchase decisions are made suggests that most buyers use a compensatory, **multiattribute model** incorporating weighted averages across desired characteristics.[3] These weighted averages incorporate (1) assessments of how well the product or supplier performs in meeting each of the specified characteristics and (2) the relative importance of each specified characteristic.

> **requests for proposals (RFPs)** A form created by firms and distributed to qualified potential suppliers that helps suppliers develop and submit proposals to provide products as specified by the firm.
>
> **multiattribute model** A procedure for evaluating suppliers and products that incorporates weighted averages across desired characteristics.

Assessment of Product or Supplier Performance

The first step in applying the multiattribute model is to rate objectively how well each characteristic of the competing products or suppliers meets the buyers' needs. Let us use the example of General Motors (GM) evaluating adhesives for use in manufacturing. The buyers have narrowed the alternatives to products proposed by three suppliers: BondIt #302, AdCo #45, and StikFast #217. As illustrated in Exhibit 3.3, the GM buying team has assessed the competitive products according to how well they perform on certain important attributes. These assessments are converted to scores as depicted in Exhibit 3.4, with scores ranging from 1 (very poor performance) to 10 (excellent performance).

As illustrated, no single product is consistently outstanding across each of the eight identified characteristics. Although BondIt #302 is easy to apply and uses the buyer's current equipment, it is also more expensive and has the shortest durability time in the field. StikFast #217 also scores well for ease of application, and it has superior durability. However, it has the longest bonding time and could negatively influence production time.

Accounting for Relative Importance of Each Characteristic

To compare these performance differences properly, each score must be weighted by the characteristic's

EXHIBIT 3.3
Important Product Information

Characteristics	BondIt #302	AdCo #45	StikFast #217
Ease of application	Excellent	Good	Very good
Bonding time	8 minutes	10 minutes	12 minutes
Durability	10 years	12 years	15 years
Reliability	Very good	Excellent	Good
Nontoxic	Very good	Excellent	Very good
Quoted price	$7 per L	$5.5 per L	$6.5 per L
Shelf-life in storage	6 months	4 months	4 months
Service factors	Good	Very good	Excellent

EXHIBIT 3.4
Product Performance Scores

Characteristics	BondIt #302	AdCo #45	StikFast #217
Ease of application	10	5	8
Bonding time	8	6	4
Durability	6	8	9
Reliability	8	10	5
Nontoxic	8	10	8
Quoted price	5	9	7
Shelf-life in storage	9	6	6
Service factors	5	8	10

overall rating for each product. The product or supplier having the highest comparative rating is typically the product selected for purchase. In this example, AdCo has the highest overall evaluation, totaling 468 points, compared with BondIt's 430 points and StikFast's 446 points.

Employing Buyer Evaluation Procedures to Enhance Selling Strategies

Understanding evaluation procedures and gaining insight as to how a specific buyer or team of buyers is evaluating suppliers and proposals is vital for the salesperson to be effective and requires the integration of several bases of knowledge. First, information gathered before the sales call must be combined with an effective needs-discovery dialogue with the buyer(s) to delineate the buyers' needs and the nature of the desired solution. This establishes the most likely criteria for evaluation. Further discussion between the buyer and seller can begin to establish the importance the buyers place on each of the different performance criteria and often yields information as to what suppliers and products are being considered. Using this information and the salesperson's knowledge of how his or her products compare with competitors' offerings allows the salesperson to complete a likely facsimile of the buyers' evaluation. With this enhanced level of preparation and understanding, the salesperson can plan, create, and deliver a more effective presentation by using the five fundamental

perceived importance. In the adhesive example, importance weights are assigned on a scale of 1 (relatively unimportant) to 10 (very important). As illustrated in Exhibit 3.5, multiplying each performance score by the corresponding attribute's importance weight results in a weighted average that can be totalled to calculate an

EXHIBIT 3.5

Weighted Averages for Performance times Importance (P × I) and Overall Evaluation Scores

Characteristics	BondIt #302			AdCo #45			StikFast #217		
	P	I	P × I	P	I	P × I	P	I	P × I
Ease of application	10	8	80	5	8	40	8	8	64
Bonding time	8	6	48	6	6	36	4	6	24
Durability	6	9	54	8	9	72	9	9	81
Reliability	8	7	56	10	7	70	5	7	35
Nontoxic	8	6	48	10	6	60	8	6	48
Quoted price	5	10	50	9	10	90	7	10	70
Shelf-life in storage	9	6	54	6	6	36	6	6	36
Service factors	5	8	40	8	8	64	10	8	80
Overall evaluation score			430			468			438

strategies that are inherent within the evaluation procedures buyers use.

- **Modify the Product Offering Being Proposed.** Often, in the course of preparing or delivering a presentation, it becomes apparent that the product offering will not maximize the buyer's evaluation score in comparison with a competitor's offering. In this case, the strategy would be to modify or change the product to one that better meets the buyer's overall needs and thus would receive a higher evaluation. For example, by developing a better understanding of the adhesive buyer's perceived importance of certain characteristics, the BondIt salesperson could offer a different adhesive formulation that is not as easy to apply (low perceived importance) but offers improved durability (high perceived importance) and more competitive price (high perceived importance).

- **Alter the Buyer's Beliefs about the Proposed Offering.** Provide information and support to alter the buyer's beliefs as to where the proposed product stands on certain attributes. This is a recommended strategy for cases in which the buyer underestimates the true qualities of the proposed product. However, if the buyer's perceptions are correct, this strategy would encourage the salesperson to exaggerate and overstate claims and, thus, should be avoided. In the instance of BondIt #302's low evaluation score, the salesperson could offer the buyer information and evidence that the product's durability and service factors actually perform much better than the buyer initially believed. By working with the buyer to develop a more realistic perception of the product's performance, BondIt #302 could become the buyer's preferred choice.

- **Alter the Buyer's Beliefs about the Competitor's Offering.** For a variety of reasons, buyers often mistakenly believe that a competitor's offering has higher level attributes or qualities than it actually does. In such an instance, the salesperson can provide information to create a more accurate picture of the competitor's attributes. This has been referred to as **competitive depositioning** and is carried out by openly comparing (not simply degrading) the competing offering's attributes, advantages,

> **competitive depositioning** Providing information to create a more accurate picture of a competitor's attributes or qualities.

and weaknesses. As an illustration, the BondIt salesperson might demonstrate the total cost for each of the three product alternatives, including a quoted price, ease of application, and bonding time. BondIt is much easier to apply and has a faster bonding time. Consequently, less of it needs to be applied for each application, which results in a significantly lower total cost and a much-improved evaluation score.

- **Alter the Importance Weights.** In this strategy, the salesperson uses information to emphasize and thus increase the importance of certain attributes on which the product offering is exceptionally strong. In the case of attributes on which the offering might be short, the strategy would be to deemphasize their importance. Continuing the adhesive purchase decision, BondIt's salesperson might offer information to influence the buyer's importance rating for ease of application and storage shelf-life—two characteristics in which BondIt is much stronger than the two competitors.

- **Call Attention to Neglected Attributes.** If it becomes apparent that significant attributes may have been neglected or overlooked, the salesperson can increase the buyer's evaluation of the proposed offering by pointing out the attribute that was missed. For instance, the BondIt #302 adhesive dries to an invisible, transparent, and semiflexible adhesive compared with the two competitors, which cure to a light grey that could detract from the final product if the adhesive flowed out of the joint. The appearance of the final product is a significant concern, and this neglected attribute could substantially influence the comparative evaluations.

PHASE SIX—EVALUATION OF PROPOSALS AND SELECTION OF SUPPLIERS

The buying decision is the outcome of the buyer's evaluation of the various proposals acquired from potential suppliers. Typically, further negotiations will be conducted with the selected supplier(s) for the purpose of establishing the final terms regarding product characteristics, pricing, and delivery. Salespeople play a central role in gaining the buyer's commitment to the purchase decision and in the subsequent negotiations of the final terms.

PHASE SEVEN—SELECTION OF AN ORDER ROUTINE

Once the supplier(s) has been selected, details associated with the purchase decision must be settled. These details include delivery quantities, locations, and times

As established in an order routine, a salesperson takes an order at the customer's site with a handheld device and then transmits the order via GSM to the applicable warehouse.

along with return policies and the routine for reorders associated with the purchase. For cases in which the purchase requires multiple deliveries over time, the routine for placing subsequent orders and making deliveries must be set out and understood. Is the order routine standardized on the basis of a prearranged time schedule, or is the salesperson expected to monitor usage and inventories to place orders and schedule shipments? Will orders be placed automatically through the use of electronic data interchange or the Internet? Regardless of the nature of the order routine, the salesperson plays a critical role in facilitating communication, completing ordering procedures, and settling the final details.

PHASE EIGHT—PERFORMANCE FEEDBACK AND EVALUATION

The final phase in the buying process is the evaluation of performance and feedback shared among all parties for the purpose of improving future performance and enhancing buyer-seller relationships. Research supports that salespeople's customer interaction activities and communication at this stage of the buying process become the primary determinants of customer satisfaction and buyer loyalty. Consequently, it is critical that salespeople continue working with buyers after the sale. The salesperson's follow-up activities provide the critical points of contact between the buyer and seller to ensure consistent performance, respond to and take care of problems, maximize customer satisfaction, create new value opportunities, and further enhance buyer–seller relationships.

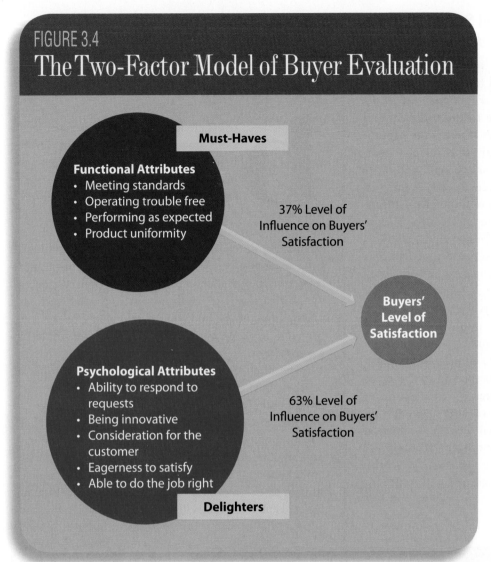

FIGURE 3.4
The Two-Factor Model of Buyer Evaluation

Must-Haves

Functional Attributes
- Meeting standards
- Operating trouble free
- Performing as expected
- Product uniformity

37% Level of Influence on Buyers' Satisfaction

Buyers' Level of Satisfaction

Psychological Attributes
- Ability to respond to requests
- Being innovative
- Consideration for the customer
- Eagerness to satisfy
- Able to do the job right

63% Level of Influence on Buyers' Satisfaction

Delighters

Buyers evaluate functional attributes and psychological attributes of a sales offering to assess overall performance and satisfaction.

LO5
Understanding Postpurchase Evaluation and the Formation of Satisfaction

Research shows that buyers evaluate their experience with a product purchase on the basis of product characteristics that fall into a **two-factor model of evaluation** as depicted in Figure 3.4.[4] The first category, **functional attributes**, refers to the features and characteristics that are related to what the product actually does or is expected to do—its functional characteristics. These functional characteristics have also been referred to as **must-have attributes**, features of the core product that the customer takes for granted. These are the attributes that must be present for the supplier or product to even be included among those being considered for purchase. Consequently, they tend to be fairly common across the set of suppliers and products being considered for purchase by a buyer. Such characteristics as reliability, durability, conformance to specifications, competitive pricing, and performance are illustrative of functional attributes.

Psychological attributes make up the second general category. This category refers to how things are carried out and done between the buyer and seller. These supplier and market offering characteristics are described as the **delighter attributes**—the augmented features and characteristics included in the total market offering that go beyond buyer expectations and have a significant positive impact on customer satisfaction. The psychological or delighter characteristics are not perceived as being universal features across the evoked set of suppliers and market offerings being considered. Rather, these are the differentiators between the competitors. The competence, attitudes, and behaviours of supplier personnel with whom the buyer has contact, as well as the salesperson's trustworthiness, consideration for the customer, responsiveness, ability to recover when there is a problem, and innovativeness in providing solutions are exemplary psychological attributes.

two-factor model of evaluation A postpurchase evaluation process buyers use that evaluates a product purchase by using functional and psychological attributes.

functional attributes The features and characteristics that are related to what the product actually does or is expected to do.

must-have attributes Features of the core product that the customer takes for granted.

psychological attributes The augmented features and characteristics included in the total market offering that go beyond buyer expectations and have a significant positive impact on customer satisfaction.

delighter attributes The augmented features included in the total market offering that go beyond buyer's expectations and have a significant positive impact on customer satisfaction.

The Growing Importance of Salespeople in Buyers' Postpurchase Evaluation

Understanding the differential impact of functional (*must-haves*) and psychological (*delighters*) attributes is important for salespeople. Functional attributes possess a close correspondence to the technical and more tangible product attributes whereas the psychological attributes are similar to the interpersonal communication and behaviours of salespeople and other personnel having contact with customers. Numerous research studies across a variety of industries evidence psychological attributes as having up to two times as much influence on buyer satisfaction and loyalty as functional attributes. This observation underscores special implications for salespeople, as it is their interpersonal communication and behaviours—what they do—that make up the psychological attributes. Although both categories of product characteristics are important and have significant influences on buyer satisfaction, the activities and behaviours of the salesperson as she or he interacts with the buyer have more impact on that buyer's evaluation than the features of the product or service itself.

straight rebuy decision A purchase decision resulting from an ongoing purchasing relationship with a supplier.

LO6
Types of Purchasing Decisions

buyers are learners in that purchase decisions are not isolated behaviours. Buyer behaviour and purchase decisions are based on the relevant knowledge that buyers have accumulated from multiple sources to assist them in making the proper choice. Internally, buyers reflect on past experiences as guides for making purchase decisions. When sufficient knowledge from past experiences is not available, buyers access external sources of information: secondary sources of information (e.g., trade journals, product test reports, advertising) and other individuals the buyer perceives as being trustworthy and knowledgeable in a given area.

The level of relevant experience and knowledge a buyer or buying organization possesses in relation to a given purchasing decision is a primary determinant of the time and resources the buyer will allocate to that purchasing decision. The level of a buyer's existing experience and knowledge has been used to categorize buyer behaviour into three types of purchasing decisions: straight rebuys, modified rebuys, and new tasks. As summarized in Exhibit 3.6, selling strategies should reflect the differences in buyer behaviours and decision-making characteristic of each type of buying decision.

STRAIGHT REBUYS

If past experiences with a product resulted in high levels of satisfaction, buyers tend to purchase the same product from the same sources. Comparable with a routine repurchase in which nothing has changed, the **straight rebuy decision** is often the result of a long-term purchase agreement. Needs have been predetermined with the corresponding specifications, pricing, and

EXHIBIT 3.6
Three Types of Buying Decisions

	Decision Type		
	Straight Rebuy	**Modified Rebuy**	**New Task**
Newness of problem or need	Low	Medium	High
Information requirements	Minimal	Moderate	Maximum
Information search	Minimal	Limited	Extensive
Consideration of new alternatives	None	Limited	Extensive
Multiple buying influences	Very small	Moderate	Large
Financial risk	Low	Moderate	High

shipping requirements already established by a blanket purchase order or an annual purchase agreement. Ordering is automatic and often computerized by using **electronic data interchange** (EDI) and e-commerce (Internet, intranet, and extranet). Mitsubishi Motor Manufacturing of America uses a large number of straight rebuy decisions in its acquisition of component parts. Beginning as a primary supplier of automotive glass components, Vuteq has developed a strong relationship with Mitsubishi Motor Manufacturing of America over several years. As a result, Vuteq's business has steadily increased and now includes door trims, fuel tanks, and mirrors in addition to window glass. These components are purchased as straight rebuys by using EDI, allowing Vuteq to deliver these components to Mitsubishi on a minute-to-minute basis, matching ongoing production.

Buyers allocate little, if any, time and resources to this form of purchase decision. The primary emphasis is on receipt of the products and their continued satisfactory performance. With most of the purchasing process automated, straight rebuy decisions are little more than record keeping that clerical staff in the purchasing office often handles.

For the in-supplier (a current supplier), straight rebuys offer the advantage of reduced levels of potential competition. Rather than becoming complacent, however, in-salespeople must continually monitor the competitive environment for advances in product capabilities or changes in price structures. They should also follow up on deliveries and interact with users as well as decision makers to make sure that product and performance continue to receive strong and positive evaluations.

Straight rebuy decisions present a major challenge to the out-salesperson. Buyers are satisfied with the products and services from current suppliers and see no need to change. This is a classic case in which the buyer perceives no difference or needs gap between their actual and desired state. Consequently, there is no active buying motive to which the out-salesperson can respond. In this case, out-salespeople are typically presented with two strategy choices. First, they can continue to make contact with the buyer so that when there is a change in the buying situation or if the current supplier makes a mistake, they are there to respond. Second, they can provide information and evidence relevant to either the desired

or actual states so that the buyer will perceive a needs gap. For example, Vuteq's competitors will find it most difficult to gain this portion of Mitsubishi's business by offering similar or equal products and systems. However, a competitor might adopt future advances in technology that would enable them to offer significant added value beyond what Vuteq offers. Effectively communicating and demonstrating their advanced capabilities holds the potential for raising the desired state and thus producing a needs gap favouring their solution over Vuteq's existing sales offering.

NEW TASKS

The purchase decision characterized as a **new task decision** occurs when the buyer is purchasing a product or service for the first time. As illustrated in Figure 3.5, new task purchase decisions are located at the opposite end of the continuum from the straight rebuy and typify situations in which buyers have no experience or knowledge on which to rely. Consequently, they undertake an extensive purchase decision and search for information designed to identify and compare alternative solutions. Reflecting the extensive nature of this type of purchase decision, multiple members of the buying team are usually involved. As a result, the salesperson will be working with several different individuals rather than a single buyer. Mitsubishi buyers and suppliers were presented with new task decisions when the new

electronic data interchange Transfer of data electronically between two computer systems.

new task decision A purchase decision that occurs when a buyer is purchasing a product or service for the first time.

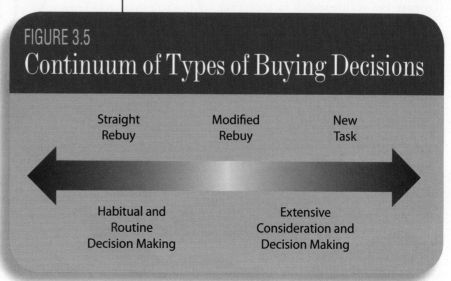

FIGURE 3.5
Continuum of Types of Buying Decisions

Straight Rebuy — Modified Rebuy — New Task

Habitual and Routine Decision Making

Extensive Consideration and Decision Making

Mitsubishi four-wheel-drive sport utility vehicle was moving from design to production. Moving from their historical two-wheel-drive to four-wheel-drive power lines and transmissions presented a variety of new needs and problems.

Relevant to a new task purchasing decision, there is no in- or out-supplier. Further, the buyer is aware of the existing needs gap. With no prior experience in dealing with this particular need, buyers are often eager for information and expertise that will assist them in effectively resolving the perceived needs gap. Selling strategies for new task decisions should include collaborating with the buyer in a number of ways. First, the salesperson can provide expertise in fully developing and understanding the need. The salesperson's extensive experience and base of knowledge is also valuable to the buyer in terms of specifying and evaluating potential solutions. Finally, top salespeople will assist the buyer in making a purchase decision and provide extensive follow-up to ensure long-term satisfaction. By implementing this type of a consultative strategy, the salesperson establishes a relationship with the buyer and gains considerable competitive advantage.

MODIFIED REBUYS

Modified rebuy decisions occupy a middle position on the continuum between straight rebuys and new tasks. In these cases, the buyer has experience in purchasing the product in the past but is interested in acquiring

additional information regarding alternative products and suppliers. As there is more familiarity with the decision, there is less uncertainty and perceived risk than for new task decisions. The modified rebuy typically occurs as the result of changing conditions or needs. Perhaps the buyer wants to consider new suppliers for current purchase needs or new products existing suppliers offer. Continuing the example of buyer-seller experiences at Mitsubishi, the company's recent decision to reexamine their methods and sources for training and education corresponds to the characteristics of a modified rebuy decision. Since its beginning, Mitsubishi Motor Manufacturing of America has used a mix of company trainers, community colleges, and universities to provide education and training to employees. Desiring more coordination across its training programs, the company has requested proposals for the development and continued management of a corporate university from a variety of suppliers, including several current and new sources.

Often a buyer enters into a modified rebuy type of purchase decision simply to check the competitiveness of existing suppliers in terms of the product offering and pricing levels. Consequently, in-salespeople will emphasize how well their product has performed in resolving the needs gap. Out-salespeople will use strategies similar to those undertaken in the straight rebuy. These strategies are designed to alter the relative positions of the desired and actual states in a way that creates a perceived gap and influences buyers to rethink and reevaluate their current buying patterns and suppliers.

Sea World worked with St. Charles-based Craftsmen Industries to develop a pod of six Shamu cruisers to meet its new task decision on a means for conducting a special Shamu promotion.

© FINITE COMMUNICATION INC.

www.seaworld.com

LO7
Understanding Communication Styles

Verbal and nonverbal messages can also provide salespeople with important cues regarding buyers' personalities and communication styles. Experienced salespeople emphasize the importance of reading and responding to customer communication styles. Effectively sensing and interpreting customers' communication styles allows salespeople to adapt their own interaction behaviours in a way that facilitates

FIGURE 3.6

Comparison of the Principal Characteristics of Assertiveness and Responsiveness

Low Assertiveness

- Slow paced
- Cooperative
- Avoids taking risks
- Supportive
- Team player
- Nondirective
- Easygoing
- Reserved in expressing opinions

High Assertiveness

- Fast paced
- Competitive
- Takes risks
- Independent
- Directive
- Confrontational
- Forcefully expresses opinions

Low Responsiveness

- Task oriented
- Guarded and cool
- Rational
- Meticulous organizer
- Inflexible regarding time
- Controlled gesturing
- Nondirective
- Formal

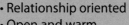
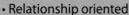

High Responsiveness

- Relationship oriented
- Open and warm
- Emotional
- Unorganized
- Flexible regarding time
- Highly animated
- Spontaneous
- Informal

Most sales training programs use a two-by-two matrix as a basis for categorizing communication styles into four primary types. The four styles are based on two dimensions: assertiveness and responsiveness.

buyer-seller communication and enhances relationship formation. Most sales training programs use a two-by-two matrix as a basis for categorizing communication styles into four primary types.[5] Figure 3.6 illustrates the characteristics based on two determinant dimensions: assertiveness and responsiveness.

Assertiveness—**Assertiveness** refers to the degree to which a person holds opinions about issues and attempts to dominate or control situations by directing the thoughts and actions of others. Highly assertive individuals tend to be fast-paced, opinionated, and quick to speak out and take confrontational positions. Low-assertive individuals tend to exhibit a slower pace. They typically hold back, let others take charge, and are slow and deliberate in their communication and actions.

Responsiveness—**Responsiveness** points to the level of feelings and sociability an individual openly displays. Highly responsive individuals are relationship oriented and openly emotional. They readily express their feelings and tend to be personable, friendly, and informal. However, low-responsive individuals tend to be task oriented and very controlled in their display of emotions. They tend to be impersonal in dealing with others, with an emphasis on formality and self-discipline.

The actual levels of assertiveness and responsiveness will vary from one individual to another on a continuum ranging from high to low. An individual may be located anywhere along the particular continuum, and where the individual is located determines the degree to which he or she possesses and demonstrates the particular characteristics associated with that dimension (refer back to Figure 3.6).

Overlaying the assertiveness and responsiveness dimensions produces a four-quadrant matrix as illustrated in Figure 3.7. The four quadrants characterize an individual as exhibiting one of four different communication styles on the basis of his or her demonstrated levels of assertiveness and responsiveness. *Amiables* are high on responsiveness but low on assertiveness. *Expressives* are defined as high on both responsiveness and assertiveness. *Drivers* are low on responsiveness but high on assertiveness. *Analyticals* are characterized as being low on assertiveness as well as responsiveness. A salesperson's skill in properly classifying customers can provide valuable cues regarding customer attitudes and behaviours. In turn, these cues allow the salesperson to be more effective by adapting his or her communication and responses to better fit the customer's style.

assertiveness The degree to which a person holds opinions about issues and attempts to dominate or control situations by directing the thoughts and actions of others.

responsiveness The level of feelings and sociability an individual openly displays.

amiables Individuals who are high on responsiveness, low on assertiveness, prefer to belong to groups, and are interested in others.

expressives Individuals who are high on both responsiveness and assertiveness, are animated and communicative, and value building close relationships with others.

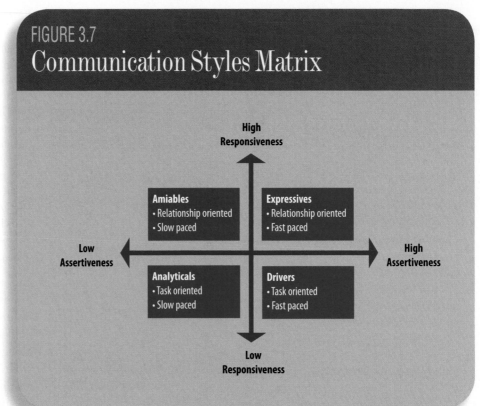

FIGURE 3.7
Communication Styles Matrix

The four quadrants characterize an individual as having one of four different communication styles on the basis of his or her demonstrated levels of assertiveness and responsiveness. A salesperson's skill in properly classifying customers can provide valuable cues regarding customer attitudes and behaviours.

Amiables—Developing and maintaining close personal relationships are important to **amiables**. Easygoing and cooperative, they are often characterized as friendly back-slappers because of their preference for belonging to groups and their sincere interest in other people—their hobbies, interests, families, and mutual friends. With a natural propensity for talking and socializing, they have little or no desire to control others but rather prefer building consensus. Amiables are not risk takers and need to feel safe in making a decision. Somewhat undisciplined with regard to time, amiables appear to be slow and deliberate in their actions. They avoid conflict and

Verbal and nonverbal messages can provide salespeople with important cues regarding buyers' personalities and communication styles.

tend to be more concerned with opinions—what others think—than with details and facts. When confronted or attacked, amiables tend to submit. In working with an amiable customer, salespeople should remember that their "must-have" is to be liked and their fundamental "want" is for attention.

Expressives—**Expressives** are animated and highly communicative. Although very competitive by nature, they also exhibit warm personalities and value building close relationships with others. In fact, they dislike being alone and readily seek out others. Expressives are extroverted and are highly uninhibited in their communication. When confronted or crossed, they will attack. Enthusiastic and stimulating, they seem to talk in terms of people rather than things and have a ready opinion on everything. Yet they remain open-minded and changeable. Expressives are fast paced in their decision making and behaviour and prefer the big picture rather than getting bogged down in details. As a result, they are very spontaneous, unconcerned with time schedules, and not especially organized in their daily lives. They are creative, comfortable operating on intuition, and demonstrate a willingness to take risks. The two keys for expressives that salespeople must keep in mind are the "must-have" of never being hurt emotionally and their underlying "want" is attention.

© JGI/JUPITER IMAGES

fundamentals that salespeople must keep in mind when working with this style are the "must-have" of being right and the underlying "want" is for analytical activities.

MASTERING COMMUNICATION STYLE FLEXING

In addition to sensing and interpreting the customer's communication style, a salesperson must also be aware of his or her own personal style. Mismatched and possibly clashing styles can be dysfunctional and present significant barriers to communication and relationship building. To minimize possible negative effects stemming from mismatched styles, salespeople can flex their own style to facilitate effective communication. For example, an expressive salesperson calling on an analytical buyer would find considerable differences in both pace and relationship/task orientation that could hinder the selling process unless adjustments are made. Flexing his or her own style to better match that of the buyer enhances communication. In our example, the salesperson would need to adjust by slowing down his or her natural pace, reining in the level of spontaneity and animation, and increasing task orientation by offering more detailed information and analysis.

Adapting to buyers by flexing their own communication style has been found to have a positive impact on salespeople's performance and the quality of buyer-seller relationships. Nevertheless, flexing should not be interpreted as meaning an exact match between a salesperson's style and that of a customer. Not only is it not required, but exact matches could even be detrimental. For example, a buyer and seller with matching expressive styles could easily discover that the entire sales call regressed to little more than a personal discussion with nothing of substance being accomplished. However, a buyer and seller matched as drivers could find it difficult, if not impossible, to reach a decision that was mutually beneficial. Rather than matching the buyer's style, flexing implies that the salesperson should adjust to the

> Expressives are animated and highly communicative.

Drivers—Sometimes referred to as the director or dictator style, **drivers** are hard and detached from their relationships with others. Described as being cool, tough, and competitive in their relationships, drivers are independent and willing to run over others to get their preferred results. As they seek out and openly demonstrate power and control over people and situations, they are difficult to get close to and appear to treat people as things. Drivers are extremely formal, businesslike, and impatient, with a penchant for time and organization. They are highly opinionated, impatient, and quick to share those opinions with those around them. When attacked or confronted, drivers will dictate. Drivers exhibit a low tolerance for taking advice, tend to be risk takers, and favour making their own decisions. Although they are highly task oriented, drivers prefer to ignore facts and figures and instead rely on their own gut feelings in making decisions—after all, they do know it all. When working with drivers, salespeople should remember that this style's "must-have" is winning, and their fundamental "want" is results.

Analyticals—The descriptive name for this style is derived from their penchant for gathering and analyzing facts and details before making a decision. **Analyticals** are meticulous and disciplined in everything they do. Logical and very controlled, they are systematic problem solvers and thus very deliberate and slower in pace. In stressful situations and confrontations, analyticals tend to withdraw. Many times, they appear to be nitpicky about everything around them. They do not readily let their feelings show nor are they spontaneous in their behaviours. As a result, they are often seen as being cool and aloof. Analyticals shy away from personal relationships and avoid taking risks. Time and personal schedules are close to being a religious ritual for the analytical. The two

drivers Individuals who are low on responsiveness, high on assertiveness, and detached from relationships.

analyticals Individuals who are low on responsiveness and assertiveness, and are analytical, meticulous, and disciplined in everything they do.

buying teams Teams of individuals in organizations that use the expertise and multiple buying influences of people from different departments throughout the organization.

initiators Individuals within an organization who identify a need.

influencers Individuals within an organization who guide the decision process by making recommendations and expressing preferences.

users Individuals within an organization who will actually use the product being purchased.

deciders Individuals within an organization who have the ultimate responsibility of determining which product or service will be purchased.

purchasers Organizational members who negotiate final terms of the purchase and execute the actual purchase.

gatekeepers Members of an organization who are in a position to control the flow of information to and between vendors and other buying centre members.

needs and preferences of the buyer to maximize effectiveness. Growmark, an agricultural product and service organization with divisions in Canada and the United States, teaches its salespeople to flex throughout their interaction with a buyer by studying different behaviours a salesperson might demonstrate with each style of buyer (see the Appendix to this chapter).[6]

Study and compare the flexing behaviours that Growmark recommends that their salespeople demonstrate when working with each different buyer communication style. Note the differences in recommended salesperson behaviour and rationalize them in terms of the specific characteristics of each buyer's style. Overlaying and integrating these two sets of information will enhance the understanding of how to flex to different buyers and why that form of flexing is recommended.

It is not always possible to gain much information about a buyer's communication style, especially if the buyer is new. If this is the case, it may be more appropriate to assume that the buyer is an analytical driver and prepare for this style. If the buyer proves to be close to an amiable expressive, then the salesperson can easily adapt. It is much more difficult to prepare for the amiable expressive and then switch to an analytical-driver style.

LO8
Buying Teams

single individual typically makes routine purchase decisions, such as straight rebuys and simpler modified rebuys. However, the more complex modified rebuy and new task purchase decisions often in-

volve the joint decisions of multiple participants within a buying centre or team. **Buying teams** (also referred to as buying centres) use the expertise and multiple buying influences of people from different departments throughout the organization. As the object of the purchase decision changes, the makeup of the buying team may also change to maximize the relevant expertise of team members. The organization's size, as well as the nature and volume of the products being purchased, will influence the actual number and makeup of buying teams. The different members of a buying team will often have varied goals reflecting their individual needs and those of their different departments.

Buying team members are described in terms of their roles and responsibilities within the team.[7]

- *Initiators*—**Initiators** are individuals within the organization who identify a need or perhaps realize that the acquisition of a product might solve a need or problem.

- *Influencers*—Individuals who guide the decision process by making recommendations and expressing preferences are referred to as **influencers**. These are often technical or engineering personnel.

- *Users*—**Users** are the individuals within the organization who will actually use the product being purchased. They evaluate a product on the basis of how it will affect their own job performance. Users often serve as initiators and influencers.

- *Deciders*—The ultimate responsibility for determining which product or service will be purchased rests with the **deciders**. Although buyers may also be deciders, it is not unusual for different people to fill these roles.

- *Purchasers*—**Purchasers** have the responsibility for negotiating final terms of purchase with suppliers and executing the actual purchase or acquisition.

- *Gatekeepers*—Members who are in a position to control the flow of information to and between vendors and other buying centre members are referred to as **gatekeepers**.

Although each of these influencer types will not necessarily be present on all buying teams, the use of buying teams incorporating some or all of these multiple influences has increased in recent years. One example of multiple buying influences is offered in the recent experience of an Executive Jet International salesperson selling a Gulfstream V corporate jet to a Chicago-based pharmaceutical company. For more than six months, the salesperson worked with a variety of individuals serving different roles within the buying organization:

- *Initiator:* The initiator of the purchase process was the chief operating officer of the corporation who found that the recent corporate expansions had outgrown the effective service range of the organization's existing aircraft. Beyond pointing out the need and thus initiating the search, this individual would also be highly involved in the final choice based on her personal experiences and the perceived needs of the company.

- *Influencers:* Two different employee groups acted as the primary influencers. First were the corporate pilots who contributed a readily available and extensive background of knowledge and experience with a variety of aircraft types. Also playing a key influencer role were members from the capital budgeting group in the finance department. Although concerned with documented performance capabilities, they also provided inputs and assessments of the different alternatives by using their capital investment models.

- *Users:* The users provided some of the most dynamic inputs, as they were anxious to make the transition to a higher performance aircraft to enhance their own efficiency and performance in working at marketing/sales offices and plants that now stretched over North and South America. Primary players in this group included the vice presidents for marketing and for production/operations, in addition to the corporate pilots who would be flying the plane.

- *Deciders:* Based on the contribution and inputs of each member of the buying team, the chief executive officer would make the ultimate decision. Primarily travelling by commercial carriers, her role as decider was based more on her position within the firm rather than her use of the chosen alternative. As the organization's highest operating officer, she was in a position to move freely among all members of the buying team and make the decision on overall merits rather than personal feelings or desires.

- *Purchaser:* Responsibility for making the actual purchase, negotiating the final terms, and completing all the required paperwork followed the typical lines of authority and was the responsibility of the corporate purchasing department, with the director of purchasing actually assuming the immediate contact role. The purchasing office typically handles purchasing contracts and is staffed to draw up, complete, and file the related registrations and legal documents.

- *Gatekeepers:* This purchase decision involved two different gatekeepers within the customer organization: the executive assistant to the chief operating officer and an assistant purchasing officer. The positioning of these gatekeepers facilitated the salesperson's exchange of information and ability to keep in contact with the various members of the buying team. The COO's executive assistant moved easily among the various executives influencing the decision and was able to make appointments with the right people at the right times. However, the assistant purchasing officer was directly involved with the coordination of each member and bringing their various inputs into one summary document for the CEO. The salesperson's positive dealings and good relationships with each gatekeeper played a significant role in Executive Jet getting the sale.

A classic and all-too-common mistake among salespeople is to make repetitive calls on a purchasing manager over a several months only to discover that a buying team exists and that someone other than the purchasing manager will make the ultimate decision. Salespeople must gather information to discover who is in the buying team, what their individual roles are, and which members are the most influential. This information might be collected from account history files, people inside the salesperson's organization who are familiar with the account sources within the client organization, and even other salespeople. A salesperson should work with all members of the buying team and be careful to address their varied needs and objectives properly. Nevertheless, circumstances sometimes prevent a salesperson from working with all members of the team, and it is important that the salesperson reaches those who are most influential.

> Gatekeepers, such as this administrative assistant, are in a position to control the flow of information to and between vendors and other buying centre members.

© CAP53/ISTOCKPHOTO

Current Developments in Purchasing

today's business organizations are undergoing profound change in response to ever-increasing competition and rapid changes in the business environment. The worldwide spread of technology has resulted in intense and increasingly global competition that is highly dynamic in nature. Accelerating rates of change have fragmented what were once mass markets into more micro and niche markets composed of more knowledgeable and demanding customers with escalating expectations. In response, traditional purchasing practices are also rapidly changing.

INCREASING USE OF INFORMATION TECHNOLOGY

Buyers and sellers alike are increasingly using technology to enhance the effectiveness and efficiency of the purchasing process. Business-to-business e-commerce is growing at a rate exceeding 33 percent per year. Although EDI over private networks has been in use for some time, nearly all the current growth has been in Internet-based transactions.

Information technology electronically links buyers and sellers for direct and immediate communication and transmission of information and data. Transactional exchanges, such as straight rebuy decisions, can now be automated with Internet- and World Wide Web-enabled programs tracking sales at the point of purchase and capturing the data for real-time inventory control and order placing. By cutting order and shipping times, overall cycle times are reduced, mistakes are minimized, and working capital invested in inventories is made available for more productive applications. Further, the automation of these routine transactions allows buyers and salespeople to devote more time to new tasks, complex sales, and postsale service and relationship-building activities.

Customer relationship management (CRM) systems integrated with the Web allow reps to have a more informed conversation with prospects and customers by helping them to better understand customers. Sales organizations know keywords searched to find the seller's company, pages clicked on the company's website, and particular products and services buyers examined before asking for more information. Additionally, data collected on customer demographics, sales and customer service histories, and marketing preferences and customer feedback can be easily accumulated through a CRM system and used to better understand customers and provide customized offerings to best serve their needs. Celanese Corporation, a leading chemicals manufacturer, credits its CRM system with allowing sales conversations to advance based on the premise that the customer has a specific need it can fulfill.[8] Social networking technologies are likely to play an important role in CRM systems, making it more convenient for customers to provide information that goes into product planning and development, as well as provide deeper insights into customer buying motives.

In addition to facilitating exchange transactions, applications integrating the Internet are also being used to distribute product and company information along with training courses and materials. Several companies have begun publishing their product catalogues online as a replacement for the reams of product brochures salespeople have traditionally had to carry with them. The online catalogues can be easily updated without the expense of obsolete brochures and can be selectively downloaded by salespeople to create customized presentations and proposals.

RELATIONSHIP EMPHASIS ON COOPERATION AND COLLABORATION

More than ever before, the business decisions one company makes directly affect decisions in other companies. Business in today's fast-paced and dynamic marketplace demands continuous and increased levels of interactivity between salespeople and buyers representing the customer organizations. This trend is further underscored by more and more buying organizations emphasizing long-term relationships with fewer suppliers so that they can forge stronger bonds and develop more efficient purchasing processes. As illustrated in "An Ethical Dilemma," this increasing level of buyer–seller interaction and interdependence can create challenging ethical decisions for the salesperson.

Rather than competing to win benefits at the expense of one another, leading organizations are discovering that it is possible for all parties to reduce their risk and increase the level of benefits each receives by sharing information and coordinating activities, resources, and capabilities.[9] These longer-term buyer–seller relationships are based on the mutual benefits received

An Ethical Dilemma

© GALLO IMAGES-HEINRICH VAN DEN BERG/JUPITER IMAGES

Sam Karmo, a key account manager with Diversified Holdings, has developed strong relationships with members of the buying teams at each of the 15 companies that compose his account list. Tungston Industries, a worldwide producer of large metal castings and forgings, has become Karmo's largest account. In fact, Tungston alone accounts for more than 30 percent of his total annual sales volume. Last week, Karmo took Tungston's director of purchasing—an avid golfer—out for a day of golf at one of Prince Edward Island's best private golf clubs. On the tenth tee, Karmo hit his best drive of the day, and the Tungston buyer began admiring Karmo's driver. It was a brand new club (the technologically advanced TaylorMade Model r7 460), for which he had paid $499 only a few days earlier. At the next tee box, Karmo handed the club to the buyer and insisted that he try it out. He did and drilled a beautiful shot straight down the fairway—and the ball went a good 40 yards longer than any previous drive. The buyer handed the driver back to Karmo with many positive exclamations including the comment that he could not wait to get one for himself. At that point, Karmo tossed the driver back to the buyer saying, "It's in your bag. Just remember to think of me every time you use it."

What do you think about Karmo's latest efforts at building relationships with the Tungston buyer? How would you have handled this situation if you were in Karmo's place?

supply chain management The strategic coordination and integration of purchasing with other functions within the buying organization as well as external organizations.

outsourcing The process of giving to a supplier certain activities that the buying organization previously performed.

Beyond a buyer-seller relationship, supply chain management emphasizes the strategic coordination and integration of purchasing with other functions within the buying organization as well as external organizations, including customers, customers' customers, suppliers, and suppliers' suppliers. Salespeople must focus on coordinating their efforts with all parties in the network—end users and suppliers alike—and effectively work to add value for all members of the network. As described in "Professional Selling in the 21st Century: Enhancing Value for the Customer through Mobile Technology,"[10] it is clear that advances in mobile communications are making it possible for salespeople to maintain more effective customer communication even while on the road travelling between accounts.

by and the interdependence between all parties in this value network. In addition to being keenly aware of changing customer needs, collaborative relationships require salespeople to work closely with buyers to foster honest and open two-way communication and develop the mutual understanding required to create the desired solutions. Further, salespeople must consistently demonstrate that they are dependable and acting in the buyer's best interests.

SUPPLY CHAIN MANAGEMENT

Having realized that their success or failure is inextricably linked to other firms in the value network, many organizations are implementing **supply chain management** across an extended network of suppliers and customers.

INCREASED OUTSOURCING

Broader business involvement and expanded integration between organizations is a natural evolution as buyers and suppliers become increasingly confident of the other's performance capabilities and commitment to the relationship. These expanded agreements often involve **outsourcing** to a supplier certain activities that the buying organization previously performed. These activities are necessary for the day-to-day functioning of

© ABSODELS/GETTY IMAGES

PROFESSIONAL SELLING IN THE 21ST CENTURY

Enhancing Value for the Customer Through Mobile Technology

Consistent, effective communication is critical for managing the buyer-seller relationships that deliver successful sales outcomes. Yet with salespeople increasingly on the road, effective communication becomes a challenge that needs to be addressed. Harprit Singh, CEO of Intellicomm, a communications services organization, discusses the variety of ways a salesperson can stay productive and work with customers while on the road.

From a communications standpoint, having broad access is probably number one. Second, you want to address the need for a cell phone so that you have a good communication channel. Then, when you have Internet access, you essentially have phone functionality via VoIP (Voice-over-Internet Protocol). You can also use faxes, email, and instant messaging—all powerful tools for keeping in touch. These combinations of communication technologies also enable the use of additional channels, such as Web conferencing and teleconferencing, which can help make your communication tasks more efficient. In today's mobile world, with the realities of increased communication requirements, applications that offer unified voice, fax, and data messaging are becoming essential tools for working successfully and staying in touch.

the buying organization but are not within the organization's core or distinct competencies. Outsourcing these activities allows the organization to focus on what it does best. However, these activities are typically among those in which the supplying organization specializes or even excels. As a result of the outsourcing agreement, the relationship gains strength and is further extended in such a way that all parties benefit

target price The price buyers determine for their final products through information gathered from researching the marketplace.

over the long term. Outsourcing agreements place increased emphasis on the role of the salesperson to provide continuing follow-up activities to ensure customer satisfaction and nurture the buyer–seller relationship. Changes in customer needs must be continually monitored and factored into the supplier's market offerings and outsourcing activities.

TARGET PRICING

Using information gathered from researching the marketplace, buyers establish a **target price** for their final products. For example, buyers determine the selling price for a new printing press should be $320,000. Next, they divide the press into its subsystems and parts to estimate what each part is worth in relation to the overall price. Using such a system, buyers might conclude that the maximum price they could pay for a lead roller platen would be $125 and then use this information when working with potential suppliers. In working with targeted pricing requirements, salespeople find they have two fundamental options. They can meet the required cost level, which often entails cutting their prices, or they can work with the buyer to better understand and possibly influence minimum performance specifications. Certain restrictive specifications might be relaxed as a trade-off for lower pricing. For example, a salesperson might negotiate longer lead times, fewer or less complex design features, or less technical support in exchange for lower prices. The latter option requires salespeople to have a high level of knowledge regarding their product's organizational capabilities, and customer applications and needs. Just as important is the ability to create feasible options and effectively communicate them to the buyer.

INCREASED IMPORTANCE OF KNOWLEDGE AND CREATIVITY

The increased interdependence between buyer and seller organizations hinges on the salesperson's capabilities to serve as a problem solver in a dynamic and fast-changing business environment. Buyers depend on the salesperson to provide unique and value-added solutions to their changing problems and needs. To shape such innovative solutions, salespeople must have broad-based and comprehensive knowledge readily available and the ability to use that knowledge in creative ways. This includes knowledge of one's own products and capabilities, as well as the products and capabilities of competitors. More important, the salesperson must possess a thorough understanding of product applications and the needs of the customer to work with the buyer in generating innovative solutions.

Visit **sell.nelson.com** to find the resources you need today!

Located at the back of the textbook are rip-out Chapter Review cards. Make sure you also go online to check out other tools that SELL offers to help you successfully pass your course.

- Flashcards
- Glossary
- PowerPoint Notes

- Role-Play Videos
- Games
- Interactive Quizzing

Recommended Flexing Behaviour for Different Communication Styles

Selling Task or Objective

SETTING AN APPOINTMENT

Selling to the Analytical

- Send a business letter with details about yourself and the company.
- Follow the letter with a phone call to confirm expectations and set an appointment.

Selling to the Driver

- Drivers may not take time to read your letter.
- Contact them by phone first and follow up with a letter.
- Keep the call businesslike and to the point by identifying yourself, explaining the business problem addressed by your product, and asking for an appointment.
- The letter should simply confirm the time and date of appointment and include materials the driver might review before the meeting.

Selling to the Amiable

- Send a letter with a personal touch stating who you are and why you are contacting him or her.
- The letter should include your experience working with clients the prospect knows by reputation or experience, your reliability and follow-through, and the quality of your product or service.
- Follow the letter with a personal phone call.
- Take time to be friendly, open, and sincere, and to establish trust in the relationship.

Selling to the Expressive

- Generally, a phone call is most appropriate.
- Make your call open and friendly, stressing quick benefits, personal service, your experience, and your company's experience with its products and services.
- If you send a letter, make it short and personal, stressing who you are, how you know of him or her, and what you are interested in talking about.

OPENING THE CALL

Selling to the Analytical

- Provide background information about you and the company.
- Approach in an advisory capacity, acknowledging buyer's expertise.
- Show evidence that you have done your homework on the buyer's situation.
- Offer evidence of having provided solutions in the past.
- Be conscious of how you are using the buyer's time.

Selling to the Driver

- Listen and focus on the driver's ideas and objectives.
- Provide knowledge and insight relevant to the driver's specific business problems.
- Be personable but reserved and relatively formal.
- Present factual evidence that establishes the business problem and resulting outcome.
- Maintain a quick pace. Drivers value punctuality and the efficient use of time.

Selling to the Amiable

- Engage in informal conversation before getting down to business.
- Demonstrate that you are personally interested in the amiable's work and personal goals.
- You will have to earn the right to learn more personally about the amiable.
- Demonstrate your product or service knowledge by referencing a common acquaintance with whom you've done business.

Selling to the Expressive

- Quickly describe the purpose of your call and establish credibility—you must earn the right to develop a business relationship with the expressive.
- Share stories about people you both know.
- Share information the expressive would perceive as exclusive.
- Share your feelings and enthusiasm for the expressive's ideas and goals.
- Once the expressive has confidence in your competence, take time to develop an open and trusting personal relationship.

GATHERING INFORMATION

Selling to the Analytical

- Ask specific, fact-finding questions in a systematic manner.
- Establish a comprehensive exchange of information.
- Encourage the buyer to discuss ideas while focusing on factual information.
- Be thorough and unhurried—listen.
- Explain that you are in alignment with his or her thinking and can support his or her objectives.

Selling to the Driver

- Ask, don't tell. Ask fact-finding questions leading to what the driver values and rewards.
- Make your line of questioning consistent with your call objective.
- Follow up on requests for information immediately.
- Support the buyer's beliefs; indicate how you can positively affect goals.
- Clarify the driver's expectations.

Selling to the Amiable

- Create a cooperative atmosphere with an open exchange of information and feelings.
- Amiables tend to understate their objectives, so you may need to probe for details and specifics about his or her goals.
- Listen responsively. Give ample amounts of verbal and nonverbal feedback.
- Verify whether there are unresolved budget or cost justification issues.
- Find out who else will contribute to the buying decision.
- Summarize what you believe to be the amiable's key ideas and feelings.

Selling to the Expressive

- Begin by finding out the expressive's perception of the situation and vision of the ideal outcome.
- Identify other people who should contribute to analysis and planning.
- Listen and then respond with plenty of verbal and non-verbal feedback that supports the expressive's beliefs.
- Question carefully the critical data you'll need.
- Keep the discussion focused and moving toward a result.
- If the expressive shows limited interest in specifics, summarize what has been discussed and begin to suggest ways to move the vision toward reality.

ACTIVATING THE NEED TO CHANGE

Selling to the Analytical

- Use the buyer's records to supply information.
- Use a logical approach.
- Illustrate with dollars and cents.

Selling to the Driver

- Be fast paced and businesslike.
- Be sure of your figures.
- Show the driver the bottom line.
- Appeal to rational thinking and avoid appealing to emotions.

Selling to the Amiable

- Address emotional needs in line with safety and comfort needs.
- Use the amiable's own figures rather than your own.
- Do not push!

Selling to the Expressive

- Support the expressive's ideas and goals.
- Work toward his or her esteem needs.
- Supply data from people seen as leaders by the expressive.

ENGAGING IN THE SALES CONVERSATION

Selling to the Analytical

- Provide a detailed written proposal as part of your presentation.
- Include the strongest cost-benefit justifications
- Support with third-party data.
- Be reserved and decisive but not aggressive.
- Limit emotional or testimonial appeals.
- Recommend a specific course of action.
- Give the buyer chance to review all documents related to purchase and delivery.

Selling to the Driver

- Present your recommendation so that the driver can compare alternative solutions and probable outcomes.
- Provide documented options.
- Offer the best quality given the cost limitations.
- Be specific and factual without overwhelming the driver with details.
- Appeal to esteem and independence needs.
- Reinforce the driver's preference for acting in a forthright manner.
- Summarize content quickly, and then let the driver choose a course of action.

Selling to the Amiable

- Define clearly in writing and make sure the amiable understands the following:
  - What you can do to support the amiable's personal goals

  - What you will contribute and what the amiable needs to contribute
  - The support resources you intend to commit to the project
- Provide a clear solution to the amiable's problem with maximum assurances that this is the best solution and that there is no need to consider others.
- Ask the amiable to involve other decision makers.
- Satisfy needs by showing how your solution is best now and will be best in the future, and support it with references and third-party evidence.
- Use testimonials from perceived experts and others close to the amiable.

Selling to the Expressive

- Provide specific solutions to the expressive's ideas—in writing.
- Build confidence that you have the necessary facts, but do not overwhelm the expressive with details.
- Do not rush the discussion. Spend time developing ways to implement ideas.
- Appeal to personal esteem needs.
- Try to get commitments to action in writing.

EARNING COMMITMENT

Selling to the Analytical

- Ask for commitment in a low-key but direct manner.
- Expect to negotiate changes.
- Pay special attention to pricing issues.
- Work for commitment now to avoid the analytical's tendency to delay decisions.
- Cite data supporting your company's service records.
- Respond to objections by emphasizing the analytical's buying principles and objectivity.

Selling to the Driver

- Ask for the order directly.
- Put your offer in clear, factual terms.
- Offer options and alternatives.
- Be prepared to negotiate changes and concessions.
- Drivers sometimes attach conditions to a sale.
- Offer the driver time to consider the options.

- Anticipate objections in advance and come prepared with facts.
- Respond to objections based on driver's values and priorities.

Selling to the Amiable

- Ask for the order indirectly—do not push.
- Emphasize the guarantees that offer protection to the amiable.
- Do not corner the amiables; he or she will want out if things go wrong.
- Guard against "buyer's remorse"—get a commitment even if you have to base it on a contingency.
- Stress your personal involvement after the sale.
- Encourage the amiable to involve others in the final purchase decision.
- Welcome objections and be patient and thorough in responding to them.
- When responding to objections,
  - Describe financial justification
  - Refer to experts or others the amiable respects
  - Keep in mind how the amiable feels about and will be affected by the purchase decision

Selling to the Expressive

- When you have enough information to understand the need and have tested the appropriateness of the recommendation, assume the sale and ask for the order in a casual and informal way.
- When the opportunity presents itself, offer incentives to encourage the purchase.
- Do not confuse the issue by presenting too many options or choices.
- Get a definite commitment. Be sure the expressive understands the decision to purchase.
- Save the details until after you have a firm buying decision. The expressive believes it is the salesperson's job to handle details.
- In handling objections,
  - Describe what others have done to get over that hurdle
  - Respond to the expressive's enthusiasm for his or her goals
  - Deal with how the recommendation meets with this buyer's options

- Restate benefits that focus on the satisfaction a buying decision will bring

PROVIDING FOLLOW-UP

Selling to the Analytical

- Provide a detailed implementation plan.
- Maintain regular contact.
- Check to confirm satisfactory and on-schedule delivery.

Selling to the Driver

- Set up a communication process with the driver that encourages quick exchange of information about checkpoints and milestones.
- Make sure you have a contingency plan to responsively implement corrections and incorporate changes.
- Make sure there are no surprises.

Selling to the Amiable

- Immediately after the purchase decision is made, make a follow-up appointment.
- Initiate and maintain frequent contacts providing services, such as the following:
  - Periodic progress reports on installation
  - Arrangements for service and training
  - Introduction of new products and services
  - Listening carefully to concerns, even those that seem trivial

Selling to the Expressive

- As soon as the order is signed, reaffirm the schedule for delivery and your personal relationship with the buyer, and introduce the implementation person or team.
- A social situation, such as a lunch, can be a very effective opportunity for following up on business with this buyer.
- Work toward becoming an ongoing member of the buyer's team.
- In case of any complaints, handle them yourself. Never refer them to another in your organization without the buyer's consent.

BEYOND SEATING, INC.

Background

You are a salesperson for Beyond Seating, Inc., working with the Toronto Centre for the Arts to replace the seating as part of a major rejuvenation of the auditorium. The remodelling project is being done because several private theatres and two universities' entertainment centres had begun to take major show bookings from the auditorium.

Current Situation

The buyers want the new auditorium seating to be as comfortable as possible and have specified units complete with arms and hinged seats/backs that allow the user to sit upright or slightly recline by leaning back 10 centimetres. The specifications also require heavy frames, hardware, and linkage assemblies to yield an expected usable life of 10 years before requiring any form of service or replacement. However, these specifications increase the cost of the chairs by 13 percent. As a result, the buyers are now requesting a lower-grade vinyl fabric in hopes of making up for some of the increased hardware costs.

With your expertise in chairs and fabrics, you have recommended the use of higher grade nylon velvet rather than vinyl. The velvet will not only be much more comfortable but also more durable than the vinyl. Although both fabrics are equally moisture and stain resistant, the velvet comes with a guaranteed usable life of 10 years compared with the vinyl's 6-year guarantee.

Questions

1. Use the multiattribute model of evaluation to develop a strategy for reselling the better-grade fabric as the best choice for the new auditorium seating.
2. What is the role of the salesperson in explaining and demonstrating that the longer-term added value of a solution with a higher initial cost can make it the lowest lifetime cost alternative?
3. What sales aids could assist the salesperson in demonstrating the longer term added value and evidencing the greater benefits to the buyer?

Role Play

Situation: Read the case.

Characters: You, salesperson for Beyond Seating, Inc.; the buyer, purchasing manager for the Toronto Centre for the Arts.

Scene:
Location—Buyer's office at the Toronto Centre for the Arts

Action—You are presenting the chairs and seating equipment that your company is proposing to sell and install in line with the desired specifications outlined by the design architect and the management for the Toronto Centre for the Arts.

Demonstrate how you might present the advantages and benefits of the higher grade nylon velvet over the lower grade vinyl fabric and gain the buyer's commitment to use the better fabric on the seating that is purchased.

Cape Breton Computer Corporation

Background

As a salesperson for Cape Breton Computer Corporation (CBCC), you have just received a call from your regional manager regarding a program now underway at one of your key accounts, Farmland Companies. Farmland is a national insurance company with agency offices spread across Canada. The company is in the early stages of designing and specifying a computer system that will place a computer in each agency office. The system will allow each agency to develop, operate, and maintain its own customer database to provide better service to customers. In addition, by linking through the CBCC mainframe, agencies, regional offices, and CBCC headquarters will be networked for improved internal communications and access to the corporate database.

Current Situation

You have serviced this account for several years, and CBCC equipment accounts for the biggest share of computers now in place at Farmland—some 35 to 40 percent of all units. As reflected in your share of this account's business, you and CBCC have a good reputation and strong relationship with Farmland. In talking with Aimee Linn, your usual contact in the Farmland purchasing office, you have learned that this agency network system is the brainstorm and pet project of Mike Hughes, a very "hands-on" CEO. Consequently, the probability of the system becoming a reality is high. While faxing a complete set of hardware specs to you, Linn has also let you know that although Kerri Nicks, director of the Farmland MIS department, is actually heading up this project, the national agency sales director, Ravi Singh, is also very active in its design and requirement specifications. His interest stems not only from wanting to make sure that the system will do what is needed at the corporate, regional, and agency levels but also from the fact that he brainstormed and spearheaded a similar project two years ago that was never implemented. The previous effort did not have the blessing of Nicks in the MIS department, and it became a political football between the two departments. Each department wanted something different, and each side accused the other of not knowing what it was doing. Primarily, because the CEO has commanded that it will be done, both sides seem to be playing ball this time.

Linn did hint at one concern, however, although corporate is designing and specifying the system, each agency has to purchase its units out of its own funds. The agencies represent Farmland Insurance products exclusively, and each agency is owned by the general agent, not Farmland. Some of the agents are not convinced that the system is worth the projected price tag of $3500 per system, and Farmland cannot force them to buy the systems.

As with other selling opportunities with Farmland, this has all the makings of a decision that will be made after multiple inputs from an assortment of individuals across the company—a buying team of sorts. As the salesperson having primary responsibility for this account, how would you go about identifying the members of the buying centre? Using the worksheet provided, how about "complete the following tasks", as one doesn't respond to an activity, per se?

Questions

1. Identify each member of the buying centre and the role each participant plays, and estimate the amount of influence (low, medium, high, very high) each has on the final decision.
2. What are the major problems, needs, and expectations that you will need to address for each of these buying centre members?

As you complete this assignment, remember that a single individual can perform multiple roles in the centre. Furthermore, it is common to find more than one individual playing the same buying centre role.

Role Play

Characters: You, salesperson for the Cape Breton Computer Corporation; Aimee Linn, purchasing manager for Farmland Companies; Kerri Nicks, director of MIS for Farmland Companies; Ravi Singh, national agency sales director for Farmland Companies; and Mike Hughes, CEO for Farmland Companies

Scene 1: *Location*—Linn's office at Farmland Companies
Action—You, as the Cape Breton Computer salesperson, are entering the first meeting with the Farmland buying team. Your goal for this first sales call is to establish rapport with each of the buying team members and identify the needs and expectations that will determine the purchases for this project. Identifying these needs and expectations is critical so that you can work with your own technology support people and develop a customized system as a solution to Farmland's needs.

Worksheet for Identifying Buying Team Members and Roles

Buying Team Role	Team Member Playing This Role	Level of Influence	Team Member's Perceived Needs and Expectations
Initiators			
Users			
Influencers			
Purchasers			
Deciders			
Gatekeepers			

Join with another group of students to role play this first sales call and demonstrate how you would (a) build rapport with the team members, (b) identify the needs and expectations the team members have for this information technology project, and (c) bridge the gap between the sales manager and the MIS director that killed the project once before.

Scene 2: *Location*—Aimee Linn's office at Farmland Companies
Action—Based on the needs and expectations discovered in your first sales call, you have worked with your support team at Cape Breton Computers to develop a customized system meeting Farmland's primary needs. You are now making a follow-up sales call to present your proposed system and make the sale.

After completing the role play, address the following questions:

1. In what way would the different communication styles of the buying team members present complications in the critical stages of building a rapport and discovering the buyers' needs and expectations?
2. How can a salesperson effectively build rapport with a team of different individuals that have large variations across their communication styles?
3. In a buying team situation, it is typical that certain needs will be championed by specific members while other members will be vocal in support of other needs the solution must address. How might a salesperson best present the proposed package of features and benefits and recognize the relevant interests of the different buying team members?
4. What suggestions do you have for improving the presentation of the proposed solution and maximizing the positive involvement and buy-in of the different team members?

GET ONLINE

The easy-to-navigate website for **SELL** offers guidance on key topics in **sales** in a variety of engaging formats. You have the opportunity to refine and check your understanding via interactive quizzes and flashcards. Videos and cases provide inspiration for your own further exploration. And to make **SELL** an even better learning tool, we invite you to speak up about your experience with

SELL by completing a survey form and sending us your comments.

Get online and discover the following resources:

- PowerPoint notes
- Flashcards
- Interactive quizzing
- Crossword puzzles
- Role-play videos

"I think this book is awesome for students of all ages. It is a much simpler way to study."

—Yasmine Al-Hashimi, Fanshawe College

Visit **www.sell.nelson.com** to find the resources you need today!

Interactive, collaborative

conversations with customers are essential for gaining critical information and insight about customers' situations and enable salespeople to offer unique, added-value solutions for customers' needs.

what do you think?

Of all the skills and activities involved in selling, the most important for salesperson success is active listening.

1 2 3 4 5 6 7
strongly disagree   strongly agree

4

Communication Skills

After completing this chapter, you should be able to

 **LO1** Explain the importance of collaborative, two-way communication in trust-based selling.

LO2 Explain the primary types of questions and how they are applied in selling.

LO3 Illustrate the diverse roles and uses of strategic questioning in trust-based selling.

LO4 Identify and describe the SPIN and ADAPT systems for effective questioning in a sales dialogue.

LO5 Discuss the four sequential steps for effective active listening.

LO6 Describe and interpret the different forms of verbal and nonverbal communication.

Introduction

When she was growing up, Kathy Collard was painfully shy and withdrawn. "I was the kid who never put their hand up in class, even if I knew the answer. I had really low self-esteem," she recalls. That lack of confidence was reflected in her demeanour, affecting the way she spoke and gestured and generally presented herself.

It wasn't until she became an adult and opened her Kingston, Ont.-based business, Home Inspirations, that she recognized the value of improving her verbal and non-verbal communication skills. "I knew I'd need to be doing presentations and workshops, and I was terrified," said Ms. Collard, a professional household organizer.

She joined a local Toastmasters group, which helped with her presentation style; but to move further out of her comfort zone, Ms. Collard sought the help of Catherine Bell, president of Prime Impressions Image Consultants in Kingston. Ms. Collard's training sessions were videotaped and reviewed each week, giving her an accurate picture of how she appeared to others and what she needed to change to better project confidence.

The tapes, for example, revealed her tendency to lean to one side and cross her feet when standing, a position that made her appear uncomfortable, unstable and less grounded. "It was a real learning experience," Ms. Collard said. Not only is she now more aware of the wordless signals her body language sends, but she's also more sensitive to the non-verbal cues of others.

"It's invaluable, especially in what I do as a organizer. A lot of times, physical clutter means emotional clutter. If I'm tuned into other people's body language—whether they're sitting facing me, looking at me, how receptive they are—it helps me help them."

Non-verbal behaviour—facial expressions, gestures, eye movement, posture, and even tone of voice—send strong signals that tell others how well you're listening and whether you're interested in them, Ms. Bell said.

"Most people are unaware that their body language speaks far louder than what they are saying. And there's a huge number of physical distractions that can certainly undermine or change your message," Ms. Bell said.

About 93 percent of all our communication is non-verbal, said Ric Phillips, president of 3V Communications Ltd. in Toronto. Understanding and using body language can be an invaluable tool to build better relationships, he said.

Whether you're managing employees, meeting with clients, making presentations or going on a job interview, both your verbal and non-verbal messages must align for effective communication, Mr. Phillips said. "People know when they see something odd; they may not be able to say exactly what that is, but they can sense when something is not right."

A recent survey by CareerBuilder Canada of 200 hiring managers found that 68 per cent said they would be less likely to hire a person who failed to make eye contact during a job interview. Forty-five percent cited the lack of a smile as a hiring deterrent, and 37 percent said poor posture would also reflect negatively on job seekers.

Other body language that spurred a negative impression with the hiring managers included crossing arms over the chest (33 per cent); fidgeting (34 per cent); a weak handshake (33 per cent); playing with something on the table (32 per cent); and playing with hair or touching the face (21 per cent).

These sorts of gestures usually stem from our anxiety in situations where we want to appear confident and capable, such as making a formal presentation or during a job interview, Ms. Bell noted. And often the moves or gestures are unconscious habits.

Women and men make the same mistakes in body language, although women are especially prone to touching their hair, brushing it off their faces or sweeping it behind their ears, signs of insecurity and nervousness.

"In any situation, you must be thinking about the message you want to send. Constantly ask yourself, 'What do I want to convey?'" Ms. Bell said.

Self-awareness is key to improving your body language, Mr. Phillips said. Of course, you need to know what mistakes you're making before you can fix them.

Your professional abilities can be undermined because of the way you look or behave, Ms. Bell notes, adding that even the smallest things can sabotage your image. "You always want to be remembered for the right reasons."

Source: Jennifer Meyers. "It's Not What You Say, It's How You Move." *Globe and Mail*, January 13, 2011.

this chapter addresses the need to better understand and master the art of collaborative, two-way communication. First, we will examine the basic nature of **trust-based sales communication**. Building on this preliminary understanding, the text breaks down trust-based sales communication into its component and subcomponent parts to facilitate study, application, and mastery. The verbal dimension of communication is examined first with an emphasis on three communication subcomponents: (1) developing effective questioning methods for use in uncovering and diagnosing buyers' needs and expectations, (2) using active listening skills to facilitate the interchange of ideas and information, and (3) maximizing the responsive sharing of information with buyers in a way that fully explains and brings to life the benefits of proposed solutions. Finally, the nonverbal dimension of interpersonal communication is examined with an emphasis on its application and meaningful interpretation.

LO1
Sales Communication as a Collaborative Process

neither people nor organizations buy products. Rather, they seek out the satisfaction and benefits that certain product features provide. Although traditional selling has been described as "talking *at* the customer," trust-based selling has been referred to as "talking *with* the customer." Trust-based sales communication is a two-way and naturally collaborative interaction that allows buyers and sellers alike to develop a better understanding of the need situation and work together to generate the best response for solving the customer's needs. Although trust-based selling has become the preeminent model for contemporary personal selling, the situation described in "An Ethical Dilemma" should serve as a reminder that some salespeople and sales organizations continue to practise more traditional and manipulative forms of selling.

Trust-based sales communication is the sharing of meaning between buying and selling parties that results from the interactive process of exchanging information and ideas. It is important to note that the purpose of sales communication is not agreement but rather the maximization of common understanding among participants. With this emphasis on establishing understanding, communication is fundamental throughout each stage of the selling process. Effective communication skills are needed to identify buying needs and to demonstrate to buyers how a salesperson's proposed solution can satisfy those needs better than competitors. The critical capabilities for

An Ethical Dilemma

© STOCKLITE/SHUTTERSTOCK

Aimee Moore is 23 years old and recently completed her undergraduate degree in marketing. She accepted a position in the fast-growing financial services field as a financial representative for one of the largest, nationwide organizations in the industry—a company focused on maintaining a growth rate that will ensure its continued dominance in the industry and sustain its large customer base. After accepting the position, Moore first completed a two-month training program (along with 18 other new recruits) at the company's headquarters in Saguenay. She describes the training program as being primarily concerned with (a) legal and industry issues to get the necessary licences and (b) product knowledge so that she understands the various products and services she was hired to sell. Coverage of basic sales skills was limited and was addressed only on the last two days in Saguenay.

On completion of the two months of training, the newly minted financial representatives returned to their resident offices and were given a list of prospects that they would use for making phone calls. Each new rep was also given a three-ring binder of selling tips to use as needed. The first page of the selling tips contained a motivational message followed by what was titled, "The 5 Keys to Successful Selling." These keys to success were as follows:

Key #1: Everybody needs a financial planner! Make your daily calls, demonstrate the benefits of our products, and ask for the appointment.

Key #2: Prospective buyers do not know what they need in terms of financial products and services! At the appointment, follow the standard selling message showing each of our products, and ask for the order each time until the buyer makes a choice.

Key #3: Always be closing! If you do not ask for the order, nobody will buy!

Key #4: Success in selling is simply a numbers game! Contact enough prospects and you will make your quota. Want to sell more? Make more contacts!

Key #5: Product knowledge is the key! Have a good opening, explain the products, handle objections, and close the sale by leading the buyer where you want them to go.

How does this company's selling philosophy compare with the trust-based, collaborative selling approach we have been discussing? How are these keys to selling success likely to work in today's marketplace? Why?

effective selling include questioning, listening, giving information, nonverbal communication, and written communication skills. Although each of these skills is pervasive in everyday life, they are literally the heart and soul of the interpersonal exchange that characterizes trust-based selling.

Successful salespeople are experts at considering what information they need to know and purposefully planning and asking the questions they need to ask.

Verbal Communication: Questioning

there are two ways to dominate or control a selling conversation. A salesperson can talk all the time, or can maintain a more subtle level of control by asking well-thought-out questions that guide the discussion. As highlighted in "Professional Selling in the 21st Century: Importance of Preparation and Well-Thought-Out Questions,"[1] successful salespeople must be masters at thinking through what they need to know and planning the questions they need to ask. They should know exactly what information they need and which type of question is best suited for eliciting that information from a prospective buyer.

Purposeful, carefully crafted questions can encourage thoughtful responses from a buyer and provide richly detailed information about the buyer's current situation, needs, and expectations. This

Salespeople use purposeful questions to encourage thoughtful and detailed responses from prospects.

additional detail and understanding is often as meaningful for the buyer as it is for the salesperson. That is, proper questioning can facilitate both the buyer's and the seller's understanding of a problem and its possible solutions.[2] For example, questions can encourage meaningful feedback regarding the buyer's attitude and the logical progression through the purchase decision process. Questioning also shows interest in the buyer and his or her needs and actively involves the buyer in the selling process. Questions can also be used tactically to redirect, regain, or hold the buyer's attention should it begin to wander during the conversation. In a similar fashion, questions can provide a convenient and subtle transition to a different topic of discussion and provide a logical guide promoting sequential thought and decision making.

Questions are categorized by the results they are designed to accomplish. Does the salesperson want to receive a free flow of thoughts and ideas or a simple yes/no confirmation? Is the salesperson seeking a general description of the overall situation or specific details regarding emergent needs or problematic experiences with current suppliers? To be effective, a salesperson must understand which type of question will best accomplish his or her desired outcome. In this manner, questions can be put into two basic categories: (1) the amount of information and level of specificity desired and (2) the strategic purpose or intent.

© KHZ/SHUTTERSTOCK

LO2
TYPES OF QUESTIONS CLASSIFIED BY AMOUNT AND SPECIFICITY OF INFORMATION DESIRED

Open-End Questions

Open-end questions, also called nondirective questions, are designed to let the customer respond freely. That is, the customer is not limited

PROFESSIONAL SELLING IN THE 21ST CENTURY

Importance of Preparation and Well-Thought-Out Questions

Successful salespeople do not rely solely on their instincts during a sales call. They know that in today's environment of sophisticated and knowledgeable buyers they cannot "wing it" without preparing a solid precall plan that outlines the information they need and the questions they will ask to acquire the information from the customer. Mark Shonka and Dan Kosch, copresidents of IMPAX Corporation and sales training consultants to Fortune 500 companies, share their comments regarding the importance of precall planning and knowing what questions you are going to ask before you make the actual sales call:

The information gained in the sales call should build on the research that a salesperson has already gathered from other sources and should provide the salesperson with more detail from the insider's perspective. As there is a limitless amount of knowledge about the target account available, keeping on track and avoiding the social conversation trap requires that the salesperson determine what information they need and what questions they might ask before actually making the sales call. Typically, the information needed from the insider's perspective can be classified into five distinct categories:

1. *Corporate Profile and Direction*
   Get a grasp of the facts and figures that describe the company and make it unique
   Investigate the issues and activities that influence the company's plans and operations
   Determine what their plans are for the future
2. *Organizational Structure*
   Formal Chart—chain of command; how the company is structured
   Informal Chart—how things actually get done: politics and power do not always follow formal titles
   Social Chart—the key relationships that affect what happens in the company
3. *Key Players and Profiles (Buying Team Roles)*
   Personal and professional background information
   Objectives and priorities
   Issues and concerns
4. *Departmental Profile and Direction*
   Profile the internal workings and how it functions
   Objectives, strategies, projects
   Issues and concerns
5. *Buying Organization—Selling Organization Business Fit*
   Addresses customer's objectives and issues
   Focuses on decision makers' concerns
   Aims for long-term, value-based relationship

closed-end questions
Questions designed to limit the customer's responses to one or two words.

dichotomous questions A directive form of questioning; these questions ask the customer to choose from two or more options.

probing questions Questions designed to penetrate below generalized or superficial information to elicit more articulate and precise details for use in needs discovery and solution identification.

evaluative questions Questions that use the open- and closed-end question formats to gain confirmation and to uncover attitudes, opinions, and preferences the prospect holds.

tactical questions Questions used to shift or redirect the topic of discussion when the discussion gets off course or when a line of questioning proves to be of little interest or value.

to one- or two-word answers but is encouraged to disclose personal business information. Open-end questions encourage buyers' thought processes and deliver richer and more expansive information than closed-end questions. Consequently, these questions are typically used to probe for descriptive information that allows the salesperson to better understand the specific needs and expectations of the customer. The secret to successfully using open-end questions lies in the first word used to form the question. Words often used to begin open-end questions include *what, how, where, when, tell, describe*, and *why*?[3] "What happens when . . .", "How do you feel . . .", and "Describe the . . ." are examples of open-end questions.

Closed-End Questions

Closed-end questions are designed to limit the customers' response to one or two words. This type of question is typically used to confirm or clarify information gleaned from previous responses to open-end questions. Although the most common form is the yes/no question, closed-end questions come in many forms—provided the response is limited to one or two words. For instance, "Do you . . .", "Are you . . .," "How many . . .", and "How often . . ." are common closed-end questions.

Dichotomous/Multiple-Choice Questions

Dichotomous questions and multiple-choice questions are directive forms of questioning. This type of question asks a customer to choose from two or more options and is used in selling to discover customer preferences and move the purchase decision process forward. An

example of this form of question would be, "Which do you prefer, the _____ or the _____?"

TYPES OF QUESTIONS CLASSIFIED BY STRATEGIC PURPOSE

Probing Questions

Probing questions are designed to penetrate below generalized or superficial information to elicit more articulate and precise details for use in needs discovery and solution identification. Rather than interrogating a buyer, probing questions are best used in a conversational style: (1) requesting clarification ("Can you share with me an example of that?" "How long has this been a problem?"), (2) encouraging elaboration ("How are you dealing with that situation now?" "What is your experience with _____?"), and (3) verifying information and responses ("That is interesting, could you tell me more?" "So, if I understand correctly, _____. Is that right?").

Evaluative Questions

Evaluative questions use open- and closed-end question formats to gain confirmation and to uncover attitudes, opinions, and preferences the prospect holds. These questions are designed to go beyond generalized fact finding and uncover prospects' perceptions and feelings regarding existing and desired circumstances as well as potential solutions. Exemplary evaluative questions include "How do you feel about _____?" "Do you see the merits of _____?" and "What do you think _____?"

Tactical Questions

Tactical questions are used to shift or redirect the topic of discussion when the discussion gets off course or when a line of questioning proves to be of little interest or value. For example, the salesperson might be exploring the chances of plant expansion only to find that the prospect cannot provide that type of proprietary information at this early stage of the buyer–seller relationship. To avoid either embarrassing the prospect or himself or herself by proceeding on a forbidden or nonproductive line of questioning, the seller uses a tactical question designed to change topics. An example of such a tactical question might be expressed as "Earlier you mentioned that _____. Could you tell me more about how that might affect _____?"

Reactive Questions

Reactive questions are questions that refer to or directly result from information the other party previously provided. Reactive questions are used to elicit additional information, explore for further detail, and keep the flow of information going. Illustrative reactive questions are "You mentioned that ____. Can you give me an example of what you mean?" and "That is interesting. Can you tell me how it happened?"

These different groupings of question types are not mutually exclusive. As depicted in the guidelines for combining question types in Exhibit 4.1, effective questions integrate elements from different question types. For example, "How do you feel about the current trend of sales in the industry?" is an open-end (classified by format) question and evaluative (classified by purpose) in nature.

Regardless of the types of questions combined, Robert Jolles, senior sales training consultant for Xerox Corporation, cautions against the natural tendency to use closed-end questions rather than open-end questions. His experience and research indicate that for every open-end question the average salesperson asks, there will be ten closed-end questions.[4] This overuse of closed-end questions is dangerous in selling. The discovery and exploration of customer needs are fundamental to trust-based selling, and discovery and exploration are best done with open-end questions.

As previously discussed, closed-end questions certainly have their place in selling, but they are best used

reactive questions
Questions that refer to or directly result from information the other party previously provided.

EXHIBIT 4.1
Guidelines for Combining Types of Questions

		Strategic Objective or Purpose of Questioning			
		Explore and Dig for Details	**Gain Confirmation and Discover Attitudes/Opinions**	**Change Topics or Re-direct Buyer's Attention**	**Follow Up Previously Elicited Statements**
Amount and Specificity of Information Desired	**Discussion and Interpretation**	*Open-end* questions designed to be *probing* in nature	*Open-end* questions designed to be *evaluative* in nature	*Open-end* questions designed to be *tactical* in nature	*Open-end* questions designed to be *reactive* in nature
	Confirmation and Agreement	*Closed-end* questions designed to be *probing* in nature	*Closed-end* questions designed to be *evaluative* in nature	*Closed-end* questions designed to be *tactical* in nature	*Closed-end* questions designed to be *reactive* in nature
	Choosing from Alternatives	*Dichotomous or multiple-choice* questions designed to be *probing* in nature	*Dichotomous or multiple-choice* questions designed to be *evaluative* in nature	*Dichotomous or multiple-choice* questions designed to be *tactical* in nature	*Dichotomous or multiple-choice* questions designed to be *reactive* in nature

for clarification and confirmation, not discovery and exploration. An additional issue in overusing closed-end questions is that when they are used in a sequence, the resulting communication takes on the demeanor of interrogation rather than conversation.

LO3
STRATEGIC APPLICATION OF QUESTIONING IN TRUST-BASED SELLING

Effective questioning skills are indispensable in selling and are used to address critical issues throughout all stages of the selling process. In practice, salespeople combine the different types of questions discussed earlier to accomplish multiple and closely related sales objectives:

- *Generate buyer involvement.* Rather than the salesperson dominating the conversation and interaction, purposeful and planned questions are used to encourage prospective buyers to participate actively in a two-way collaborative discussion.

- *Provoke thinking.* Innovative and effective solutions require cognitive efforts and contributions from each participant. Strategic questions stimulate buyers and salespeople to think thoroughly and pragmatically about and consider all aspects of a given situation.

- *Gather information.* Good questions result from advance planning and should be directed toward gathering the information required to fill in the gap between "What do we need to know?" and "What do we already know?"

- *Clarify and emphasize.* Rather than assuming that the salesperson understands what a buyer has said, questions can be used to clarify meaning further and to emphasize the important points within a buyer-seller exchange further.

- *Show interest.* In response to statements from buyers, salespeople ask related questions and paraphrase what the buyer has said to demonstrate their interest in and understanding of what the buyer is saying.

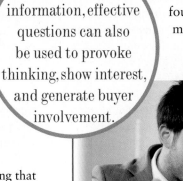

Besides gaining information, effective questions can also be used to provoke thinking, show interest, and generate buyer involvement.

- *Gain confirmation.* The use of simple and direct questions allow salespeople to check back with the prospective buyer to confirm the buyer's understanding or agreement and gain his or her commitment to move forward.

- *Advance the sale.* Effective questions are applied in a fashion that guides and moves the selling process forward in a logical progression from initiation through needs development and through needs resolution and follow-up.

With the aim of simultaneously targeting and achieving each of these objectives, several systems have been developed to guide salespeople in properly developing and using effective questions. Two of the more prominent questioning systems are SPIN and ADAPT. Both of these systems use a logical sequencing—a sort of funnelling effect—that begins with broad-based, nonthreatening, general questions. Questioning progressively proceeds through more narrowly focused questions designed to clarify the buyer's needs and to propel the selling process logically toward the presentation and demonstration of solution features, advantages, and benefits.

LO4
SPIN QUESTIONING SYSTEM

The **SPIN** system sequences four types of questions designed to uncover a buyer's current situation and inherent problems, enhance the buyer's understanding of the consequences and implications of those problems, and lead to the proposed solution.[5] SPIN is actually an acronym for the four types of questions making up the multiple question sequence: situation

© PEEPO/ISTOCKPHOTO

questions, problem questions, implication questions, and need-payoff questions.

- *Situation questions.* This type of question solicits data and facts in the form of general background information and descriptions of the buyer's existing situation. **Situation questions** are used early in the sales call and provide salespeople with leads to develop the buyer's needs and expectations fully. Situation questions might include "Who are your current suppliers?" "Do you typically purchase or lease?" and "Who is involved in purchasing decisions?" Situation questions are essential, but they should be used in moderation as too many general fact-finding questions can bore the buyer. Further, their interrogating nature can result in irritated buyers.

- *Problem questions.* **Problem questions** follow the more general situation questions to probe further for specific difficulties, developing problems, and areas of dissatisfaction that might be positively addressed by the salesperson's proposed sales offering. Some examples of problem questions include "How critical is this component for your production?" "What kinds of problems have you encountered with your current suppliers?" and "What types of reliability problems do you experience with your current system?" Problem questions actively involve the buyer and can assist the person in better understanding his or her own problems and needs. Nevertheless, inexperienced and unsuccessful salespeople generally do not ask enough problem questions.

- *Implication questions.* **Implication questions** follow and relate to the information flowing from problem questions. Their purpose is to assist the buyer in thinking about the potential consequences of the problem and understand the urgency of resolving the problem in a way that motivates him or her to seek a solution. Typical implication questions might include "How does this affect profitability?" "What impact does the slow response of your current supplier have on the productivity of your operation?" "How would a faster piece of equipment improve productivity and profits?" and "What happens when the supplier is late with a shipment?" Although implication questions are closely linked to success in selling, even experienced salespeople rarely use them effectively.

- *Need-payoff questions.* Based on the implications of a problem, salespeople use **need-payoff questions** to propose a solution and develop commitment from the buyer. These questions refocus the buyer's attention on solutions rather than problems and get the buyer to think about the positive benefits derived from solving the problems. Examples of need-payoff questions are "Would more frequent deliveries allow you to increase productivity?" "If we could provide you with increased reliability, would you be interested?" "If we could improve the quality of your purchased components, how would that help you?" and "Would you be interested in increasing productivity by 15 percent?" Top salespeople effectively incorporate a higher number of need-payoff questions into sales calls than do less successful salespeople.

ADAPT QUESTIONING SYSTEM

As Figure 4.1 illustrates, the **ADAPT** questioning system uses a logic-based funnelling sequence of questions, beginning with broad and generalized inquiries designed to identify and assess the buyer's situation. Based on information gained in this first phase, further questions are generated to probe and discover more details regarding the needs and expectations of the buyer. In turn, the resulting information is incorporated in further collaborative discussion in a way that activates the buyer's motivation to implement a solution and further establishes the buyer's perceived value of a possible solution. The last phase of ADAPT questioning transitions to the buyer's commitment to learning about the proposed solution and grants the salesperson permission to move forward into the presentation and demonstration of the sales offering. ADAPT is an acronym for the five stages of strategic questioning and represents what the salesperson should be doing at each stage: assessment

situation questions
One of the four types of questions in the SPIN questioning system used early in the sales call that provides salespeople with leads to develop the buyer's needs and expectations fully.

problem questions One of the four types of questions in the SPIN questioning system that follows the more general situation questions to further probe for specific difficulties, developing problems, and areas of dissatisfaction that might be positively addressed by the salesperson's proposed sales offering.

implication questions
One of the four types of questions in the SPIN questioning system that follows and is related to the information flowing from problem questions; they are used to assist the buyer in thinking about the potential consequences of the problem and understanding the urgency of resolving the problem in a way that motivates him or her to seek a solution.

need-payoff questions
One of the four types of questions in the SPIN questioning system that is based on the implications of a problem; they are used to propose a solution and develop commitment from the buyer.

ADAPT A questioning system that uses a logic-based funnelling sequence of questions, beginning with broad and generalized inquiries designed to identify and assess the buyer's situation.

FIGURE 4.1

Funnelling Sequence of ADAPT Technique for Needs Discovery

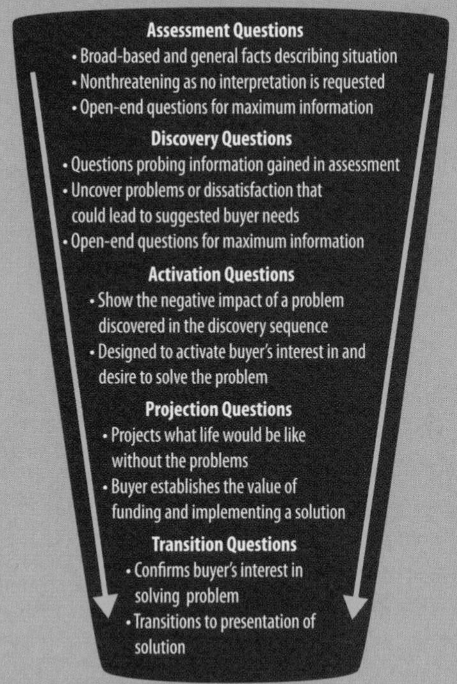

Assessment Questions
- Broad-based and general facts describing situation
- Nonthreatening as no interpretation is requested
- Open-end questions for maximum information

Discovery Questions
- Questions probing information gained in assessment
- Uncover problems or dissatisfaction that could lead to suggested buyer needs
- Open-end questions for maximum information

Activation Questions
- Show the negative impact of a problem discovered in the discovery sequence
- Designed to activate buyer's interest in and desire to solve the problem

Projection Questions
- Projects what life would be like without the problems
- Buyer establishes the value of funding and implementing a solution

Transition Questions
- Confirms buyer's interest in solving problem
- Transitions to presentation of solution

The ADAPT questioning technique logically sequences questions from broad and general inquiries through increasingly detailed questions for effective needs discovery.

questions, discovery questions, activation questions, projection questions, and transition questions.[6]

- *Assessment questions.* This initial phase of questioning is designed to be nonthreatening and to spark conversation that elicits factual information about the customer's current situation that can provide a basis for further exploration and probing. As illustrated in Exhibit 4.2, **assessment questions** do not seek conclusions—rather, at a macro or treetop level of focus, these questions should address the buyer's company and operation, goals and objectives, market trends and customers, current suppliers, and even the buyer as an individual. The information sought should augment or confirm precall research. Examples would include "What is the current level of your production?" "How long has the current equipment been in place?" "How many suppliers are currently being used?" "What are the growth objectives of the company?" and "What individuals have input into purchase decisions?"

- *Discovery questions.* As portrayed in Exhibit 4.3, these questions follow up on the responses gained from the preceding assessment questions. At a more micro and ground-level focus, **discovery questions** should drill down and probe for further details needed to fully develop, clarify, and understand the nature of the buyer's problems. Facts as well as the buyer's interpretations, perceptions, feelings, and opinions are sought about the buyer's needs, wants, dissatisfactions, and expectations relevant to product, delivery requirements,

assessment questions
One of the five stages of questions in the ADAPT questioning system that do not seek conclusions but rather should address the buyer's company and operations, goals and objectives, market trends and customers, current suppliers, and even the buyer as an individual.

discovery questions
One of the five stages of questions in the ADAPT questioning system that follows up on the assessment questions; they should drill down and probe for further details needed to develop, clarify, and understand the nature of the buyer's problems fully.

EXHIBIT 4.2

Assessment Questions

These questions are designed to elicit factual information about the customer's current situation. These questions do not seek conclusions; rather, they seek information that describes the customer and his or her business environment. The information sought should augment or confirm precall research.

Examples:

1. **Question—"What types of operating arrangements do you have with your suppliers?"**
   Answer—We use a just-in-time (JIT) system with our main suppliers.

2. **Question—"Who is involved in the purchase decision-making process?"**
   Answer—I make the decisions regarding supplies . . . .

Assessment questions are generally open end; however, closed-end questions are used when seeking confirmation or basic descriptive information. For example, "So, you currently work with 10 different suppliers?" or "How many years have you been in business?" Assessment questions are necessary for drawing out information early in the sales cycle.

EXHIBIT 4.3
Discovery Questions

Discovery questions are used to uncover problems or dissatisfactions the customer is experiencing that the salesperson's product or company may be able to solve. Basically, these questions are used to distill or boil down the information gained from the preceding assessment questions and from precall research into suggested needs.

Examples:

1. **Question—"I understand you prefer a JIT relationship with your suppliers—how have they been performing?"**
   Answer—Pretty well . . . an occasional late delivery . . . but pretty well.

2. **Question—"How do you feel about your current supplier occasionally being late with deliveries?"**
   Answer—It is a real problem . . . for instance . . . .

The *suggested* needs gained from discovery questions are used as a foundation for the rest of the sales call. Yet a *suggested* need is usually not sufficient to close the sale. Often, a customer will believe that a particular problem does not cause any significant negative consequences. If this is the case, finding a solution to the problem will be a very low priority. The professional salesperson must then help the customer to reevaluate the impact of the *suggested* need by asking activation questions.

activation questions
One of the five stages of questions in the ADAPT questioning system used to activate the customer's interest in solving discovered problems by helping him or her gain insight into the true ramifications of the problem and to realize that what may initially seem to be of little consequence is, in fact, of significant consequence.

budget and financing issues, and desired service levels. The goal is to discover needs and dissatisfactions that the salesperson's sales offering can resolve. Examples of discovery questions might include "How often do these equipment failures occur?" "How well are your current suppliers performing?" "What disadvantages do you see in the current process?" "How satisfied are you with the quality of components you are currently purchasing?" and "How difficult are these for your operators to use?"

- *Activation questions.* The implied or suggested needs gained from discovery questions are not usually sufficient to gain the sale. Often, a buyer will believe that a particular problem does not cause any significant negative consequences; hence, the motivation to solve the problem will carry a low priority. Successful

salespeople help the customer realistically evaluate the full impact of the implied need through the use of **activation questions**. As detailed in Exhibit 4.4, the objective is to activate the customer's interest in solving discovered problems by helping him or her gain insight into the true ramifications of the problem and to realize that what may initially seem to be of little consequence is, in fact, of significant consequence. Examples include "What effects do these equipment breakdowns have on your business operations?" "To what extent are these increases in overtime expenses affecting

EXHIBIT 4.4
Activation Questions

Activation questions are used to show the impact of a problem, uncovered through discovery questions, on the customer's entire operation. The objective is to activate the customer's interest in solving the problem by helping him or her to gain insight into the true ramifications of the problem and realize that what may seem to be of little consequence is, in fact, of significant consequence.

Examples:

1. **Question—"What effect does your supplier's late delivery have on your operation?"**
   Answer—It slows production . . . . Operating costs go up.

2. **Question—"If production drops off, how are your operating costs affected, and how does that affect your customers?"**
   Answer—Customer orders are delayed . . . . Potential to lose customers.

Activation questions show the negative impact of a problem so that finding a solution to that problem is desirable. Now the salesperson can help the customer to discover the positive impact of solving the problems by using projection questions.

profitability?" "How will the supplier's inability to deliver on time affect your planned expansion?" and "When components fail in the field, how does that failure influence customer satisfaction and repurchase?"

- *Projection questions.* As a natural extension of the activation questions, **projection questions** encourage and facilitate the buyer in "projecting" what it would be like without the problems that have been previously discovered and activated. The use of good projection questions accomplishes several positive outcomes. First, the focus is switched from problems and their associated consequences to the upside—the benefits to be derived from solving the problems. What were initially perceived as costs and expenses are now logically structured as benefits to the buyer and his or her organization—the payoff for taking action and investing in a solution. Second—and equally important—the benefit payoff allows the buyer to establish the realistic value of implementing a solution. In this manner, the benefit payoff is perceived as a positive value received and serves as the foundation for demonstrating what the solution is worth—what the buyer would be willing to pay. As illustrated in Exhibit 4.5, projection questions

encourage the buyer to think about how and why he or she should go about resolving a problem. In essence, projection questions assist the buyer by establishing the worth of the proposed solution. The customer, rather than the salesperson, establishes the benefits of solving the problem. This reinforces the importance of solving the problem and reduces the number of objections that might be raised. Examples of projection

EXHIBIT 4.5
Projection Questions

Projection questions help the customer to project what life would be like without the problems or dissatisfactions uncovered through activation questions. This helps the customer to see value in finding solutions to the problems developed earlier in the sales call.

Examples:

1. **Question—"If a supplier was never late with a delivery, what effects would that have on your JIT operating structure?"**
   Answer—It would run more smoothly and at a lower cost.

2. **Question—"If a supplier helped you meet the expectations of your customers, what impact would that have on your business?"**
   Answer—Increased customer satisfaction would mean more business.

These questions are used to let the customer tell the salesperson the benefits of solving the problem. By doing so, the customer is reinforcing in his or her mind the importance of solving the problem and reducing the number of objections that might be raised.

projection questions
One of the five stages of questions in the ADAPT questioning system used to encourage and help the buyer project what it would be like without the problems that have been previously discovered and activated.

transition questions
One of the five stages of questions in the ADAPT questioning system used to smooth the transition from needs discovery into the presentation and demonstration of the proposed solution's features, advantages, and benefits.

questions include "If a supplier was never late with a delivery, what effects would that have on your overall operation?" "What would be the impact on profitability if you did not have problems with limited plant capacity and the resulting overtime expenses?" "How would a system that your operators found easier to use affect your business operations?" and "If component failures were minimized, what impact would the resulting improvement in customer satisfaction have on financial performance?"

- *Transition questions.* **Transition questions** are used to smooth the transition from needs discovery into the presentation and demonstration of the proposed solution's features, advantages, and benefits. As shown in Exhibit 4.6, transition questions are typically closed end and evaluative in format. These questions confirm the buyer's desire to seek a solution and give consent for the salesperson to move forward with the selling process. Examples include "So, having suppliers that are consistently on time is important to you—if I could show you how our company ensures on-time delivery, would you be interested?" "It seems that increasing capacity is a key to reducing overtime and increasing profitability—would you be interested in a way to increase capacity by 20 percent through a simple addition to your production process?" and "Would you be interested in a system that is easier for your operators to use?"

EXHIBIT 4.6
Transition Questions

Transition questions are simple closed-end questions that confirm the customer's desire to solve the problem(s) uncovered through the previous questions.

Examples:

1. **Question—"So, having a supplier who is never late with deliveries is important to you?"**
   Answer—Yes, it is.

2. **Question—"If I can show you how our company ensures on-time delivery, would you be interested in exploring how it could work for your organization?"**
   Answer—Yes, if I am convinced your company can guarantee on-time delivery.

The primary function of these questions is to make the transition from need confirmation into the sales presentation. In addition, these questions can lead to a customer commitment, provided the salesperson adequately presents how his or her company can solve the customer's problems.

Verbal Communication: Listening

Listening is the other half of effective questioning. After all, asking the customer for information is of little value if the salesperson does not listen. Effective listening is rated among the most critical skills for successful selling. Yet most of us share the common problem of being a lot better at sending messages than receiving them. Considerable research identifies effective listening as the number-one weakness of salespeople.[7]

Poor listening skills have been identified as one of the primary causes of salesperson failure.[8] To get the information needed to best serve, identify, and respond to needs, and nurture a collaborative buyer–seller relationship, salespeople must be able to listen to and understand what was said *and* what was meant. Nevertheless, situations similar to the one depicted in "An Ethical Dilemma" are all too common. As Figure 4.2 illustrates, effective listening can

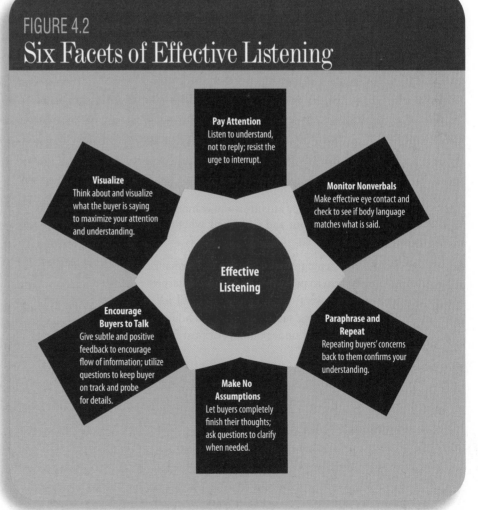

FIGURE 4.2
Six Facets of Effective Listening

Pay Attention
Listen to understand, not to reply; resist the urge to interrupt.

Monitor Nonverbals
Make effective eye contact and check to see if body language matches what is said.

Visualize
Think about and visualize what the buyer is saying to maximize your attention and understanding.

Effective Listening

Encourage Buyers to Talk
Give subtle and positive feedback to encourage flow of information; utilize questions to keep buyer on track and probe for details.

Paraphrase and Repeat
Repeating buyers' concerns back to them confirms your understanding.

Make No Assumptions
Let buyers completely finish their thoughts; ask questions to clarify when needed.

The six facets of effective listening enable salespeople to better pick up, sort out, and interpret buyers' verbal and nonverbal messages

be broken down into six primary facets:

1. *Pay attention*—Listen to understand, not to reply. Resist the urge to interrupt, and receive the full message the buyer is communicating.

2. *Monitor nonverbals*—Make effective eye contact and check to see if the buyer's body language and speech patterns match what is being said.

3. *Paraphrase and repeat*—Confirm your correct understanding of what the buyer is saying by paraphrasing and repeating what you have heard.

4. *Make no assumptions*—Ask questions to clarify the meaning of what the buyer is communicating.

5. *Encourage the buyer to talk*—Encourage the flow of information by giving positive feedback and help the buyer stay on track by asking purposeful, related questions.

6. *Visualize*—Maximize your attention and comprehension by thinking about and visualizing what the buyer is saying.

The practised listening skills of high performance salespeople enable them to pick up, sort out, and interpret a greater number of buyers' verbal and nonverbal messages than lower performing salespeople can. In addition to gaining information and understanding critical to the

An Ethical Dilemma

People describe Brian Reed as an enthusiastic and very outgoing person. He graduated with a double major in applied computer systems and marketing and is very knowledgeable in the areas of computer technology, software applications, and networking systems. Bringing together his personality traits and educational background, Reed works as a salesperson for Business Systems & Solutions, a major technology consultancy and business systems design organization. Even though Reed finished his training at the top of his class, his sales success in the field has been consistently below average, and a number of his existing accounts have been lost to the competition. Hoping to assist Reed in realizing his true potential, his sales manager recently spent several days with him out in the field calling on new prospects as well as existing customers. During these ride-alongs, the sales manager has observed that Reed has a tendency to interrupt when the buyer is discussing problems and desired outcomes. Rather than allowing buyers to describe the nature of a given situation or need fully, Reed interjects his own opinions based on his own knowledge and experience. Although he continues to close sales successfully, Reed's hit ratio is considerably below average and needs to improve if he is to remain in his current position with Business Systems & Solutions.

What is going on in terms of Reed's sales conversations with his customers that might explain his below average performance? If you were Reed's sales manager, what changes would you suggest to him? Why?

relational selling process, a salesperson's good listening behaviours provide the added benefits of positively influencing the formation and continuation of buyer-seller relationships. A salesperson's effective use and demonstration of good listening skills is positively associated with the customer's trust in the salesperson and the anticipation of having future interactions with the salesperson.[9] Clearly, effective listening is a critical component in trust-based, relational selling, and success requires continuous practice and improvement of our listening skills.

Effective listening requires more than just hearing what is being said.

LO5
USING DIFFERENT TYPES OF LISTENING

Communications research identifies two primary categories of listening: *social and serious.*[10] **Social listening** is an informal mode of listening that can be associated with day-to-day conversation and entertainment. Social listening is characterized by low levels of cognitive activity and concentration and is typically used in conversation with a friend or a store clerk or listening to music, a concert, a television program, or even a play. The received messages are taken at face value and do not require a high degree of concentration or thinking to sort through, interpret, and understand. However, **serious listening** is associated with events or topics in which it is important to sort through, interpret, understand, and respond to received messages. The serious form of listening is often referred to as *active listening*, as it requires high levels of concentration and cognition about the messages being received. *Concentration* is required to break through the distractions and other interference to facilitate receiving and remembering specific messages. *Cognition* is used to sort through and select the meaningful relevant messages and interpret them for meaning, information, and response.

ACTIVE LISTENING

Active listening in a selling context is defined as "the cognitive process of actively sensing, interpreting, evaluating, and responding to the verbal and nonverbal messages of present or potential customers."[11] This definition is very useful to those wanting to master active listening skills. First, it underscores the importance of receiving and interpreting both verbal and nonverbal cues and messages to better determine the full and correct meaning of the message. Second, it incorporates a well-accepted model of listening. As illustrated in Figure 4.3,[12] the **SIER** model depicts active listening as a hierarchical, four-step sequence of sensing, interpreting, evaluating, and responding.[13] Effective active listening requires each of these four hierarchical process activities to be carried out successfully and in proper succession.

- *Sensing.* Listening is much more than simply hearing. Nevertheless, the first activities in active listening are sensing (i.e., hearing and seeing) and receiving (i.e., paying attention to) the verbal and nonverbal components of the message being sent. Sensing does not occur without practice and should not be taken for granted. In fact, research indicates that most of us listen at only 25 percent of our capacity. Think about yourself. How often have you had to ask someone to repeat what he or she said or perhaps assumed you knew what the sender was going to say before he or she could say it? Increased concentration and attention can improve sensing effectiveness. Taking notes, making eye contact with the sender, and not interrupting can improve sensing skills. Let the sender finish and provide the full content of the message. This not only improves the concentration of the receiver but also encourages the sender to provide more information and detail.

social listening An informal mode of listening that can be associated with day-to-day conversation and entertainment.

serious listening A form of listening that is associated with events or topics in which it is important to sort through, interpret, understand, and respond to received messages

active listening The cognitive process of actively sensing interpreting, evaluating, and responding to the verbal and nonverbal messages of present or potential customers.

SIER A model that depicts active listening as a hierarchical, four-step sequence of sensing, interpreting, evaluating, and responding.

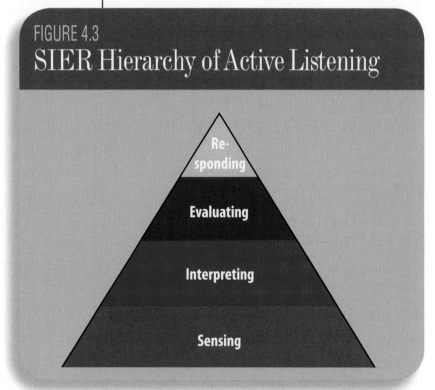

FIGURE 4.3
SIER Hierarchy of Active Listening

Active listening is a cognitive process of actively sensing, interpreting, evaluating, and responding to verbal and nonverbal messages from buyers and prospects.

- *Interpreting.* After the message is received, it must be correctly interpreted. Interpreting addresses the question of "What meaning does the sender intend?" Both content and context are important. That is, in addition to the semantic meaning of the words and symbols, we must consider the experiences, knowledge, and attitudes of the sender to understand fully what was meant. Hold back the temptation to evaluate the message until the sender is through speaking. Note the nonverbal and verbal cues along with possible consistencies and inconsistencies between them. Incorporate knowledge of the sender's background and previous relevant statements and positions into the message interpretation.

- *Evaluating.* Active listening requires the receiver to decide whether he or she agrees with the sender's message. The results from the interpretation stage are evaluated to sort fact from opinion and emotion. Too often, receivers complete this activity before receiving the full message, and on hearing something with which they disagree, the sender is effectively tuned out. As a result, communication is stifled. Evaluating can be improved through concentration and thoughtful consideration of the full message. Summarizing the key points as if they were going to be reported to others can further enhance evaluation skills. Searching for areas of interest rather than pre-judging the message can also facilitate the evaluation process.

- *Responding.* Responding is both an expectation and a requirement for active listening to be effective. Collaborative, two-way communication requires that the listener respond to the sender. Responses provide feedback to the other party, emphasize understanding, encourage further elaboration, and can serve as a beginning point for the receiver to transition into the role of sender for the next message sent. Responses can take many forms. Nonverbal cues, such as nodding and smiling, can indicate that the sender's message was received. Responses in the form of restating and paraphrasing the sender's message can provide strong signals of interest and understanding. Asking questions can elicit additional details and clarification.

The SIER model provides a useful framework for evaluating communication accuracy and pinpointing the sources of problems. Similarly, it can be effectively used for planning activities and behaviours designed to improve communication effectiveness. As the SIER

Salespeople maximize interpersonal communication by using active listening to show interest, evaluate, and respond to what the prospect is saying.

© MICHAELDELEON/ISTOCKPHOTO

model depicts, active listening is a hierarchical and sequential process. A person must sense the message before it can be interpreted. In turn, the message must be interpreted before it can be evaluated. Finally, it must be effectively evaluated before a proper response can be generated. When diagnosing a listening breakdown, look for the lowest level in the hierarchy where the breakdown could have originated and take proper action to remedy the problem. Exhibit 4.7[14] describes ten specific keys to effective listening that can be used in conjunction with the SIER model to pinpoint and improve listening problems.

LO6
Interpreting the Different Forms of Verbal and Nonverbal Communication

VERBAL COMMUNICATION: GIVING INFORMATION

Verbal information refers to statements of fact, opinions, and attitudes that are encoded in the form of words, pictures, and numbers in such a way that they convey meaning to a receiver. However, many words and

EXHIBIT 4.7
Ten Keys to Effective Listening

The Key Practice	The Weak Listener	The Strong Listener
1. Find areas of interest	Tunes out dry subjects	Actively looks for opportunities of common interest
2. Judge content, not delivery	Tunes out if the delivery is poor	Skips over delivery errors and focuses on content
3. Hold your fire until full consideration	Evaluates and enters argument before completion of message	Does not judge or evaluate until message is complete
4. Listen for ideas	Listens for facts	Listens for central themes
5. Be flexible	Takes intensive and detailed notes	Takes fewer notes and limits the theme to the central theme and key ideas presented
6. Work at listening	Shows no energy output; attention is faked	Works hard at attending the message and exhibits active body state
7. Resist distractions	Is distracted easily	Resists distractions and knows how to concentrate
8. Exercise your mind	Resists difficult expository material in favour of light recreational materials	Uses complex and heavy material as exercise for the mind
9. Keep an open mind	Reacts to emotional words	Interprets colour words but does not get hung up on them
10. Capitalize on the fact that thought is faster than speech	Tends to daydream with slow speakers	Challenges, anticipates, mentally summarizes, weighs evidence, and listens between the lines

Sales aids, such as samples, brochures, and charts, reinforce the verbal message and enhance the receivers' understanding and recall.

symbols mean different things to different people. Different industries, different cultures, and different types of training or work experience can result in the same word or phrase having multiple interpretations. For instance, to a design or production engineer, the word *quality* might mean "manufactured within design tolerance." However, to a customer it might be translated as "meeting or exceeding expectations." To maximize clarity and minimize misunderstandings, understand and use the vocabulary and terminology that corresponds with the perspective of the customer.

Understanding the Superiority of Pictures over Words

Studies in cognitive psychology have found that pictures tend to be more memorable than their verbal counterparts.[15] The fact that pictures enhance understanding and are more easily recalled than abstract words and symbols has several implications for effective selling.

- The verbal message should be constructed in a manner that generates a mental picture in the receiver's mind. For example, the phrase "Tropicana juices are bursting with flavour" is more visual than the more abstract version "Tropicana juices have more flavour." This can also be accomplished by providing a short and illustrative analogy or illustrative story to emphasize a key point and bring it alive in the buyer's mind.

- Rather than abstract words that convey only a broad general understanding, use words and phrases that convey concrete and detailed meaning. Concrete expressions provide the receiver with greater information and are less likely to be misunderstood than their abstract counterparts. For example, "This Web transfer system will increase weekly production by 2,100 units" provides more detail than "This Web transfer system will increase production by 10 percent." Similarly, "This conveyor is faster than your existing system" does not deliver the same impact as "This conveyor system will move your product from production to shipping at 15 metres per second as compared with your current system's 6 metres per second."

- Integrate relevant visual sales aids into verbal communication. Sales support materials that explain and reinforce the verbal message will aid the receiver's understanding and enhance recall of the message. As an additional benefit, such sales aids as samples, brochures, graphs, and comparative charts can be left with the buyer to continue selling until the salesperson's next call on the buyer.

Impact of Grammar and Logical Sequencing

Grammar and logical sequencing are also important in the process of giving information to others. The use of proper grammar is essential in business and social communication. In its absence, the receiver of the message tends to exhibit three closely related behaviours. First, the meaning and credibility of the message are significantly downgraded. Second, the receiver begins to focus on the sender rather than the message, which materially reduces the probability of effective communication. Last, the receiver dismisses the sender and the sender's organization as being unqualified to perform the role of an effective supplier and partner. The importance of proper grammar should not be overlooked.

Similarly, whether one is engaged in simply explaining details or making a formal proposal, logical sequencing of the material is critical. The facts and details must be organized and connected in a logical order. This is essential to clarity and assists the receiver in following the facts. A discussion or presentation that jumps around runs the risk of being inefficient and ineffective. At best, the receiver will have to ask many clarification questions. At worst, the receiver will dismiss the salesperson as incompetent and close off the sales negotiation. Advance planning and preparation can improve organization. Outline what needs to be covered and organize it into a logical flow. The outline becomes the agenda to be covered and can serve as an aid for staying on track.

NONVERBAL COMMUNICATION

Nonverbal behaviours have been recognized as an important dimension of communication since medieval times. As early as 1605, Francis Bacon focused on the messages conveyed by *manual language*. Verbal communication deals with the semantic meaning of the message itself, whereas the nonverbal dimension consists of the more abstract message conveyed by how the message is delivered. **Nonverbal communication** consists of the conscious and unconscious reactions, movements, and utterances that people use in addition to the words and symbols associated with language. This dimension of communication includes eye movements and facial expressions; placement and movements of hands, arms, head, and legs as well as body orientation; the amount of space maintained between individuals; and variations in vocal characteristics. Collectively, the various forms of nonverbal communication carry subtle and explicit meanings and feelings along with the linguistic message and are frequently more informative than the verbal content of a message.[16]

Research indicates that highly successful salespeople are capable of picking out and comprehending a higher number of behavioural cues from buyers than less successful salespeople are able to sense and

nonverbal communication The conscious and unconscious reactions, movements, and utterances that people use in addition to the words and symbols associated with language.

Eye Movements

In North America and Western Europe, avoiding eye contact results in a negative message and is often associated with deceit and dishonesty. However, a sender's increased eye contact infers honesty and self-confidence. Increased eye contact by the receiver of the message signals increasing levels of interest and concentration. However, when eye contact becomes a stare and continues unbroken, either by glances away or blinking, it is typically interpreted as a threat or inference of power. A blank stare or eye contact directed away from the conversation can show disinterest and boredom. Repeated glancing at a watch or possibly an exit door often indicate that the conversation is about to end.

Placement and Movements of Hands, Arms, Head, and Legs

Smooth and gradual movements denote calm and confidence, whereas jerky and hurried movements are associated with nervousness and stress. Uncrossed arms and legs signal openness, confidence, and cooperation. However, crossed arms and legs psychologically close out the other party and express disagreement and defensiveness. Increased movement of the head and limbs hints at increasing tension, as does the tight clasping of hands or fists. The placement of a hand on the chin or a tilted head suggests increased levels of evaluation, whereas nodding of the head expresses agreement. Growing impatience is associated with drumming of the fingers or tapping of a foot. Fingering the hair and rubbing the back of the neck signify increasing nervousness and apprehension.

Body Posture and Orientation

Fidgeting and shifting from side to side is generally considered to be a negative message associated with nervousness and apprehension. Leaning forward or sitting forward on the edge of a chair is a general sign of increasing interest and a positive disposition in regard to what is being discussed. Similarly, leaning away can indicate disinterest, boredom, or even distrust. Leaning back with both hands placed behind the head signifies a perceived sense of smugness and superiority. A rigid erect posture can convey inflexibility or even defensiveness, whereas sloppy posture suggests disinterest in the topic. Similar to sitting backward in a chair, sitting on the edge of the table or the arm of a chair is an expression of power and superiority.

Fifty percent or more of the meaning conveyed in interpersonal communication comes through nonverbal behaviours. What nonverbal messages are being conveyed here?

interpret. In addition, evidence shows that 50 percent or more of the meaning conveyed within the communication process stems from nonverbal behaviour.[17] As the nonverbal components of a message carry as much or more meaning than the language portions, it is critical for salespeople to sense effectively, interpret accurately, and evaluate fully the nonverbal elements of a message as well as the verbal components. In addition to sensing verbal messages, learn to sense between the words for the thoughts and feelings not being conveyed verbally.

Facial Expressions

Possibly reflecting its central point of focus in interpersonal communication, the various elements of the face play a key role in giving off nonverbal messages. Frowning, pursed lips, and squinted eyes are common in moments of uncertainty, disagreement, and even outright skepticism. Suspicion and anger are typically accompanied by tightness along the jaw line. Smiles are indicative of agreement and interest, whereas biting of the lip can signal uncertainty. Raised eyebrows can signify surprise and are often found in moments of consideration and evaluation.

Proxemics

proxemics The personal distance that individuals prefer to keep between themselves and other individuals; an important element of nonverbal communication.

Proxemics refers to the personal distance that individuals prefer to keep between themselves and other individuals and is an important element of nonverbal communication. The distance that a person places between himself or herself and others implies a meaningful message and affects the outcome of the selling process. If a salesperson pushes too close to a prospect who requires more distance, the prospect may perceive the salesperson to be manipulative, intimidating, and possibly threatening. However, salespeople who put too much distance between themselves and the customer risk being perceived as rigidly formal, aloof, or even apprehensive.

Proxemics differs across cultures and regions of the world. For example, in North Africa and Latin America business is conducted at a much closer distance than in North America. As depicted in Figure 4.4, North Americans generally

> As trust develops, salespeople are able to use interpersonal space to communicate and positively affect the sales outcome.

recognize four distinct proxemic zones. The *intimate zone* is reserved for intimate relationships with immediate family and loved ones. The *personal zone* is for personal relationships with close friends and associates. The *social zone* is for business client relationships and is the zone in which most business is conducted. The *public zone* is for the general public and group settings such as classrooms and presentations.

It is critical that salespeople understand proxemics and monitor the progression of their buyer–seller relationships so as to position themselves with different customers properly. Typically, salespeople begin working with a prospect at the far end of the *social zone*. As the salesperson-buyer relationship develops, the salesperson is in a position to move closer without violating the customer's space and causing him or her to become defensive.

Variations in Vocal Characteristics

Nonverbal vocal characteristics, such as speaking rates, pause duration, pitch or frequency, and intensity, have been linked to communication effectiveness and selling performance. These voice characteristics convey direct as well as subtle and implied meanings and feelings that can complement or accent the corresponding verbal message.[18]

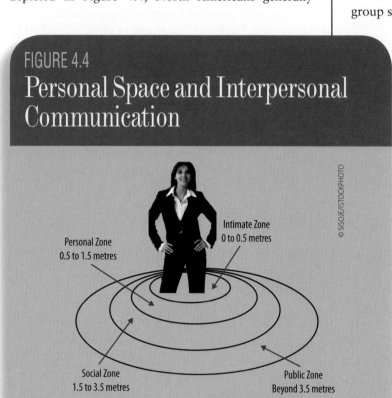

FIGURE 4.4
Personal Space and Interpersonal Communication

Intimate Zone
0 to 0.5 metres

Personal Zone
0.5 to 1.5 metres

Social Zone
1.5 to 3.5 metres

Public Zone
Beyond 3.5 metres

© SISOJE/ISTOCKPHOTO

Individuals use four preferred spatial zones for interaction in different social and business situations.

Speaking Rates and Pause Duration Within normal speaking rates, faster speakers are generally evaluated more favourably than slower speakers. Contrary to the often-cited fast-talking salesperson being perceived as high pressure, faster rates of speech and shorter pause duration are actually associated with higher levels of intelligence, credibility, and knowledge.19 Slower speakers are perceived as being less competent as well as less benevolent. However, speech rates that are jerky and beyond normal rates of speech can present problems in sensing and interpreting the complete message. Varying the rate of speech has also been found to be conducive to maintaining interest.

Pitch or Frequency Vocal pitch carries a great deal of information to the receiver. Varying pitch and frequency during the course of a message encourages attentiveness of the listener and accents certain forms of statements. A rising pitch during the message is associated with questions and can often be perceived as reflecting uncertainty. Just the opposite, a falling pitch is associated with declarative statements and completion of the message. Overall, high-pitched voices are judged as less truthful, less emphatic, less potent, and more nervous. Lower-pitched voices are considered more persuasive and truthful and have a positive impact on selling performance.

Intensity and Loudness Dominance, superiority, intensity, and aggression are commonly associated with loud voices, whereas soft voices characterize submission and uncertainty. However, it is the variability of intensity that has been found to be most effective in communication. Varying levels of loudness allow the sender to adapt to different situations and environments. Variation also increases the receiver's attention and can provide additional information inputs by accenting key points of a message.

Using Nonverbal Clusters

Nonverbal clusters are groups of related expressions, gestures, and movements. Similar to a one-word expression, a single isolated gesture or movement should not be taken as a reliable indication of the true intent or meaning of a message. Sensing and interpreting groups or clusters of nonverbal cues provides a more reliable indicator of the message and intent. When the individual behaviours and gestures begin to fit together, they form a common and unified message that the salesperson should consider. Common nonverbal clusters applicable to selling communication are described in Exhibit 4.8.[20]

Just as salespeople can interpret nonverbal messages to better understand communication with prospects and buyers, those same prospects and buyers can also sense and interpret the nonverbal messages the salesperson is sending. Consequently, it is important that salespeople monitor the nonverbal cues they are sending to ensure consistency with and reinforcement of the intended message.

EXHIBIT 4.8
Common Nonverbal Clusters

Cluster Name	Cluster Meaning	Body Posture and Orientation	Movement of Hands, Arms, and Legs	Eyes and Facial Expressions
Openness	Openness, flexibility, and sincerity	• Moving closer • Leaning forward	• Open hands • Removing coat • Unbuttoning collar • Uncrossing arms and legs	• Slight smile • Good eye contact
Defensiveness	Defensiveness, skepticism, and apprehension	• Rigid body	• Crossed arms and legs • Clenched fists	• Minimal eye contact • Sideways glances • Pursed lips
Evaluation	Evaluation and consideration of message	• Leaning forward	• Hand on cheek • Stroking of chin • Chin in palm of hand	• Tilted head • Glasses dropping to tip of nose
Deception	Dishonesty and secretiveness	• Patterns of rocking	• Fidgeting with objects • Increasing leg movements	• Increased eye movement • Frequent gazes elsewhere • Forced smile
Readiness	Dedication or commitment	• Sitting forward	• Hands on hips • Legs uncrossed • Feet flat on floor	• Increased eye contact
Boredom	Lack of interest and impatience	• Leaning head in palm of hands • Slouching	• Drumming fingers • Swinging a foot • Brushing and picking at items • Tapping feet	• Poor eye contact • Glances at watch • Blank stares

CANADIAN SEATING COMPANY AND THE ALBERTA MUSIC ARTS ASSOCIATION

Background

This case involves a salesperson representing the direct sales department of Canadian Seating Company (CSC) and Rodney Moore, the head architect representing the Alberta Music Arts Association (AMAA). Although there are some 12 major manufacturers of auditorium seating in Canada, CSC's market share of 21 percent makes the company the industry leader. CSC's selling efforts are organized on a basis of market types: one department sells direct to end-users and a second department sells to distributors who in turn sell to retailers of business furniture. Direct sales to end users are restricted to minimum orders of $200,000.

Current Situation

As an integral part of a major remodelling project, AMAA wants to replace the seats in the Northern Alberta Jubilee Auditorium. Based on engineering reports and information about AMAA's auditorium, CSC estimates the seat replacement represents a potential sale of between $350,000 and $500,000. This range represents differences in both quantity and types of seating desired. According to the available information, funding for this project is being provided through bonds that have already been issued. The funds for construction and remodelling are already available and the plans are in the initial stage of development—an ideal time for CSC to get involved in the buying decision process for seating. Engineering Designs, a Winnipeg-based architectural firm, is in charge of this remodelling project and has primary responsibility for specifying materials and components that will go into the job.

In preparation for an initial meeting with Rodney Moore at Engineering Designs, the CSC sales representative is outlining information needs and developing a draft set of needs discovery questions. These needs discovery questions will be the focus of the meeting with Engineering Designs and enable CSC to better identify and confirm the actual needs, desires, and expectations regarding seating.

Questions

1. What information does the CSC salesperson need to fully understand the seating needs of the AMAA project?

2. Following the ADAPT methodology for needs discovery questioning, develop a series of salesperson questions and anticipated buyer responses that might apply to this selling situation.

Role Play

Situation: Read the case and review the ADAPT questions you developed in response to the questions associated with this case.

Characters: You, salesperson for Canadian Seating Company (CSC); Rodney Moore, head architect for Engineering Designs and representative for the Northern Alberta Jubilee Auditorium Association

Scene: *Location*—Rodney Moore's office at Engineering Designs
Action—As a salesperson for CSC, you are making an initial sales call to Moore for the purpose of identifying and detailing the specific needs and expectations AMAA has for seating in the new auditorium. Role play this needs discovery sales call and demonstrate how you might use SPIN or ADAPT questioning sequences to identify the needs for seating.

MidMobile Inc.

Background

MidMobile Inc. specializes in providing cell phones and wireless services for small businesses with 10 to 500 employees having needs that call for mobile, wireless communication. As an account development specialist for MidMobile, you are making an initial sales call to Jim Smith, director of the Facilities Maintenance Division at Memorial University. The purpose of this initial call is to assess the division's current use and needs for wireless mobile communication services. According to the initial information you gained from a short phone conversation with Smith, they are currently using Aliant cellular service for a number of their maintenance supervisors. Having staff members wirelessly linked and able to communicate from anywhere on campus has proven beneficial in terms of increasing efficiency and productivity. You have further learned that the university is considering rolling cell phones out to all building maintenance workers. They have been pleased with the positive aspects of wireless communication but, during your phone conversation, Smith made a couple of comments indicating that there might be some problems with the present vendor and expressed concerns about potential employee misuse of the phone services.

Role Play

Location—Jim Smith's office at the university
Action—Role play this needs discovery sales call and demonstrate how you might use SPIN or ADAPT questioning sequences to identify the needs and concerns of the prospect.

MORE BANG FOR YOUR BUCK

SELL has it all, and you can, too. Between the text and our online offerings, you have everything at your fingertips. Make sure you check out all that **SELL** has to offer:

- Printable and interactive flashcards
- Interactive quizzing
- Crossword puzzles
- Role-play videos

"I really like how you use student's opinions on how to study and made a website that encompasses everything we find useful. Seeing this website makes me excited to study!"

—Abby Boston, Fanshawe College

Visit **www.sell.nelson.com** to find the resources you need today!

Spending time with

the best prospects and customers is one
of the keys to salesperson success.

5

Strategic Prospecting and Preparing for Sales Dialogue

Introduction

mike Lipkin is an author, a sales coach, and a motivational speaker who has helped more than 500 different companies. He describes his role as bringing out "the best in their people so their people can bring out their best for their customers." Lipkin observes that although people often forget what is said to them, they rarely forget how someone makes them feel. This can be the deciding factor when two vendors are competing for business.

Lipkin stresses the importance of listening and explains that "the way you listen to others becomes [people's] impression of themselves." He also believes in being as authentic as possible to earn trust among colleagues and customers. By not "placing artificial constraints on yourself," you can instead focus on the potential customer you are interacting with.

Colleen Francis, the founder and president of Engage Selling Solutions, also offers some important advice for salespeople. She states that the traditional model of prospecting and making cold calls is becoming increasingly outdated. Salespeople must think about ways of getting customers to come to them by being recognizable experts in their field. When a potential client is searching for a solution to a problem, a salesperson needs to be immediately visible. Creating this expertise can include publishing case studies, white papers, vendor comparisons, and return-on-investment tools. Francis explains that "we have to give away our value for free to attract buyers to ourselves."

Among her rules for successful selling are putting yourself in front of clients every 30 days to stay top of mind, as well as banishing all "corporate speak" in marketing material and replacing it with client testimonials. According to Francis, "Very few people trust what you say about yourself"; having customers speak highly of you is invaluable.

Sources: "Attracting Clients by Hanging Off Their Every Syllable," *Ottawa Business Journal*, May 2, 2011, http://objmags.newspaperdirect.com/epaper/viewer.aspx, accessed May 17, 2011; Mike Lipkin, "Home page," http://www.mikelipkin.com, accessed May 17, 2011.

After completing this chapter, you should be able to

LO1 Discuss why prospecting is an important and challenging task for salespeople.

LO2 Explain strategic prospecting and each stage in the strategic prospecting process.

LO3 Describe the major prospecting methods and give examples of each method.

LO4 Explain the important components of a strategic prospecting plan.

LO5 Discuss the types of information salespeople need to prepare for sales dialogue.

most salespeople have to cultivate new business if they are to sustain the sales growth objectives their company establishes. However, salespeople typically achieve sales growth objectives by finding the right balance between getting new customers and generating additional business from existing customers. A variety of prospecting approaches are available, with each having advantages and disadvantages. New technological advances are increasing the number of tools salespeople can use to determine the best sales opportunities. The purpose of this chapter is to examine the importance and challenges of prospecting, introduce the strategic prospecting process, present different prospecting methods, and discuss preparation for sales dialogue.

LO1
The Importance and Challenges of Prospecting

prospecting is extremely important to most salespeople. Salespeople who do not regularly prospect are operating under the assumption that the current business with existing customers will be sufficient to generate the desired level of future revenue. This is a shaky assumption in good times, but it is especially questionable in the tough economic environment of recent years. As market conditions change, existing customers may buy less. Or customers may go out of business. Some customers might be acquired by another firm, with the buying decisions now being made outside the salesperson's territory.

The salesperson could also simply lose customers because of competitive activity or dissatisfaction with the product, the salesperson, or the selling firm. Because there is typically a considerable time lag between the commencement of prospecting and the conversion of prospects to customer status, salespeople should spend time prospecting on a regular basis. Otherwise, lost sales volume cannot be regained quickly enough to satisfy the large majority of sales organizations—those that are growth oriented.

Despite its importance, salespeople often find it difficult to allocate enough time to prospecting. Many salespeople do not like to prospect because of their fear of rejection. Today's buyers are busy, and many are reluctant to see salespeople. Buyers may not want to take the time to see a salesperson for several reasons:

1. They may have never heard of the salesperson's firm.
2. They may have just bought the salesperson's product category and presently have no need.
3. Buyers may have their own deadlines on other issues, and not be in a receptive mood to see any salespeople.
4. Buyers are constantly getting calls from salespeople and do not have time to see them all.
5. Gatekeepers in any organization screen their bosses' calls and sometimes are curt and even rude.

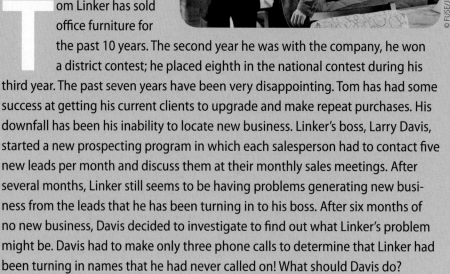

An Ethical Dilemma

Tom Linker has sold office furniture for the past 10 years. The second year he was with the company, he won a district contest; he placed eighth in the national contest during his third year. The past seven years have been very disappointing. Tom has had some success at getting his current clients to upgrade and make repeat purchases. His downfall has been his inability to locate new business. Linker's boss, Larry Davis, started a new prospecting program in which each salesperson had to contact five new leads per month and discuss them at their monthly sales meetings. After several months, Linker still seems to be having problems generating new business from the leads that he has been turning in to his boss. After six months of no new business, Davis decided to investigate to find out what Linker's problem might be. Davis had to make only three phone calls to determine that Linker had been turning in names that he had never called on! What should Davis do?

© FUSE/JUPITER IMAGES

Salespeople can overcome the challenges of prospecting and become more effective in determining the best sales opportunities by following a strategic sales prospecting process, using a variety of prospecting methods, developing a strategic prospecting plan, and preparing for sales dialogue with prospects. Sometimes the stress of prospecting can produce difficult situations as presented in "An Ethical Dilemma."

LO2
The Strategic Prospecting Process

the first step in the trust-based sales process presented in Chapter 1 is strategic prospecting. **Strategic prospecting** is a process designed to identify, qualify, and prioritize sales opportunities, whether they represent potential new customers or opportunities to generate additional business from existing customers. The basic purpose of strategic prospecting is to help salespeople determine the best sales opportunities in the most efficient way. Effective strategic prospecting helps salespeople spend their valuable selling time in the most productive manner.

The strategic prospecting process (illustrated in Figure 5.1) is often viewed as a **sales funnel** or **sales pipeline** because it presents the entire trust-based sales process and the strategic prospecting process in the form of a funnel. The funnel is very wide at the top, as salespeople typically have a large number of potential sales opportunities. As salespeople move through the strategic prospecting process and the other stages in the trust-based sales process, the funnel narrows because only the best sales opportunities are pursued and not all sale opportunities result in a sale or new

customer relationship. For the most productive salespeople, the sales funnel is normally much wider at the bottom than it is for less productive salespeople. The most productive salespeople pursue the best sales opportunities and translate a larger percentage of these opportunities into actual sales than less productive salespeople do. We will now discuss each step in the strategic prospecting process.

strategic prospecting A process designed to identify, qualify, and prioritize sales opportunities, whether they represent potential new customers or opportunities to generate additional business from existing customers.

sales funnel or **pipeline** A representation of the trust-based sales process and strategic sales prospecting process in the form of a funnel.

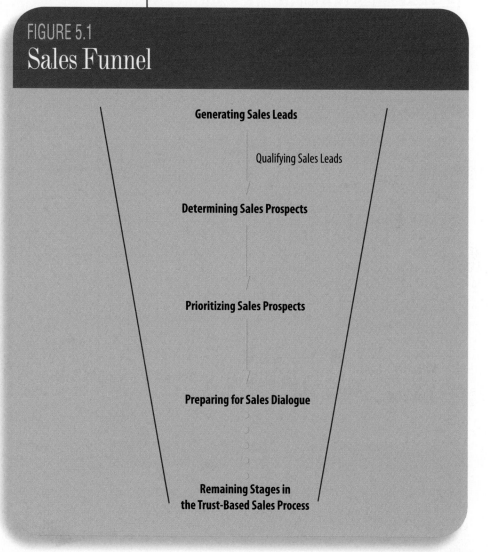

FIGURE 5.1
Sales Funnel

Generating Sales Leads

Qualifying Sales Leads

Determining Sales Prospects

Prioritizing Sales Prospects

Preparing for Sales Dialogue

Remaining Stages in the Trust-Based Sales Process

The sales funnel presents the trust-based sales process and highlights the major steps of the strategic prospecting process.

GENERATING SALES LEADS

The first step in the strategic prospecting process is to identify sales leads. **Sales leads** or **suspects** are organizations or individuals who might possibly purchase the product or service a salesperson offers. This represents the realm of sales opportunities for a salesperson. For example, if a salesperson sells copiers in business markets, any organization that might need a copier would be a sales lead. Although more sales leads are usually better than fewer leads, the identified organizations represent different types of sales opportunities. For example, large organizations might represent better sales

> The most productive salespeople pursue the best sales opportunities and translate a larger percentage of these opportunities into sales than less productive salespeople do.

opportunities because they probably need more copiers than smaller organizations. Other organizations may have just purchased copiers or are very satisfied with their current copiers, which would mean they do not represent good sales opportunities. If salespeople merely generate leads and pursue most of them, they are likely to be spending a great deal of their time with organizations that are unlikely to purchase from them.

DETERMINING SALES PROSPECTS

The most productive salespeople evaluate sales leads to determine which ones are true prospects for their product or service. This evaluation process is usually called **qualifying sales leads**. Salespeople search for,

collect, analyze, and use various types of screening procedures to determine if the sales lead is really a good sales prospect. Although specific companies define sales prospects in different ways, a **sales prospect** is typically an individual or organization that

- has a need for the product or service
- has the budget or financial resources to purchase the product or service
- has the authority to make the purchase decision

Those that meet these criteria move down the sales funnel (see Figure 5.1) into the sales prospect category, while those that do not are set aside. Salespeople who spend the time and effort qualifying their leads limit the time wasted on making calls with a low probability of success and focus their efforts on the more fruitful opportunities.

PRIORITIZING SALES PROSPECTS

Even though the qualifying process has culled out the least promising sales leads, the remaining prospects do not all represent the same sales opportunity. The most productive salespeople prioritize their sales prospects to ensure that they spend most of their time on the best opportunities. One approach is to create an **ideal customer profile** and then analyze sales prospects by comparing them with this ideal customer profile. Those that most closely fit the profile are deemed to be the best sales prospects. Another approach is to identify one or more criteria, evaluate sales prospects against these criteria, and either rank all of the sales prospects based on this evaluation or place the sales prospects into A, B, and C categories, with A sales prospects representing the best sales opportunities.

PREPARING FOR SALES DIALOGUE

The final step in the strategic prospecting process is to prepare for the initial contact with a sales prospect by planning the sales dialogue. The information accumulated to this point in the process is helpful, but additional information is usually required to increase the chances of success in the initial sales dialogue. The types of additional information required are discussed later in this chapter.

---

sales leads or **suspects** Organizations or individuals who might possibly purchase the product or service a salesperson offers.

qualifying sales leads The salesperson's act of searching out, collecting, and analyzing information to determine the likelihood of the lead being a good candidate for making a sale.

sales prospect An individual or organization that has a need for the product or service, has the budget or financial resources to purchase the product or service, and has the authority to make the purchase decision.

ideal customer profile The characteristics of a firm's best customers or the perfect customer.

LO3
Prospecting Methods

many different sources and methods for effective strategic prospecting have been developed for use in different selling situations. A good selling organization and successful salespeople will have a number of ongoing prospecting methods in place at any given time. The salesperson must continually evaluate prospecting methods to determine which methods are bringing in the best results. New methods must also be evaluated and tested for their effectiveness. Many popular prospecting methods are presented in Exhibit 5.1.

COURTESY OF LINKEDIN CORPORATION

COLD CANVASSING

Cold canvassing occurs when salespeople contact a sales lead unannounced with little if any information about the lead. **Cold calling** is the most extreme form of cold canvassing because salespeople merely knock on doors or make telephone calls to organizations or individuals. This is a very inefficient prospecting method. Typically, a very small percentage of cold calls produce, or lead to future sales dialogue with, qualified prospects. Because there is so much rejection, many salespeople do not like to cold call sales leads.

Using referrals or introductions can improve the success of cold calling. A **referral** is a sales lead a customer or some other influential person provides. Salespeople are often trained to ask customers and others for the names and contact information of potential prospects. Sometimes salespeople can also obtain sufficient information to qualify the lead as a good sales prospect. Additionally, salespeople can get permission to use the person's name when contacting

> Salespeople can network for prospects electronically.

cold calling Contacting a sales lead unannounced and with little or no information about the lead.

referral A name of a company or person given to the salesperson as a lead by a customer or even a prospect who did not buy at this time.

EXHIBIT 5.1
Prospecting Methods

Cold Canvassing	Networking	Company Sources	Published Sources
• Cold calling	• Centres of influence	• Company records	• Directories
• Referrals	• Noncompeting salespeople	• Advertising inquiries	• Commercial lead lists
• Introductions	• Electronic networking	• Telephone inquiries	
		• Trade shows	
		• Seminars	

PROFESSIONAL SELLING IN THE 21ST CENTURY

Getting Appointments over the Phone

John O'Neill, an agent for Guiney's Financial Services in Saint John, New Brunswick understands the importance of prospecting to gain new business. Here are a few of his thoughts on how he uses the telephone in his prospecting process:

I need to make two appointments per day to be successful and meet my personal selling targets. Many times it takes 25 to 40 phone calls to make those two good appointments. I understand that the phone is my lifeline. If I don't get a commitment in a matter of seconds, I have lost the prospect. This means that my primary points have to be direct, compelling, and brief—very brief. I have to be well organized. I don't use a script, but I do have my key points outlined on paper and in front of me when I make my prospecting calls.

My philosophy is to keep my opening short and sweet. I briefly introduce myself. I mention referrals right away when I can, and I resist the temptation to make a full-blown sales presentation over the phone. I try to sell the appointment. It may sound obvious, but always be polite. One last thought, if someone already has a good relationship with an agent, I thank him or her for their time and let them know that I'm available if anything changes.

the prospect. In some cases, the person might agree to provide an **introduction** by writing a letter or making a phone call to introduce the salesperson to the prospect. An example of cold calling with referrals is presented in "Professional Selling in the 21st Century: Getting Appointments over the Phone."

NETWORKING

Salespeople can use various types of networking as effective methods for prospecting. Many salespeople join civic and professional organizations, country clubs, or fraternal organizations, and these memberships provide the opportunity for them to build relationships with other members. Sometimes these relationships yield prospects. Some members might be influential people in the community or other organizations, making them **centres of influence** for the salesperson and potentially providing help in locating prospects. Accountants, bankers, attorneys, teachers, business owners, politicians, and government workers are often good centres of influence.

Networking with salespeople from noncompeting firms can also be a good source of prospects. Business Networking International (BNI), which has several active chapters throughout Canada, is a formal organization with each local group consisting of **noncompeting salespeople**. The basic purpose of this organization is for the members to generate prospects for one another. There are other sales and marketing organizations that salespeople can join to create the opportunity to identify prospects by networking with members.

It is important for salespeople to strike up conversations with other sales representatives while waiting to see buyers. Noncompeting salespeople can be found everywhere and can help in getting valuable information about prospects. An example of how noncompeting salespeople can help each other was demonstrated when a Hershey Chocolate salesperson went out of his way to tell a noncompeting sales representative from Hormel Foods about a new grocery store going into his territory. Hormel Foods is a manufacturer of food and meat products for consumers throughout the world. The Hormel representative was the first of his competitors to meet with the new grocery store management team and was given valuable shelf space that his competitors could not get. A few months later, the Hormel sales representative returned the favour when he found out that an independent convenience store was changing hands. The Hershey salesperson was able to get into the new owner's store early and added valuable shelf space for his products. The operating principle of "you scratch my back and I scratch yours" works when information flows in both directions.

Electronic Networking

New developments in technology have produced a variety of websites that allow salespeople to engage in **electronic networking**. Some of the sites are free, but others charge fees for some or all services provided. The specifics of each site differ, but all make it possible for salespeople to network online for prospects and obtain various types of information about the prospects. The most popular sites include: Linkedin (http://www.linkedin.com), Jigsaw (http://www.jigsaw.com), Spoke Software (http://www.spoke.com), and Plaxo (http://www.plaxo.com). The use of electronic networking is likely to increase in the future as technology continues to advance.

Personal Selling and Social Media Various forms of social media, such as Facebook, MySpace, Twitter, and blogs have become mainstream forms of communication for individuals and businesses alike. Since social media is top of mind for most businesses, and with sales organizations' emphasis on external communications, the pressure to stay current is high. However, sales experts agree that sale reps and managers must apply some type of filter so that social media remains a sales tool and not a distraction to the sales rep.[1]

"Social networking is a strategy for marketing promotions and relationship management. It is not a prospecting

tool. A lot of the maintenance functions involved with social media tools are going to slide down to the lowest paid person who is competent to do them."[2] In other words, sales reps should not be focusing on daily tweets and Facebook updates. Some experts believe that these new communication tools are doing a disservice to salespeople; they are tools of communication and not meant to replace the sales process.

© STOCKBYTE/JUPITER IMAGES

Participating in trade shows is an effective prospecting method.

COMPANY SOURCES

Many companies have resources or are engaged in activities that can help their own salespeople with strategic prospecting. **Company records** can be a useful source of prospects, as illustrated in this chapter's opening vignette. Salespeople can also review company records to identify previous customers who have not placed an order recently. Contacting previous customers to determine why they have stopped ordering could provide opportunities to win back business. Examining the purchasing behaviour of existing customers can also help in identifying opportunities to sell additional products to specific customers.

Advertising inquiries are potentially a good source of prospects. For example, one manufacturer's rep in the natural gas industry speaks highly of his company's advertising plan. The company advertises only in trade magazines that it believes buyers read. The salesperson's territory includes Alberta, Manitoba, and Saskatchewan. The advertising message is simply "If we can help you with any of your natural gas needs (e.g., flow meters, odorizers), please give us a call." These leads are then turned over to the salesperson who calls on that territory. One salesperson cannot cover territories of this size. The advertising program qualifies the prospect (with the help of the telephone) before the salesperson is sent out on the call.

inbound telemarketing A way to locate prospects in which the prospect calls the company to get information.

outbound telemarketing A way to locate prospects in which the salesperson contacts the prospect by telephone.

trade shows Events at which companies purchase space and set up booths that clearly identify each company and its offerings and that are staffed with salespeople who demonstrate the products and answer questions.

seminars A presentation salespeople give to generate leads and provide information to prospective customers who are invited to the seminar by direct mail, word of mouth, or advertising on local television or radio.

directories Electronic or print sources that provide contact and other information about many different companies or individuals.

Many organizations today use both inbound (prospect calls the company) and outbound (salesperson contacts the prospect) telemarketing. **Inbound telemarketing** involves a telephone number (usually a toll-free number) that prospects or customers can call for information. Companies distribute toll-free numbers by direct mail pieces (brochures), advertising campaigns, and their **outbound telemarketing** program. Some companies use both inbound and outbound telemarketing to serve their market. They use outbound telemarketing to generate and then qualify leads for their salesforce. Qualified leads are turned over to experienced salespeople. Usually, interns do all the outbound telemarketing. Inbound telemarketing is used to resolve problems, answer questions from prospects, and take orders from existing customers.

Attending conventions and **trade shows** presents salespeople with excellent opportunities to collect leads. Generally, the company purchases booth space and sets up a stand that clearly identifies the company and its offerings. Salespeople are available at the booth to demonstrate their products or answer questions. Potential customers walk by and are asked to fill out information cards indicating an interest in the company or one of its products. The completed information card provides leads for the salesperson. Trade shows can stimulate interest in products and provide leads. For example, bank loan officers attend home improvement trade shows and can offer the homeowner immediate

credit to begin a project. Those who sign immediately may be offered a lower interest rate.

Firms can use **seminars** to generate leads and provide information to prospective customers. For example, a financial planner will set up a seminar at a local hotel to give a presentation on retirement planning, inviting prospects by direct mail, word of mouth, or advertising on local television and radio. The financial consultant discusses a technique or investment opportunities that will prepare the audience for retirement. Those present will be asked to fill out a card expressing their interest for follow-up discussions. The financial consultant hopes this free seminar will reward him or her with a few qualified prospects.

PUBLISHED SOURCES

Published lists and **directories** offer an inexpensive, convenient means of identifying leads. Telephone books today contain a business section that lists all the community's businesses. This list is usually broken down further by business type. Manufacturers, medical facilities, pharmacies, and grocery stores, to name a few, can be easily identified by using the business pages of the phone book. Many other directories exist, such as Board of Trade directories, chamber of commerce directories, trade association lists, *Moody's Industrial Directory*, and *Standard & Poor's Register of Corporations, Directors, and Executives*. Directories are a wealth of information if used correctly. A salesperson must remember that when these lists are published they become obsolete. Companies change their names, merge with others, and even change addresses. Salespeople must verify information from published sources before using it. Exhibit 5.2 lists some of the directories that salespeople have at their disposal.

> Directories provide salespeople with useful information for prospecting.

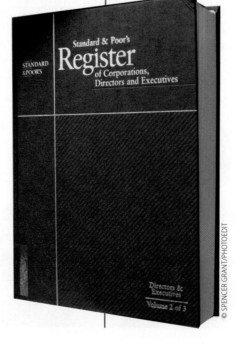

© SPENCER GRANT/PHOTOEDIT

A large variety of list providers offer **commercial lead lists** designed to focus on virtually any type of business or individual. Available on paper or in convenient computer formats, commercial lead lists range from simple listings of names, addresses, and phone numbers to more detailed listings with a full profile of the different entities included in the list. Leading providers include infoCANADA (http://www.infocanada.ca), Scott's Directories (http://www.scottsdirectories.com), *Canada Business Directory* (http://canadabusinessdirectory.ca.), and Industry Canada (http://www.ic.gc.ca).

commercial lead lists
Lists that focus on virtually any type of business or individual; they range from simple listings of names, addresses, and phone numbers to more detailed listings with a full profile of the different entries included in the list.

EXHIBIT 5.2
List of Secondary Lead Sources

1. *Canadian Business Resource*, published by Canadian Newspaper Services International, maintains a database of 2500 of Canada's largest firms and all firms listed on the TSX and TSX Venture exchanges. It also maintains more than 40,000 contact names that are downloadable to subscribers' contact management software from http://www.cbr.ca.

2. *Moody's Industrial Directory* is an annual publication with a wide range of statistical information about particular firms that might be prospects for a specific product or service. Names of executives, description of the company business, and a brief financial statement for more than 10,000 publicly held firms are available at http://www.moodys.com.

3. *Standard & Poor's Register of Corporations, Directors, and Executives* is an excellent source of personal information about individuals in companies. Such information can be used for qualifying prospects and for learning enough about them to plan an effective approach and presentation. This annual publication lists names, titles, and addresses for 50,000 firms. See http://www.standardandpoors.com.

4. *Canadian Trade Index*, published by Canadian Manufacturers and Exporters, is available in print, on CD-ROM, and online at http://www.ctidirectory.com. It lists more than 30,000 manufacturers, distributors, and industrial service companies and features nearly 100,000 product listings under 20,000 headings.

5. *Polk City Directory* supplies detailed information on individuals living in specific communities. Polk publishes more than 1,100 directories covering 6,500 communities throughout Canada and the United States. The local chamber of commerce should have access to this directory. See http://www.citydirectory.com.

6. Canadian Key Business Directory, available from Dun and Bradstreet Canada in print form or on CD, lists and profiles more than 20,000 of Canada's largest companies and maintains more than 60,000 key contact names. See http://www.dnb.ca/salesmarketing/keybusinessdir.html.

7. *World Scope: Industrial Company Profiles* (Wright Investor's Service) provides extensive coverage of 5,000 companies from 25 countries, within 27 major industry groupings. See http://www.wisi.com.

8. Frasers.com provides a comprehensive online directory and search tool for Canadian manufacturers and industrial distributors and their products and services. It also lists international companies that sell in the Canadian marketplace. A separate website lists trade shows in Canada and the United States. See http://www.frasers.com/public/home.jsf.

9. Scott's Directories publishes separate directories for many sectors: corporate (140,000 manufacturers, distributors, banks, construction companies, etc.), medical (100,000 doctors, dentists, hospitals, etc.), government (federal, provincial and territorial, municipal), associations (10,000 listings), schools (various types), and residential (12 million listings, available by segment). Directories are available in print, on CD-ROM, or online. See http://www.scottsinfo.com.

LO4
Developing a Strategic Prospecting Plan

t he most productive salespeople use a variety of prospecting methods and follow the strategic prospecting process by generating leads, qualifying them to identify true prospects, and then prioritizing these prospects so that they pursue the best sales opportunities. The use of a strategic prospecting plan can help salespeople continually improve their prospecting effectiveness.

A **strategic prospecting plan** should fit the individual needs of the salesperson. As illustrated in Figure 5.2, the focal point of a prospecting plan should be the goal stating the

strategic prospecting plan A salesperson's plan for gathering qualified prospects.

tracking system Part of the strategic prospecting plan that records comprehensive information about the prospect, traces the prospecting methods used, and chronologically archives outcomes from any contacts with the prospect.

FIGURE 5.2
Prospecting Plans Are the Foundation for Effective Prospecting

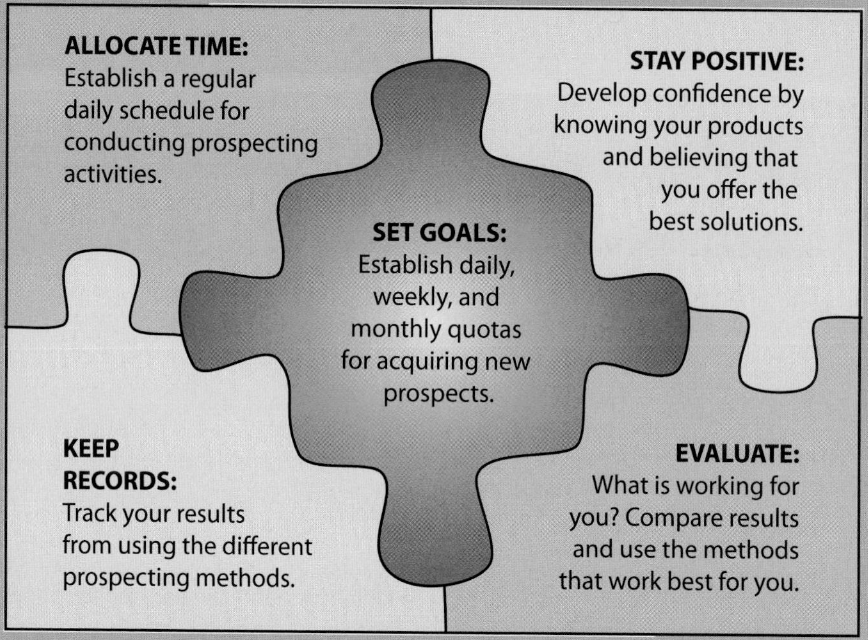

ALLOCATE TIME: Establish a regular daily schedule for conducting prospecting activities.

STAY POSITIVE: Develop confidence by knowing your products and believing that you offer the best solutions.

SET GOALS: Establish daily, weekly, and monthly quotas for acquiring new prospects.

KEEP RECORDS: Track your results from using the different prospecting methods.

EVALUATE: What is working for you? Compare results and use the methods that work best for you.

The strategic prospecting plan sets goals, allocates specific times to be used for prospecting, and continuously evaluates results to maximize the effectiveness of prospecting time and effort.

number of qualified prospects to be generated. Formalized goals serve as guides to what is to be accomplished and help to keep a salesperson on track. The plan should also allocate an adequate and specific daily or weekly time period for prospecting. Having specific times set aside exclusively for prospecting helps to prevent other activities from creeping in and displacing prospecting activities. A good **tracking system** should also be a part of the prospecting plan. A tracking system can be as low-tech as a set of index cards or employ one of the many computerized and online contact management or customer relationship management software applications. Exhibit 5.3 shows an example of a simple, but effective, paper and pencil tracking form. The tracking system should record comprehensive information about the prospect, trace the prospecting methods used, and chronologically archive outcomes from any contacts with the prospect. A fourth element of the prospecting plan is a system for analyzing and evaluating the results of prospecting activities. Continuous evaluation should be employed to ensure the salesperson is meeting prospecting goals and using the most effective prospecting methods. The fifth and final element of a prospecting plan should be a program to review and stay up-to-date on product knowledge and competitor information to emphasize and underscore that the salesperson's products and services offer the best solutions to customer needs and problems. Self-confidence is critical to success in selling, and a base of comprehensive knowledge and understanding is the key to believing in yourself.

As with all phases of the sales process, salespeople must exercise judgment and set priorities in prospecting. A limited amount of time is available for prospecting, and a better understanding of the concepts and practices illustrated in this chapter can help a salesperson be more productive. An added bonus is that the sales process is

EXHIBIT 5.3
Personal Prospecting Log

PERSONAL PROSPECTING LOG

Name Tom Jenkins

Team Charlottetown commercial   Date 4/16

1st Contact	Organization	Contact Person	Source of Lead	Phone	Date of Appointment	Outcome of Call	Follow-Up Activity
3/02/12	Cummins Engine	Tyler Huston	Personal contact	902-444-1234	4/11 8:30 a.m.	Need info on printer	Send in mail
9/01/11	Costco	Katya Epstein	Referral Tom Oats John Deere	902-888-4111	Will call with dates/times	Liked our numbers; decision next week	Send info on satisfied customers
9/02/11	Ball-Foster	MaryLou Hinkle	Called in on 800#	902-365-4242	4/13 Lunch	Great lunch, need proposal	Will work up proposal, set date and present
4/19/12	Ontario Systems	Darrell Beaty	Referral	902-223-4117	4/19 4 p.m.		
4/17/12	Tom's Grocery	Sharon Bristow	Referral Stacey Jones Saskatoon Saskatchewan	905-452-4422	4/17 8 a.m.		
2/02/12	Shopper's Drug Mart	Isabelle Chen	Direct mail sent back 6/02	905-663-2214	4/16 Lunch	Didn't seem impressed, need more work	Need more contact with Alice PACER GAME?
2/03/12	Davis & Davis	Frank Chapman	800# call in	905-211-8811	Bob Evans 4/15 Breakfast	Will include their DP department at next call	Schedule DP
3/03/12	ABB	Jerome Parker	Personal contact	905-927-4321	4/14 2 p.m.	Liked our proposal	Call Monday for answer
3/03/12	Thomson Consumer Electronics	Doug Lyon	Phone	905-212-4111	4/15 3 p.m.	Had bad experience with us several years ago	This one will take time

more enjoyable for salespeople calling on bona fide prospects who can benefit from the salesperson's offering.

LO5
Gathering Prospect Information to Prepare for Sales Dialogue

Once potential customers are identified, the salesperson must begin the process of collecting information. During this stage, the salesperson gathers information about the prospect that will be used to formulate future sales interactions. Buyer's needs, buyer's motives, and details of the buyer's situation should be determined. Some organizations spend a great amount of time determining the salesperson's and buyer's communication styles. Effectively sensing and interpreting customers' communications styles allows salespeople to adapt their own interaction behaviours in a way that facilitates buyer–seller communication and enhances relationship formation.

The more a salesperson knows about a prospect, the better chance a salesperson has to make a sale. Over time, the salesperson should be able to accumulate knowledge about the prospect. The information that the salesperson needs varies with the kind of product that he or she is selling. As a rule, a salesperson needs to know a few basic things about his or her customers (e.g., the prospect's name, correct spelling, and correct pronunciation). A salesperson can learn a great deal about a customer over time by collecting bits and pieces of information, sorting them out, and developing a personalized presentation for the customer.

OBTAINING INFORMATION ON THE BUYER

A salesperson must do some preliminary homework once a company has been identified as a potential client. The first stage of information gathering is to concentrate on the individual prospect. Several questions need to be answered that will identify how the buyer will behave toward the salesperson. Exhibit 5.4 details some of the questions that a salesperson needs to ask.

EXHIBIT 5.4
Information to Gather on a Prospect and Whom to Contact

Information Needed	How to Collect Information
The prospect's name.	Correct spelling and pronunciation can be gathered by asking the receptionist or secretary to verify information.
The prospect's correct title.	This can be determined by asking the gatekeepers to verify.
Is this prospect willing to take risks? Are they confident with decision making?	The salesperson may have to ask the prospect about willingness to take risks.
Is the prospect involved in the community? Does the prospect belong to any clubs or professional organizations?	The salesperson may be able to observe club or organizational honours displayed in the office.
Does the prospect have hobbies or interests he or she is proud of (e.g., coin collector, sports enthusiast)?	Observation of the office might give away this information.
What is the prospect's personality type? Easygoing? All business?	Observation and experience with the buyer will give the answer to the salesperson.
Where was the prospect educated? Where did this prospect grow up?	Look for a degree or diploma on the wall. The salesperson may have to ask for this information.

An Ethical Dilemma

Naomi Beaupré had just completed her sales training for small engines, and she really took to heart the importance of precall information gathering. Her company kept a customer profile and planning sheet that gathered information such as the one shown at right.

She had only been in her territory two weeks when her sales manager, Ted Hart, started receiving complaints from Beaupré's prospects and customers. The callers complained that she had been aggressively collecting information on their company and buyers by interviewing everyone in their respective companies that would agree to see her. One caller, Jane VanWay (the lead buyer for Ontario Power Corporation and a key account for Foster Supply) even termed one of her sales calls an "interrogation." After reviewing her profile sheets, Hart was amazed at how complete they were. Nevertheless, there was still the problem in how Beaupré was going about getting the information. If you were Beaupré, how might you go about researching and collecting the needed company and individual buyer information in a fashion that would not be perceived as so intrusive and aggressive?

Name _____
Address _____
Type of Business _____
Name of Buyer _____
Buyer's Hobbies _____
Decision Maker _____
Key Influences in the Company _____
Buyer Profile _____
Buyer Personality Type _____
Name of Owner _____
Age of Company _____
Primary Products Produced, etc. _____

GATHERING INFORMATION ON THE PROSPECT'S ORGANIZATION

Gathering information about the prospect's company helps salespeople better understand the environment in which they will be working. Exhibit 5.5 details some of the questions that provide useful information about the prospect's organization. Is the prospect presently buying from a single supplier? How long has the prospect been buying from this supplier? If the answer is 20 years and he or she is extremely satisfied with the current salesperson, products, and services, then the prospect should be thanked for his or her time, and the salesperson should move on to other accounts.

It is not unusual for gatekeepers to prohibit the salesperson access to the buyer over the phone if the salesperson mispronounces the buyer's name. Mail is thrown away without being opened if the name is misspelled or the title is incorrect.

Precall information should be used to develop a rapport with the prospect and eventually to tailor the presentation to fit the buyer's needs. A salesperson can establish a relationship with a prospect by discussing such mutual points of interest as an alumni association with the same university or support for the same athletic team. As illustrated in "An Ethical Dilemma," information gathering must be done thoughtfully. It can take many sales calls and months to gather all the useful information a salesperson needs.

> Salespeople often have to call prospects to gather information.

SOURCES OF INFORMATION

A good salesperson uses all available information sources to gather valuable information. Lists and directories will have names, addresses, phone numbers, and other key information. The Web can be a valuable tool as companies provide more than enough vital information for a salesperson. Quite often, companies have employees responsible for seeking critical Web information daily about the company's clients and competitors. Salespeople have access to a large quantity of current information and should use it to gain an edge over their competitors.

Secretaries and receptionists can be a friendly source of information and can certainly be used to verify name, title, pronunciation, and correct spelling. Also, noncompeting salespeople can help a salesperson fill in information on accounts.

© RUBBERBALL/MIKE KEMP/JUPITER IMAGES

EXHIBIT 5.5
Gathering Information about the Organization

Information Needed	How to Collect Information
What type of business are we dealing with: manufacturer, wholesaler, retailer, government, educational, medical, financial institution?	This can be gathered from a directory.
To what market does the company sell? Who are the organization's primary competitors? What does the company make and sell?	Annual reports may be helpful in answering these questions.
From whom does the prospect presently buy? Do they buy from a single vendor? Multiple vendors? How long have they purchased from their suppliers? What problems does the company face? In what volume does the company buy? What is the organization's financial position?	The salesperson may have to ask for this information.

Finally, a salesperson should be gathering information about each of its companies and buyers. Some companies provide the salesforce with contact management software like ACT or Goldmine. Salespeople may develop their own system for gathering pertinent information. Exhibit 5.6 illustrates the types of information that can be gathered in a customer profile.

DETERMINING OTHER BUYERS' INFLUENCES

As products become more complex, we often see an increase in the number of buying influencers and decision makers involved in the purchase. The salesperson should attempt to determine the various buying influencers.

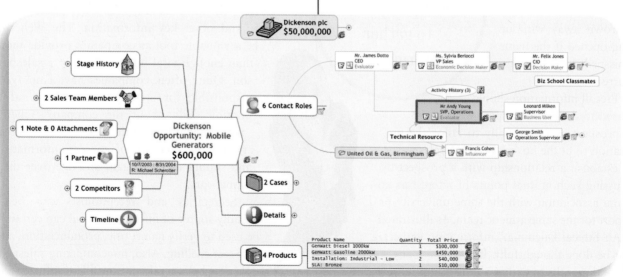

Salespeople can use different software programs to assemble information about prospects.

PR NEWSWIRE/AP IMAGES

EXHIBIT 5.6
Customer Profile

1. Name of Business _____
2. Address _____
3. Phone _____
4. Name of Buyer(s) _____ Title _____
   Personality, Hobbies, Interests _____
   _____
   _____
   _____
5. Source of Prospect (i.e., referral, cold call) _____
6. Other Key People
   Receptionists _____
   Personality, Hobbies, Interests _____
   Secretaries _____
   Personality, Hobbies, Interests _____
   Department Heads _____
   Personality, Hobbies, Interests _____
   Other Influencers—Who? _____
   Personality, Hobbies, Interests _____
7. What products does the company produce? _____
8. History and current standing in the industry _____
9. How many employees? _____
10. Extent of operations—local, regional, national, international _____
11. Is buying done by individuals or committee? _____
12. Does the company buy from single or multiple sources? _____

For example, if a salesperson concentrates on the purchasing agent in an organization and ignores other key players (e.g., department head, data processing) in the decision-making process, the salesperson risks selling to the wrong person.

The salesperson must use observation and questioning to determine the role of each member of the buying team and the amount of influence each exerts; each member's needs should be determined before or during the presentation. Department heads may be interested in how the product will benefit their department, whereas the CFO may care only about the price. During group presentations, all the members of the buying party must feel involved. The salesperson must be sure to direct questions and comments to all potential decision makers in the group.

If a salesperson has only one contact (e.g., purchasing agent) in an organization, he or she runs the risk that the key contact could die, get fired, change jobs, get transferred, or retire. By having contact with many influencers in an organization, the salesperson will always have a number of people who have had previous experiences to pass on to the new purchasing agent or team member. In the first instance, the salesperson must start the entire relationship process again; in the second, the salesperson will have help keeping the relationship in place.

HOW TO PROSPECT FOR NEW CUSTOMERS

Background

Pete Tsuleff has been interested in the food and beverage industry since he was a little boy. His father owned a restaurant/tavern. Tsuleff spent his evenings, weekends, and summers working in the restaurant. At age 21, he began to work as a bartender. He had firsthand experience ordering food, hiring, firing, and running the entire operation by the time he was 25. At age 30, he bought his father out.

During the next 10 years, he opened another restaurant/bar and two package liquor stores. Tsuleff's first love was experimenting with new recipes. He had a chili that won competitions in his hometown. He made a spaghetti sauce that was world class. His garlic bread and garlic cheese bread were legendary. Tsuleff decided to get out of the tavern and liquor business and opened a line of spaghetti shops. Sales over the first five years were outstanding and he opened a new store every six months.

Tsuleff continued to experiment with recipes and developed a line of barbecue sauces. He believes that he is the first to dual-franchise spaghetti and barbecue in the same building.

Current Situation

Tsuleff is convinced that a good market exists (e.g., groceries, restaurants, gas stations) for his garlic bread and spaghetti and barbecue sauces. He has seen his sales grow by 18 percent per year over the past five years, and the trend is expected to continue for at least the next three years.

One of his first problems is to obtain a list of prospects.

Questions

1. What prospecting methods should Tsuleff use?
2. How can Tsuleff qualify the leads he receives? What qualifying factors will be most important?
3. How can Tsuleff organize his prospecting activities?
4. How should he keep records of his prospects?
5. What precall information does Tsuleff need? How will he collect this information?

Role Play

Situation: Read the case.

Characters: Pete Tsuleff, owner and salesperson for Specialty Foods & Sauces; Sue Almont, specialty products buyer for Cub Food Stores

Scene:

Location—Pete Tsuleff's office at Specialty Foods & Sauces

Action—In the course of Tsuleff's prospecting activities, Sue Almont and Cub Food stores have scored a high priority as a qualified prospect for his new line of garlic breads and sauces. Cub Food stores is a major supermarket chain with significant market penetration in Alberta, Manitoba, New Brunswick, and Saskatchewan

Role play the phone conversation between Tsuleff and Almont as Tsuleff introduces himself and his company to Almont, gathers needed information about the prospect, and asks for an appointment for an initial sales call.

Prospecting and Gaining Prospect Information

Background

Preston Adams has just completed the sales training program for the Office Equipment Division of Xerox. Adams has been assigned a territory in New Brunswick that includes the metro areas of Fredericton, Saint John, and Moncton. The company once commanded a significant market share in these markets. However, because of a problem with a previous salesperson in these markets three years ago, Xerox has not been directly working this particular region of central Illinois. Although a large number of Xerox machines are still in use across this territory, it has been a while since a salesperson has called on any accounts. As with any geographic area, a lot of changes have likely occurred, with existing companies moving or even going out of business and new companies opening up.

Current Situation

Adams's sales manager, Eric Waits, is coming in two weeks to spend three days in the field with Adams calling on prospective accounts. Adams is working to develop a list of leads that he can qualify and then contact to set up the sales calls he will be making with his manager.

Role Play

Situation: Read the role play.

Characters: Preston Adams, salesperson for Xerox Business Machines Division; Jerri Spencer, office manager with purchasing responsibilities for Moncton-based McKelvey and Walters, Attorneys-at-Law.

Scene: *Location*—Preston Adams's office at Xerox Business Machines Division. *Action*—In the course of Adams's prospecting activities, Spencer and the McKelvey and Walters law firm have come up as a strong prospect for Xerox's new line of professional copiers. McKelvey and Walters operate a large office in Moncton that occupies most of two floors in the Planter's Bank Building and a branch office in Saint John. They were previously a customer of Xerox, but the information that Adams has obtained indicates that they are using an unspecified variety of different brands of copiers.

Role play the phone conversation between Adams and Spencer as Adams introduces himself and his company to Spencer, gathers needed information to better qualify the prospect, and asks for an appointment for an initial sales call.

In sales,

you have to show up to be successful. But before
you show up, you have to do your homework.

what do you think?

**Salespeople with
great presentation
skills can overcome
a lack of planning for
sales calls.**

1 2 3 4 5 6 7
strongly disagree   strongly agree

6

Planning Sales Dialogues and Presentations

After completing this chapter, you should be able to

LO1 Explain why it is essential to focus on the customer when planning sales calls.

LO2 Understand alternative ways of communicating with prospects and customers through canned sales presentations, written sales proposals, and organized sales dialogues and presentations.

LO3 Discuss the nine components of the sales dialogue template that can be used for planning an organized sales dialogue or an organized sales presentation.

LO4 Explain how to write a customer value proposition statement.

LO5 Link buying motives to benefits of the seller's offering, support claims made for benefits, and reinforce verbal claims made.

LO6 Engage the customer by setting appointments.

Introduction

n its quest to take multichannel retailing to new levels, Circuit City Stores envisioned creating a "boundless selling environment." At the heart of this project was an army of associates who could deliver infinite knowledge, regardless of merchandise category or department—similar to the service shoppers receive online. The chain quickly realized that isolated customer-service departments and employees that possessed specialized technical knowledge would not support its endeavours.

By developing an interactive, wireless tablet PC-based selling tool, Circuit City is not only assisting store-level employees to become more knowledgeable and deliver more customer service, it is also helping the chain differentiate itself among competitors.

The chain wanted a tool that could achieve three goals: to uphold its boundless selling, guide shoppers to make the best buying decision, and feature top-notch training.

Circuit City connected the tablets to Web-based information. Linked to proprietary software, the tablets wirelessly communicated with Circuit City's network. "Associates carried the tablets as they walked throughout the store. It enabled them to answer questions, provide digital-merchandise demonstrations and service shoppers beyond the sales counter," explained Matt M. Johnson, manager of Circuit City's concept development/store experience.

"The units definitely helped us improve our guest service, and helped our partners perform better from a selling standpoint," said Brian Leach, Circuit City's VP, New Concepts.

The biggest strides came when the chain wanted to augment the multichannel experience through the units. "We have tied our Web presence very closely with our business units and merchandising departments," Dave Romero, the chain's senior manager, New Concepts, said.

"We wanted the next tablet generation to give partners visibility into offers, promotions, and merchandise available enterprisewide," he said. "Our past versions focused on the merchandise. The newest version had to focus on providing solutions."

Source: Deena M. Amato-McCoy. "The New Power Tool." *Chain Store Age*. September 30, 2008. Reprinted with permission of Chain Store Age.

LO1

Customer-Focused Sales Dialogue Planning

buyers are generally well informed and have little time to waste. This means that salespeople must invest a significant amount of time in planning sales calls on prospective and existing customers so that they can communicate in a clear, credible, and interesting fashion. A **sales call** takes place when the salesperson and buyer or buyers meet in person to discuss business. This typically takes place in the customer's place of business, but it may take place elsewhere, such as in the seller's place of business or at a trade show.

As defined in Chapter 1, **sales dialogue** comprises business conversations between buyers and sellers that take place over time as salespeople attempt to initiate, develop, and enhance customer relationships. The term *sales conversation* is used interchangeably with sales dialogue. Some sales calls involve **sales presentations** as part of the dialogue. Sales presentations are comprehensive communications that convey multiple points designed to persuade the prospect or customer to make a purchase.

Ideally, sales presentations focus on customer value and only take place after the salesperson has completed the ADAPT process (introduced in Chapter 4). As a reminder, the ADAPT process means the salesperson has **a**ssessed the customer's situation; **d**iscovered his or her needs, buying processes, and strategic priorities; **a**ctivated the buyer's interest in solving a problem or realizing an opportunity; helped the buyer **p**roject how value can be derived from a purchase; and then made a **t**ransition to the full sales presentation. Salespeople who

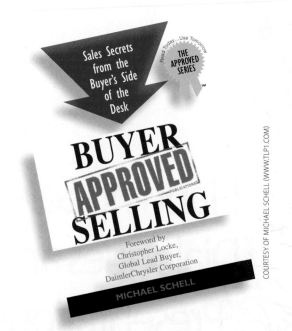

The importance of focusing on the customer when planning sales dialogues is reflected in the popular trade book **Buyer Approved Selling** by Michael Schell.

attempt to make a sales presentation before building a foundation through sales dialogue risk being viewed as noncustomer oriented and overly aggressive.

Consistent with the trust-based sales process introduced in Chapter 1 (see Figure 1.5), sales dialogue planning efforts should focus on customer value. Salespeople must have a basic understanding of the value they and their companies can deliver to customers. Further, they must recognize that what constitutes value will typically vary from one customer to the next. Finally, as the process continues and relationships are established with customers, salespeople must work continually to increase the value their customers receive. Throughout the process, selling strategy must focus on customer needs and how the customer defines value.

To better understand the process of planning sales dialogues and presentations, we will now discuss the three most common approaches: the canned sales presentation, the written sales proposal, and organized sales dialogues and presentations. Each of these alternatives varies greatly in terms of how much customization and customer interaction is involved. A planning template that serves as a guide for sales dialogues and comprehensive presentations will then be presented. The chapter concludes with a discussion of how to foster better sales dialogues when attempting to initiate relationships with customers.

sales call An in-person meeting between a salesperson or sales team and one or more buyers to discuss business.

sales dialogue Business conversations between buyers and sellers that occur as salespeople attempt to initiate, develop, and enhance customer relationships. Sales dialogue should be customer focused and have a clear purpose.

sales presentations Comprehensive communications that convey multiple points designed to persuade the customer to make a purchase.

LO2
Sales Communications Formats

in planning customer encounters, salespeople must decide on a basic format, such as a canned sales presentation, a written sales proposal, or an organized sales dialogue. Exhibit 6.1 summarizes the types of communications sales professionals use. A salesperson might use one or more of these formats with a particular customer. Each format has unique advantages and disadvantages. To be successful, these communications must be credible and clear. In addition, the salesperson must communicate in the right environment at an appropriate time to maximize the probability of a successful outcome.

For any of the three communications types, salespeople must plan to be as specific as possible in developing their sales message. For example, it is better to tell a prospect "This electric motor will produce 4800 RPM and requires only one hour of maintenance per week" than to say "This motor will really put out the work with only minimum maintenance."

CANNED SALES PRESENTATIONS

Canned sales presentations include scripted sales calls, memorized presentations, and automated presentations. The telemarketing industry relies heavily on scripted sales calls, and memorized presentations are common in trade show product demonstrations. Automated presentations rely heavily on computer images, movies, tapes, or slides to present the information to the prospect.

When done right, canned presentations are complete and logically structured. Objections and questions can be anticipated in advance, and appropriate responses can be formulated as part of the presentation. The sales message varies little from customer to customer, except that some sales scripts have "branches" or different salesperson responses based on how the customer responds. Canned presentations can be used by relatively inexperienced salespeople, and using this format might boost the confidence of some salespeople. Canned sales presentations should be tested for effectiveness, ideally with real customers, before they are implemented with the entire salesforce.

Canned sales presentations make an implicit assumption that customer needs and buying motives are essentially homogeneous. Therefore, canned presentations fail to capitalize on a key advantage of personal selling—the ability to adapt to different types of customers and various selling situations. The salesperson can only assume the buyer's need and must hope that a lively presentation of product benefits will cause the prospect to buy. The canned presentation can be effective, but is not appropriate for many situations—simply because customer opportunity to interact is minimized. During a memorized presentation, the salesperson talks 80 to 90 percent of the time, only occasionally allowing the prospect to express his or her feelings, concerns, or opinions. Canned presentations do not handle interruptions well, may be

> **canned sales presentation** Sales presentations that include scripted sales calls, memorized presentations, and automated presentations.

EXHIBIT 6.1
Types of Sales Communications

Canned Presentations
- These include scripted sales calls, and memorized and automated presentations.
- They can be complete and logically structured.
- The downside is that to not vary from buyer to buyer; they should be tested for effectiveness.

Written Sales Proposals
- The proposal is a complete self-contained sales presentation.
- Written proposals are often accompanied by sales calls before and after the proposal is submitted.
- Thorough customer assessment should take place before a customized proposal is written.

Organized Sales Dialogues and Presentations
- They address individual customer and different selling situations.
- They allow flexibility to adapt to buyer feedback.
- They are the most frequently used format by sales professionals.

MARTIN MEISSNER/AP IMAGES

Canned sales presentations include scripted presentations to customers at industry trade shows.

explain the proposal and provide answers to questions. Alternatively, preliminary sales dialogues may lead to a sales proposal. In any event, the sales proposal should be prepared after the salesperson has made a thorough assessment of the buyer's situation as it relates to the seller's offering.

The sales proposal has long been associated with important, high-dollar-volume sales transactions. It is frequently used in competitive bidding situations and in situations involving the selection of a new supplier by the prospect. One advantage of the proposal is that the written word is usually viewed as being more credible than the spoken word. Written proposals are subject to careful scrutiny with few time constraints, and specialists in the buying firm often analyze various sections of the proposal.

Sales proposal content is similar to other comprehensive sales presentations, focusing on customer needs and related benefits the seller offers. In addition, technical information, pricing data, and perhaps a timetable are included. Most proposals provide a triggering mechanism, such as a proposed contract to confirm the sale, and some specify follow-up action to be taken if the proposal is satisfactory.

With multimedia sales presentations becoming more routine, it is natural to think that written sales proposals would be declining in importance. Actually, the opposite is true. With the widespread use of multimedia, the standards for all sales communication continue to rise. Buyers expect clear, informative sales messages, and they are less tolerant of sloppy communication. Because everyone knows that word processing programs have functions to check spelling and grammar, for example, mistakes are less acceptable than ever.

Because written communication provides a permanent record of claims and intentions, salespeople should be careful not to overpromise but still maintain a positive and supportive tone. No buyer wants to read a proposal full of legal disclaimers and warnings, yet such information may be a necessary ingredient in certain written communication. As with all communication, salespeople should try to give buyers the information they need to make informed decisions.

awkward to use with a broad product line, and may alienate buyers who want to participate in the interaction.

Despite its limitations, the canned sales presentation can be effective in some situations. If the product line is narrow and the sales force is relatively inexperienced, the canned presentation may be suitable. Also, many salespeople find it effective to use a sales dialogue to introduce their company, to demonstrate the product, or for some other limited purpose.

Buyers expect clear, informative sales messages, and they are less tolerant of sloppy communication.

WRITTEN SALES PROPOSALS

The second basic type of sales communication is the **written sales proposal**. The proposal is a complete self-contained sales presentation, but it is often accompanied by sales dialogues before or after the proposal is delivered. In some cases, the customer may receive a proposal and then request that the salesperson make a sales call to further

written sales proposal
A complete self-contained sales presentation on paper, often accompanied by other verbal sales presentations before or after the proposal is delivered.

Writing Effective Proposals

Whether the proposal is in response to a buyer's request for proposals (RFP) or generated to complement and strengthen a sales presentation, it is essential that the proposal be correctly written and convey the required information in an attractive manner. Tom Sant, an author and consultant who works with many Fortune 100 companies, gives these reasons why proposals may fail:[1]

1. The customer does not know the seller.
2. The proposal does not follow the specified format.
3. The executive summary does not address the customer's needs.
4. The proposal uses the seller's (not the customer's) company jargon.
5. The writing is flat and technical and without passion.
6. Generic material contains another customer's name.
7. The proposal is not convincing.
8. The proposal contains glaring grammatical errors.
9. The proposal does not address key decision criteria.
10. The proposal does not build a persuasive value proposition.

Clearly, developing a quality proposal takes time and effort. When beginning the proposal-writing process, it is important for the salesperson to adopt the right mindset with a key thought of "Okay, this will take some time to get the details down, but it will be worth it." To reinforce this mindset, consider the advice given in Exhibit 6.2: Tips for Creating Effective Sales Proposals.[2]

Breaking the proposal down into its primary and distinct parts can simplify the process of writing an effective proposal. Five parts common to most proposals are an executive summary, customer needs and proposed solution, seller profile, pricing and sales agreement, and an implementation section with a timetable.

Executive Summary This summary precedes the full proposal and serves two critical functions. First, it should succinctly and clearly demonstrate the salesperson's understanding of the customer's needs and the relevance of the proposed solution. An effective summary

EXHIBIT 6.2
Tips for Creating Effective Sales Proposals

- When writing a proposal, pretend you are one of the buyer's decision makers and decide what you need to know to make a decision.
- Think of the proposal as an in-depth conversation with the buyer's decision makers.
- Give the decision makers all the information they need to make an informed decision.
- Avoid boilerplate proposals that use the same wording for all customers.
- Avoid so-what proposals that do not give customers the financial justification for buying your product.
- Realize that you must educate the buyer and provide information accordingly.
- Ensure that your proposal has a logical flow that the customer can easily follow.

will spell out the customer's problems, the nature of the proposed solution, and the resulting benefits to the customer. A second function of the summary is to build a desire to read the full proposal. This is important as many key members of the organization often read little more than the information provided in the summary. A question new salespeople commonly ask refers to the length of the executive summary. A good rule of thumb is that an executive summary should be limited to two typewritten pages—especially if the main body of the report is fewer than 50 pages.

Customer Needs and Proposed Solution This section is typically composed of two primary parts. First, the situation analysis should concisely explain the salesperson's understanding of the customer's situation, problems, and needs. Second, the recommended solution is presented and supported with illustrations and evidence on how the proposed solution uniquely addresses the buyer's problems and needs. The emphasis in this section should be on the benefits resulting from the solution and not on the product or service being sold. It is important that these benefits be described from the perspective of the customer. Proprietary information required in the proposal can be protected in a number of ways. The most common method is to place a notice on the cover (i.e., "Confidential" or "For Review Purposes Only"). Many technology companies ask the prospect to sign a nondisclosure agreement that is part of the overall document and, in some instances, the selling organization will even copyright the proposal.

Seller Profile This section contains information that the customer wants to know about the selling company. This section offers a succinct overview and background of the firm, but the emphasis should be on the company's capabilities. Case histories of customers for whom the company solved similar problems with similar solutions have proved to be an effective method to document and illustrate organizational capabilities and past successes.

Pricing and Sales Agreement The previous sections are designed to build the customer value of the proposed solution. Once this value has been established, the proposal should "ask for the order" by presenting pricing information and delivery options. This information is often presented in the form of a sales agreement for the buyer to sign off on and complete.

Implementation and Timetable The purpose of this section is to make it as easy as possible for the buyer to make a positive purchase decision. In effect, this section should say "if you like the proposal and want to act on it, this is what you do." There may be a contract to sign, an order form to fill out, or instructions regarding whom to call to place an order or request further information. A timetable that details a schedule of key implementation events should also be included.

Evaluating Proposals before Submission In the customer's eyes, the standards for written sales proposals are high. Poor spelling and grammatical mistakes send a negative message that the seller has little regard for attention to detail. The quality of a salesperson's written documents is a surrogate for that salesperson's competence and ability as well as the capabilities and overall quality of the organization. If the proposal does

not properly interpret the buyer's needs or fails to make a compelling case to justify the purchase, the odds of success are low. Although a well-written proposal is no guarantee of making the sale, a poorly written proposal will certainly reduce the probability of success.

Since the stakes are usually high when written sales proposals are used, it is a best practice to evaluate proposals carefully before they are submitted to the customer. In fact, it is a good idea to build the evaluative criteria into the proposal writing process early on, then use the criteria shown in Exhibit 6.3[3] as a final check before submitting a sales proposal.

ORGANIZED SALES DIALOGUES

In most situations, the process of converting a prospect into a customer will take several sales conversations over multiple encounters. These conversations constitute an **organized sales dialogue**. For example, salespeople often speak by telephone with a qualified prospect to get an appointment for a later meeting. The second conversation with the customer typically focuses on fact finding and parallels the ADAPT process. The next step would come after the salesperson has developed a tailored solution for the customer. The salesperson may make a comprehensive sales presentation but, in this case, it is designed for dialogue with the customer throughout. To reiterate, this is not a one-way presentation or monologue—it is a sales dialogue with a high level of customer involvement. This type of comprehensive presentation is commonly called an **organized sales presentation**.

> Before making comprehensive sales presentations, salespeople often have several conversations with prospects to better understand their situation and needs.

© IMAGE SOURCE/JUPITER IMAGES

EXHIBIT 6.3
Evaluating Sales Proposals

It is a best practice to evaluate sales proposals before they are submitted to the customer. Five important dimensions for evaluating proposals are reliability, assurance, tangibles, empathy, and responsiveness.

Reliability reflects your (the seller's) ability to identify creative, dependable, and realistic solutions and strategies and match them to the buyer's needs and wants.

Does the proposal

1. Clearly articulate proposed solutions and strategies?
2. Provide creative and innovative solutions and strategies for the buyer?
3. Present solutions and strategies appropriate for the buyer's business operation and organization?
4. Provide financial justifications that support the proposed solutions and strategies?

Assurance builds the buyer's trust and confidence in your ability to deliver, implement, produce, and provide the benefits.

Does the proposal

1. Provide adequate specifications and benefits that substantiate ability and capability statements?
2. Present techniques, methodologies, or processes for ensuring quality performance?
3. Concisely and adequately define project or implementation roles and responsibilities?
4. Clearly identify and define all fees, prices, and expenses for completing the project?

Tangibles enhance and support the communication of your message and invite readership by its overall appearance, content, and organization.

Does the proposal

1. Provide a logical flow of information and ideas and sense of continuity for solving the buyer's business problems?
2. Convert the intangible elements of the solutions or strategies into tangibles?
3. Demonstrate high standards for excellence in format, structure, grammar, spelling, and appearance?
4. Provide positive indicators to differentiate the proposing organization from their competition?

Empathy confirms your thorough understanding of the buyer's business and his or her specific needs and wants.

Does the proposal

1. Clearly identify the buyer's specific needs and wants?
2. Demonstrate a thorough understanding of the buyer's business operation and organization?
3. Provide solutions and strategies that fit within the buyer's business goals?
4. Identify and discuss financial and nonfinancial benefits in terms of their impact on the buyer's unique operation and organization?

Responsiveness developed in a timely manner demonstrates a willingness to provide solutions for the buyer's needs and wants and to help measure results.

Does the proposal

1. Reflect a genuine willingness to understand the buyer's business operation and organization and provide viable and flexible solutions and strategies?
2. Reflect the proposing organization's willingness to work closely with the buyer by enthusiastically asking questions, gathering information, presenting options, and reviewing draft proposals?
3. Lead to the proposing organization thoroughly reviewing the final proposal with the buyer and responding to his or her questions or clarifying any outstanding issues and concerns?
4. Describe the proposed solutions or strategies within the buyer's budget and implementation time frames?

An Ethical Dilemma

Tom Lawrence was not one who liked to do a lot of precall planning or ask questions of his prospects. Lawrence had a good idea about which of his products' features were hot buttons for most prospects. During each of his sales calls, he hammered home those features that he thought were important to most of his prospects. His sales manager made calls with him for a few days and made the observation that Lawrence should do more questioning and listening and sell only those features and benefits that were relevant to each prospect. Lawrence stated: "I feel that is a waste of time. Most of my buyers are busy. They don't have time to answer questions all day. I'm the expert; I should know what they need." What are the dangers in the way Lawrence thinks? What can his sales manager do to help Lawrence change?

Organized sales dialogues may precede or follow other sales communications, such as a written sales proposal. Sales dialogues are much more than mere conversation—they are a chance for the salesperson to seek information or action from the prospect and to explore the business reasons the prospect has for continuing the dialogue with the salesperson (e.g., solving a problem or realizing an opportunity). Feedback from the prospect is encouraged, and therefore this format is less likely to offend a participation-prone buyer. "An Ethical Dilemma" demonstrates the problem for a salesperson who is not willing to ask questions and gain feedback.

When the situation calls for a full sales presentation, the organized sales presentation is usually favoured over both the canned presentation and the written proposal. Such an approach allows much-needed flexibility to adapt to buyer feedback and changing circumstances during the presentation. Organized presentations may also include some canned portions. For example, a salesperson for Caterpillar may show a videotape to illustrate the earth-moving capabilities of a bulldozer as one segment of an organized presentation. Because of its flexibility during the sales call and its ability to address various sales situations, the organized presentation is the most frequently used format for professional sales presentations.

One reality of this presentation format is that it requires a knowledgeable salesperson who can react to questions and objections from the prospect. Stephanie Cooper, president of Enriched Insurance Services, confirms this in "Professional Selling in the 21st Century: Being Prepared for My Sales Calls." Further, this format may extend the time horizon before a purchase decision is reached, and it is vulnerable to diversionary delay tactics by the prospect. Presumably, those who make these arguments think that a canned presentation forces a purchase decision in a more expedient fashion. Overall, however, most agree that the organized presentation is ideal for most sales situations. Its flexibility allows a full exploration of customer needs and appropriate adaptive behaviour by the salesperson. By fully participating in the dialogue, both buyer and seller have an opportunity to establish a mutually beneficial relationship.

The trust-based relational selling presentation often referred to as the need-satisfaction/consultative model is a popular form of an organized presentation. Figure 6.1 highlights the three stages of the trust-based selling process and the participation levels of the salesperson and buyer.

The first stage of the process, the need development stage, is devoted to a discussion of the buyer's needs. During this phase the buyer should be talking 60 to 70 percent of the time. The salesperson accomplishes this by using the first four questioning techniques of the ADAPT process.

The second stage of the process (need awareness) is to verify what the buyer thinks his or her needs are and to make the buyer aware of potential needs that may exist. For instance, fast-food restaurants were generally slow to recognize the need to offer more low-fat and low-carbohydrate menu items until their sales volume suffered. Others, such as Subway, gained a competitive advantage by working with their suppliers to formulate a significant number of menu alternatives for the health-conscious consumer. The need-awareness stage is a good time to restate the prospect's needs and to clarify exactly what the prospect's needs are. During this stage, the participation level for the buyer and salesperson has reached a balance in which both individuals are interacting equally.

In the final stage, the need fulfillment, the salesperson must show how his or her product and its benefits will meet the needs of the buyer. During this stage, the salesperson will do more of the talking by indicating what specific product will meet the buyer's needs. For this stage to be successful, the salesperson has to identify the features of a product and explain the advantages of those features to demonstrate the benefits of the product. By letting the customer talk and practising active listening, the salesperson will better understand the needs of the customer. The salesperson, by being a good listener early in

PROFESSIONAL SELLING IN THE 21ST CENTURY

Being Prepared for My Sales Calls

Stephanie Cooper, president of Enriched Insurance Services in Regina, Saskatchewan, knows the importance of planning and organizing each of her sales calls.

My clients are very knowledgeable; they want answers to questions and I must be prepared to answer them. It may sound simple but my clients want to know what I am selling and why they need it. If they have high schoolers, it's my job to explain the postsecondary savings plan and how it works. I represent many different companies so my clients want to know what company I am recommending and why. It is not unusual to be asked if I have other satisfied clients using the product. I have to be prepared to talk about my satisfied clients and how I helped them. Yes, price always comes up and my clients want to know if my prices are truly competitive. We're not always the lowest, but we'd better be close. Many of my clients are not confident in their decision making. I must be prepared to explain why they need to act now and not wait. I cannot go into my sales calls having not thought about these questions. As a professional salesperson, I must plan for them before the fact and be ready to answer them.

the process, will now have a better chance to gain the buyer's interest and trust by talking about specific benefits the buyer has confirmed as being important.

By fully participating in the dialogue, both buyer and seller have an opportunity to establish a mutually beneficial relationship.

FIGURE 6.1

The Trust-Based Selling Process: A Need-Satisfaction Consultative Model

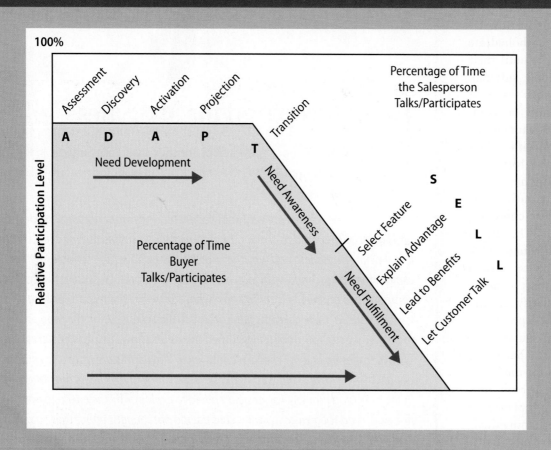

At some points in the two-way sales dialogue, the customer will do more talking; at other points, the salesperson will do more of the talking.

LO3
SALES DIALOGUE TEMPLATE

Sales dialogues are not scripted in advance as canned sales presentations are; however, salespeople should think ahead about what questions and statements to include in the conversation and be prepared to hold up their end of the conversation with an appropriate amount of detail. **A sales dialogue template** (see Exhibit 6.4) is a useful tool to ensure that all pertinent content areas are covered with each prospect. The template is flexible and can be used

sales dialogue template A flexible planning tool that assists the salesperson in assembling pertinent information to be covered with the prospect.

either to plan a comprehensive organized sales presentation or to guide sales dialogues of a more narrow scope. The template is not meant to be a script for a sales encounter, but rather an aid in planning and assembling the information required of the salesperson.

By addressing the issues noted in the template, salespeople can facilitate trust-building by demonstrating their competence and expertise, customer orientation, candour, dependability, and compatibility. It is true that trust is built through behaviour not just by planning and having good intentions; however, salespeople who are aware of what it takes to earn the customer's trust in the planning stages have a better chance of earning that trust in subsequent encounters with the customer. The sales dialogue template is organized into nine sections, each of which is discussed individually.

Section 1: Prospect Information

This section is used to record specific information on the prospect, such as the company name, key decision maker's name and job title, and the type of business. In most business-to-business situations, it is critical to know who else is involved in the buying decision and what role he or she plays, such as gatekeeper, user, or influencer. (Refer to Chapter 3 if you need to review the buying team concept.) It is also important that the salesperson make sure that all the key players are receiving the appropriate information and getting the proper attention they deserve. A mistake salespeople often make is not identifying all the buying influencers.

EXHIBIT 6.4
Sales Dialogue Template

1. Prospect Information

A. Company Name: _____ Type of Business: _____

Key-Person Information

B. Prospect's Name (Key Decision Maker) _____ Job Title: _____

C. Other people involved in the purchase decision:

Names/Job Title	Departments	Role in Purchase Decision

2. Customer Value Proposition: A brief statement of how you will add value to the prospect's business by meeting a need or providing an opportunity. Include a brief description of the product or service:

A. Product/Service That Delivers Value:

B. Value Proposition Statement:

3. Sales Call Objective (must require customer action, such as making a purchase, supplying critical information, etc.):

Continued

EXHIBIT 6.4

Sales Dialogue Template—*Continued*

4. Linking Buying Motives, Benefits, Support Information, and Other Reinforcement Methods.
(Repeat for each person who will be involved in the upcoming sales call.)

A. *Buying motives:* What is most important to the prospect(s) in making a purchase decision? **Rational** motives include economic issues, such as quality, cost, service capabilities, and the strategic priorities of the prospect's company. **Emotional** motives include fear, status, and ego-related feelings. List all relevant buying motives in order of importance.	B. *Specific benefits matched to buying motives:* Benefits to be stressed are arranged in priority order (sequence to be followed unless prospect feedback during the presentation indicates an alternative sequence). Each benefit should correspond to one or more buying motives.	C. *Information needed to support claims for each benefit.*	D. *Where appropriate, methods for reinforcing verbal content* (Audio/ visual, collateral material, illustrations, testimonials, etc.).
1. ⟶	⟶	⟶	
2. ⟶	⟶	⟶	
3. ⟶	⟶	⟶	
4. ⟶	⟶	⟶	

5. Current Suppliers (If Applicable) and Other Key Competitors:

Competitors	Strengths	Weaknesses

6. Beginning the Sales Dialogue:

Plans for the first few minutes of the sales presentation:

Introduction, thanks, agenda agreement, then begin ADAPT as appropriate or transition into other sales dialogue or presentation:

Assessment _____

Discovery _____

Activation _____

Project _____

Transition to Presentation _____

Note: The ADAPT process may take place over several sales conversations during multiple sales calls. In other cases, it may be concluded in a single sales call, then immediately followed by a sales presentation during the same sales call.

Continued

EXHIBIT 6.4

Sales Dialogue Template—*Continued*

7. Anticipating Prospect Questions and Objections, with Planned Responses:

Questions/Objections	Responses

8. Earning Prospect Commitment

A preliminary plan for how the prospect will be asked for a commitment related to the sales call objective:

9. Building Value through Follow-Up Action

Statement of follow-up action needed to ensure that the buyer–seller relationship moves in a positive direction:

LO4

Section 2: Customer Value Proposition

In this section, the salesperson develops a preliminary **customer value proposition**, which is a statement of how the sales offering will add value to the prospect's business by meeting a need or providing an opportunity. Essentially, the customer value proposition summarizes the legitimate business reason for making the sales call by answering the prospect's question, "Why should I spend my time with you?" A good customer value proposition clearly states why the customer will be better off by doing business with the salesperson and his or her firm but at this point does not try to list all of the reasons.[4]

At the planning stage, the customer value proposition is preliminary. The salesperson has good reason to believe that customer value can be enhanced by delivering

customer value proposition A statement of how the sales offering will add value to the prospect's business by meeting a need or providing an opportunity.

on the contents of the proposition, but the true value of the proposition will be accepted or rejected by the customer as the sales process moves along. It is during this sales dialogue process that the actual customer value to be delivered will be refined and modified. This section of the template provides a point of departure for planning purposes and assumes that the value proposition is likely to be modified before the purchase decision. In writing the preliminary customer value proposition, salespeople should attempt the following:

1. Keep the statement fairly simple so that the direction for upcoming sales dialogues is clear.

2. Choose the key benefit(s) likely to be most important to the specific customer who is the audience for this particular dialogue or presentation. (At this point, it is not necessary to list all the benefits of their offerings.)

3. Make the value proposition as specific as possible on tangible outcomes (e.g., improvements to revenues, cost containment or reduction, market share, process speed and efficiency) or the enhancement of the customer's strategic priority.

4. Reflect product or service dimensions that add value, whether or not the customer pays for them. For example, some companies offer delivery, installation, and training along with the purchase of their products. Added value may also accrue from what the seller's sales team provides (e.g., work in the field with a distributor's salespeople or certification training for the buyer's technicians).

5. Promise only what can be consistently delivered. Strictly speaking, a customer value proposition in the planning stage is not a guarantee; rather, it is a belief based on the salesperson's knowledge and best judgment. As the sales process moves along, appropriate guarantees can be made.

Using these points as a guide, the following is an example of a customer value proposition that could provide clear direction for planning an upcoming sales presentation or a series of sales dialogues:

"ABC Company can improve its market share by a minimum of four percentage points in a one-year period in its Vancouver and Calgary markets by implementing our customer satisfaction and retention training for its customer service personnel."

In contrast, here is an example of a poorly constructed customer value proposition:

"By adopting our customer satisfaction and retention programs, ABC Company will see a dramatic increase in its market share."

This second proposition opens the salesperson to a potential barrage of questions:

Dramatic increase in market share? What's dramatic?

We operate in 22 markets. Are you saying that we will increase market shares in all 22 markets?

What do you mean by programs? Are you referring to training programs?

In the planning stages, salespeople may or may not be fully aware of the prospect's needs and priorities—and, until they are aware of these needs and priorities, the sales dialogue should focus on the first two stages of the ADAPT process: assessing the prospect's situation and discovering his or her needs. Unless these stages are completed, the customer value proposition will not contain enough detail to be useful.

Section 3: Sales Call Objective

Section 3 asks the salesperson to determine the objective for his or her sales call. Salespeople must have an objective for each sales call. Basically, sales call objectives state what salespeople want customers to do as a result of the sales call. The objectives should be specific enough to know whether or not they have been accomplished at the conclusion of the call, and they should require customer actions, such as placing an order, agreeing to participate in a test market, or supplying specific information useful to the salesperson. Many salespeople think that they have only one objective: to get an order. Other legitimate sales call objectives do exist. For instance, during an introductory call the objective may be simply to introduce the salesperson and his or her company and to gather information on the buyer's needs. Eventually, the major sales presentation objective will be to earn a commitment from the customer by making a sale, but this is not always the only objective.

After the sale is made, the objective may be to follow up and determine whether or not the customer is satisfied with the salesperson's efforts. The salesperson can also look for openings to cover additional objectives. Gwen Tranguillo of Hershey's always looks for ways to introduce other products in her presentation if the buyer expresses interest. Tranguillo made a major sales presentation on a Halloween display of king-size candies and found that the buyer was very interested in adding more king sizes immediately. She shifted gears and gained a commitment on the new king-size display and later in the presentation went back to her

Halloween proposal. At the very least, the heart of any presentation should be to advance the process toward an order.

LO5

Section 4: Linking Buying Motives, Benefits, Support Information, and Other Reinforcement Methods

In Section 4 of the planning template, the prospect's buying motives are linked to specific benefits offered. For each benefit identified, the salesperson will also assemble the information needed to support the claims to be made in the upcoming dialogue or presentation. In some cases, verbal claims must be reinforced with audio-visual portrayal, illustrations, printed collateral material, or testimonials from satisfied customers, as appropriate to the situation.

Buying motives refer to the most important factors from the customer's perspective in making a purchase decision. In other words, what will motivate the buyer to make a purchase? Buying motives may be rational or emotional, or a combination of both rational and emotional. **Rational buying motives** typically relate to the economics of the situation, including cost, profitability, quality, services offered, and the total value of the seller's offering that the customer perceives. **Emotional motives**, such as fear, the need for security, the need for status, or the need to be liked, are sometimes difficult for salespeople to uncover as prospects are generally less likely to share such motives with salespeople. In business-to-business selling, rational motives are typically the most important buying motives, but salespeople should not ignore emotional motives if they are known to exist.

In linking benefits to buying motives, benefits should be distinguished from features. **Features** are factual statements about the characteristics of a product or service, such as "This is the lightest electrical motor in its performance category." **Benefits** describe the added value for the customer—the favourable outcome derived from a feature. For example, "The lightweight motor supports your mobile repair service strategy in that it is very portable. The ease of use allows your technicians to complete more service calls per day, thus increasing your profitability." To make such a claim about increasing profitability, the salesperson would need to gather specific information to support it. For example, in this case the claim that technicians can complete more service calls per day because the motor

is easy to use might call for competitive comparisons and actual usage data or a demonstration.

Some situations may lead the salesperson to decide that a product demonstration and testimonials from satisfied customers will reinforce the spoken word. In other cases, third-party research studies or articles in trade publications might be used to reinforce oral claims. Another powerful option is material developed by the salesperson, such as a break-even chart showing how quickly the customer can recoup the investment in the new product or service. A note of caution: It is always a good idea to use these types of sales support materials sparingly—some prospects do not react positively to information overload. Chapter 7 discusses in greater detail sales tools and how they can enhance the sales effort.

Section 5: Competitive Situation

Understanding the competitive situation is essential in planning sales dialogues and presentations. Because buyers make competitive comparisons in their decision processes, salespeople should be prepared for it. This section of the planning template asks the salesperson to identify key competitors and to specify their strengths and weaknesses. By knowing their own product's strengths and weaknesses as well as those of their competitors, salespeople are better equipped to articulate customer value relative to their competitors. This competitive positioning is important, as most major purchase decisions are made in a highly competitive business environment. If the prospect is already buying a similar product, knowledge about the current supplier can give the salesperson critical insight into which buying motives and product attributes are likely to be affecting the buyer's decisions.

buying motives A need-activated drive to search for and acquire a solution to resolve a need or problem; the most important factors from the customer's perspective in making a purchase decision.

rational buying motives Typically relate to the economics of the situation, including cost, profitability, quality, services offered, and the total value of the seller's offering as perceived by the customer.

emotional buying motives Includes such motives as security, status, and the need to be liked; sometimes difficult for salespeople to uncover these motives.

features Qualities or characteristics of a product or service that are designed to provide value to a buyer.

benefits The added value or favourable outcome derived from features of the product or service the seller offers.

Section 6: Beginning the Sales Dialogue

Section 6 addresses the critical first few minutes of the sales call. During this period, salespeople will greet the prospect and introduce themselves, if necessary. There is typically some brief polite conversation between the salesperson and buyer as the salesperson is welcomed to the buyer's office, then both parties are usually eager to get down to business as quickly as possible. It is recommended that the salesperson propose an agenda, to which there may or may not have been previous agreement. Then, depending on the situation, the salesperson will proceed with questions designed to assess the prospect's situation, discover their needs, or make a transition into a sales dialogue or presentation. A typical first few minutes might sound like this:

Buyer: Come on in, Pat. I am John Jones. Nice to meet you. *(Introduction/greeting.)*

Seller: Mr. Jones, I am Pat Devlin with XYZ Company. Nice to meet you, too. I appreciate the time that you are spending with me today. *(Thanks, acknowledges importance of the buyer's time.)*

Buyer: Glad you could make it. We have had a lot of cancellations lately because of the bad weather. Did you have any problems driving over from Montreal? *(Polite conversation may last for several minutes depending on the buyer-seller relationship and on how much the buyer wants to engage in this sort of conversation.)*

Seller: Not really, it was pretty smooth today. I know you are busy, so I thought we could talk about a couple of key ways I think we can really help you build market share with your end-user market. How does that sound? *(A simple illustration of getting the buyer to agree to the agenda.)*

Buyer: Sure, let us get right to it. What do you have in mind?

Seller: Well, based on our phone call last week, I believe that our training programs for your customer service representatives can improve your customer satisfaction ratings and customer retention. I can share the details with you over the next 20 minutes or so. *(Transition to a sales dialogue or presentation based on customer needs and customer value.)*

In planning the first few minutes of the sales call, salespeople should remind themselves to be friendly and positive. They should also remain flexible in terms of their proposed agenda—customers like to have an agenda but sometimes want to modify it. The salesperson should be prepared to make an adjustment on the spot. For example, in the previous dialogue, the prospect might have said, "Yes, I want to hear about your training programs for our customer service reps, but I am also interested in your thoughts on how we can build a service-based culture across our entire marketing organization." The salesperson might respond accordingly, "I would be happy to do that. In fact, let me start with an overview that shows you the big picture from a strategy and company culture perspective, then later I will show you how the customer service training piece fits into the overall strategy. How does that sound?"

These first few minutes are critical in the trust-building process. By showing sensitivity to customer needs and opinions, and by asking questions to clarify the customer's perspective, salespeople demonstrate a customer orientation. Salespeople can demonstrate their expertise and competence by being sharp and well prepared. First impressions are crucial in all human interactions, so time spent on planning the first few minutes is a good investment on the salesperson's part. But remember that the planning template is not intended as a script. It is imperative that salespeople think logically—and from the buyer's point of view—in planning what to say after greeting the customer.

Planning the first few minutes of a sales dialogue can help the salesperson make a positive impression and build trust by exhibiting a customer orientation and demonstrating his or her sales expertise.

Initiating Contact Kim Davenport, district manager for Shering-Plough, discusses the importance of making a good first impression and looking professional in "Professional Selling in the 21st Century: Making a Good First Impression."

In planning the first few minutes of the sales dialogue or presentation, there are few ironclad rules. Instead, the situation and the prospect's preferences the appropriate sequence—but a few general rules do apply:

- Following an adequate introduction of the salesperson and the salesperson's company, the salesperson should use questions, careful listening, and confirmation statements to clarify and define explicit customer needs and motives as related to his or her offering.

- The salesperson should present benefits in order of importance according to the prospect's needs and motives, and these benefits may be repeated during the presentation and at the conclusion of the presentation.

- If the sales presentation is a continuation of one or more previous sales calls, the salesperson should make a quick summary of what has been agreed on in the past, moving quickly into the prospect's primary area of interest.

- As a general rule, the salesperson should not focus on pricing issues until the prospect's needs have been defined and the salesperson has shown how those needs can be addressed with the product or service being sold. After prospects fully understand how the product or service meets their needs, they can make informed judgments on price/value issues.

Obviously, the first few minutes of the sales call will be greatly influenced by previous interaction (if any) between the buyer and the salesperson. For example, if

PROFESSIONAL SELLING IN THE 21ST CENTURY

Making a Good First Impression

Kim Davenport, district manager for Shering-Plough, has seen his industry change since 1977 regarding what is accepted as professional appearance. Salespeople are allowed to wear beards and mustaches as long as they are groomed properly (i.e., short, neatly trimmed, not shaggy). What salespeople are allowed to wear has changed dramatically over the years. Today (particularly during the summer season) men and women sales representatives routinely wear short-sleeve golf shirts that have Shering-Plough's name on the front for identification. Davenport says it is almost a necessity in cities like Toronto, where temperatures can reach 80°C or more in the summer. First impressions are still important according to Davenport, and looking professional is the key. Dressing attractively and giving special attention to grooming will always pay off.

previous sales calls have established buyer needs and the buyer has agreed to a sales presentation, the first few minutes will be quite different than if this is the first sales call on this prospect. The ADAPT questioning process (refer to Chapter 4) can be used in part or whole to acquire needed information and make a transition to the sales dialogue or presentation. As a guide, the salesperson should respect the buyer's time and get to the presentation as soon as circumstances allow. The salesperson should not rush to get to the presentation and certainly should not launch into a presentation without establishing buyer needs and interest in it.

Section 7: Anticipating Questions and Objections

For reasons to be explained fully in Chapter 8, prospects will almost always have questions and objections that salespeople must be prepared to answer. In the planning stages, salespeople can prepare by asking themselves, "If I were the buyer, what would I want to be certain about before I make a purchase?" By anticipating these issues and preparing responses, salespeople can increase their chances of ultimate success.

Section 8: Earning Prospect Commitment

As sales dialogues and presentations progress, there eventually comes a critical time to ask for a customer's purchase decision. In many cases, this is an obvious point in the sales conversation, but at other times the salesperson may feel the need to probe to see if the timing is right. Earning a commitment from a customer as discussed in Chapter 8 should be a natural step in the conversation, not a forced or high-pressure attempt by the salesperson. Although circumstances will dictate exactly when and how commitment will be sought, a preliminary action plan for seeking customer commitment should be part of the overall planning process. Most buyers expect the salesperson to seek a commitment—and, if the commitment is sought at the right time, buyers appreciate that effort from the salesperson.

Section 9: Building Value through Follow-Up Action

Finally, the salesperson must always be looking for ways to enhance the relationship and move it in a positive direction. The salesperson should always make a note of any promises that he or she has made during the sales calls and especially during the proposal presentation. The buyer may ask for information that the salesperson is not prepared to give during the presentation. By taking notes, the salesperson ensures that the appropriate follow-up activities will happen.

This planning template for sales dialogues and presentations is an extremely useful tool for all salespeople, especially inexperienced salespeople. It guarantees that all the appropriate steps are covered and that all the pertinent information needed is collected. Using this template will make the task of customizing sales dialogues and presentations easier.

LO6
Engaging the Customer

most initial sales calls on new prospects require an appointment. Requesting an appointment accomplishes several desirable outcomes. First, the salesperson is letting the prospect know that he or she thinks the prospect's time is important. Second, there is a better chance that the salesperson will receive the undivided attention of the prospect during the sales call. Third, setting appointments is a good tool to assist the salesperson in effective time and territory management. The importance of setting appointments is clearly proclaimed in a survey of secretaries, administrative assistants, and other "gatekeepers" responsible for scheduling appointments. A majority of respondents thought that arriving unannounced to make a sales call is a violation of business etiquette.[5] Given this rather strong feeling of those who represent buyers, it is a good idea to request an appointment if there is any doubt about whether one is required. The "An Ethical Dilemma" demonstrates the importance of trust and why doing an end run around a gatekeeper is unacceptable.

© DEAN MITCHELL/SHUTTERSTOCK

An Ethical Dilemma

Mary Munoz has been selling computer systems for more than ten years. She has not had the success she once had in telephoning prospects and setting appointments. She stumbled onto a technique one day to get past the gatekeeper by suggesting to the secretary that she was conducting research and their company had been selected to participate. All she needed was a few minutes of the data processing manager's time. Munoz was surprised to find how easy it was now to get past the gatekeeper. She was having a great deal of success with this method. What do you think of Munoz's tactics? Is there any potential for future problems?

A salesperson can request an appointment by phone, mail (including email), or personal contact. By far, setting appointments by telephone is the most popular method. Combining mail and telephone communications to seek appointments is also commonplace. Regardless of the communication vehicle used, salespeople can improve their chances of getting an appointment by following three simple directives: give the prospect a reason why an appointment should be granted; request a specific amount of time; and suggest a specific time for the appointment. These tactics recognize that prospects are busy individuals who do not spend time idly.

In giving a reason that the appointment should be granted, a well-informed salesperson can appeal to the prospect's primary buying motive as related to one of the benefits of the salesperson's offering. Be specific. For example, it is better to say that "you can realize gross margins averaging 35 percent on our product line" than "our margins are really quite attractive."

Specifying the amount of time needed to make the sales presentation alleviates some of the anxiety a busy prospect feels at the idea of spending some of his or her already scarce time. It also helps the prospect if the salesperson suggests a time and date for the sales call. It is very difficult for busy individuals to respond to a question such as, "What would be a good time for

© I LOVE IMAGES/JUPITER IMAGES

Most buyers and gatekeepers prefer that salespeople make an appointment for their initial sales call. Telephone calls are the most popular means of arranging appointments.

you next week?" In effect, the prospect is being asked to scan his or her entire calendar for an opening. If a suggested time and date is inconvenient, the interested prospect will typically suggest another. Once a salesperson has an appointment with the prospect and all the objectives have been established, the salesperson should send a fax or an email that outlines the agenda for the meeting and reminds the buyer of the appointment.

Visit **sell.nelson.com** to find the resources you need today!

Located at the back of the textbook are rip-out Chapter Review cards. Make sure you also go online to check out other tools that SELL offers to help you successfully pass your course.

- Flashcards
- Glossary
- PowerPoint Notes

- Role-Play Videos
- Games
- Interactive Quizzing

PREPARING FOR A SALES CALL
Background

Pat Strickland is a highly successful independent sales consultant who works with companies that are trying to sell into major retail chains, such as Walmart, Home Depot, and Rona. Pat's brother, Steve Strickland, is a recent university graduate and a member of a sales team for John Deere. His team sells riding lawn mowers and recently the sales team targeted Home Depot as a potential customer. The sales team has met with Beth Jackson, Home Depot's lead

buyer for riding mowers, and established that Home Depot is interested in at least discussing the possibility of stocking John Deere's products.

Current Situation

In a recent conversation, Steve asked Pat to take a look at some key parts of his sales team's plan for an upcoming meeting with Beth Jackson. Steve's team is using the Sales Dialogue Template that he learned about in his professional selling course in university to produce a written plan for selling to Home Depot. Steve's team has completed the first four sections of the template (see Exhibit A).

EXHIBIT A
John Deere's Partial Plan for Selling to Home Depot

1. Prospect Information
A. Key person information

Company Name: Home Depot	**Type of Business:** Equipment Manufacturer
Prospect's Name: Key Decision Maker: Beth Jackson	**Job Title:** Corporate Product Buyer

2. Customer Value Proposition: A brief statement of how you will add value to the prospect's business by meeting a need or providing an opportunity. Include a brief description of the product or service:

Our product will provide the Home Depot chain with a sellable product that is backed by a dependable and well-recognized company. John Deere can also provide Home Depot's customers with the highest quality mowers and superior product support. The product we propose Home Depot sells is the EZtrak Series Zero-Turn Mower: It features a heavy-duty frame for unmatched durability and mowing performance. This mower series contains engines that feature overhead valves and vertical crankshafts, which lead to a longer engine life.

3. Specific objective for this sales call (must require customer action):

To influence the Home Depot chain to carry the EZtrak Series Zero-Turn John Deere Mower. We would like to establish a 12-month contract with Home Depot for the sale of this product. John Deere is seeking to supply the chain with a quality residential series of mowers.

Continued

John Deere's Partial Plan for Selling to Home Depot—
Continued

4. Linking buying motives, benefits, support information, and reinforcement methods. This section should address the buying motives of all people who will be involved in the upcoming sales call.

A. *Buying motives:* What is most important to the prospect(s) in making a purchase decision? **Rational** motives include economic issues, such as quality, cost, service capabilities, and the strategic priorities of the prospect's company. **Emotional** motives include fear, status, and ego-related feelings. List all relevant buying motives in order of importance.	B. *Specific benefits matched to buying motives:* Benefits to be stressed are arranged in priority order (sequence to be followed unless prospect feedback during the presentation indicates an alternative sequence). Each benefit should correspond to one or more buying motives.	C. *Information needed to support claims for each benefit.*	D: *Where appropriate, methods for reinforcing verbal content (AV, collateral material, illustrations, testimonials, etc.)*
1. Service capabilities	1. Help stress customer service by handling complaints through John Deere 2. Less responsibility for Home Depot because John Deere holds warranties, etc.	1. Home Depot is a retail store—it deals with many companies and cannot handle specific product complaints 2. Home Depot is a retail store—it deals with many companies and cannot stay current on one specific product's warranties'	1. Internet (website), hotline, and internet, hotline & e-training (give Home Depot training manuals/videos) 2. John Deere will provide Home Depot with marketing materials that provide customers with warranty information
2. Quality product lines	1. Home Depot customers recognize brand names backed by a quality company	1. John Deere's marketing department (using independent researchers) does national surveys on brand recognition	1. Consumer reports, national marketing and advertising
3. Shared advertising expenses	1. Home Depot gets the benefit of John Deere's existing and current marketing of their product line OR Home Depot and John Deere could advertise together	1. John Deere is a nationally recognized company and it does provide its own advertising for its products (less expense for Home Depot and this specific product line)	1. Website, TV, brochures, magazines, etc.

Continued

John Deere's Partial Plan for Selling to Home Depot—*Continued*

4. Cost incentives	1. John Deere's ability to provide financing for Home Depot's customers	1. Home Depot's employees receive training on how to set up financing for customers who are purchasing a John Deere product	1. Training from John Deere, support hotlines for employees and customers

Steve explained that his sales manager at John Deere wanted to review the plan in a few days and that he would appreciate having Pat's expert opinions before his sales team met with the sales manager. When Steve turned over the partial plan to Pat, he said: "The plan is tentative at this point, so anything you can tell us to make it better will be much appreciated. We know it may take more than one sales call on Home Depot to get the business, so this plan may have to change as we move along." Pat promised to read the plan over the weekend and give Steve some feedback on Monday morning.

Questions

1. What else does the John Deere team need to know to be well prepared for upcoming sales calls with Home Depot?
2. In the role of Pat Strickland, what specific comments do you have on the template he gave you?

The Overhead Door Company

Background

Manon Dion sells for The Overhead Door Company. She has sold garage doors to contractors and individual home owners for two years. When Dion first began selling, she used to introduce herself and the name of her company. Next, she made a brief opening remark and then moved quickly into her presentation. Although this resulted in selling many garage doors, Dion thought that there must be a better method.

Role Play

Characters: Manon Dion, sales representative; customer

Scene 1: *Location*—Dion is on the phone calling a new prospect.
Action—Dion introduces herself. Role-play Dion's introduction and try different approach techniques.

Questions

After completing the role play, address the following questions:

1. Do you think some openings are more effective than others?
2. Which ones do you find effective?
3. Which approach techniques do you find difficult to use? Why?

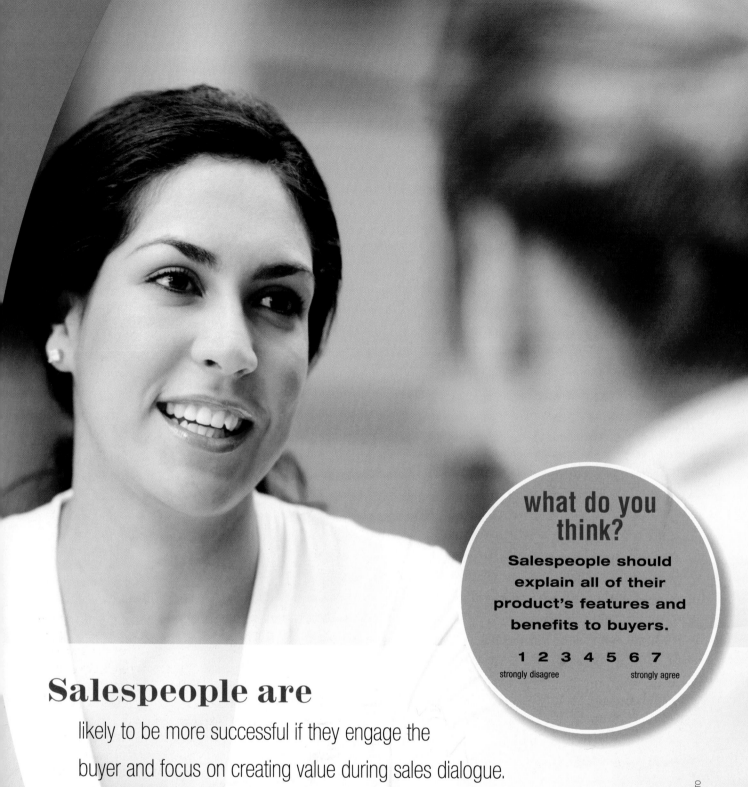

what do you think?

Salespeople should explain all of their product's features and benefits to buyers.

1 2 3 4 5 6 7

strongly disagree   strongly agree

Salespeople are

likely to be more successful if they engage the buyer and focus on creating value during sales dialogue.

7

Sales Dialogue: Creating and Communicating Value

After completing this chapter, you should be able to

LO1 Describe the key characteristics of effective sales dialogue.

LO2 Describe the differences among features, potential benefits, and confirmed benefits, and describe the role they play in benefits selling.

LO3 Describe how verbal support can be used to communicate value in an interesting and understandable manner.

LO4 Discuss how sales aids can engage and involve buyers.

LO5 Explain how salespeople can support product claims.

LO6 Discuss the special considerations involved in sales dialogue with groups.

Introduction

The past 10 years have witnessed a remarkable transformation in the professional selling landscape. Competition is tougher, buyers are more demanding, and pressures on margins have increased, while product differences have been steadily whittled nearly out of existence.

Faced with these daunting challenges, many savvy sales organizations have turned to outside sales-training consultants to deliver the skills and knowledge necessary to gain an edge over ever-shifting customer demands. By working with hundreds of companies in a broad range of industries, top sales trainers enjoy a rare perspective on what does—and doesn't work—in the 21st-century sales marketplace.

Sam Reese, president and CEO of Miller Heiman, one of the world's top sales training organizations, says that his clients frequently comment on losing business when, with no apparent warning, a familiar buying process will erode, leaving them out in the cold.

"That's the number one thing we hear," Reese explains. "They'll say, 'Hey, I've been doing business with this client for 10 years, and then somehow we find we're not in the position we need to be in. New people are involved in the buying process. We now have all these new restrictions placed on us, and our guy in purchasing isn't calling the shots anymore.' That's a big one."

Naturally, two straight years of economic stagnation have only hastened this trend, driving upper-level executives to pay much closer attention to every dollar going out the door. As upper-level decision makers take greater interest in every purchase, product evaluators and purchasing agents located lower on the corporate ladder lose much of the power they once wielded to make value-based buying decisions.

Effective value selling today requires leapfrogging the low-level customer agents to sell to those upper-level folks who are genuinely empowered to buy based on more than simply product specs and price. But as Reese notes, selling to senior-level executives is a game with a different set of rules; success frequently means abandoning some of the tried and no-longer-true tactics that have been drilled into salespeople for generations.

"All the tactics and techniques around manipulation are out," he says. "That doesn't work anymore. You have to have the right product and the right solution, and it's a gradual process of making sure you meet all the customer's requirements. If you're selling the right way, you're not dealing with people who can be manipulated that way."

In contrast with the traditional hard-close route, Reese emphasizes the greater need today for respect and openness in the buyer-seller interaction.

"If you really believe in what you do, you want companies to make their decisions with all the information available. You want that because you passionately believe your company is the best at providing them with a solution. If you don't want that, then you need to take a hard look at what you're doing and what your company's doing. To me that's the definition of manipulation—hoping things don't surface for you to address that might put you at a disadvantage and make you weak because you can't deliver what the customer needs.

"Sales-training organizations have often spent most of their time teaching people how to know their products, their company and their competitors very well," he explains. "That needs to change. We need to teach people how to understand their customers' businesses. That's what makes the difference in whether you're perceived by the customer as yet another vendor peddling product—which is where you don't want to be—or as a true strategic resource who understands the customer's issues, challenges and opportunities."

Effective sales training today may be more forward-thinking, customer-focused and sophisticated than ever before, but it's also more complex, more demanding and frankly, more challenging to implement across a sales organization than the manipulative, hard-closing approaches that used to predominate. That's why sales trainers themselves have to work harder today, Reese says, not only to get the salespeople on board, but to create company-wide change that supports the new approach.

Ultimately, says Reese, what strategy a company employs to train its sales force reflects that company's attitude about the sales function and the job the salespeople themselves perform.

"For a long time, a lot of companies have really considered their salespeople as little more than glorified order-takers," he says. "But now that's changing and we're saying, 'No, they're not just order-takers, they're a real strategic asset.' Smart companies recognize that the sales force can be their most powerful strategic weapon. The way you sell can provide a huge strategic advantage—or disadvantage, for that matter. In the past, very few companies even understood this. But today that's changing, and the organizations that understand the concept and are putting powerful tools in the hands of the salespeople are the ones that are succeeding. And that's no coincidence."

Source: Malcolm Fleschner "The Value-Added Ladder." *Selling Power.* http://www.sellingpower.com/content/article.php?a=6242.

t he purpose of this chapter is to examine the keys to effective sales dialogue. The chapter provides an opportunity to apply what has been learned about building trust (Chapter 2), understanding buyers (Chapter 3), and communication skills (Chapter 4). It also builds on the information gathered during the prospecting stage of the sales process (Chapter 5) and the Sales Dialogue Template and section on "Beginning the Sales Dialogue" presented in Chapter 6. Chapter 8 expands on this chapter by addressing how to resolve buyer concerns and earn a commitment from a sales dialogue.

LO1
Effective Sales Dialogue

p reparing and completing this phase of the sales process successfully has been compared to doing surgery in that it is complex and requires preparation, knowledge, and skill.[1] Before conducting surgery, the doctor has acquired a great deal of relevant information from a variety of sources and developed a comprehensive understanding of the patient's problems and needs. Based on this understanding of the patient's needs, the surgeon uses his or her training and skills in combination with an assortment of tools to conduct a surgical procedure unique to the individual patient's needs. Continuing the analogy, up to the point of the presentation in the selling process the salesperson has been developing his or her knowledge and understanding of the buyer's situation and needs. Now, in the form of an effective presentation, the salesperson presents a solution that is specific and customized to the needs of the buyer, illustrates and demonstrates the benefits of the solution, and confirms the buyer's belief in and desire to obtain the benefits.

Good salespeople are very much like good surgeons in that they are serious in what they do and leave nothing to chance. They work with the prospective buyer to identify, diagnose, and clarify unsatisfied needs or problems and then show the buyer how much better the situation would be by purchasing the proposed product or service. As discussed previously, it will normally take several sales calls to complete a sales dialogue. Many firms plan for multiple sales calls in their sales process. For example, salespeople at Northwestern Mutual Financial Network conduct an initial "fact finding" sales call to identify the financial situation and objectives of potential clients. Then, one or more subsequent sales

© YURI ARCURS/SHUTTERSTOCK

LO2
Needs-Gap Analysis

the simple fact that a qualified prospect has a need that can be met by the salesperson's product or service does not necessarily translate into a purchase. Need alone is not sufficient. A prospect will buy after concluding that by purchasing the salesperson's product, he or she will be substantially better off. Given the high level of competition in most industries, salespeople must have a clear understanding of their customers' needs to be considered seriously. Using a questioning sequence, such as SPIN or ADAPT (for a full discussion of these see Chapter 4, "Communication Skills"), the salesperson explores the buyer's situation to identify missed opportunities, dissatisfactions, needs, and problems. The salesperson must ask questions, probe for details, and listen carefully to what the prospective buyer says. This may take more than one sales call, depending on the amount of probing and clarifying that must take place to understand the prospect's needs. The salesperson's primary goal is to uncover the prospect's specific needs or problems and then focus on what products or services will solve the problem or meet the specific needs.

Based on the prospective buyer's identified and confirmed needs, the salesperson reviews possible product and service options to select or create a solution that best satisfies the buyer's requirements. The salesperson describes and builds desire for the recommended solution by detailing features of the solution as they relate to the prospective buyer's specific needs and demonstrating the benefits provided by each relevant feature. Features and benefits are linked to the buyer's specific needs in a way that generates the buyer's desire to purchase and acquire the recommended solution.

calls are used to present strategies for achieving these financial objectives.

Professional selling classes often require students to role play a sales dialogue. This has been found to be an effective way for students to learn about and develop skills for a sales dialogue. We will cover a complete sales dialogue in one sales call in this chapter and Chapter 8.

The keys to effective sales dialogue are presented in Exhibit 7.1. The importance of planning and practising were emphasized in Chapter 6. This planning and practice should focus on an organized sales dialogue and not a canned sales presentation. Salespeople who practise asking questions, getting different responses, and adapting to these responses appropriately are better prepared to be successful in a real sales dialogue. Proper planning and practice provide an important foundation for effective sales dialogue. We discuss the remaining keys in the rest of this chapter.

> Salespeople must diagnose customer problems before prescribing solutions.

LINKING SOLUTIONS TO NEEDS

It is unlikely that the customer will be interested in every detail of the salesperson's product or service offering, and certainly some aspects will be more important to a particular prospect than will others. Essentially, salespeople

---

EXHIBIT 7.1
Keys to Effective Sales Dialogue

The most effective sales dialogues

1. Are planned and practised by salespeople.
2. Encourage buyer feedback.
3. Focus on creating value for the buyer.
4. Present value in an interesting and understandable way.
5. Engage and involve the buyer.
6. Support customer value through objective claims.

© From INGRAM/LAFORGE/AVILA/SCHWEPKER. *Professional Selling*, 4E. © 2008 South-Western, a part of Cengage Learning, Inc. Reproduced by permission. www.cengage.com/permissions.

should strive to communicate three crucial factors: (1) how buyer needs will be met or how an opportunity can be realized as a result of a purchase, (2) how the product features translate, in a functional sense, into benefits for the buyer, and (3) why the buyer should purchase from you as opposed to a competitor salesperson. To assist salespeople in effectively communicating these three factors, most sales training programs emphasize a form of benefit selling, sometimes referred to as **FAB** (for features, advantages, and benefits).

Benefit Selling

any given product or service comprises multiple features that have the capability to produce different potential benefits and confirmed benefits. **Features** are traditionally defined as a quality or characteristic of a product or service that is designed to provide value to a buyer. Features answer the question, "What is it?" A benefit is the value provided by a feature to the buyer, and addresses the always present question, "What's in it for me?" However, not all benefits will be valued at the same level by all buyers, thus the categorization of *potential benefits* versus *confirmed benefits*. A **potential benefit** describes a general form of value that is assumed to be of importance by the salesperson but is not yet acknowledged as such by the buyer. Once the prospective buyer acknowledges the importance of a benefit to his or her buying situation, it is a **confirmed benefit**. Because confirmed benefits represent customer value that is provided by the proposed solution, some sales programs refer to one or more confirmed benefits as the value proposition.

Research tells us that buyers do not purchase products and features. Rather, buyers purchase the value and satisfaction provided to them in the form of relevant benefits. Consequently, features have very little persuasive power. Salespeople can be more effective by selling benefits rather than features. However, to be most effective and gain the buyer's confirmation, stated benefits must be relevant to the prospective buyer's needs and phrased in a format that clearly translates the benefit from a generic one-size-fits-all description to a unique and customized benefit that has immediate meaning for the prospective buyer. While the one-size-fits-all benefit statements do not require much thinking on the part of the salesperson, they typically do not pass from potential benefits to confirmed benefits. As illustrated in Exhibit 7.2, benefit statements that build on the salesperson's understanding and appreciation of the buyer's situation and are tailored to the individual buyer's needs and expectations are more likely to be confirmed by the buyer as being important.

By themselves, features and potential benefits risk the buyer thinking or asking, "So what?" Confirmed benefits are persuasive and advance the sale forward on the basis of creating added value for the buyer. This is the foundation of benefit selling. In benefit selling, the salesperson describes the benefits as they relate to specific needs of the prospective buyer and limits the role of features to simply supporting and evidencing the presence of confirmed benefits. This combination of a specific feature and its meaningful benefit statement is referred to as a selling point. As the following illustrate, selling points should be phrased in a conversational tone and clearly describe the benefit in a manner that emphasizes its applicability and importance to the individual buyer:

- "This copier automatically selects the paper size that best matches your original document. Based on the experience of other customers using this model, it will speed up reproduction of longer reports and reduce waste. Not only will this save you money by reducing waste, but it will also increase the efficiency of your office staff, which you expressed as one of your major concerns."

- "The design of this golf club will give you an expanded sweet spot for maximum ball contact. This will not only increase the distance of your shots but will also provide the improved accuracy that you are looking for."

- "Our unique use of overnight express for merchandise delivery reduces your need for backup inventory while eliminating the possibility for being out of stock and disappointing customers, which you mentioned was costing you business."

Most sales trainers and successful salespeople agree that showing the buyer potential benefits of relevant features will sometimes lead to successful sales calls. A sale may be made but, if not, at least the dialogue has been advanced in a positive manner, which sets the stage for subsequent sales calls. However, without question, the chances of a successful sales call are greatly improved by getting the buyer to agree that one or more benefits are indeed important to him or her.

The use of confirmed benefits is further explained in "Professional Selling in the 21st Century: Using Confirmed Benefits."[2] In selecting specific features and benefits to be stressed, salespeople should focus on any unique benefits not offered by the competition, as long as the benefits are of interest to the prospective buyer. These might include product benefits and nonproduct benefits, such as delivery, financing, extraordinary customer service, or additional sales support available to the buyer.[*]

Encouraging Buyer Feedback

In a productive sales dialogue, the salesperson continually assesses and evaluates the reactions and responses of prospective buyers. The SPIN or ADAPT questioning processes are designed to get the buyer to provide feedback to specific questions the salesperson asks. During the presentation portion of a sales dialogue, the most successful salespeople encourage buyer feedback. In contrast, less successful salespeople often rush through the entire presentation from beginning to end and never stop to invite feedback from the buyer. Feedback from the prospective buyer provides the salesperson with important information measuring the climate between the salesperson and the buyer, the buyer's level of interest in the product's features and benefits, whether the salesperson has successfully responded to the buyer's concerns, and how well the presentation is progressing toward the buyer making a purchase decision.

EXHIBIT 7.2
Features, Potential Benefits, and Confirmed Benefits

Salesperson in golf shop selling Titleist golf balls to a weekend golfer.	Confirmed Benefit?	Explanation
Feature: Solid 1.58" diameter core		
Potential Benefit: Higher initial velocity and launch angle.	No	The typical weekend golf customer would not immediately see how the benefit of higher velocity and launch angle will benefit him or her.
Feature: Solid 1.58" diameter core		
Potential Benefit: Provides more distance on shots for the typical golfer and lowers your score.	Yes	Longer shots and lower scores are a primary interest of the typical weekend golfer. Customers can immediately understand the benefit to themselves.

Selling a new Frito-Lay snack to a regional supermarket chain.	Confirmed Benefit?	Explanation
Feature: Daily delivery		
Potential Benefit: Retailer can reduce inventory costs.	No	This prospective buyer considers inventory costs a regular cost of doing business. The potential benefit is not perceived as being important.
Feature: Daily delivery		
Potential Benefit: Assures product freshness, which will lead to high customer satisfaction.	Yes	Prospective customer places tremendous emphasis on customer satisfaction. Consequently, this potential benefit is confirmed as being valuable.

© From INGRAM/LAFORGE/AVILA/SCHWEPKER. *Professional Selling*, 4E. © 2008 South-Western, a part of Cengage Learning, Inc. Reproduced by permission. www.cengage.com/permissions.

---

*Page 163–165: INGRAM/LAFORGE/AVILA/SCHWEPKER. *Professional Selling*, 4E. © 2008 South-Western, a part of Cengage Learning, Inc. Reproduced by permission. www.cengage.com/permissions.

© KEMALBAS/ISTOCKPHOTO

Using Confirmed Benefits

Jamie Howard, vice president of Active Solutions, emphasizes selling confirmed benefits rather than features to advance the sale.

In today's competitive business environment, it has become more difficult for sales professionals to separate their solutions from the competition. It is important to realize that what advances the sale to the next step is not always directly related to the features of the product, but instead to the value the benefits of the product creates.

The contract furniture industry is as competitive as any other industry. When a large corporation is in the market for new furniture, as many as five competitors will be asked to bid. In one high-profile project last year, creating value through showing our solution's benefits was the only chance to win. The products being proposed had very similar features and our price was slightly higher. My team had to develop a strategic plan to create value for what we were offering. When everything is perceived to be similar, features will not be the deciding factor in the client's decision. The majority of the time the client will make his or her decision based on other variables. In this case, our price was higher and the features were similar. We had to create value for our product by focusing on the benefits rather than the features. The benefits had to be tied to the buyer's needs, which we developed during the questioning phase of the sales cycle. By identifying the client's needs, we were able to present the confirmed benefits that created added value over the competition. The customer's perceived value of our solution separated us from the competition. Following months of strategic meetings, we won the high-profile project—the largest in our company's history. The client acknowledged that understanding how our solution benefited them was the key in their decision-making process because we had solved a problem for them instead of just offering a product.

As detailed and discussed in Chapter 4, the observant salesperson can receive a great deal of continual feedback in the form of the buyer's nonverbal cues. In addition to observing nonverbal cues, high-performing salespeople incorporate verbal probes at key points to evaluate the buyer's interest and assess the progress of the sales dialogue. These verbal probes are typically confirmatory forms of questions in search of simple "yes" or "no" responses from the buyer.

The phrases **check-backs** or **response checks** have become common names for this form of questioning—seeking feedback from the buyer. Although feedback can be sought at any point in the conversation, checkbacks are commonly employed at two key points: (1) after a specific feature-benefit sequence in to confirm the benefit and better assess the prospective buyer's level of interest and (2) following the response to an objection in order to evaluate the level to which the salesperson has handled the problem. Exhibit 7.3

check-backs or response checks Questions salespeople use throughout a sales dialogue to generate feedback from the buyer.

EXHIBIT 7.3
Illustrative Examples of Check-Backs

- "How does this sound to you?"
- "Does this make sense to you so far?"
- "Would this feature be useful to you in your current operations?"
- "What do you think?"
- "So is this something that would be valuable to you?"
- "Isn't that great?"
- "Do you like this colour?"
- "From your comment, it sounds as if you would want the upgraded memory. Is that correct?"
- "Does that answer your concern?"
- "Would this be an improvement over what you are doing right now?"
- "Is this what you had in mind?"

advance the presentation toward gaining the buyer's purchase commitment. A series of positive response-checks indicates that the buyer is nearing a purchase decision. The more positive affirmations a salesperson receives in relation to his or her response-checks, the easier the final purchase decision becomes and the more confident the prospective buyer is in having made the appropriate decision. Specific examples of check-backs within a sales dialogue will be presented at appropriate places in the remainder of this chapter.

verbal support The use of voice characteristics, examples and anecdotes, and comparisons and analogies to make sales dialogue interesting and understandable.

provides an illustrative selection of check-back examples that salespeople indicate are typical of those they commonly use.

The effective use of check-backs offers a number of advantages. Probably the most evident is increased buyer interaction. Asking for buyer feedback helps to ensure that the dialogue remains a two-way, collaborative exchange. The effective use of response-checks also helps the salesperson evaluate the level of the buyer's understanding and keeps the salesperson on the right track. If feedback indicates a lack of understanding—or even worse, a lack of interest—on the part of a prospective buyer, the salesperson must make changes to improve alignment with the needs and expectations of the buyer. In contrast, positive feedback indicating a high level of understanding and interest on the part of the buyer would signal the salesperson to stay the course and

Salespeople need to vary the pitch and speed of their speech during sales dialogue.

© U.P.IMAGES_PHOTO/SHUTTERSTOCK

LO3
Interesting and Understandable Sales Dialogue

Once confirmed benefits have been identified, the salesperson needs to present key selling points in a manner that is interesting and understandable to the buyer. The presentation should focus on the buyer and is intended to gain and hold the buyer's attention, and to increase the buyer's understanding and retention of the information provided by the salesperson. **Verbal support** elements include voice characteristics, examples and anecdotes, and comparisons and analogies. Using these elements appropriately can produce interesting and understandable sales dialogue.

VOICE CHARACTERISTICS

The key aspects of **voice characteristics** are the pitch and speed of speech. Varying and changing pitch on key words adds emphasis and increases impact. It is analogous to putting different colours and hues into your voice. The increased intensity and vividness grab attention, hold interest, and help the buyer remember what is said. Fluctuating the speed of speech can add emphasis and guide the buyer's attention to selected points of the presentation. Important details—especially quantitative information—should be provided at a slower, more careful pace. Less critical information can be presented at a faster pace to grab the buyer's attention and redirect his or her interest. Changes in volume can be used to add emphasis to an important phrase or topic, and a softer volume— almost a whisper—can build intrigue and pull the prospect into the conversation. Altering volume from loud to soft can better grab and hold the buyer's interest while simultaneously adding clarity and emphasis to increase understanding.

As emphasized in "Professional Selling in the 21st Century: Energizing Sales Dialogues," a salesperson can know his or her product inside and out, but if there is no energy and passion in his or her voice, the potential for making the sale will be seriously impaired. As voice coach Jeffrey Jacobi emphasizes, "Your voice and how you use it determines how people respond to you. The sound of your voice relays to people whether you are confident, likable, boring, unpleasant, honest, or even dishonest."[3] Voice quality can be used to bring excitement and drama to the presentation by doing three things: varying the pitch, fluctuating the speed, and altering the volume.

EXAMPLES AND ANECDOTES

An **example** is a brief description of a specific instance used to illustrate features and benefits. Examples may

© SMITH COLLECTION/GETTY IMAGES

voice characteristics
The pitch and speed of speech, which salespeople should vary to emphasize key points.

example A brief description of a specific instance used to illustrate features and benefits of a product or service.

be either real or hypothetical and are used to further explain and emphasize a topic of interest. A production equipment salesperson might further explain the purpose of an infrared guidance control by using the following example:

If the feedstock coming off the main paper roll gets out of line by as little as 1.5 millimetres, the infrared guidance control will sense it and automatically make the correct adjustments. This prevents a paper jam from shutting down your package printing line and costing lost time and wasted product.

An **anecdote** is a type of example presented in the form of a story describing a specific incident or occurrence. Stories can be very effective in keeping a buyer interested and helping the buyer understand the solution a salesperson presents. The production equipment salesperson might use an anecdote such as the following:

One of my customers was having a problem with paper jams that were shutting down the firm's package printing line. Similar to your situation, there was a lot of lost production time and wasted product. We installed the infrared guidance control, which automatically adjusts the paper roll when it gets off by as little as 1.5 millimetres. This reduced paper jams, resulting in less wasted product and more production time for the customer.

A salesperson's use of examples and anecdotes keeps the buyer interested, brings clarity into the presentation, and improves the buyer's understanding and retention of what the salesperson is presenting. The use of an example and anecdote in a sales dialogue example for customer service training follows.

Seller: Customized training programs can be very effective. For example, one of our clients increased customer satisfaction ratings by 25 percent after we implemented a customized program for their reps. (*Example*). Is this the type of improvement you are looking for? (*Check-back*)

Seller: Customers of the XYZ Company were very dissatisfied with the service the firm's reps provided. We reviewed the customers' complaints, met with the customer service reps, identified the main problems, and created a specific training program to deal with the key problems. After completion of the sales training program, customer complaints decreased by 75 percent

(*anecdote*). What do you think about these results? (*Check-back*)

COMPARISONS AND ANALOGIES

A **comparison** is a statement that points out and illustrates the similarities between two points. Comparisons increase the buyer's level of interest and understanding of information. A salesperson wanting to add emphasis and meaning to his or her verbal description of the Honda S2000's performance capabilities might use a direct comparison to the performance capabilities of a competitive model that the prospective buyer might also be considering:

You have the performance specifications on both cars, and as you can see . . . the 6-second 0 to 60 performance of the S2000 outperforms the Audi TT by a good 10 percent. This is a large difference in performance.

A salesperson for Newell-Rubbermaid might illustrate the benefits of setting up an end-of-aisle display of special occasion containers by using the following comparison to the store manager's sales goals for the product category:

Sales data from stores similar to yours indicate that adding an end-of-aisle display for these seasonal containers will increase their sales by 35 to 40 percent during the fourth quarter holiday season. This would certainly help you achieve— and possibly exceed—the store's goal of a 20-percent increase for this general product category.

anecdote A type of example that is provided in the form of a story describing a specific incident or occurrence.

comparison A statement that points out and illustrates the similarities between two points.

Salespeople can use comparisons to communicate effectively with buyers.

© JM5 WENN PHOTOS/NEWSCOM

analogy A special and useful form of comparison that explains one thing in terms of another.

sales aids The use of printed materials, electronic materials, and product demonstrations to engage and involve buyers.

An **analogy** is a special and useful form of comparison that explains one thing in terms of another. Analogies are useful for explaining something complex by allowing the buyer to better visualize it in terms of something familiar that is easier to understand. A BMW salesperson presenting to an Air Force pilot the option of an in-car global positioning system map and tracking system might use the following analogy:

Having the onboard map and tracking system is like having a friendly flight controller with you on every trip. You will always know exactly where you are and what route you should travel to reach your destination. You will never get lost or be delayed because you took the wrong turn.

An example of a comparison and an analogy in a sales dialogue example is presented here.

Seller: We will incorporate your reps throughout the design and execution of our training program. This gives the reps some ownership in the program. Our competitors, in contrast, develop their programs based on what management tells them is important. (*Comparison*). Do you think your reps would respond well to being included in all aspects of the training program? (*Check-back*)

Seller: Developing a customized sales training program is like planning for a family vacation. Everyone in the family is likely to be more excited about the vacation if they are involved in all aspects of the planning process. (*Analogy*) What do you think about involving your reps in all aspects of the training program? (*Check-back*)

LO4
Engaging and Involving the Buyer

Simply informing the prospect about the benefits and their value to the buyer is seldom sufficient to generate the level of interest and desire required to result in a purchase decision. To maximize the effectiveness of the sales dialogue, salespeople use various **sales aids** to engage and involve the buyer throughout the sales interaction. These sales aids also help to capture and hold the buyer's attention, boost the buyer's understanding, increase the believability of the claims, and build the buyer's retention of information (see Exhibit 7.4). Not all sales aids are suitable for all products, selling situations, or buyers. Nor should a salesperson feel the need to use each and every tool in any given sales call. A salesperson should use the sales aids that will engage and involve each buyer most effectively in a particular sales dialogue. Many times, the selling organization provides these sales tools. However, experienced salespeople are quick to comment that some of their most effective sales aids are those that they developed themselves for specific prospects and selling situations.

TYPES OF SALES AIDS

Sales aids allow the salesperson to involve one or more of the buyer's senses in the presentation, help to illustrate features and confirmed benefits, and add clarity and dramatization to increase the effectiveness of a sales dialogue. The types of sales aids available to a salesperson include visual materials, electronic materials, and product demonstrations.

EXHIBIT 7.4
Reasons for Using Sales Aids

- Capture prospective buyer's attention.
- Generate interest in the recommended solution.
- Make presentations more persuasive.
- Increase the buyer's participation and involvement.
- Provide the opportunity for collaboration and two-way communication.
- Add clarity and enhance the prospect's understanding.
- Provide supportive evidence and proof to enhance believability.
- Augment the prospect's retention of information.
- Enhance the professional image of the salesperson and selling organization.

Visual Materials

Visual materials represent a variety of sales aids intended to engage and involve buyers visually. The major types of visual materials are printed materials, photographs and illustrations, and charts and graphs. Exhibit 7.5 provides salespeople with a number of tips for preparing printed materials and visuals.

Printed materials include such items as brochures, pamphlets, catalogues, articles, reprints, reports, testimonial letters, and guarantees. Well-designed printed materials can help the salesperson communicate, explain, and emphasize key points during a sales dialogue. They are designed to summarize important features and benefits and can be effectively used not only during the presentation but also left behind as reminder pieces for the buyer after the salesperson has left. When printed materials are left with a buyer, the salesperson's name and contact information should be clearly printed on the material or an attached business card.

Photographs and illustrations are easy to produce and relatively inexpensive. Using images

© ART DIRECTORS & TRIP/ALAMY

> Printed materials are effective sales aids.

allows the salesperson to present a realistic portrayal of the product or service. Many products cannot be taken into a prospective buyer's office because of their size. A detailed image can give the prospect an idea of the product's appearance and size. Line drawings and diagrams can show the most important details of a product. Images are most effective when they illustrate and simplify a more complex product or feature and make it easy to communicate information about size, shape, construction, and use.

Charts and graphs are useful in showing trends and illustrating relationships. As such, they can show the prospect what the problem is costing them or how a solution might work. Charts and graphs often illustrate relationships by using bars, lines, circles, or squares. For example, a salesperson for an office equipment vendor might get the cost figures associated with the buyer's use of an outside copy centre for the previous two years. The salesperson could then use this information in a comparative bar graph to better illustrate the savings possible if the buyer owned a copier. Salespeople for a leading medical technology company use a chart format to compare the features and benefits of their product versus the competitors' equipment the buyer is considering.

visual materials Printed materials, photographs and illustrations, and charts and graphs used as sales aids.

EXHIBIT 7.5
Tips for Preparing Visual Materials

- Visual materials should be kept simple.
- When possible, use phrases and let the buyer's mind complete the sentences.
- Use the same layout and format throughout to tie the presentation together.
- Check for typographical and spelling errors.
- Use colours sparingly and for functional rather than decorative purposes.
- Leave plenty of white space; do not crowd the page.
- Each visual should present only one idea.
- Try to use a maximum of seven words per line and seven lines per visual.
- Where possible, use graphics (charts and graphs) rather than tables.
- Use bullet points to emphasize key points.
- Never read the presentation directly from the visual.
- Clearly label each visual with titles and headings to guide the prospective buyer.

The chart format succinctly and effectively supports statements of superiority made during the presentation.

Electronic Materials

Electronic materials include all sales aids in electronic format. These span individual slides and videos to complete multimedia presentations. As technology continues to develop, more options to use electronic materials become available to salespeople. Two examples are customized electronic presentations and online sales aid libraries.

Salespeople today can customize graphic presentations for each buyer. Customizing and enriching presentations by using electronic multimedia can be done inexpensively and in a fairly short time. Microsoft PowerPoint, for example, allows the salesperson to quickly build a complete, high-impact graphic presentation customized for an individual prospect. These powerful multimedia presentations might include pictures of products, as well as product demonstrations and competitive comparisons. The use of video has the advantage of both sound and action. The buyer can be taken on a virtual tour of the selling organization and see the product being produced or simultaneously see and hear a personal message from the president of the selling organization as well as testimonials from satisfied customers.

A rapidly growing trend is the development and use of online libraries of sales aids. Selling organizations typically develop these libraries for their salespeople's exclusive use. For example, GlaxoSmithKline provides salespeople with before-and-after slides to depict the effectiveness of a topical cream product. The slides show how the skin of most patients clears up after using the cream for three days. Hewlett-Packard maintains an extensive online database and library of sales aids that include product brochures and specification sheets, graphics, proposal templates, competitive comparisons, and an archive of PowerPoint presentations. Content can be downloaded and printed as is or customized to better fit a specific need.

Product Demonstrations

The product itself is often the most effective sales tool because it provides the prospective buyer with an opportunity for hands-on experience. When the actual product does not lend itself to being demonstrated, models can be used to represent and illustrate key features and benefits of the larger product. The value of an actual product demonstration is applicable to all types of products and services. For example, Boeing salespeople use scale models to give the buyer a detailed and realistic feel for the aircraft, which cannot be tucked into the salesperson's briefcase. As the sale progresses, the prospective buyer's team will be given actual hands-on experience with the real product. Simmons and Sealy, leading manufacturers of quality sleep products, require that their registered dealers have demonstration models of mattress sets on display and available for customers to try out. Major vendors of office furniture will set up a model office so that the prospective client can experience its actual use. Pharmaceutical companies provide doctors with samples of the product for trial use with selected patients.

As detailed in Exhibit 7.6, the salesperson should make sure the product being demonstrated is typical of what is being recommended. Furthermore, it should be checked to ensure that it is in good working order before the demonstration and that setup and removal do not detract from the presentation. The last thing the salesperson wants is to have to apologize for poor appearance or inadequate performance.

> Multimedia sales aids are being used more in sales dialogue.

© PR NEWSWIRE/NEWSCOM

EXHIBIT 7.6
Guidelines for Product Demonstrations

- Ensure the appearance of the product is neat and clean.
- Check for problem-free operation.
- Be confident and able to demonstrate the product skillfully.
- Practise using the product before the demonstration.
- Anticipate problems and have backup or replacement parts on hand.
- Make sure that setup and knockdown are easy and quick.

Whenever possible, it is important to have the buyer use the product instead of the salesperson demonstrating its use. For example, buyers often realize that many new software products have features that could be valuable to their firm. However, they may be reluctant to make a purchase because they think it will be too hard for their employees to learn to use the software. A salesperson could demonstrate the software to show how easy it is to use, but it would be more effective to have the buyer use the software to experience firsthand its ease of use.

USING SALES AIDS IN THE PRESENTATION

Practise! Practise! Practise! Rehearsal of the presentation is the final key to conducting effective sales dialogue. Understand what features are relevant and what benefits are meaningful to the prospective buyer in terms of value to be realized. Be confident in developing and using multiple sales aids to add impact to the presentation itself. Using the SPES Sequence can facilitate the effectiveness of presentation tools and sales aids: S = *State selling point and introduce the sales aid*; P = *Present the sales aid*; E = *Explain the sales aid*; S = *Summarize.*[5]

State the Selling Point and Introduce the Sales Aid

State the full selling point, including the feature and potential benefit, and then introduce the sales aid. For instance, "To demonstrate this benefit, I would like you to take a look at this video" or "This graph summarizes the increased performance you will experience with the Honda S2000." This prepares the buyer for the visual aid and informs him or her that attention is required.

Present the Sales Aid

Present the sales aid to the customer and allow a few moments for examination and familiarization before saying anything. For example, when using printed materials, place the material directly in front of the customer and allow it to be reviewed momentarily in silence. Allow the customer to review the sales aid and satisfy his or her natural curiosity before using it.

Explain the Sales Aid

No matter how carefully a sales aid is prepared, it will not be completely obvious. The customer will not necessarily understand the significance unless the salesperson provides a brief explanation. Do not rely on a chart or graph to illustrate fully the points being supported. Similarly, a prospect might enjoy a product demonstration yet totally miss the information or experience supporting the presentation. The salesperson should

> Salespeople can increase the success of a sales dialogue by using appropriate sales aids effectively.

point out the material information and explain how it supports his or her points.

Summarize

When you have finished explaining the significance of the sales aid, summarize its contribution and support and remove the sales aid. If not removed, its presence can distract the prospective buyer's attention from subsequent feature and benefit points.

The use of the SPES Sequence to use a sales aid in a customer service training program sales dialogue is presented here.

Seller: You mentioned earlier that your reps are not well prepared to deal with irate customers. I would like to show you a short video from a training program we developed for another firm. The video illustrates how we use role plays to help reps develop the skills to interact with irate customers effectively. (*State the selling point and introduce the sales aid*)

(*The salesperson shows the video to the buyer*)

Seller: Did you notice how everyone involved in the training program watched the role play carefully and was able to contribute comments to improve the interaction with the irate customer? (*Explain the sales aid*)

Buyer: The role play exercise did get everyone involved and produced some good ideas for improvement.

Seller: Although this is just one type of exercise we employ in our training programs, the role play produced some guidelines that all reps could use to deal with irate customers more effectively. (*Summarize*). Do you think this type of exercise would be valuable to your reps? (*Check-back*)

LO5
Supporting Product Claims

as discussed earlier in this chapter, confirmed benefits answer the buyer's question, "What is in it for me?" In a similar fashion, **proof providers**, such as statistics, testimonials, and case histories, can be used to preempt the buyer from asking, "Can you prove it?" or "Who says so?" Claims of benefits and value produced and provided to the buyer need to be backed up with evidence to highlight their believability.

STATISTICS

Statistics are facts that lend believability to claims of value and benefit. When available, statistics from authoritative, third-party sources carry the highest credibility. Among others, third-party sources include independent testing organizations and labs (e.g., *Consumer Reports*, Underwriters Laboratory), professional organizations (e.g., Risk and Insurance Management Society), research companies (e.g., PricewaterhouseCoopers), institutions (e.g., University of Toronto), and various governmental entities (e.g., Statistics Canada, Industry Canada). Statistics prepared by the selling organization as well as the salesperson can also be useful in providing evidence for claims. Facts and statistics are most powerful when they fairly represent all sides to the story and are presented in printed form rather than simply stated orally. Not only does the printed word carry more credibility but it is also convenient and can be left as a reminder to aid the prospect's retention of information.

TESTIMONIALS

Testimonials are similar to statistics, but in the form of statements from satisfied users of the selling organization's products and services. Supportive statements from current users are excellent methods to build trust and confidence. They predispose the prospective buyer to accept what the salesperson says about the benefits and value a recommended solution offers, and they reduce the prospect's perceived risk in making a purchase decision. Written testimonials are especially effective when they are on the recommending user's letterhead and signed. However, testimonials that list customers, trade publications, trade associations, and independent rating

> Salespeople can use testimonials to support their product claims.

PR NEWSWIRE/AP IMAGES

organizations along with one-sentence comments in a presentation can also be effective. For instance:

- "The Canadian Dental Association has endorsed the new Laserlite drilling system as being safe and painless for the patient."
- "In January, *Fortune* magazine recognized CDW as the top-rated technology vendor on the basis of services provided to the buying customer."
- "The *RIMS Quality Scorecard* rated Arthur J. Gallagher & Co. as the highest-rated insurance broker in North America in terms of value and service provided to its clients."

As shown in "An Ethical Dilemma," the power of testimonials sometimes tempts salespeople to misuse them.

Testimonials are used extensively across industry and product/service types. To maximize their effectiveness, testimonials should be matched according to relevance and recognition to the prospective buyer. It is critical that the organization or person providing the supporting testimony be known or recognized by the prospect, above reproach, and in a position of respect.

CASE HISTORIES

Case histories are basically a testimonial in story or anecdotal form. Their added length allows more detail to be presented to further clarify an issue or better itemize the proof for a given statement. Case histories can also break the monotony of a long presentation. Like their counterpart testimonials, case histories should be used only when they clearly illustrate a particular point and are appropriate for the prospective buyer. Unrelated or tangential stories not only distract the customer but also can be a source of irritation that works against credibility building. Case histories should be short and to the point, lasting no

more than a minute. They should support the presentation rather than becoming the centre of attention.

LO6
Group Sales Dialogue

Sales dialogue with groups is fairly commonplace in business-to-business selling. For example, retail chains often employ buying committees when considering the addition of new products for their stores. Hospitals

© LISEGAGNE/ISTOCKPHOTO

An Ethical Dilemma

Jane Rafael is an account manager for International Supply and Uniform (ISU), a major provider of work wear and uniforms to companies, institutions, and individuals throughout Canada. During her recent sales presentation to the Ottawa-based Waits Manufacturing Corp., Rafael was well into the presentation of her proposed weekly uniform supply program when the buyer asked about the quality of the uniforms. Rafael responded that J. D. Powers (a well-known organization rating product and service quality) had recently rated them as one of the highest-quality providers of work uniforms. This appeared to satisfy the buyer and the sale was closed. On leaving the buyer's office, the sales assistant working with Rafael that day asked about the J. D. Powers rating, commenting "I can't believe I missed something that important. Where can I get a copy of it?" Rafael replied, "Actually, J. D. Powers has never rated uniform suppliers that I know of. The buyer was ready to make a commitment and just needed some kind of quality reference to help him make the decision. Don't worry about it. Nobody ever checks things like that. Besides, our quality is excellent. There will be no problems." What are the dangers in how Rafael uses references and testimonials? How might the sales assistant help Rafael change this habit?

© FUSE/JUPITER IMAGES

use cross-functional teams comprising medical and administrative personnel to choose vendors such as food service providers. A group of marketing and up-per-management people usually make the decision about which advertising agency will be chosen. Corporations often depend on repre-sentatives from several departments to make purchase decisions that affect all employees, such as the choice of insurance providers.

Interacting with groups presents special challenges and opportunities. In addition to the basic fundamen-tals of planning and delivering sales dialogue to indi-vidual buyers, there are additional strategies and tactics that can enhance sales dialogue with groups.

When selling to groups, salespeople can expect tough questions and should prepare accordingly. Al-though buyer questions are part of most sales dialogues, whether with individuals or groups, they are particularly crucial when multiple buyers are involved. Most buy-ing groups are assembled to tap the individual exper-tise and interests of the group members. For example, a buying committee for a company's computer informa-tion system could include technical specialists; finance and accounting personnel; and representatives from production operations, logistics, management, and mar-keting. All of these individuals are experts and demand in-depth information to make a decision. In some situa-tions, this calls for a sales team to address all ques-tions adequately, while in other cases, an individual salesperson has the cross-functional expertise re-quired to make the sale.

preselling Salespeople present their product or service to individual buyers before a major sales dialogue with a group of buyers.

> Salespeople are increasingly involved in group sales dialogue.

When selling to a group, salespeople should take every opportunity of **preselling** to individual group members before the group presentation. Preselling to individual buyers or subgroups of buyers takes place before a major sales presentation to the entire group. Buying procedures in a given company may or may not allow preselling. If it is an option, the salesperson should work with the individuals composing the buying group before presenting to the group as a whole. By do-ing so, the salesperson can better determine individual and group interests and motives and possibly build a positive foundation for the group presentation. Preselling can also reveal the roles of the in-dividuals in the buying centre as discussed in Chapter 3. Knowing who the decision maker is, along with the other roles, such as users and influencers, is crucial for success in group sales interactions. In the following discussion, we will focus on two key areas: tactical suggestions for group presentations and handling ques-tions in group settings.

SALES TACTICS FOR SELLING TO GROUPS

Assuming that the salesperson or sales team has planned a comprehensive sales dialogue and done as much preselling as possible, some specific sales tactics can enhance presentations to groups. Sales tactics for group presentations fall into three general categories: arrival tactics, eye contact, and communication tips for presentation delivery.

Arrival Tactics

Try to arrive at the location for the meeting before the buying group arrives. This provides an opportunity to set up and check audio-visual equipment, prepare col-lateral material for distribution to the group, and be-come familiar and comfortable with the surroundings. It also sets the stage for the salesperson to greet indi-viduals from the buying team personally as they enter the room. In a symbolic way, it also signals territorial command, or that the salesperson is in charge of the meeting. Although the control of the meeting is typi-cally shared with the buying group, arriving first sends a message that the salesperson is prepared to start promptly at the appointed time, thus showing respect for the buyer's time.

From the very beginning, the salesperson is hoping to connect with each individual in the group, rather than connecting only at the group level. By arriving first, the salesperson may have the opportunity to talk briefly with each individual. If nothing more, a friendly greeting, handshake, and introduction can help establish a rapport with individuals in the group. When not allowed to arrive first, salespeople should attempt individual introductions when joining the group. If that is not practical, salespeople must try and engage each individual through eye contact and, if appropriate, introductory remarks early in the presentation that recognize the individual interests of those present. For example, a salesperson for a food service company might begin a presentation to a hospital with the following:

> *Thank you for the opportunity to discuss our food service programs with you today. In planning for our meeting, I recognize that the dietary group is most concerned about the impact of any proposed change on the quality of patient care. Linda [the head dietician], I believe we have a program that will enhance the quality of care that your patients receive. John [the head of finance], we will also propose an efficient, cost-effective alternative . . . .*

Opening remarks such as these, when kept brief, can be most effective in building involvement with all individuals in a small group.

Eye Contact

For both small and large groups, establishing periodic eye contact with individuals is important. With small groups, this is easily accomplished. With larger groups, especially formal presentations in which the salesperson is standing and the group is sitting, there may be a tendency to use the so-called overhead approach. This method calls for looking just over the heads of the group, with the idea that those seated farthest from the presenter will feel included as part of the group. This method should be avoided. It might be fine for a formal speech to a large audience in a convention hall, but it is far too impersonal for groups of 10 to 25 individuals. Also avoid a rapid scanning from side-to-side. This gives the appearance of nervousness and is ineffective in connecting with individual group members. The most effective eye contact is to try to connect with each individual or small subgroups for a few seconds, moving through the entire group over the course of the presentation. Professional entertainers often use this method

to connect with audience members, and salespeople can do the same.

Communications Tips

When selling to groups, it is essential to make all members of the group feel that their opinions are valuable. It is also important to avoid being caught in the middle of disagreements between members of the buying group. For example, if one member likes the salesperson's proposal and another thinks it is too expensive, any resolution of this disagreement must be handled carefully. Although the salesperson may present information that resolves the issue, in some cases, disagreements among group buying members may be resolved outside the meetings. It is to the salesperson's advantage if disagreements can be handled during the presentation, as it keeps the sales process moving; unresolved issues can stall the sales process. As an example of how salespeople can play a peacemaker role, consider this exchange:

Buyer A: "I really like this system and think we should install it as soon as possible."

Buyer B: "I like it too, but it is way too expensive. Is there a less expensive alternative?"

Buyer A: "Sure, but it will not do the job."

Salesperson: (Directed to Buyer B) "Could I add something here? I believe we have a cost-effective system and that our lease-to-purchase plan reduces the capital expenditure and allows a favourable payback period. Could we take another look at the numbers?"

Salespeople must be diplomatic as participants in discussions that might develop between members of the buying group. This sometimes means remaining silent while the discussion comes to a resolution, and sometimes it means playing an active role. There are no hard and fast rules in this area, and salespeople must simply use their best judgment to guide their actions.

In delivering group presentations, it is important to maintain contact with group members. Thus, reading or overreliance on densely worded slides should be avoided. Think of slides and other audio-visual aids as support tools, not as a "roll-and-scroll" presentation to be read to the group. Natural movement can also enhance contact with the group. Too much pacing about can be detrimental to holding the group's attention, just as remaining tethered to a laptop can detract from group communication. When possible, salespeople should stand to the left of visual aids, as people read right-to-left. When standing to the left, it is easier to direct attention to the visual aids while momentarily deflecting attention away from the speaker. In this way, the salesperson becomes an unobtrusive narrator and the visual aid has maximum impact.

Body language can add to or detract from sales effectiveness in the group setting. In general, your posture should reflect an energetic, relaxed person. Conventional wisdom dictates that presenters should avoid contact with their own bodies while presenting. Salespeople who stuff their hands in their pockets, scratch their heads, or cross their arms are creating distractions to their own messages.

HANDLING QUESTIONS IN GROUP DIALOGUE

Just as is the case with sales dialogue to individuals, questions from buyers in a group are an important part of the buyer-seller interaction that leads to a purchase decision. Salespeople should recognize that questions fill information gaps, thus allowing buyers to make better decisions. In a group setting, questions can also add a dramatic element, making the presentation more interesting for those in attendance. To the extent that it is possible, salespeople should anticipate group questions and then decide whether to address the question before it arises or wait and address the question should it arise during the presentation.

To effectively handle questions that arise during the meeting, salespeople should listen carefully. Questions should be answered as succinctly and convincingly as possible. By listening carefully to the question, salespeople show respect for the person asking the question. At the same time, they are helping direct the attention of the group to the question. As the question is posed, it is important for the salesperson to maintain eye contact with the person asking the question. Again, this demonstrates respect for the person and for his or her right to ask questions. This may require some practice, as salespeople may be tempted to glance at sales materials or perhaps their watch when the attention is shifted to the person asking the question. To do so could insult the questioner, who may feel slighted by the lack of attention.

In many cases, it is a good idea to repeat or even restate the question. This will ensure that everyone understands the question. It also signals a shift from the individual back to the group. Additionally, it allows the salesperson to state the key issue in the question succinctly. This is often important because not all questions are well formulated and they are sometimes accompanied by superfluous information. Consider this dialogue:

Buyer: "You know, I have been thinking about the feasibility of matching our Brand X computers with Brand Y printers. Not too long ago, matching multiple brands would have been a disaster. Are you telling me now that Brand X computers are totally compatible with Brand Y printers?"

Seller: "You are asking whether your computers compatible with our printers. Is that right? Yes, they are—with no special installation requirements."

When restating questions, salespeople must be careful to capture the essence of the buyer's concern accurately. Otherwise, they could be perceived as avoiding the question or trying to manipulate the buyer by putting words in his or her mouth. Therefore, when in doubt, it is a good practice when restating a question to seek buyer confirmation that the restated question is an accurate representation of the original question. For example, salespeople might say, "Ms. Jackson, as I understand the question, you are concerned about the effectiveness of our seasonal sales promotion programs. Is that correct?"

When answering questions, there are three guidelines. First, salespeople should not attempt to answer a question until he or she and the group members clearly understand the question. Second, salespeople should not attempt to answer questions that they are

> In answering questions during a group dialogue, salespeople should listen carefully, answer directly, and address the individual asking the question as well as the others in the group.

not prepared to answer. It is far better to make a note and tell the group you will get back to them with the answer than to speculate or give a weak answer. Third, salespeople should try to answer questions as directly as possible. Politicians are often accused of not answering the questions posed during press conferences, but rather steering the answer toward what they want to talk about. Salespeople will quickly lose credibility if they take a long time to get to the point in their answer. To answer convincingly, start with a "yes" or "no," then explain the exceptions to the general case. For example, say, "Yes, that is generally the case. There are some exceptions, including . . ." is preferred to answering, "Well that depends . . ." then explaining all of the special circumstances only to conclude with "but, generally, yes, that is the case."

When answering questions, it is important to address the entire group rather than just the individual who asked the question. Otherwise, salespeople may lose the attention of other group members. When salespeople conclude their answers, they have the option of going back to the person who asked the question, continuing their presentation, or taking a question from another group member. Salespeople can rely on their common sense and experience to decide what is appropriate in a given situation.

In larger groups, it is particularly important to avoid getting locked into a question-and-answer dialogue with one person if other people are showing an interest in asking questions. Indeed, it is important to take all questions, but it is also important to spread the opportunity to ask questions around the room, coming back to those who have multiple questions until all questions are answered. If one person is a dominant force within the buying group, other group members will typically defer their questions until that person has asked all of their questions at different points in the presentation.

When selling to a group, salespeople should have a clear objective for their presentation. To get the group to take the desired action, salespeople must make a convincing case, motivate the group to take action, and make it easy for the group to take the desired action. Some of the methods for handling buyer objections and earning a commitment as will be discussed in Chapter 8 will prove useful for accomplishing these tasks.

In some cases, the group will want to deliberate and let the salesperson know of their decision at a later time. This is not uncommon, because the group may need a frank discussion without outsiders to reach a final decision. Should this occur, salespeople should be certain that the group has all the information they need or offer to provide the needed information promptly and offer to follow-up within a specified time period.

The process for planning and delivering a group sales dialogue is much the same as it is for sales dialogue with individuals. By paying attention to the special considerations in this section, salespeople can build on their experience with sales interaction with individuals and engage in effective sales dialogue with groups.

Visit **sell.nelson.com** to find the resources you need today!

Located at the back of the textbook are rip-out Chapter Review cards. Make sure you also go online to check out other tools that SELL offers to help you successfully pass your course.

- Flashcards
- Glossary
- PowerPoint Notes
- Role-Play Videos
- Games
- Interactive Quizzing

PETERBOROUGH PAINT & COATINGS (PPC)

Background

Peterborough Paint & Coatings (PPC) is a producer of specialty paints and coatings for industrial and agricultural equipment manufacturers. In business for more than 25 years, PPC has established a strong reputation as a competitive supplier of high-quality acrylic and resin-based coatings. Working with the National Research Council (NRC) in Ottawa, PPC is rolling out a breakthrough self-priming paint product that offers several significant benefits to equipment manufacturers. By eliminating the need for a primer coat, the new product can cut application time in half and can eliminate about one-third of the material cost involved in the typical paint process. The self-priming paint can be directly applied to any clean metal surface by using either a low-pressure spray or roller. An additional benefit is its flash-drying characteristic, which means it dries and cures after only three to five minutes of exposure to room temperature air. In just five minutes after application, it is fully cured, rock hard, and highly scratch, chemical, and fade resistant.

Current Situation

Richard Henry is an account manager for PPC and has been working to establish John Deere's Lethbridge, Alberta, facility as an account. With the previous line of traditional paint products, he had been successful in gaining about 10 percent of the plant's annual paint requirements. However, that seemed to be the limit. Even with the great relationship he has established with Tim Dickerson, head paint and coating buyer for Deere's Lethbridge construction equipment plant, Henry has not been able to gain additional share of the plant's paint requirements.

Henry sees the self-priming product as his path to capturing a majority share of the plant's paint needs. The cost and time savings will certainly be a major item of interest. But first, he must convince Dickerson that the new paint meets and even exceeds the performance specifications. As he is looking through the information he has in his database, he sees that there is a wealth of NRC test data and competitive information that will document the performance of the new coating, but he is pondering how he might organize and present it in a way that will be most effective. He is also trying to think of an effective demonstration he might provide that will give Dickerson a hands-on experience with the paint's superior performance.

Questions

1. What are the benefits of self-priming paint?
2. What different sales aids might Henry use to enhance his presentation of the new self-priming paint?
3. Once he has established the superior performance of the new paint, what should Henry do?

Role Play

Situation: Read the case.

Characters: Richard Henry, salesperson for Peterborough Paint & Coatings; Tim Dickerson, head paint and coating buyer for John Deere, Lethbridge

Scene: *Location*—The office of Tim Dickerson at John Deere, Lethbridge
Action—As described, Henry is presenting a revolutionary new self-priming paint. Although cost savings will be important, his first concern is to establish that the new paint exceeds all performance requirements.

Role play how Henry might incorporate different sales aids to make his presentation to Dickerson more effective.

Role play how Henry might collaborate with Dickerson to illustrate the possible cost savings provided by the new paint.

After completing the role plays, address the following questions:

1. What other sales aids might prove useful in demonstrating the performance of the new paint?
2. What information will Henry need in order to substantiate the possible cost savings to Dickerson? Where and how might he get this information?

All Risk Insurance and National Networks

Background

The All Risk Insurance Company has 3200 sales agents spread across five regions that cover entire Canada. The company is moving toward the development of a national network that would tie each of the agent offices together with the regional offices and corporate headquarters. The improved communication capability will allow all company personnel to have full access to customer records and form the core of a comprehensive customer relationship management system that is to be rolled out in 18 months.

Current Situation

Jim Roberts is a network account specialist for National Networks, a specialist in large corporate network solutions, and has been working with the technology-buying group at All Risk Insurance for several months now. Roberts has worked through several meetings with the buying group members and has a meeting scheduled for next Wednesday to present his recommendations and demonstrate why they should select National Networks as the supplier for this sizable project. Joyce Fields (director of information systems), John Harris (comptroller and CFO), Javid Quadri (director of agent services), and Dianne Sheffield (director for customer services) will make the final decision. Roberts also knows that one other competitor will be making a presentation in hopes of landing the project. The equipment both vendors are proposing is virtually identical because of the detailed specifications that All Risk Insurance had included in the RFP. Prices are also likely to be pretty similar. The decision will most likely come down to the services each competitor includes in the proposals. Based on the information that Roberts has collected from different sources, he has come up with a comparison of customer services National Networks and the competitor offer (see the table on the following page).

Role Play

Situation: Read the role play Background and Current Situation.

Characters: Jim Roberts—salesperson for National Networks; Joyce Fields—director of information systems for All Risk Insurance; John Harris—comptroller and CFO for All Risk Insurance; Javid Quadri—director of agent services for All Risk Insurance; Dianne Sheffield—director for customer services for All Risk Insurance

Scene: *Location*—A conference room at All Risk Insurance
Action—As described, Jim Roberts is presenting the National Networks proposal for a corporate computer network linking All Risk Insurance's corporate offices with each of its five regional offices and 3200 sales agents out in the field.

Role play Roberts's presentation of each of the feature-benefit sets incorporating sales aids suitable for use in the group presentation.

Features	Capability of National Networks	Capability of Competitor	Benefits
Service and repair centres	175 affiliated service and repair centres across Canada	21 affiliated service and repair centres across Canada	Ensures fast and reliable repairs for hardware and software
Installation and testing	Installation and testing done by National Networks employees	Installation and testing outsourced to several different companies	Knowledge that all installations will be done the right way
Customer call centre	24 hours, 7 days per week, and staffed by National Networks employees	24 hours, 7 days per week, and staffed by an outsource commercial provider	Knowledgeable staff always available to assist All Risk Insurance employees with problems

Questions

After completing the role plays, address the following questions:

1. What other sales tools and aids might prove useful to Roberts in presenting his proposed solution to the All Risk Insurance buying team?
2. How might Roberts employ other tactics for selling to a group to increase the effectiveness of his presentation and advance the sale toward getting an order?

89% of students surveyed found the interactive online quizzes valuable.

LEARNING YOUR WAY

We know that no two students are alike. **SELL** was developed to help you learn **sales** in a way that works for you.

Not only is the format fresh and contemporary, but it's also concise and focused. And **SELL** is loaded with a variety of supplements, like chapter review cards, flashcards, and more!

At **www.sell.nelson.com** you will find **flashcards, crossword puzzles, role-play videos, a glossary**, and **more** to test your knowledge of key concepts. It includes plenty of resources to help you study, no matter what learning style you like best!

"I enjoy the cards in the back of the book and the fact that it partners with the website."

—Cassandra Jewell, Sir Sandford Fleming College

Visit **www.sell.nelson.com** to find the resources you need today!

what do you think?

The best salespeople are the best closers.

1 2 3 4 5 6 7

strongly disagree   strongly agree

Sales resistance

is a normal part of any sales conversation. It should not be looked on as a negative.

8

Addressing Concerns and Earning Commitment

After completing this chapter, you should be able to

LO1 Explain why it is important to anticipate and overcome buyer concerns and resistance.

LO2 Understand why prospects raise objections.

LO3 Describe the five major types of sales resistance.

LO4 Explain how the LAARC method can be used to overcome buyer resistance.

LO5 Describe the recommended approaches for responding to buyer objections.

LO6 List and explain the techniques for earning commitment that secure commitment and closing.

Introduction

f or most entrepreneurs, sales calls aren't a laughing matter. But maybe they should be.

Making humor a part of your pitch can work wonders, says Burt Teplitzky, a stand-up comedian, author and corporate trainer in Los Angeles. Jokes can help establish a rapport with customers, release tension and increase your "likability factor"—all of which can make it a lot easier to close a deal.

"Your main job is to create an environment where the customer wants to buy from you," says the 52-year-old Mr. Teplitzky, who once headed the corporate-training arm of the Improv comedy-club chain, among a range of other sales-related jobs, including real estate. Humor, he says, "helps to open lines of communication because you are both comfortable with each other and you are communicating back and forth.... Your points are coming across loud and clear."

Teplitzky says jokes can help seal deals.

"I use humor to reinforce a point in selling a product or service. My formula is punch them with the joke, stick them with the point and leave them with the benefit. When you take a joke and incorporate it into a conversation or a presentation, it carries a lot more power. It carries the power to change people's minds, reinforce what they think or feel, and to sell something. That chosen joke is no longer just a joke. It becomes a gem, a humor gem.

"Remember, your audience wants humor and they fear that if they don't laugh, you will stop using it. They don't want to have to suffer through a dry presentation.

"The point and benefit should be stated simply and take just 10 seconds to deliver. Whatever your product or service is, you should know the features and benefits of it thoroughly. List the features and benefits so that you have at least 10 of them. You should attach a humor gem or story to each one. This applies whether you are speaking in front of a group or presenting one on one.

"However, just because an individual likes a joke doesn't mean the audience will like it. The material could be offensive or not relevant to the sales material. Presenters should avoid jokes about money, politics, religion, sexual orientation and ethnicity. Also, cursing and words that could be taken the wrong way shouldn't be used.

"Adopt this motto: When in doubt, leave it out.

"And salespeople should use only proven, clean jokes—don't ad lib. Let the comedians and humorists worry about creating original

sales resistance A buyer's objections to a product or service during a sales presentation.

stories. You concentrate on selling or using the tools necessary to bring in the money. Always credit the comedian who originated the joke."

Teplitzky says that sometimes humor can help overcome objections in sales calls "One time a potential client couple told me they had to interview other real-estate agents even though they were sure that I could do the job. I said, "Let's say you go grocery shopping to buy eggs. If you open a box and all of the eggs are unbroken, do you check all of the other boxes to see if they are unbroken as well?

"This made the client realize how silly it was to interview others, at least at that instant, and I was able to get them to sign a contract while they were laughing."

Source: Barbara Haislip, "Make 'Em Laugh," *The Wall Street Journal*, May 16, 2011. Reprinted by permission of *Wall Street Journal*, Copyright © (2011) Dow Jones & Company, Inc. All Rights Reserved Worldwide. License number 2743691029130.

Addressing Concerns

an objection or **sales resistance** is anything the buyer says or does that slows down or stops the buying process. The salesperson's job is to uncover these objections and answer them to the prospect's or client's satisfaction. It is very difficult for a salesperson to earn commitment if doubt or concern remain on the buyer's part. Thus, the salesperson must uncover and overcome any and all objections. In doing so, the salesperson strengthens the long-term relationship and moves the sales process closer to commitment.

Good salespeople will anticipate their buyers' concerns.

At the very least, it creates open dialogue between the salesperson and the prospect.

A brief discussion follows on why it is important for salespeople to anticipate and negotiate buyer concern. Following a discussion of why prospects raise objections, this chapter covers the five major types of objections. Next, different approaches to handling sales resistance are explained. Finally, techniques to earn commitment are reviewed.

LO1

Anticipating and Negotiating Concerns and Resistance

Over the years, many sales forces were taught that sales resistance was bad and would likely slow down or stop the selling process. Salespeople were also told that if they received resistance, then they had not done a good job explaining their product or service.

These notions have changed over the years, and objections are now viewed as opportunities to sell. Salespeople should be grateful for objections and always treat them as questions. The buyer is just asking for more information. It is the salesperson's job to produce the correct information to help buyers alleviate their concern. Inexperienced salespeople need to learn that sales resistance is a normal, natural part of any sales conversation. The prospect that does not question price, service, warranty, and delivery concerns is probably not interested.

Although many salespeople fear sales resistance from their prospects or customers, it should be viewed as a normal part of the sales process. At a minimum, the salesperson has the prospect involved. The salesperson can now start to determine customer interest and measure the buyer's understanding of the problem. In some situations, a salesperson cannot overcome resistance (e.g., delivery dates do not match; technology does not fit). Under these circumstances, the successful salesperson gracefully ends the sales call while leaving open the option for further business.[1] Finally, if the sales resistance is handled correctly, the outcome can lead to customer acceptance.

LO2

REASONS WHY PROSPECTS RAISE OBJECTIONS

There are many reasons why prospects will raise objections.

1. The prospect wants to avoid the sales interview. Some prospects do not want to create any more

work for themselves than they already have. Granted, a sales interview takes time and buyers already have a busy schedule handling normal day-to-day tasks. Buyers may want to avoid the salesperson because they view his or her call as an interruption in their day. Most buyers do not have the time to see every salesperson that knocks on their door.

2. The salesperson has failed to prospect and qualify properly. Sometimes, poor prospects slip through the screening process. The prospect may have misunderstood the salesperson's intentions when asked for the interview. The salesperson should attempt to qualify the prospect during the sales call. For example, a computer software company used telemarketing to qualify prospects. Leads were turned over to the salesforce for in-person visits. The major product line was an inventory control package that cost $20,000. The salesperson asked the owner of the company if she had a budget for this project. The owner answered $5,000. The salesperson gave the owner the names of a couple of inexpensive software companies, thanked the owner for her time, and moved on. The owner was not about to spend $20,000 and said so early in the sales conversation. That resistance actually helped the salesperson. What if this condition had stayed hidden for four to six weeks while the salesperson continued to call on the owner? Both the salesperson's and owner's time would have been wasted.

3. Objecting is a matter of custom. Many purchasing agents have a motto never to buy on the first call with a salesperson. Trust has not yet been developed and a thorough understanding of the salesperson, his or her company, and the products has not been created. The buyer will need most of this information to make a decision. Many buyers may say no during the first few calls to test the salesperson's persistence.

4. The prospect resists change. Many buyers like the way that they are presently doing business. Thus, buyers will tell the salesperson that they are satisfied with what they have now. Many prospects simply resist change because they dislike making decisions. Prospects may fear the consequences of deciding and dread disturbing the status

quo. A purchase usually involves dismissing the present supplier and handling all of the arrangements (price, terms, delivery, and product specifications) to move the new supplier in smoothly. Once a buyer is comfortable with his or her suppliers, he or she will generally avoid new salespeople until a major need arises.

5. The prospect fails to recognize a need. The prospect may be unaware of a need, uninformed about the product or service, or content with the present situation. In any case, the lack of need creates no motivation to change suppliers. Many purchasing agents were content with their overnight mail service and were slow to recognize the fax machine as a viable solution to getting information to their customers quickly. The poor quality of the reproduced document also turned away many buyers. Only when the need for the information outweighed the aesthetics of the document did the buyers readily embrace the fax machine.

6. The prospect lacks information. Ultimately, all sales resistance comes back to the fact that the prospect simply lacks the information he or she needs to make a decision comfortably. The salesperson must view this as an opportunity to put the right information in front of the buyer. If the salesperson diagnoses correctly and presents the right information, then the resistance problem can be more easily overcome. Exhibit 8.1 summarizes why prospects raise objections and lists strategies for dealing with them.

EXHIBIT 8.1
Why Prospects Raise Objections and Strategies for Dealing with Them

- Buyer wants to avoid the sales interview.
  Strategy: Set appointments to become part of the buyer's daily routine.

- Salesperson has failed to prospect and qualify properly.
  Strategy: Ask questions to verify prospect's interest.

- Buyer will not buy on the first sales call.
  Strategy: A regular call on the prospect lets the prospect know the salesperson is serious about the relationship.

- Prospect does not want to change the present way of doing business.
  Strategy: Salesperson must help the prospect understand there is a better solution than the one the prospect is presently using.

- Prospect has failed to recognize a need.
  Strategy: Salesperson must show evidence that sparks the prospect's interest.

- Prospect lacks information on a new product or on the salesperson's company.
  Strategy: Salesperson must continually work to add value by providing useful information.

© IMAGE SOURCE/JUPITER IMAGES

Secretaries, assistants, receptionists, and even voicemail can block the access to your prospect; they can be the gatekeepers.

It is not unusual for salespeople to encounter product objections. Most buyers have fears associated with buying a product. The buyer may be afraid that the product will not be as reliable as the salesperson said it would. Not only do the salespeople have to demonstrate that their product will perform at the level they say it will, but they must also show how it stacks up to the competition. A competitor introducing a new technology (e.g., e-commerce) may change the way a salesperson competes on a particular product line (e.g., office products).

Many buyers are constantly assessing their supplier on service (e.g., delivery, follow-up, warranties, guarantees, repairs, installation, and training). If the service is good and department heads are not complaining, the buyer is likely to stay with the status quo. Service is one variable that companies and salespeople can use to differentiate their product. Enterprise Rent-a-Car will deliver cars to the home of the renter and has made this difference a factor in its advertising. A salesperson for a wholesale distributor may make the point to a prospect that their fresh fruit, fish, and meat can be delivered daily when their competitors only deliver three times per week.

Many buyers will feel intense loyalty to their present suppliers and use this as a reason not to change. Buyers may be equally committed to the salesperson from whom they are presently buying. As a nonsupplier to the company, the salesperson must continue to call on the buyer and look for opportunities to build trust with the prospect. The salesperson may want to investigate whether the buyer has had any previous bad experience with his or her company that is causing the buyer not to do business with the company. Some salespeople and their buyers will not hit it off. The salesperson has to recognize these feelings and move on if several calls do not result in a sale.

At first glance, an inexperienced salesperson may be overwhelmed with the thought of how he or she will handle all the different types of objections buyers will raise. Salespeople need to develop skills in evaluating objections.[2] It does not take long, however, for a salesperson to learn that most objections fall into just a few categories. When preparing to buy a product or service, a prospect generally obtains information in five areas: need, product or service features, company or source, price, and timing of the buy. Objections could come from any of these areas, as shown in Exhibit 8.2. A more detailed look at each of these areas follows.

LO3
TYPES OF SALES RESISTANCE

Although there appears to be an infinite number of objections, most fall into five or six categories. Buyers use delay techniques to avoid taking immediate action. Comments such as "Give me a couple of weeks to think it over" can save the buyer the discomfort of saying no at the end of a presentation. "Your price is too high" or "I have no money" are easy ways for purchasing agents not to buy a salesperson's offering. Price is probably the most often cited objection and usually is not the most important issue. It is obvious that buyers do not buy merely based on price; if this were true, then the lowest price supplier would get all of the business and eventually be the only supplier left selling the product. "No need at this time" is another typical objection. The buyer may not be in the market to purchase at this time.

EXHIBIT 8.2
Types of Objections

No need	Buyer has recently purchased or does not see a need for the product category. "I am not interested at this time."
Product or service objection	Buyer may be afraid of product reliability. "I am not sure the quality of your product meets our needs." Buyer may be afraid of late deliveries, slow repairs, etc. "I am happy with my present supplier's service."
Company objection	Buyer is intensely loyal to the present supplier. "I am happy with my present supplier."
Price is too high	Buyer has a limited budget. "We have been buying from another supplier that meets our budget constraints."
Time or delay	Buyer needs time to think it over. "Get back with me in a couple of weeks."

need objection Resistance to a product or service in which a buyer says that he or she does not need the product or service.

product or **service objection** Resistance to a product or service in which a buyer does not like the way the product or service looks or feels.

Need Objections

Without a need, prospects have little or no reason to talk to a salesperson. If the prospect has been qualified properly, the salesperson believes the prospect has a need for the product. Many buyers have been conditioned to say automatically, "I do not need your product" (i.e., **need objection**). This may be the result of the buyer being out of budget or not having the time to look at your product or proposal. Other buyers may respond, "We are getting along just fine without your product. No one in my company is asking for your product. Call back in a few months and maybe something will change."

The salesperson has a tough challenge ahead if the buyer sincerely believes they have no need. It is the salesperson's job to establish a need in the buyer's mind; if the salesperson cannot do this then, logically, an objection can be expected.

Many prospects do not know they have a specific need for a product until a situation occurs that makes them aware of it (i.e., engineering calls and needs a special software package). Therefore, objections to the need require the salesperson to stimulate the need awareness of the prospect with relevant information—features and benefits that pique the prospect's interest. Exhibit 8.3 summarizes a number of the no-need objections.

Product or Service Objections

Often the product or service lacks something that the buyer wants and the salesperson cannot deliver. A competitive advantage for a large software firm (Ontario) is that they have 24-hour 800 service available to all their customers. Their number-one competitor offers only 8:00 a.m. to 8:00 p.m. call-in phone service. For those clients that run three shifts and need 24-hour service, their choice is easy: they buy from Ontario.

Other prospect objections could be simply emotional—the prospect does not like the way the product looks or feels (i.e., **product or service objection**). Still others have a problem with the product's performance characteristics (i.e., "I need a copier that has colour and staples in the bin"). The salesperson also must do an adequate job of fact-finding and qualifying. Many of these issues can be resolved by knowing what the prospect is looking for.

EXHIBIT 8.3
Possible Need Objections

"I have all I can use (all stocked up)."

"I do not need any."

"The equipment I have is still good."

"I am satisfied with the company we use now."

"We have no room for your line."

company or **source objection** Resistance to a product or service that results when a buyer has never heard of or is not familiar with the product's company.

price objection Resistance to a product or service based on the price of the product being too high for the buyer.

Objections toward the product centre on understanding the fit between the product and the customer's needs. The salesperson's job is to learn what product features are important to the buyer and sell those features. Products are bundles of benefits that customers seek to fit their needs. Tying the benefits to the customer's needs helps the prospect bridge the gap from no-need to need. Exhibit 8.4 summarizes a number of product or service objections.

Company or Source Objections

Marty Reist is a manufacturer's representative for a small company in the sporting goods industry. He has to sell against many large competitors. Sales representatives from Nike, Titleist, and Reebok probably do not have to work as hard to get past the gatekeepers. Reist, in contrast, must justify his existence every day. "I have never heard of your company" (i.e., **company or source objection**) is something Reist must continually overcome.

Other buyers may be happy with their present supplier. It is not unusual for buyer–seller relationships to last

EXHIBIT 8.4
Possible Product or Service Objections

"I do not like the design, colour, or style."

"A maintenance agreement should be included."

"Performance of the product is unsatisfactory (e.g., the copier is too slow)."

"Packaging is too bulky".

"The product is incompatible with the present system (e.g., we prefer Apple over IBM)."

"The specifications do not match what we have now."

"How do I know if you will meet our delivery requirements?"

"The product is poor quality."

EXHIBIT 8.5
Company or Source Objections

"Your company is too small to meet my needs."

"I have never heard of your company."

"Your company is too big. I will get lost in the shuffle."

"Your company is pretty new. How do I know you will be around to take care of me in the future?"

"Your company was recently in the newspaper. Are you having problems?"

10 to 15 years and even longer. Robert Carroll, a former sales representative from Monsanto Agricultural Division, heard the following quote from many of his farmers and farm co-ops, "I'm perfectly happy with Monsanto; my crops look good. I've been buying from them for years, and they have always treated me right." This is one of the hardest objections to overcome, especially if the prospect feels genuine loyalty to his or her present supplier.

Professional salespeople never criticize their competitors. The salesperson can point out any superior features their product or service might have. They can also ask for a single order and ask for an evaluation against the present supplier.

Another form of source objection is a negative attitude a buyer might have about the salesperson's company or the poor presentation of a previous salesperson. A buyer might remember a late or damaged order the company did not properly handle. A former salesperson may have made promises to the buyer and did not follow through on them. The salesperson must investigate any and all source objections. The salesperson may uncover source problems that can be overcome with time. Exhibit 8.5 outlines typical company or source objections.

Price Objections

Most sales experts agree that price is the most common form of buyer resistance.[3] This objection has the prospect saying that they cannot afford the product, the price is too high, or the product is not in their budget at this time (i.e., **price objection**). This objection may be a request for the salesperson to justify to the prospect how they can afford the product or how they can work it into their budget. Most salespeople feel the price objection is an attempt by the buyer to get the salesperson to lower his or her price. The salesperson must address the price objection by citing how the benefits (value) outweigh the cost. To do this, the product's value must be established before the salesperson spends time discussing price.[4] Many companies never sell as the low-cost option. Stryker Medical sells hospital beds and stretchers to hospitals and emergency rooms. Stryker never offers the lowest cost. Stryker's salespeople almost always hear the price objection. First, they have to educate their prospects and customers that their products last 25 to 50 percent longer than their competitor's products. They can demonstrate with evidence their product will still be around 5 to 10 years after their competitor's has been discarded. If one of their stretchers is $1500 more than their competitor's, they must break down the price over the entire life of the stretcher. They can actually show a savings over time. By providing the right information, Stryker can show value over the competitor's offering.

Price objections probably occur more frequently than any other type. Price objections may be used to cover the real reason for a reluctance to buy. Probing and asking questions are the salesperson's tools to get to the real reasons for a buyer's objection. Exhibit 8.6 summarizes a number of price objections.

Time Objections

Buyers use the **time objection**, or as some salespeople call it, the stalling objection, to put off the decision to buy until a later date. Many inexperienced salespeople

hear this technique and believe the prospect is going to buy in the future but not today. Some buyers use this technique to get rid of salespeople so that the buyer does not have to reject the salesperson and his or her sales proposal formally. Sometimes proposals are very complex and the buyer does need time to think them over. The salesperson must be sensitive to this and not push too hard to get an answer until the buyer has had adequate time to make a decision. It is acceptable for the salesperson to review the reasons to act now or soon. Waiting can have consequences (e.g., prices rise, a new tax begins the first of the year) and the buyer should be made aware of these. Exhibit 8.7 illustrates possible time objections.

LO4
USING LAARC: A PROCESS FOR NEGOTIATING BUYER RESISTANCE

The term **LAARC** is an acronym for listen, acknowledge, assess, respond, and confirm and describes an effective process for salespeople to follow to overcome sales resistance. The LAARC method is a customer-oriented way to keep the sales dialogue positive. In the early days of sales, buyers and sellers were not always truthful with each other, and manipulation was the norm. Although being persuasive is necessary to be an

time objection Resistance to a product or service in which a buyer puts off the decision to buy until a later date.

LAARC An acronym for listen, acknowledge, assess, respond, and confirm that describes an effective process for salespeople to follow to overcome sales resistance.

effective sales representative, having such a singular focus can have a detrimental effect on customer rapport and relationships.[5] Salespeople who said whatever it took to get an order—who overpromised and underdelivered and misrepresented their offering—were sometimes looked on favourably by their selling organization. Professional sellers today want to keep the dialogue open and build goodwill by adding value to their proposition. By listening to buyers' concerns and negotiating through open dialogue, the seller increases the likelihood of purchase decisions being made on a favourable basis, and this leads to long-term relationships. Thus, it is the salesperson's job to communicate and demonstrate value when sales resistance arises.

Here is a description of LAARC:

- *Listen:* Salespeople should listen to what their buyers are saying. The ever-present temptation to anticipate what buyers are going to say and cut them off with a premature response should be avoided. Learning to listen is important—it is more than just being polite or professional. Buyers are trying to tell the salesperson something that they consider important.

- *Acknowledge:* As buyers complete their statements, salespeople should acknowledge that they received the message and that they appreciate and can understand the concern. Salespeople should not jump in with an instantaneous defensive response. Before responding, salespeople need a better understanding about what their buyers are saying. By politely pausing and then simply acknowledging their statement, a salesperson establishes that he or she is a reasonable person—a professional who appreciates other people's opinions. It also buys a salesperson precious moments for composing his or her thoughts and thinking of questions for the next step.

- *Assess:* This step is similar to assessment in the ADAPT process of questioning. This step in dealing with buyer resistance calls for salespeople to ask assessment questions to gain a better understanding of exactly what their buyers are saying and why they are saying it. Equipped with this information and

An Ethical Dilemma

Mila Santiago has lost several orders to competitors who are stretching the truth on their product reliability. She knows her product lasts at least as long as her competitors' and in most cases even longer. She heard a competitor say he was not going to stick around to deal with the customer when a claim about his product did not come true. Santiago was not sure what to do. Was it time to blow the whistle on her competitor? If so, how?

© INFLUX PRODUCTIONS/GETTY IMAGES

understanding, salespeople are better able to make a meaningful response to the buyer's resistance.

- *Respond:* Based on his or her understanding of what and why the buyer is resisting, the salesperson can respond to the buyer's resistance. Structuring a response typically follows the method that is most appropriate for the situation. In "An Ethical Dilemma," Mila Santiago has to choose her words carefully when responding to her prospects and customers about a competitor that is less than forthright with the information they provide to their prospects. The more traditional methods of response (see Exhibit 8.8) include forestalling, direct denial, indirect denial, translation (or boomerang), compensation, question, third-party reinforcement (or feel-felt-found), and "coming to that."

These techniques have been used both positively and negatively. Professional salespeople use these techniques to add value to their proposal. For instance, the translation or boomerang technique can be used quite effectively if the salesperson has gathered the appropriate information to support his or her response. The buyer might state, "Your company is too big, and we might slip through the cracks as a small customer." The salesperson might respond, "That is exactly why you want to do business with us. We are larger, and we are going to be able to offer you all of the levels of expertise you said you needed. Smaller companies will not be able to do this, and you will eventually have to search for another supplier. We are one-stop shopping, and we will make sure you will not fall through the cracks." Here, the salesperson took a reason not to buy and translated

EXHIBIT 8.8
Techniques to Answer Concerns

Technique	How It Works	Example
Forestalling	Take care of the objection before the prospect brings it up.	Many of my customers have had a concern going into my presentation that we do not have a warranty program. Let me put this to rest: we have one-, three-, and five-year warranty programs that match our competitors. I hope this answers your concern.
Direct denial	A rather harsh response that the prospect is wrong.	You have heard incorrectly. We are not raising prices.
Indirect denial	Softening the blow when correcting a prospect's information.	We have heard that rumour, too—even some of our best customers asked us about it. Our senior management team has guaranteed us our prices will hold firm through the rest of the year.
Translation or boomerang	Turn a reason not to buy into a reason *to* buy.	Buyer: Your company is too small to meet our needs. Salesperson: That is just the reason you want to do business with us. Because we are smaller, you will get the individual attention you said you wanted.
Compensation	Counterbalance the objection with an offsetting benefit.	Yes, our price is higher, but you are going to get the quality you said that you needed to keep your customers happy.
Questioning or asssessing	Ask the buyer assessment questions to gain a better understanding of what they are objecting to.	Your concern is price. Can you please tell me who you are comparing us with, and does that quote include any service agreement?
Third-party reinforcement	Use the opinion or data from a third-party source to help overcome the objection.	Bill Middleton from Dial Electronics had the same concern going in. Let me tell you why he is comfortable with our proposal. . . .
Feel-felt-found	Salesperson relates that others actually found their initial opinions to be unfounded.	Buyer: I do not think my customers will want to buy a product with all those features. We generally sell scaled-down models. Salesperson: I can certainly see how you *feel*. Lisa Richardson down the road in Brandon *felt* the same way when I first proposed that she go with these models. However, after she agreed to display them in the front of her store, she *found* that her customers started buying the models with more features—and that, in turn, provided her with larger margins. In fact, she called me less than a week later to order more!
Coming-to-that	The salesperson tells the buyer that he or she will be covering the objection later in his or her presentation.	Buyer: I have some concerns about your delivery dates. Salesperson: I am glad you brought that up. Before fully discussing our delivery, I want to go over the features that you said were important to you that will help you better understand our product. Is that okay?

it into a reason to buy. Much dialogue had to go on before this for the salesperson to be able to provide the proper information to overcome the concern. Exhibit 8.8 includes examples of how a salesperson might respond to buyer concerns in a professional manner.

- *Confirm:* After responding, the salesperson should ask confirmatory questions—response-checks to make sure that the buyer's concerns have been adequately met. Once this is confirmed, the presentation can proceed. In fact, experience indicates that this form of buyer confirmation is often a sufficient buying signal to warrant the salesperson's attempt to gain a commitment.

LO5
RECOMMENDED APPROACHES FOR RESPONDING TO OBJECTIONS

A brief description of traditional methods for responding to objections follows. Exhibit 8.8 summarizes how each technique works.

Forestalling

When salespeople hear an objection arising repeatedly, they may decide to include an answer to the objection within their sales presentation before it is voiced by the prospect (i.e., **forestalling**). Marty Reist of MPRS Sales, Inc., often tells his prospects he realizes he is not Nike, Titleist, or Reebok, but his size has not kept him from providing outstanding service to his customers. Reist can add a third-party testimonial to back up his statements and put his prospect's mind at ease. This technique should be used only when there is a high probability that the prospect will indeed raise the objection.[6]

Direct Denial

When using the **direct denial** technique to handle sales resistance, the salesperson is directly telling the customer that he or she is mistaken.

> **forestalling** A response to buyer objections in which the salesperson answers the objection during the presentation before the buyer has a chance to ask it.
>
> **direct denial** A response to buyer objections in which the salesperson tells the customer that he or she is wrong.
>
> **indirect denial** A response to buyer objections in which the salesperson takes a softer, more tactful approach when correcting a prospect or customer's information.
>
> **translation** or **boomerang** A response to buyer objections in which the salesperson converts the objection into a reason the prospect should buy.

Prospects may have incorrect facts or may not understand the information they have.

The prospect might say the following:

> **Prospect:** I hear you do not offer service agreements on any of your products.

The salesperson, knowing this is not true, cannot soft-pedal his or her answer. In this situation, the prospect is clearly incorrect and the direct denial is the best solution.

> **Salesperson:** I am sorry, that is not correct. We offer three- and five-year service contracts, and our warranty is also five years.

The important part of using the direct denial is not to humiliate or anger the prospect. The direct denial should be used sparingly, but it may be easier to use when the salesperson has a good feel for the relationship that he or she has with the buyer.

Indirect Denial

Sometimes it is best not to take an objection head on. The indirect approach takes on the objection, but with a softer, more tactful approach. With the **indirect denial**, the salesperson never tells the prospect directly that he or she is wrong. The best way to use this method is to think of it as offering sympathy with the prospect's view and still managing to correct the invalid objection of the buyer. An example follows:

> **Prospect:** I heard that your emergency room beds are $4000 more than your competitor's.
> **Salesperson:** Many of our customers had a similar notion that our beds are much more expensive. The actual cost is only $1200 higher. I have testimonials from other hospitals stating that our beds last up to five years longer. You actually save money.

The salesperson here tries to soften the blow with the opening sentence. Then the salesperson must correct the misconception. Techniques can be combined as the salesperson adds information from a third party to lend credibility to his or her statement.

Translation or Boomerang

The **translation** or **boomerang** method converts the objection into a reason that the prospect should buy.

What the salesperson is trying to do is to take a reason not to buy and turn it into a reason to buy. Marty Reist of MPRS Sales, Inc., offers the following advice:

> Whenever I hear the objection "I don't think your company is large enough to meet our service needs," I immediately come back with "that is exactly the reason you should do business with us. We are big enough to meet your service needs. In fact, you will be calling an 800 number with a larger company and you won't know who you'll get to help you. With our company, anytime you have a problem, question, or concern, you'll call me and talk to a familiar voice."

Another example using the price objection might go like this:

Buyer: "Your price appears to be high."
Salesperson: "Our high price is an advantage for you; the premium sector of the market not only gives you the highest margin but it is also the most stable sector of the market."

The goal of the translation or boomerang method is to turn an apparent deficiency into an asset or reason to buy.

Compensation

There may be a time when a salesperson has to admit that his or her product does have the disadvantage that the prospect has noticed. The **compensation** technique is an attempt to show the prospect that a benefit or an advantage compensates for an objection. For example, a higher product price is justified by benefits, such as better service, faster delivery, or higher performance.

A buyer may use the objection that your company's lead time is 14 days compared with 10 days for your leading competitor. The salesperson's response could be: "Yes, our required lead time is 14 days, but we ship our orders completely assembled. This practically eliminates extra handling in your warehouse. My competitor's product will require assembly by your warehouse workers."

With the compensation method, the objection is not denied at all—it is acknowledged and then balanced by compensating features, advantages, and benefits.

Questioning or Assessing

Another potentially effective way to handle buyer resistance is to convert the objection into a question. This technique calls for the salesperson to ask **questions** or **assess** to gain a better understanding of the precise nature of the buyer's objections. Sometimes it is difficult for the salesperson to know the exact problem. This technique is good for clarifying the real objection. This technique can also be effective in resolving the objection if the prospect is shooting from the hip and does not have a strong reason for the objection. John Huff, in "Professional Selling in the 21st Century: Sales Resistance Is Good," describes that it is critical for him to assess his doctors' present situations and problems with their patients before he does anything else during the sales calls. Exhibit 8.9 illustrates the questioning method as a tool to overcome sales resistance.

> **compensation** A response to buyer objections in which the salesperson counterbalances the objection with an offsetting benefit.

> **questioning** or **assessing** A response to buyer objections in which the salesperson asks the buyer assessment questions to gain a better understanding of what the buyer is objecting to.

EXHIBIT 8.9
Questioning (Assessing) to Overcome Sales Resistance

Example 1

Buyer: I am not sure I am ready to act at this time.

Salesperson: Can you tell me what is causing your hesitation?

Example 2

Buyer: Your price seems to be a little high.

Salesperson: Can you tell me what price you had in mind? Have other suppliers quoted you a lower price?

Example 3

Buyer: Your delivery schedule does not work for us.

Salesperson: To whom are you comparing me? Can you please tell me what delivery schedule will work for your company?

PROFESSIONAL SELLING IN THE 21ST CENTURY

© CUSTOM MEDICAL STOCK

Sales Resistance Is Good

John Huff, a Schering-Plough sales representative, states, "Sales resistance is good; it means your doctor is pondering your proposal. Some of my doctors are so busy with their patients that they can't keep up on every medication and the changes that take place day to day in my industry. The first part of my sales call is to assess their situation and the types of patients they are seeing and the types of problems their patients are having. Then it's my job to get the doctors the correct information so they can make an informed decision. It's not easy to overcome every doctor's objection, but I know if they are questioning cost of my drug, delivery of samples, dosage, etc., at the very least they are showing interest and I've got an opportunity to win them over."

found their initial beliefs to be unfounded after they tried the product. Salespeople need to practise this method—when used in the correct sequence, it can be very effective. Again, the strength of the person and company being used as an example is critical to how much influence the reference will have on the prospect.

Coming-to-That or Postpone

Salespeople need to understand that objections may and will be made to almost everything concerning them, their products, and their company. Good salespeople anticipate these objections and develop effective answers, but sometimes it may make sense to cover an objection later in the presentation, after additional questioning and information is provided. The salesperson should evaluate how important the concern is to the prospect—and, if the objection seems to be critical to the sale, the salesperson should address it immediately.

Once the salesperson has answered all the buyer's questions and has resolved resistance issues that have come up during the presentation, the salesperson should summarize all the pertinent buying signals (i.e., fair price, acceptable delivery dates, and good service agreement).

Third-Party Reinforcement: Feel-Felt-Found

The **third-party reinforcement** technique uses the opinion or research of a third person or company to help overcome and reinforce the salesperson's sales points. Salespeople today can use a wide range of proof statements. Consumer reports, government reports, and independent testing agencies can all be used to back up a salesperson's statement. Secondary data such as this, or experience data from a reliable third party, could be all that is needed to turn around a skeptical prospect. A salesperson must remember that this technique will work only if the buyer believes in the third-party source that the salesperson is using.

A version of using third-party reinforcement is the feel-felt-found method. Here, the salesperson goes on to relate that others

third-party reinforcement A response to buyer objections in which the salesperson uses the opinion or data from a third-party source to help overcome the objection and reinforce the salesperson's points.

LO6
Securing Commitment and Closing

Ultimately, a large part of most salespeople's performance evaluation is based on their ability to gain customer commitment, often called closing sales. Because of this close relationship between compensation and getting orders, traditional selling has tended to overemphasize the importance of gaining a commitment.[7] In fact, there are those who think that just about any salesperson can find a new prospect, open a sale, or take an order. These same people imply it takes a trained, motivated, and skilled professional to close a sale. They go on to say that the close is the keystone to a salesperson's success, and a good salesperson will have mastered many new ways to close the sale. This outmoded emphasis on closing skills is typical of transaction selling techniques that stress making the sales call at all costs.

Another popular but outdated suggestion to salespeople is to "close early and often." This is particularly bad advice if the prospect is not prepared to make a decision, responds negatively to a premature attempt to consummate the sale, and then (following the principles of cognitive consistency) proceeds to reinforce the prior negative position as the salesperson plugs away, firing one closing salvo after another at the beleaguered prospect. Research tells us that it will take several sales calls to make an initial sale, so it is somewhat bewildering to still encounter such tired old battle cries as "the ABCs of selling, which stand for Always Be Closing." Research based on more than 35,000 sales calls over a 12-year period suggests that an overreliance on closing techniques actually reduces the chance of making a sale.[8]

Manipulative closing gimmicks are less likely to be effective as professional buyers grow weary of the cat-and-mouse approach to selling that a surprising number of salespeople still practise. It is also surprising to find many salespeople who view their customers as combatants over whom victory is sought. Once salespeople who have adversarial, me-against-you attitudes make the sale, the customer is likely to be neglected as the salesperson rides off into the sunset in search of yet another battle with yet another lowly customer.

One time-honoured thought that does retain contemporary relevance is that "nobody likes to be sold, but everybody likes to buy." In other words, salespeople should facilitate decision making by pointing out a suggested course of action but should allow the prospect plenty of mental space within which a rational decision can be reached.[9] Taken to its logical conclusion, this means that it may be acceptable to make a sales call without asking for the order. Salespeople must be cognizant, however, of their responsibility to advance the relationship toward a profitable sale, lest they become the most dreaded of all types of salespeople—the paid conversationalist.

It has already been mentioned that the salesperson has taken on the expanded roles of business consultant and relationship manager, which is not consistent with pressuring customers until they give in and say yes. Fortunately, things have changed to the point that today's professional salesperson attempts to gain commitment when the buyer is ready to buy. The salesperson should evaluate each presentation and attempt to determine the causes of its success or failure with the customer. The difference between closing and earning commitment is that commitment is more than just securing an order. Commitment signals the beginning of a long-term relationship.

GUIDELINES FOR EARNING COMMITMENT

Earning commitment is the culmination of the selling process. However, it should not be viewed as a formal stage that comes only at the end of the presentation. Many salespeople fail to recognize early buyer commitment by focusing on their presentation rather than on the comments the buyer is making. **Commitment signals** are favourable statements that may be made by the buyer, such as

- "I like that size."
- "That will get the job done."
- "The price is lower than I thought it would be."
- "I did not realize you delivered every day."

These statements should be considered green lights that allow the salesperson to move the process forward. They also may come in the form of trial commitments.

Throughout the presentation, it is appropriate to determine a prospect's reaction to a particular feature or product. At this time, a trial commitment is a question designed to determine a prospect's reaction without forcing the prospect to make a final "yes or no" buying decision. The trial commitment is an effort to elicit how far along the prospect is in his or her decision making. Confirmation on the prospect's part on key features helps the salesperson determine how ready the prospect is to buy.

Open-end questions are a good way to test a prospect's readiness to buy. A salesperson might ask during his or her presentation, "What do you

commitment signals
Favourable statements a buyer makes during a sales presentation that signal buyer commitment.

think of our computer's larger memory capacity?" The answer to this will help direct the salesperson to his or her next sales points. However, many statements buyers make should be considered red lights, or formal objections. The salesperson must consider each of these objections and work to overcome them. Red light statements might include the following:

- "I am not sure that will work."

- "The price is higher than I thought it would be."

- "Your delivery schedule does not work for us."

- "I do not see the advantage of going with your proposal."

Red light statements are commitment caution signals and must be resolved to the buyer's satisfaction before asking for a commitment. Closing early and often and having a closing quota for each sales call are traditional methods that buyers do not like. Richard Crist in "Professional Selling in the 21st Century: Tighten Up the Use of Closing Techniques," states that it is better to replace numerous closing efforts with better listening skills. The salesperson should put himself or herself in the buyer's shoes and think about how he or she would like to be hammered with many closes throughout a sales presentation, particularly if a few red lights are introduced. Many times, the best method for earning commitment is simply to ask for the business. If the prospect has been qualified properly and a number of confirmed benefits have been uncovered, then naturally the next step is to ask for the business.

direct commitment A selling technique in which the salesperson asks the customer directly to buy.

© DMITRIY SHIRONOSOV/SHUTTERSTOCK

TECHNIQUES TO EARN COMMITMENT

Some sales trainers will try to teach their salesforces literally hundreds of commitment techniques. One trainer recommended to his salesforce that the salespeople learn two new commitment techniques per week. Then at the end of the year, they would have more than 100 commitment techniques ready to use. Relationship managers today do not need many commitment techniques. A few good ones will suffice. Five techniques that are conducive to relationship building follow:

1. **Ask for the Order/Direct Commitment.**
   It is not unusual for inexperienced salespeople to lose an order simply by not asking the customer to buy. Professional buyers report that an amazing number of salespeople fear rejection. When the buyer is ready to buy, the salesperson must be prepared to ask for the buyer's commitment. The **direct commitment**

technique is a straightforward request for an order. A salesperson should be confident if he or she has covered all the necessary features and benefits of the product and matched these with the buyer's needs. At this time, the salesperson cannot be afraid to ask "Tom, can we set up an office visit for next week?" or "Mary, I would like to have your business; if we can get the order signed today, delivery can take place early next week." Many buyers appreciate the direct approach. There is no confusion as to what the salesperson wants the buyer to do.

2. **Legitimate Choice/Alternative Choice.**
The **alternative or legitimate choice** technique asks the prospect to select from two or more choices. For example, "Will the HP 400 or the HP 600 work best for you?" An investment broker might ask his or her prospect, "Do you feel your budget would allow you to invest $1000 a month or would $500 a month be better?" The theory behind this technique suggests buyers do not like to be told what to do but do like making a decision among limited choices.

3. **Summary Commitment.**
A very effective way to gain agreement is to summarize all the major benefits the buyer has confirmed during the sales calls. Salespeople should keep track of all the important points covered in previous calls so they can emphasize them again in summary form.

In using the summary commitment technique, a computer salesperson might say, "Of course, Tom, this is an important decision, so to make the best possible choice, let us go over the major concepts we have discussed. We have agreed that Thompson Computers will provide some definite advantages. First, our system will lower your computing costs; second, our system will last longer and has a better warranty, thus saving you money; and finally, your data processing people will be happier because our faster system will reduce their workload. They will get to go home earlier each evening."

The **summary commitment** is a valuable technique because it reminds prospects of all the major benefits that have been mentioned in previous sales calls.

4. **The T-Account or the Balance Sheet Commitment.**
The **T-account commitment** or **balance sheet commitment** is essentially a summary commitment on paper. With the T-account commitment, the sales representative takes out a sheet of paper and draws a large "T" across it. On the left-hand side, the salesperson and buyer brainstorm the reasons to buy. Here, the salesperson will list with the buyer all the positive selling points (benefits) they discussed throughout the selling process. Once this is completed, the salesperson asks the buyer for any reasons that he or she would not want to purchase. Visually, the left-hand side should help the buyer make his or her decision, as seen in Exhibit 8.10. This will not work if the weight of the reasons not to buy outweighs the reasons to buy. In the example in Exhibit 8.10, the buyer wants to act but does not have the money at this time.

> Good salespeople are never in a hurry to earn commitment!

alternative or legitimate choice A selling technique in which the salesperson asks the prospect to select from two or more choices during a sales presentation.

summary commitment A selling technique in which the salesperson summarizes all the major benefits the buyer has confirmed during the sales calls.

T-account or **balance sheet commitment** A selling technique in which a salesperson asks the prospect to brainstorm reasons on paper of why to buy and why not to buy.

EXHIBIT 8.10
T-Account Close

Reasons to Buy	Reasons Not to Buy
• Daily delivery schedule meets our needs	• Because of extra services
• Warranty agreement is longer than the one I have now (five years versus three years)	• Your price *is too high*
• You provide a training program	
• Your service department is located in our city	

5. Success Story Commitment.

Every company has many satisfied customers. These customers started out having problems, and the sales representative helped solve these problems by recommending the product or products that matched the customer's needs. Buyers are thankful and grateful when the salesperson helps solve problems. When the salesperson relates a story about how one of his or her customers had a similar problem and solved it by using the salesperson's product, a reluctant buyer can be reassured that the salesperson has done this before successfully. If the salesperson decides to use the customer's name and company, then the salesperson must be sure to get permission to do so. A **success story commitment** may go something like this:

Tom, thanks for sharing your copier problems with me. I had another customer you might know, Betty Brown, who had the same problem over at Thompson Electronics. We installed the CP 2000 and eliminated the problem completely. Please feel free to give Betty a call. She is very happy with our solution.

Some companies will use the success story commitment by actually taking the prospect to a satisfied customer. The salesperson may leave the prospect alone with the satisfied customer so the two can talk confidentially. A satisfied customer can help a salesperson earn commitment by answering questions a reluctant prospect needs answered before he or she can purchase. Exhibit 8.11 shows a summary of relationship-building earning commitment techniques.

PROBE TO EARN COMMITMENT

Not every attempt to earn commitment will be successful. Successful salespeople cannot be afraid to ask a prospect why he or she is hesitating to make a decision. It is the salesperson's job to uncover the reason why the prospect is hesitating by asking a series of questions that reveal the key issues. For instance, a buyer may state that he or she is not ready to sign an order. The salesperson must ask, "Mary, there must be a reason why you are reluctant to do business with me and my company. Do you mind if I ask what it is?" The salesperson must then listen and respond

success story commitment A selling technique in which a salesperson relates how one of his or her customers had a problem similar to the prospect's and solved it by using the salesperson's product.

EXHIBIT 8.11
Techniques to Earn Commitment

1. Direct commitment—Simply ask for the order.
2. Legitimate choice/alternative choice—Give the prospect a limited number of choices.
3. Summary commitment—Summarize all the confirmed benefits to which there has been agreement.
4. T-account/balance sheet commitment—Summary close on paper.
5. Success story commitment—Salesperson tells a story of a business that successfully solved a problem by buying his or her products.

---

accordingly. A salesperson cannot be afraid to ask why a prospect is reluctant to purchase.

TRADITIONAL METHODS

Sales trainers across the nation teach hundreds of techniques to earn commitment. Exhibit 8.12 is a summary of the traditional commitment techniques. The vast majority of these are not conducive to building a strong buyer–seller relationship. As prospects become more sophisticated, most will be turned off by these techniques and they will be ineffective. "An Ethical Dilemma" asks the question, "What happens when the buyer determines the salesperson is less than truthful when attempting to close?"

Research has clearly shown that buyers are open to consultative techniques of handling objections (e.g., questioning and assessing, direct denial with facts, and so on) and earning commitment (e.g., asking for the order in a straightforward manner, summarizing key benefits). However, buyers have stated that standard persuasive (traditional) tactics that have been used for years are unacceptable. They now view traditional techniques of handling objections (e.g., forestalling, postponing) and earning commitment (e.g., standing-room only, fear) as overly aggressive and unprofessional.[10]

EXHIBIT 8.12
Traditional Commitment Method

Method	How to Use It
Standing-room-only close	This close puts a time limit on the client in an attempt to hurry the decision to close. "These prices are good only until tomorrow."
Assumptive close	The salesperson assumes that an agreement has been reached. The salesperson places the order form in front of the buyer and hands him or her a pen.
Fear or emotional close	The salesperson tells a story of something bad happening if the purchase is not made. "If you do not purchase this insurance and you die, your wife will have to sell the house and live on the street."
Continuous yes close	This close uses the principle that saying yes gets to be a habit. The salesperson asks a number of questions, each formulated so that the prospect answers yes.
Minor-points close	Seeks agreement on relatively minor (trivial) issues associated with the full order. "Do you prefer cash or charge?"

standing-room only close A sales closing technique in which the salesperson puts a time limit on the client in an attempt to hurry the decision to close.

assumptive close A sales closing technique in which the salesperson assumes that an agreement has been reached, places the order form in front of the buyer, and hands him or her a pen.

fear or emotional close A sales closing technique in which the salesperson tells a story of something bad happening if the purchase is not made.

continuous yes close A sales closing technique that uses the principle that saying yes gets to be a habit; the salesperson asks a number of questions formulated so that the prospect answers yes.

minor-points close A sales closing technique in which the salesperson seeks agreement on relatively minor issues associated with the full order.

An Ethical Dilemma

Kelly Orlando has just returned from a training session where the sales trainer told all the associates they had to use the standing-room-only close (i.e., better order today—we are about to run out!) because inventory has been piling up in the company's warehouses and they must move the product out immediately. They are to tell their prospects that the special pricing is going to go on for only one week and then it will be over until next year. Kelly is very uncomfortable with this, knowing her company has plenty of products in the warehouse. What should she do?

© PAUL TAYLOR/JUPITER IMAGES

DATA COMPUTERS

Background

Steve Thomas sells for Data Computers. Thomas has recently completed his training seminars and has been back in the field for three months. He has been anxious to try out the selling processes his company uses. He is equally excited about the techniques he has been taught on how to handle sales resistance and earn commitment. His trainers were very impressed with his ability to use the T-account method to earn commitment. Thomas feels this technique is very pragmatic and visually shows his prospects why they should use his products. He has been surprised at how ineffective this technique has been on recent sales calls. He is beginning to wonder if he should try some other earning commitment techniques.

Current Situation

Here is a copy of Thomas's notes from a prospect he has been working on.

Thomas's Notes:

Client: Anderson Printing, Anwar Martin, purchasing agent

Prospect looks good—looks like a good fit

Potential to earn business—B+/A-

Present equipment—four years old

Fact-finding call on 9/1, buyer went to local college, two kids

9/15 Took engineers in and looked at his present system. Basically it is ready to be replaced. Purchased in 2005.

9/22 Made major proposal to Anwar Martin, could not get engineers to attend. They had all-day meetings. Gave proposal to Martin and made appointment to come back in two days to review proposal.

9/24 Overall good meeting. I used the T-account method with Martin.

Thomas is afraid he is going to lose the order. He did not leave Martin with a good feeling.

Questions

1. Look over the notes from each one of Thomas's sales calls. Can you make any recommendations on what Thomas might have done differently?
2. Thomas and Martin came up with five reasons to buy and two reasons not to act. What is holding Martin back?

Reasons to Act	Reasons Not to Act
1. New system is faster; saves time and energy.	1. Still thinks the price is high, even with the cost savings
2. Can have immediate delivery; does not have to wait	2. Needs to talk over decision with engineers
3. Really likes the cost savings	
4. Can save up to $100 per month in operating cost	
5. Quality looks great	

Role Play

Situation: Read the case.
Characters: Steve Thomas, sales representative; Anwar Martin, purchasing agent

Scene 1:
Location—Martin's office.

Action—Thomas is going to review the proposal with Martin.

Role play the T-account earning commitment with Martin.

Scene 2:
Location—Martin's office.

Action—Thomas has just asked for the order after the T-account earning commitment technique has been used.

Role play Martin telling Thomas he needs time to think it over and Thomas's response.

After completing the role plays, address the following questions:

1. Can you find any fault in Thomas's logic that there are more reasons to act than not to act?
2. What are the problems with relying on one earning commitment technique?

Muncie Fencing

Background

Muncie Fencing has been a family-run business for more than 100 years. Jerome Johnson's great-grandfather started the business by putting up fences for farmers. Today they do commercial and residential fencing and over the past two years added an invisible fence franchise that has turned into about a third of their business. Muncie Fencing takes an advertisement out in the Sunday newspaper that encourages people who are interested in a fence to call in. Muncie Fencing has a long list of customers and prospects that they can cold call. They do have a small ad in the yellow pages and they have relied on word of mouth. With the downturn of the economy, business has slowed quite a bit and Jerome has found prospects are very hesitant to spend money at this time. Jerome has two university interns in his office who answer the phone and follow up on leads that come in.

The two interns also make outbound calls to customers and leads they have secured from their ads. The interns are very frustrated because they have encountered a great deal of sales resistance. Jerome asked them to keep track of the objections they have encountered and they reported to him the following:

"I'm not sure I'm ready to buy at this time. I'll need to think it over."

"Your price is much higher than I thought it would be!"

"One of my friends said you didn't do a very good job on his fence."

Role Play

Location: Jerome Johnson's office

Action: Role play Jerome and his interns discussing the sales resistance and how they are going to overcome each objection (use LAARC).

what do you think?

Business customers are eager to develop relationships with suppliers.

1 2 3 4 5 6 7

strongly disagree   strongly agree

Repeat business

is the lifeline of an organization.

9

Expanding Customer Relationships

Introduction

t he slow economy has companies scrambling to find more profitable customers. As sales continue to move at a snail's pace, CFOs are pushing budget cuts as a top priority. In the struggle to regain lost ground, many companies make one major mistake: They fail to improve customer relationships.

According to Gartner Dataquest, worldwide customer relationship management spending on software and services reached $23 billion in 2000. Ideally, this huge investment should deliver greater insight into customers, smoother customer communications, greater customer loyalty and healthier profits. However, independent research paints a different picture.

Customer satisfaction has not improved. According to a study by the University of Michigan Business School, between 1994 and 2000 customer satisfaction declined an average of 7.9 percent. Companies ignore customer behavior. Forrester Research Inc. found that only 23 percent of companies currently improve their online operations by making use of the data associated with how customers use their Websites. A study by Broadbase Software Inc. found that 90 percent of online shoppers click to a competitor's site if they experience poor customer service.

Companies fail to weed out unprofitable customers. According to Newton, Massachusetts-based Meridien Research, 20 percent of a bank's customers generate about 150 percent of unadjusted revenues. At the bottom end, about 30 percent of the customers actually drain 50 percent of the gains realized. But cutting the bottom end without analyzing customer data can backfire. For example, First Union Corporation found that what it had considered the lowest fifth of its customer base in income was actually its most profitable segment.

Companies fail to boost customer loyalty. A customer loyalty study by Deloitte Research showed that when manufacturers set targets for retaining customers and strive to exceed loyalty goals, they are 60 percent more profitable than competitors that don't track customer loyalty well. All that insight had little impact on this year's trend of eroding loyalty. Carlson Marketing Group reported in its annual Relationship Builder survey that in 2000 four in ten customers showed a genuine commitment to brands or companies. In 2001, that commitment has dropped to just three in ten customers. Frederick F. Reichheld writes in his book *Loyalty Rules*, "Outstanding loyalty is the direct result of the words and deeds—the decisions and practices—of committed

After completing this chapter, you should be able to

LO1 Explain how to follow up to assess and take action to ensure customer satisfaction by using the latest technology.

LO2 Discuss how to expand collaborative involvement.

LO3 Explain how to add value and enhance mutual opportunities.

top executives who have personal integrity." This insight confirms that while CRM technology does not ensure customer loyalty, people do.

The road to recovery begins with the realization that customer expectations have gone up while the economy has declined. Last year more customers found it difficult to buy, hence the decline in loyalty. This year buyers make it far more difficult to sell. The message is clear: Sales won't improve until customer relationships improve. It's time to return to such core principles as treating customers well and saying thank you. It's time to return to such core values as honesty and integrity. When that happens, customer satisfaction shall again be king.

Source: Gerhard Gschwandtner. "Customer Relationships in a Slow Economy." *Selling Power.* http://www.sellingpower.com/content/article.php?a=5812.

I n traditional selling, salespeople too often thought that their job was over when they closed the sale. Once the order was obtained, they moved on to the next prospect. Any follow-up or customer service was minimal. The lifeline of an organization today is repeat business. It is important to acquire new customers, but it is critical to keep your existing customer base happy. In research involving 80,000 business customers, the number-one characteristic found to define a world-class salesperson is someone who personally manages the customer's satisfaction by being accountable for the customer's desired results.[1] Not following up with a new customer is a shortsighted attitude toward selling, for it fails to consider the importance of developing and maintaining a customer for your company.

Research indicates that successfully retaining customers is critical for all companies' success. Relationship marketing efforts can lead to longer term, broader, and deeper customer relationships, which results in increases in sales, profits, and positive word of mouth.[2] Companies that invest 10 percent or more of their revenue in customer experience have greater referral rates, superior customer satisfaction scores, and better retention rates than those companies that invest less in customer experience.[3] Another study finds that it takes only a slight decline in attention from a salesperson to lead to an opportunity to consider alternative suppliers.[4]

A salesperson can convert new customers into highly committed lifetime customers in several ways. Examples include (1) **building goodwill** by continually **adding value** to the product or service through appropriate follow-up, (2) handling complaints in a timely and thoughtful manner, and (3) processing requests for rush deliveries willingly and assuring the customer that the salesperson will do everything possible to make that request happen. However, it is just as easy for a salesperson to alienate a new customer by putting the focus on the short-term order and not the long-term activities that create a partnership. This can be done by overpromising and underdelivering, using exaggeration to get an order, and blaming everyone else for problems. Exhibit 9.1 reviews relationship enhancers and detractors that can strengthen or destroy a relationship.

Relationship-oriented salespeople are creating bonds with their customers that will partially isolate them from competitive pressures or at least minimize the importance of easily altered and matched competitive variables, such as price. This chapter explains the importance of follow-up to assess customer satisfaction. Next, harnessing technology to enhance follow-up and buyer–seller relationships is covered. This is followed by a discussion of why it is the salesperson's job to take action (i.e., be proactive) before problems

EXHIBIT 9.1
Relationship Enhancers and Detractors

Enhancers	Detractors
Focus on long term	Focus on short term
Deliver more than promised	Overpromise and/or underdeliver
Call regularly	Call sporadically
Add value	Show up only for another order
Keep communication lines open	Are unavailable to the customer
Take responsibility for problems	Lie, exaggerate, blame someone else

arise and not wait for complaints (i.e., be reactive) to ensure customer satisfaction. We then discuss the importance of collaborative involvement and working to add value for the buyer. Finally, we review the value of customer service.

LO1
Assess Customer Satisfaction

Keeping customers satisfied is important as it leads to customer trust and, ultimately, share of customer. Research shows that customer satisfaction is in part affected by salespeople's reliability and responsiveness as demonstrated by returning phone calls promptly, fulfilling commitments, satisfying customer requests, and being readily available. Furthermore, salespeople who regularly, clearly, and concisely communicate product information to customers can enhance their satisfaction.[5] Such research points to the need to be diligent in following up and properly communicating with customers to build, maintain, and enhance customer relationships.

Unfortunately, many companies do a poor job understanding and satisfying their customers. Results from an annual study of business executives conducted by the Strativity Group, Inc., include the following:[6]

- More than 65 percent do not have a dedicated customer experience management role.

- Nearly 73 percent of respondents do not have a clear definition of the customer experience that is well communicated in their companies.

- Less than one-third (28.8 percent) of respondents provide employees with the tools and authority to solve customer problems.

- Nearly 76 percent do not have employees who are well-versed in how to delight customers.

- Slightly more than 56 percent believe that their companies do not deserve their customers' loyalty.

John Haack, senior vice president of marketing and sales for Saint-Gobain Containers (a glass container manufacturer), knows the importance of enhancing customer relationships as opposed to focusing solely on current sales. With such customers as Anheuser-Busch, Quaker Oats, and Kraft, Haack says, "Making the sale is only the beginning. After that, you have to keep track of the process every step of the way. You have to make sure the product gets delivered on time and that everyone involved with the customer knows their customer's expectations." Haack continues, "Anybody can move product. I can go out and sell a ton of something, but if it is not right for that particular customer, it is just going to end up back on my doorstep as a major problem."[7]

Clearly, professional salespeople, such as John Haack, view their customer base as far too valuable an asset to risk losing it through neglect. In maintaining and enhancing customer relationships, salespeople are involved in performing routine postsale follow-up activities and in enhancing the relationship as it evolves by anticipating and adapting to changes in the customer's situation, competitive forces, and other changes in the market environment. For instance, many salespeople do field research, conduct brainstorming sessions, and provide sales leads obtained through a network of business contacts. Activities like these demonstrate a service commitment. The objective in this step is to create a strong bond with customers that will diminish the probability of customers terminating the relationship. In effect, the salesperson earns the business through a number of successive trials and strengthens his or her position as time passes through follow-up calls and by adding value.

Furthering this notion, Darrell Beaty of Ontario Systems (a collections

> Salespeople today use several technologies to stay in touch with customers.

software company) states, "We spend too much time and effort learning about our prospects to not follow through and assess satisfaction." Figure 9.1[8] demonstrates the time and commitment Beaty puts in to earn an order from a prospect. Beaty states, "We cannot be afraid to ask a customer, 'How are we doing?'" This practice should go on monthly, quarterly, and yearly. Sometimes, the salesperson will not like the answers that he or she gets from the customers. New customers generally feel special because they have received a lot of attention. Long-term customers may feel neglected because the salesperson has many new customers and cannot be as attentive as he or she was previously. Routine follow-up questions, such as "How are we doing?" can go a long way in letting a customer know that the salesperson cares and is willing to make sure that the customer is satisfied.

HARNESS TECHNOLOGY TO ENHANCE FOLLOW-UP AND BUYER–SELLER RELATIONSHIPS

Building buyer–seller relationships is easier said than done. Developing and nurturing customer relationships demands that salespeople do more than simply discover the buyer's needs and respond to them with a sales offering that resolves those needs. Relationships are formed over time through multiple buyer-seller interactions in which the seller wins the trust of the buyer. One survey found that one of the most important things buyers look for in sellers is accountability. They want someone who they can rely on during the entire sales process and who will not abandon them after the sale is finalized.[9] Another study uncovered nearly 80 reasons why customers dislike salespeople, with the fourth most important ranked reason being a lack of salesperson follow-up.[10] The results of these studies emphasize the importance of effective follow-up by the salesperson. As discussed in this chapter and illustrated in Figure 9.2, effective salesperson follow-up should include specific components designed to interact with, connect with, know, and relate with customers.

- **Interact**—The salesperson acts to maximize the number of critical encounters with buyers to encourage effective dialogue and involvement between the salesperson and buyer.

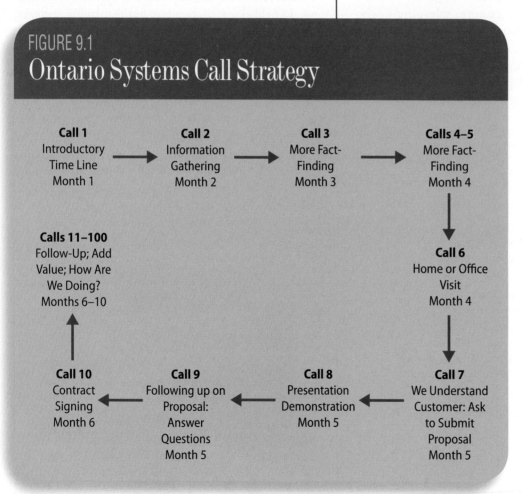

FIGURE 9.1
Ontario Systems Call Strategy

Call 1
Introductory
Time Line
Month 1

Call 2
Information
Gathering
Month 2

Call 3
More Fact-
Finding
Month 3

Calls 4–5
More Fact-
Finding
Month 4

Call 6
Home or Office
Visit
Month 4

Calls 11–100
Follow-Up; Add
Value; How Are
We Doing?
Months 6–10

Call 10
Contract
Signing
Month 6

Call 9
Following up on
Proposal:
Answer
Questions
Month 5

Call 8
Presentation
Demonstration
Month 5

Call 7
We Understand
Customer: Ask
to Submit
Proposal
Month 5

It takes many calls to earn commitment from a prospect. It can take months and even years to establish the trust needed to earn an order.

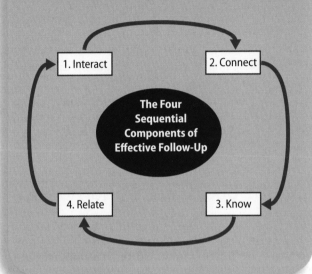

FIGURE 9.2
The Four Sequential Components of Effective Follow-Up

The Four Sequential Components of Effective Follow-Up

1. Interact
2. Connect
3. Know
4. Relate

Effective salesperson follow-up should include specific components designed to interact with, connect with, know, and relate with his or her customers.

- **Connect**—The salesperson maintains contact with the multiple individuals in the buying organization influencing purchase decisions and manages the various touch points the customer has in the selling organization to ensure consistency in communication.

- **Know**—The salesperson coordinates and interprets the information gathered through buyer-seller contact and collaboration to develop insight regarding the buyer's changing situation, needs, and expectations.

- **Relate**—The salesperson applies relevant understanding and insight to create value-added interactions and generate relationships between the salesperson and buyer.

Salespeople employ a variety of technology-based salesforce automation tools to better track the increasingly complex combination of buyer-seller interactions and to manage the exchange, interpretation, and storage of diverse types of information. Among the more popular salesforce automation tools are the many competing versions of PC- and Internet-based software applications designed to record and manage customer contact information. PC-based software applications, such as Maximizer, Goldmine, and ACT!, and Internet-based applications, such as Netsuite and Salesforce.com enable salespeople to collect, file, and access comprehensive databases detailing information about individual buyers and buying organizations. In addition to providing explicit details about customers and the multiple individuals influencing purchasing decisions within any given account, these databases also provide an archive of the interactions and purchasing decisions taking place over time. Salespeople using these systems have found them to be invaluable in helping them track and better service their accounts to ensure and enhance customer satisfaction. By better understanding every transaction and buyer-seller interaction, salespeople can be more effective in communicating with each individual customer throughout the lifetime of the account.

The advent of the Internet has allowed these customer contact management tools to be used in multiorganization intranets and extranets. An **intranet** is an organization's dedicated and proprietary computer

connect The salesperson maintains contact with the multiple individuals in the buying organization who influence purchase decisions and manages the various touch points the customer has in the selling organization to ensure consistency in communication.

know The salesperson coordinates and interprets the information gathered through buyer–seller contact and collaboration to develop insight regarding the buyer's changing situation, needs, and expectations.

relate The salesperson applies relevant understanding and insight to create value-added interactions and generate relationships between the salesperson and buyer.

intranet An organization's dedicated and proprietary computer network that offers password-controlled access to people within and outside the organization (e.g., customers and suppliers).

> Relationships are formed over time through multiple buyer–seller interactions in which the seller wins the trust of the buyer.

network offering password-controlled access to people within and outside the organization (e.g., customers and suppliers). **Extranets** are proprietary computer networks created by an organization for use by the organization's customers or suppliers and linked to the organization's internal systems, informational databases, and intranet.

Internet-activated and integrated with an organization's intranet and extranets, customer contact systems are transposed to full **customer relationship management (CRM) systems**. These systems dynamically link buyers and sellers into a rich communication network. Salespeople and buyers have immediate, 24/7 access to one another and one another's organizations. Problems can be resolved online, routine ordering procedures can be automated, and information, such as product brochures and spec sheets, inventory availability, price lists, and order status, can be exchanged. Salespeople can use the Web to view everything that is relevant to any account. This can include information in the organization's databases (e.g., purchasing history, credit rating) as well as pertinent information such as news stories, stock prices, and research reports from sources outside the organization (e.g., Hoovers, Standard & Poor's, etc.).

CRM systems enable salespeople to build and integrate multiple forms of customer information and create highly influential customer interactions that establish and reinforce long-term, profitable relationships. The benefits to salespeople learning to use these advanced, integrated systems effectively are self-evident. Every time a salesperson and buyer interact in a positive manner, the corresponding relationship is enriched. This enrichment translates to improved service levels, increased customer satisfaction, and enhanced revenues from loyal customers. For example, after a series of mergers and acquisitions, Honeywell Aerospace found customers telling them that it was difficult to do business with them. Two different Honeywell sales reps, for instance, might call on the same customer in the same day. After implementing a CRM system, customer satisfaction with Honeywell improved 38 percent, its on-time service request closure rate improved from 45 to 83 percent, and its sales opportunity rate improved. Moreover, Honeywell credits the CRM system with a 100 percent annual revenue improvement from $45 million to $100 million in the sales of its after-market spare parts.[11]

ENSURE CUSTOMER SATISFACTION

Exhibit 9.2 illustrates the partnership-enhancement activities and the salesperson's responsibility that goes

EXHIBIT 9.2
Relationship-Enhancement Activities

Partnership-Enhancement Activities	Salesperson Responsibility
Provide useful information	• Relevant • Timely • High quality
Expedite orders/monitor installation	• Track orders • Inform on delays • Help with installation
Train customer personnel	• Train even when contract does not call for it
Correct billing errors	• Go over all orders • Correct problem before customer recognizes it
Remember the customer after the sale	• Set up a regular call schedule • Let customer know you will be back
Resolve complaints	• Preferably prevent the need to complain • Ask customer how he or she wants complaint resolved

along with them. Specific relationship-enhancement activities vary substantially from company to company but are critical to the success of building long-term relationships. These activities include the following:

- Providing useful information
- Expediting orders and monitoring installation
- Training customer personnel
- Correcting billing errors
- Remembering the customer after the sale
- Resolving complaints

Traditional selling focuses on getting the order. In a sense, the sales process was over once the order was signed. The salesperson's job was to focus on getting the next order, and it was left to others in the organization to deliver and install the product. However, the relational sales process shown in Figure 9.3 indicates that many activities must take place after the sale, and it is the salesperson's responsibility to oversee and participate in all of the follow-up activities. By being actively involved during this stage, the salesperson increases the odds that a long-term relationship will develop.

PROVIDE USEFUL INFORMATION

Many buyers feel neglected once they place an order with a company. They were given a lot of attention before they placed the order, but after the order was placed, the salesperson disappeared. Once an economic relationship is established, the salesperson must continually provide timely, relevant, high-quality information to his or her customers. The job of educating the buyer never stops, and salespeople are responsible for updating customers and pointing out additional opportunities that will benefit them. Information that will help customers solve their problems also is a must.

By providing useful information, the salesperson is demonstrating a commitment to the buyer. The salesperson

FIGURE 9.3

Traditional versus Relational Sales Process

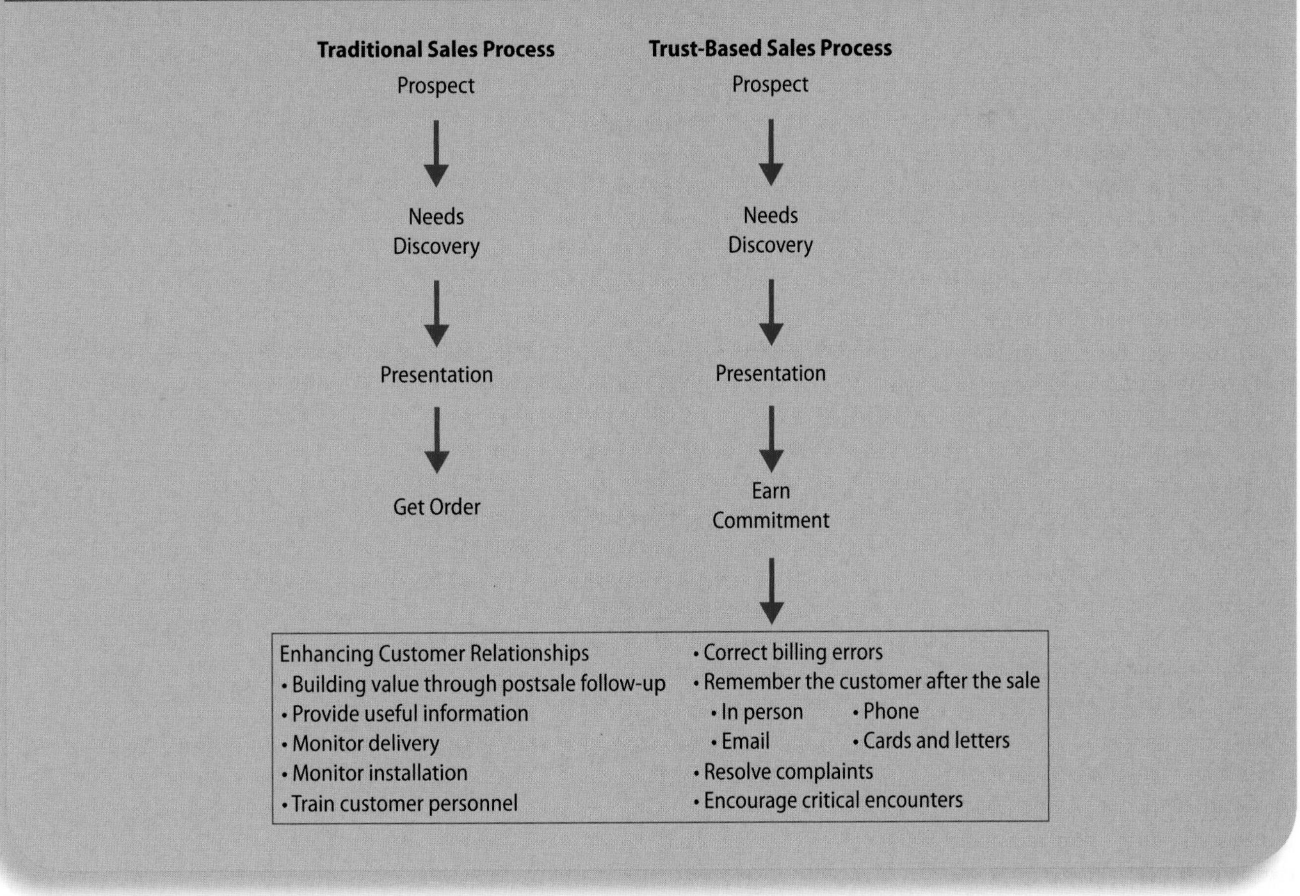

Traditional Sales Process

Prospect
↓
Needs Discovery
↓
Presentation
↓
Get Order

Trust-Based Sales Process

Prospect
↓
Needs Discovery
↓
Presentation
↓
Earn Commitment
↓

Enhancing Customer Relationships
- Building value through postsale follow-up
- Provide useful information
- Monitor delivery
- Monitor installation
- Train customer personnel

- Correct billing errors
- Remember the customer after the sale
  - In person   • Phone
  - Email   • Cards and letters
- Resolve complaints
- Encourage critical encounters

Traditional selling focuses on getting the order. The relational sales process indicates that many activities must take place after the sale.

is showing that he or she is in the relationship for the long term and that he or she values the partnership. The salesperson should remember to provide information not only to the buyer but also to the secretaries, receptionists, administrative assistants, department heads, and other influential members of the buyer's organization.

Several postsale follow-up methods can be used to provide helpful information. The best way to provide useful information is by a personal visit. After the sale is made, it is critical to follow up personally and make sure that the customer is completely satisfied with all the promises that have been made (e.g., delivery, installation done properly, courteous installers). This is the only strategy that provides face-to-face communication. When a salesperson takes the time to make a well-planned personal follow-up visit, he or she indicates to the prospect that he or she really cares. A good salesperson will use the follow-up call to keep the customer informed of new developments in the industry, new products, or new applications. Providing this information may bring about future sales. When a salesperson makes a follow-up call, he or she should always have an objective for the sales call. The salesperson should be sure not to spend too much time on gossip sessions or chitchat. It is the salesperson's job to add value, not waste the customer's time.

An efficient option for providing useful information after a sale is to use the telephone. The telephone is a quick and efficient way to contact customers. The cell phone has provided salespeople with an opportunity to stay in touch with customers while on the road. A salesperson can easily make 7 to 10 phone calls per hour, and the cost is minimal. Although a personal note to a customer is always appropriate, the telephone has the advantage of a two-way exchange of information. The phone can be used to verify delivery, inform the customer of any changes (e.g., price, delivery schedule), and check for problems in general.

Email is another way to stay in touch with a customer. Most individuals and companies have email addresses. The salesperson

has to make this part of his or her information-gathering process. When getting pertinent company and buyer information, the salesperson should also get email addresses. Some buyers will check their email and respond daily; others will not check or respond for weeks. The salesperson must determine which buyers like to use email and make it part of his or her follow-up process when dealing with these customers.

Finally, a handwritten thank-you card to a customer is an inexpensive and convenient form of customer follow-up. It should always be used in conjunction with the other follow-up methods. The mail can also be used to send out new promotional material, information about new products, and trade publication articles that may be of interest to customers. Periodically, a salesperson could send his or her customers a short survey that asks "How are we doing?" Exhibit 9.3 summarizes the strengths and weaknesses of follow-up methods. Checking the customer's level of satisfaction might highlight an area of concern that the salesperson can take care of before it becomes a major problem.

EXHIBIT 9.3
Methods to Provide Useful Information

Method	Strength	Weakness
1. Personal call	Best for interactive face-to-face communication; view body language	Most time consuming Most expensive Customers will not always see salesperson
2. Telephone	Can make 7–10 calls per hour Cell phones allow call to be made from anywhere Inexpensive Immediate feedback	May interrupt your customers Cannot evaluate facial expressions
3. Mail	One more touch that lets the customers know you are thinking about them	Customers get a lot of mail Customer may not see it if secretary opens and tosses mail One-way communication
4. Email	Easy to get many touches Inexpensive Not time consuming	Customer may not read email every day One-way communication

Postsale Communications at R.R. Donnelly

Kelly Osterling, a sales representative for R.R. Donnelly, knows that personalized service is the best way to stay in touch with her customers:

I work hard at understanding how my customers want to communicate with me. Some respond well to email, others in person, and some by phone. I have a few customers that only want to hear from me by fax. I have learned to use technology as a bridge to my customers and not as a wall.

I essentially have email addresses and fax numbers for all of my customers. When we have new product introductions, I attempt to see all of my customers in person. I can then follow up with other information, such as price changes and delivery dates through email and voice mail.

My customers know I check my emails daily, and they can send me questions, requests, and complaints. I must follow up immediately. There are times when my customers can't see me or take my phone calls; by knowing how they prefer their information delivered, I can use other forms of communication (email, voice mail, and fax) to respond to them. I want my customers to know I care.

Customer preference should determine the method of communication. The salesperson should find the methods that work with individual customers and stay with them. In "Professional Selling in the 21st Century: Postsale Communications at R.R. Donnelly," Kelly Osterling of R.R. Donnelly describes how she communicates with her customers.

EXPEDITE ORDERS AND MONITOR INSTALLATION

Generally, salespeople will set estimates on product delivery times. The salesperson must work to prevent a delay in delivery. The salesperson's job is to track the order status and inform the customers when delays occur. It is unpleasant to inform a buyer of a delay, but the information allows buyers to work around the inconvenience and plan accordingly. Waiting until the delivery date to announce a delay is inconsiderate and hurts the trust built between the salesperson and buyer.

Many problems with shipping and the delivery of an order are out of the salesperson's control. However, today's sophisticated tracking systems allow salespeople to track orders and find out what is causing the delay. The salesperson must keep the customer up-to-date on the delivery status and any possible delays.

Monitoring order processing and after-sale activities is critical to enhancing the relationship with a customer. Customers often have done a poor job of forecasting, run short of product, and may expect their salesperson to bring their emergency to a happy conclusion. Although it is not always possible to speed up orders, the salesperson should investigate and attempt to do everything possible to help the customers. If the buyer sees concern on the salesperson's part and knows that the salesperson is attempting to help the buyer, then the relationship will be strengthened, even if the order cannot be pushed through as quickly as the buyer had hoped.

Depending on the industry, salespeople generally do not help with installation. Nevertheless, some salespeople believe that it is in their best interest to supervise the installation process and to be available when customers have questions. Typically, installers do not have the same relationship with the customer and may not have the type of personality to deal with difficult situations. The salesperson can act as the buffer between the installation team and the customers.

TRAINING CUSTOMER PERSONNEL

Companies are always looking for ways to gain a competitive advantage. Once the order is placed, traditional salespeople are happy to get their commission or bonus and move on to their next conquest. Relationship managers understand the real work begins once the order is signed. Training customer personnel may or may not be included in the price terms of the agreement. Salespeople may use this to gain the competitive edge they need. For example, instead of training only one person as stated in the sales terms, the salesperson gladly trains three people for the same price. Adding value should always be a priority with any salesperson.

When the product is technical, customer training may require the assistance of the company trainer or engineer. The salesperson still has a key role as he or she knows the customer best and should serve as the facilitator to ensure that all the parties have been properly introduced and start off in a positive manner. The salesperson should schedule the training sessions as conveniently as possible for the customer. Customer education is an integral part of the marketing strategy of Ontario Systems Corporation, a collections software company. What separates Ontario from its competitors is its ability to provide timely training and education for all its

Corken, a worldwide manufacturer and marketer of compressors and pumps, provides yearly in-house product training programs, as well as assistance for initial startups and on-site training for plant personnel.

customers. Ontario knows that service after the sale is crucial, which is why it provides an 800 telephone number for 24-hour service. Each year, Ontario strengthens its relationship with customers by providing one week of training, seminars, and goodwill at its home office. Ontario understands the importance of the team approach to providing outstanding customer service.

An Ethical Dilemma

Susan Preston works for a manufacturer of ball bearings that sells to a variety of manufacturers and retail outlets. As she was reviewing the latest invoice scheduled to go out to one of her largest and longest-standing customers, Preston noticed that her customer was being billed at the newly increased prices even though she had sold the product before the price increases. Preston's customer knew that a price increase was coming but was unaware if it would be on this shipment or the next. Preston would stand to gain a significantly larger commission on this order at the new higher prices. It was questionable whether her customer would even catch the price change, much less be aware that this order was supposed to be at the older lower prices. If you were Preston, what would you do?

CORRECT BILLING ERRORS

Billing errors could turn into customer complaints if not found in a timely fashion and corrected. A salesperson should go over all orders and billing records to ensure proper billing has been sent to the customer. A customer will know the salesperson has his or her best interests in mind if the salesperson corrects problems without being prompted by the customer. As seen in "An Ethical Dilemma," it is possible that a billing error may result in an ethical dilemma.

REMEMBER THE CUSTOMER AFTER THE SALE

Customer follow-up methods should be used to express appreciation for the purchase and to develop the relationship after the sale further. Customers consistently cite poor service and lack of follow-up as the primary reasons that buyers stop buying. At one branch office of Wallace Computer Services, a saying hangs above the door: "Remember the Customer between Calls." Personal visits should be the primary method to follow up after the sale. It is the most costly but also the most effective. This method allows face-to-face, two-way communication. The customer's body language can also be observed.

The telephone can also be used to follow up a sale. Most salespeople send a written follow up thanking the customer for his or her business. The telephone can then be used to reinforce the written message. The customer can give verbal feedback, and the salesperson can ask questions and use probing techniques that cannot be used with written correspondence. It is important not to forget the customer after the sale.

RESOLVE COMPLAINTS AND ENCOURAGE CRITICAL ENCOUNTERS

Complaints will never be completely eliminated by any company. Nevertheless, it is every company's hope that it can reduce the frequency of complaints. Complaints typically arise because the product did not live up to the buyer's expectations. Buyers complain for any number of reasons: (1) late delivery, (2) wrong order sent (e.g., too many, too few), (3) product performs poorly, or (4) nobody at the salesperson's company takes the buyer's problems seriously. See Exhibit 9.4 for a more comprehensive list of complaints.

Many times, the complaint is not the fault of the salesperson (e.g., late delivery, wrong order, product performs poorly). "An Ethical Dilemma" demonstrates a typically difficult complaint a salesperson has to overcome. However, this is not a concern to buyers as they expect the salesperson to resolve it. Traditional salespeople have been known to pass the blame when complaints arise. A salesperson would be better off to tackle the complaint by accepting responsibility and promptly fixing the problem. Salespeople get into trouble by overpromising what their product can do, being overly optimistic about delivery dates, and not being attentive to their customers when they do complain. Many complaints can be avoided by giving customers a reasonable expectation of what a company's product or service can do for them.

If periodic meetings are taking place between the buyer and seller after the sale, then in all probability, most of the important issues are being discussed.

> Complaints will never be completely eliminated by any company, but they must be addressed and resolved.

Salespeople must ask their buyers to be candid with them and encourage the buyer to discuss tough issues (e.g., late deliveries, damaged products), especially in areas where the salesperson's organization is providing less than satisfactory performance. Some buyers will not complain

EXHIBIT 9.4
Typical Customer Complaints

1. Late delivery
2. Damaged merchandise
3. Invoice errors
4. Out of stock—back orders
5. Shipped incorrect product
6. Shipped incorrect order size
7. Service department unresponsive
8. Product does not live up to expectations
9. Customer not informed of new developments
10. Customer's problems not taken seriously
11. Improper installation
12. Need more training
13. Price increase—no notice
14. Cannot find the salesperson when needed

An Ethical Dilemma

Tim Sanders of Technology Unlimited has sold five personal computers to a small firm in his hometown. He secured the order by guaranteeing he could meet the customer's desired delivery date of two weeks. Sanders called his home office and was given the green light to sign the order with the delivery conditions, even though the home office knew there was only a slight chance of meeting these delivery conditions. He was very excited with his order until the two-week delivery deadline had passed, and his home office needed two more weeks before the PCs could be shipped. Sanders' customer was furious. What would you do if you were Sanders? What else could he have done when talking to his home office about delivery dates?

because they feel it will not do any good. Others will not complain because they feel that the salesperson should be in tune with their problems or concerns and recognize these problems on their own. If a salesperson encourages **critical encounters** and acts accordingly to defuse a situation in which the buyer's expectations have not been met, then this will help with future meetings and sessions where critical encounters are discussed. If the salesperson does not act on these issues, then future meetings with the buyer will not uncover problem areas because the buyer is convinced nothing will be done to solve them.

Some salespeople tell the customer what he or she wants to hear to get the order but cannot deliver on promises made. Complaints can be avoided by being truthful when presenting a product's capabilities. Providing sales support can eliminate problems with late deliveries, wrong orders being sent, and the feeling that the salesperson does not care about the customer's complaints. The following section provides an outline on how to handle customer complaints.

A Procedure to Handle Complaints

Customer complaints must be handled quickly and with great sensitivity. Customers do not care about all the problems the company is experiencing and the reasons why the salesperson is providing less-than-stellar customer service. The reason that relationship selling is such a critical part of retaining customers is because the salesperson must have an open communication line with the customer and encourage feedback, either positive or negative. Research has shown that 96 percent of customers will not complain and 63 percent of these dissatisfied customers will not repurchase.[12] Thus, salespeople must build relationships to the point where buyers will not hesitate to speak their mind if they are unhappy with the service. If the customer does not complain, then the salesperson does not know what it is that he or she needs to fix.

One study has indicated that, if a company fails to deal with customers and prospects who complain, those customers will tell on average up to 10 people about their bad experience; with email and Internet, this negative feedback can spread to an even larger number of people. Satisfied customers, in contrast, tell only four or five others about their positive experience.[13] Another study showed that a company has a 40 percent chance of winning back upset customers—which indicates that the effort to make amends is worth it.[14] Recent research in consumer services suggests that satisfactory handling of customer complaints is key to customer recommendations of a firm to others.[15] A general procedure for handling customer complaints follows.

Build the Relationship to the Point That Your Customers are Comfortable Complaining

Salespeople have been overheard saying to their customers, "Had I known that you were unhappy with our service, I could have fixed it." The buyer typically responds, "Well, I gave you plenty of signals; why were

I'M SORRY, COULD YOU STEP A LITTLE CLOSER TO ME? I CAN'T QUITE HEAR WHAT YOU'RE SAYING...

© JON CARTER

whom he or she talked to at the salesperson's company about the problem, and this information may be helpful to the salesperson in solving the complaint. This is a good time to show empathy. The salesperson should apologize for any inconvenience and let the buyer know that he or she is happy that the problem was brought up. The salesperson must make the buyer aware that he or she is anxious to resolve the problem and keep the buyer as a satisfied customer.

Ask Customers How They Would Like Their Complaint Resolved

Many salespeople attempt to solve the complaint without understanding what the customer wants them to do. For example, a salesperson may reason that the last customer wanted a 20 percent discount to make things better. "Thus, I will offer this unhappy buyer the same thing." The salesperson may be surprised to find out the buyer wanted something totally different to resolve the problem. The salesperson cannot be afraid to ask the customer what it will take to make him or her happy. A salesperson could say something like, "Theresa, we value you and your company's business. I am sorry for the inconvenience we caused you. Can you please tell me what we can do to solve this problem and keep you as a satisfied customer?" Then, the salesperson must listen carefully. The buyer may simply want an apology. He or she may want a discount; still other buyers might ask for another product to be substituted until the regular shipment arrives. Salespeople typically find that the customer is not demanding as much as they thought he or she might have been, considering the circumstances of the complaint. The solution should centre on what the customer wants and not what the salesperson thinks is appropriate. When salespeople provide customers with choice in the complaint resolution process, they are likely to increase customers' perceived control over the process and ultimately enhance customer satisfaction.[16]

you not aware of the problems I was having when we were doing business?" The buyer and salesperson must work together to develop a trust so that whenever something comes up, either person feels comfortable speaking up. Open communication channels are a must for good customer service. Companies today cannot be afraid to ask their clients, "How are we doing?" Some companies are conducting 30-, 60-, and 90-day customer satisfaction follow-up visits after the sale. Beyond that, salespeople maintain quarterly follow-ups, even if only by phone. This at least tells customers that the salesperson is interested in them and wants to service their account well.

> Salespeople don't want to make customers feel like the one in this picture! They need to make customers feel welcome to complain.

Listen Carefully and Get the Whole Story

The salesperson must listen carefully to what is being said and what is not being said. Good salespeople let the customer know that they are happy the complaint has been brought to their attention. Chances are that the customer will not complain again if he or she is made to feel uncomfortable with the initial complaint. The salesperson must be careful not to interrupt early in the discussion. The customer must be allowed to vent his or her frustration. Once the customer stops complaining, the salesperson may have to probe and ask follow-up questions to get the whole story. For instance, the buyer may not have told the salesperson

Gain Agreement on a Solution

Once the salesperson hears what the customer wants, they must agree on a solution. Sometimes, the salesperson can do exactly what the customer asks. Other times, the buyer may be asking for an unrealistic solution. The salesperson's focus should always be on trying to do exactly what the customer wants. When that is not possible, the salesperson's message should concentrate on what he or she can do for the customer and then do it in a timely manner.[17] The conversation might sound like, "Jim, I'm sorry for the inconvenience we caused you. Thanks for your suggestions on what we need to do to resolve the problem. Here are a couple of things we can do—which of these will work better for you?" The salesperson is telling the buyer that he or she cannot do exactly what the buyer asked, but the salesperson can do the following. Good salespeople always focus on the positive.

Take Action—Educate the Customer

Once an agreement is reached, the salesperson must take action and solve the customer complaint in a timely fashion. The communication lines must be kept open to the customer (e.g., letting him or her know when the repair people will be arriving). When time permits, the repair work should be monitored and the customer should be kept up-to-date on the progress.

If customers have unrealistic expectations of the services provided, then this would be a good time to educate the customers so that they have realistic expectations of the services the company will provide. Some salespeople promise the moon to secure an order and then let the customer down when the product or service does not

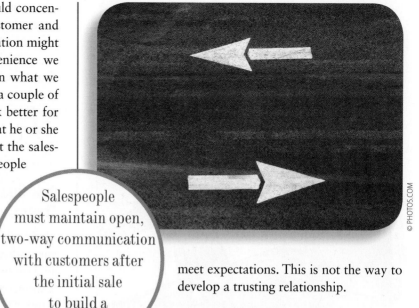

© PHOTOS.COM

Salespeople must maintain open, two-way communication with customers after the initial sale to build a relationship.

meet expectations. This is not the way to develop a trusting relationship.

Follow Through on All Promises—Add Value

Whatever promises are made, good salespeople must make sure that they are kept, and this is a good time to go beyond what has been promised. Those salespeople who overdeliver what is promised will truly impress their customers and build stronger relationships faster than their competitors.[18] By exceeding expectations and adding value, the salesperson helps ensure repeat business. Exhibit 9.5 summarizes the procedures for handling complaints.

LO2
Expand Collaborative Involvement

early in the selling process, the salesperson determines the specific needs of the buyer so that a good match can be made between the product's attributes and the needs of the buyer. This is done through effective questioning and listening to the buyer. Once the sale is made, the salesperson must continue to maintain open, two-way communication with the buyer. Periodic meetings with the buyer allow for this feedback. Furthermore, the methods discussed for obtaining information can be used to keep the line of communication between the buyer and seller open. Collaborative discussion becomes the most effective tool when dealing with customers and their problems. If the customer

---

EXHIBIT 9.5
General Procedures for Handling Complaints

1. Build the relationship to the point that the customer is comfortable complaining.
2. Listen carefully and get the whole story.
3. Ask the customer what he or she would like you to do.
4. Gain agreement on a solution. Tell the customer what you can do; do not focus on what you cannot do.
5. Take action; educate the customer so he or she has realistic expectations.
6. Follow through on all promises. Add value.

believes the salesperson is sincere, listens carefully, and responds accordingly to his or her concerns, then an already trusting relationship will become stronger.

A salesperson's goal is to work with customers who have entered into a strategic alliance with the salesperson's firm. This is done by building trust over a long time. The salesperson should always be looking for ways to take the relationship to a higher level and create a stronger bond. One way to accomplish this goal is to expand the **collaborative involvement** between the buyer's and salesperson's organizations. The salesperson may take a group of engineers along on a sales call and introduce them to the buyer's engineers. It may be possible for the engineers to work together to enhance the product offering. Customers often know the strengths and weaknesses of the product they use and can provide some insight into how improvements can be made.

Another example of a company's attempt to expand collaborative involvement is to host a week-long series of seminars, training sessions, and social engagements with its customers to expand the relationship. Brainstorming sessions with customers demonstrate a willingness to listen, show that the company cares, and often result in better ways to serve customers. Anytime the salesperson can involve additional personnel from the buyer's company during relationship building, chances are that the relationship will become stronger.

L○3
Work to Add Value and Enhance Mutual Opportunities

To build mutually satisfying relationships between buyers and sellers, professional salespeople must work toward adding value and enhancing mutual opportunities for the customer. This can be done by reducing risk through repeated displays of the seller's ability to serve the customer. By demonstrating willingness to serve the customer, the seller reduces the buyer's risk—both real and perceived. A good relationship is one that has few, if any, unpleasant surprises.

Salespeople must also establish high standards and expectations. Many relationships fail because of unmet expectations. The higher the customer's expectations,

the better, provided the seller can meet or exceed those expectations. Salespeople should ensure that the customer's expectations are reasonable by clearly and honestly conveying the firm's offering, and continually work to improve performance.

Finally, salespeople must monitor and take action to improve customer satisfaction. Salespeople must never let up on this. Doing so only invites competitor challenges. A good salesperson must always look for cracks in the relationship and patch them before insurmountable problems occur. All relationships require work, and taking a good customer for granted is foolish. It should be remembered that the salesperson must continually add value to the relationship or he or she will run the risk of losing the customer.

PROVIDE QUALITY CUSTOMER SERVICE

Every salesperson is looking for a competitive edge to help him or her differentiate his or her products in the eyes of customers.

> Great salespeople work hard to provide quality customer service.

collaborative involvement A way to build on buyer–salesperson relationships in which the buyer's organization and the salesperson's organization join together to improve an offering.

© ASEEV/ISTOCKPHOTO

service quality Meeting and or exceeding customer service expectations.

Many of the products that a salesperson sells have essentially the same features and benefits as the competitors. Chris Crabtree of Lanier once said, "A copier is a copier, is a copier. There is just no difference between what I have to offer and my competitors. We all charge about the same price. In fact, I can match any price my competitor puts on the table. That leaves only one attribute for me to differentiate on—service."

More and more companies are turning to **service quality** as a strategy to acquire and maintain customers. A salesperson must be able to convince a customer that service is important, demonstrate service quality, and then maintain a high level of service over an extended time.

The problem is that every salesperson claims to provide outstanding service. The goal today is not to meet customer expectations but to exceed them. Salespeople will rarely be given a second chance to prove that they provide outstanding service if they do not get it right the first time. A sign in a small-town business reads,

Service is advertised . . .
Service is talked about . . .
But the only time service really counts . . .
Is when it is delivered . . .
And we promise your experience with us will be outstanding.

Customers do not care about slogans and service claims until something happens to them. This is called a moment of truth. Each salesperson experiences daily moments of truth—brief moments that occur whenever a customer comes into contact with a salesperson, the training staff, installers, field engineers, or service personnel and has an opportunity to form an impression. These moments of truth are when the customer will determine if promises are being kept by the sales organization, and whether the salesperson truly cares about the customer or is simply an order getter!

Four benefits of service enthusiasm allow the sales organization to gain an advantage over its competitors. First, reputation is an important part of any organization's ability to attract and keep new customers. Reputation allows a salesperson to distinguish himself or herself from the competition. A solid reputation tells customers that you care and will help a salesperson build a loyal relationship in his or her market. Reputa-tions take a long time to establish and only one negative event to destroy.

Second, by providing good customer service the first time, an organization makes the profit that it needs to stay in business. Whenever mistakes are made (e.g., wrong order, short order delivered), service personnel have to sort out the problem and fix it. The result could lead to a lost customer. In any event, it does not take long to go into the red when people have to be added to fix problems. Efficient operations, cost savings, and doing things right the first time increase the chances for increased profits.

The third benefit of service enthusiasm is convenience. It is critically important to put the customer's convenience first. For example, most customers are uncomfortable complaining. Thus, a salesperson must make it easy for his or her customers to discuss problems or complaints. Since customers can be reluctant to complain, the salesperson must be vigilant in asking customers to express their problems or concerns. Building a strong, trusting relationship with open communication will make it easier for customers to voice their concerns. To be convenient, salespeople must be readily accessible to customers. This involves using technology (e.g., cell phone, email) to stay accessible, quickly acknowledging customer requests, and then responding in an appropriate and expedient manner.[19] When it comes to servicing customers, salespeople often must accommodate customers' schedules rather than their own. Naturally, this may pose some inconvenience to the salesperson, but customer needs must be considered first.

Salespeople must design user-friendly feedback systems. Periodically inquiring about customer satisfaction can greatly enhance a customer's feelings toward a salesperson and his or her organization. Ontario Systems (http://www.ontariosystems.com) provides a Client Resource Centre as one of its links on its website. Clients can easily get up-to-date information on product support, training, industry links, and discussion lists. Ontario Systems is always looking for ways to provide more services to its clients.

Finally, service enthusiasm goes hand in hand with spirit. A customer can be turned onto an organization by meeting many caring "can-do" people. The spirit must start with an enthusiastic, service-minded corporate culture. The salesperson, sales manager, field engineer, installer, and CSR (customer service representative) must all have the same service enthusiasm to generate the benefits of service enthusiasm. That is why the salesperson must monitor and coordinate all the people who have access to the account to ensure that good customer service is taking place.

The most difficult aspect of customer service is the potential for inconsistency. For instance, field engineer A, who has a great understanding of service enthusiasm, may be called into an account early in the week. The customer is very impressed. Three weeks later, the customer calls for help again. Field engineer A is out on another account, and field engineer B, who has little or no service skills, is sent out on the next call. Field engineer B is good at fixing the problem but has a hard time relating to customers; in fact, he is downright cold! As a result of this unevenness, the customer's level of satisfaction decreases.

The inconsistency of customer service is a problem for every sales organization. By understanding the benefits of service enthusiasm and the rewards of proper spirit, the sales organization can ensure consistency and exceed customer expectations.

MEET CUSTOMER EXPECTATIONS

A salesperson must meet the needs of his or her customer. At a minimum, customers expect a warm and friendly salesperson. Buyers have enough things going on during their day that it would not be a plus to have to deal with a surly salesperson. Warmth and friendliness are the building blocks of a successful relationship.

Reliability is another attribute that buyers look for in choosing a salesperson with whom to do business. Customers must have the confidence that the expected service will be delivered accurately, consistently, and dependably. Helpfulness and assistance are two more variables that buyers expect when working with a salesperson. Will the customer be able to find his or her salesperson when he or she needs to do so? Can the salesperson provide the speed and promptness needed by the customer? The salesperson can solve this issue by developing a regular call routine so that the customer knows when to expect the salesperson. Other customer expectations include follow-through as promised; empathy; and resolution of complaints, mistakes, or defects. The customer must know that if anything goes wrong, the salesperson will move in quickly and solve the problem. Ultimately, the customer is looking for someone who is personally accountable for their desired results.[20] Exhibit 9.6 summarizes what customers expect from their salesperson.

EXHIBIT 9.6
Customer Expectations of Salespeople

1. Warmth and friendliness
2. Reliability
3. Helpfulness/assistance
4. Speed or promptness
5. Assurance
6. Accuracy
7. Follow-through (as promised)
8. Empathy
9. Resolution of complaints, mistakes, or defects
10. Tangibles

DEVELOP A SERVICE STRATEGY

Salespeople can calculate the lifetime value of their customers. For example, Hershey Foods Corporation knows exactly how much candy it has sold at the Wal-Mart in Muncie, Indiana. It is easy for Hershey to calculate the loss if any customer decides to replace it. It is imperative for Hershey to provide the service level that each of its customers demands. Less than quality service can lead to the loss of a customer.

Developing a **service strategy** allows a salesperson to plan his or her actions for each customer. A service strategy asks a salesperson to identify his or her business and customers and what the customers want and what is important to them. The salesperson also has to determine how his or her customers' needs and perceptions are changing. The salesperson cannot be afraid to ask how the customers rate him or her in terms of their expectations. What does the salesperson's company do best, and what can the organization do better? The salesperson, ultimately, must determine how to position his or her company in the market to differentiate its products and services. All this must be done while directing efforts against

service strategy A plan in which a salesperson identifies his or her business and customers and what the customers want and what is important to them.

communication A two-way flow of information between the salesperson and the customer.

resilience The ability of a salesperson to listen to a customer's complaint and always answer with a smile.

service motivation The desire of a salesperson to service customers each day.

the competitors. Exhibit 9.7 is an example of a checklist for developing a service strategy.

CUSTOMER SERVICE DIMENSIONS

The most important customer service dimension is **communication**. Most problems arise because the customer was not informed of a change in plans (e.g., late delivery, price increase). Salespeople are extremely busy and many times do not have the time to communicate with all their customers. Communication tools, such as email, can be used to quickly do mass communication to inform customers of these changes. Over time, the telephone and personal visits can be used to confirm that the customers are aware of the changes.

Another customer service dimension is **resilience**. Resilience is the ability of a salesperson to listen to a customer's complaint and always answer with a smile. A salesperson cannot lose his or her cool just because a customer does. A tired salesperson must treat late-afternoon, difficult customers the same way that he or she would treat an early-morning dilemma while full of energy. They must both be treated well.

Finally, **service motivation** is another important customer service dimension. Salespeople must be motivated to find time each day to deal with difficult customers and problems that exist. Ignoring these activities will not make them go away. Working diligently on behalf of the customer indicates to him or her that the salesperson truly cares about the partnership. If a salesperson has a complaint from a customer and gladly fixes it, the customer becomes a more committed customer.

> Salespeople who take great care of their customers are a little bit like superheroes.

EXHIBIT 9.7
Checklist for Developing a Service Strategy

Questions a salesperson must ask when developing a service strategy:

- What is our business?
- Who are our customers?
- What do our customers want, and what is important to them?
- How are our customers' needs and perceptions changing?
- How are social, economic, and political factors affecting current and future customer needs and our ability to respond to them? How are competitors responding to these factors?
- How do customers rate us in terms of their expectations?
- For what are we best known?
- What do we do best?
- What can we do better?
- How can we position ourselves in the market to differentiate our services?

THE RELUCTANT SALESFORCE

Background

Gary O'Brien, sales manager for a large engineering firm, cannot get his salespeople into the field. He summarized his problems as follows:

1. Lack of outgoing calls or emails to prospects and customers
2. Lack of planning on a daily basis
3. No use of a follow-up program to generate additional customer contacts
4. Lack of overall planning strategy for a particular customer or group of customers
5. Reactive salesforce instead of proactive

Current Situation

O'Brien thinks his problem is that his staffs are technical in nature and want to be thought of as experts, not salespeople. He goes on to say that his staff members do great when the customers call them but do not plan for outside sales opportunities. His reps say that they are too busy with everything else to make outside calls.

O'Brien had the following conversation with his top salesperson, Ted (who happens to be his brother).

O'Brien: Ted, have you had any luck making new contacts?

Ted: Not really.

O'Brien: What is the problem?

Ted: What do you mean, man—what is the problem? I spend all day on the phone talking to our existing customers. They need me. I cannot be out of the office all day. My customers would never be able to find me.

O'Brien: I'm not talking about being out of the office all day. I need you to spend one day per week following up on existing customers to build goodwill and another half-day per week looking for new business.

Ted: That sounds good, but I do not see how I can get that done. I am already overloaded.

Questions

1. What would you do if you were O'Brien?
2. Can you force your salespeople out of the building?

Role Play

Situation: Read the case.

Characters: Gary O'Brien, sales manager; Ted O'Brien, salesperson

Scene 1:
Location—O'Brien's office.
Action—Continuation of O'Brien and Ted's conversation. Ted just replied, "I am already overloaded." Role play O'Brien's response to Ted and Ted's feedback.

Scene 2:
Location—Conference room
Action—O'Brien and the rest of the salesforce are having a meeting (3 to 5 salespeople). Role play O'Brien going over points 1 through 5 in the case background information with the salesforce.

After completing the role plays, address the following question:

What are the pros and cons of addressing each sales representative individually or having all of them in for a sales meeting?

Whatever It Takes to Get the Order

Background

Roberta Thomas has seen the good life. Her company is paying high bonuses to bring in new customers. Thomas has earned more than $100,000 per year over the past three years. Thomas has been given increasingly higher quotas during the past two years to reach her bonus. She feels that her company is putting her in an awkward position. She wants to continue to reach her quota, but in doing so, she will spend more than 90 percent of her time trying to bring in new business. Just over two years ago, she spent half of her time keeping her present customers satisfied. Her customers have been complaining about how little attention they receive. Thomas knows that she is not spending enough time with them. She brought her dilemma to her boss, Salisha Barrett, who seemed less than sympathetic.

Current Situation

Their conversation follows:

Thomas: I am really having a problem with the quota I have been assigned this year.

Barrett: Is that so? What is the problem?

Thomas: I think it is too high. I have to spend way too much time going after new business.

Barrett: That is what we pay you to do; your job is to bring in new business.

Thomas: It was not that way many years ago when I spent at least half of my time keeping my present customers happy. I enjoyed following up with them and building strong relationships.

Barrett: Times change, you know. We have to bring in new business or face laying some of you off.

Thomas: You can look over some of these phone messages I have received. These are some of our best customers, and they do not think we are taking very good care of them.

Barrett: Roberta, we have a big contest going on, and I do not intend to lose it. You had better bring in your share of the new business to win or you will let down your entire branch.

Thomas could see she was not getting anywhere and changed the subject.

Questions

1. What would you do if you were Thomas?
2. What would you do if you were Barrett?

Role Play

Situation: Read the role play.

Characters: Roberta Thomas, salesperson; Salisha Barrett, her boss

Scene: *Location*—Barrett's office
Action—Continuation of Roberta and Salisha's conversation. Role play Thomas not changing the subject and pursuing her concerns.

After completing the role play, address the following questions:

1. Thomas is not getting anywhere with Barrett; should she go to Barrett's boss?
2. Why can Thomas not go back to her old way of doing things and spend the time with her existing customers like she wants to?

Not having sufficient time

to get everything done is not the problem. We need
to reprioritize the time we have so as to maximize
that time and invest it where it accomplishes the most.

IO

Adding Value: Self-Leadership and Teamwork

After completing this chapter, you should be able to

LO1 Explain the five sequential stages of self-leadership.

LO2 Identify the four levels of sales goals and explain their interrelationships.

LO3 Describe two techniques for account classification.

LO4 Interpret the usefulness of different types of selling technology and automation.

LO5 Delineate six skills for building internal relationships and teams.

Introduction

d ave Kahle, a consultant and trainer who helps his clients increase their sales and productivity says that he often overhears salespeople proclaiming, "I have my own style of selling."

From his perspective, "that idea is more detrimental to that salesperson's success than almost any other. Not only that, but that idea holds down entire sales forces, renders sales management impotent, and dissipates the sales team's potential. Of all the ideas that detract from sales performance, this is the most malignant.

"Here's why. In the profession of sales, just like in every other profession, there is a set of best practices—specific things to do, behaviors and processes that are proven to produce results.

"'Planning for every sales call,' for example, is a best practice. Those salespeople who adhere to that discipline achieve better results than those who don't. That's an easy example. The truth is, though, that there are literally dozens of best practices, impacting every aspect of the sales process. There are proven ways to identify your highest potential prospects, to approach a prospect, to uncover opportunities, to present your solutions, to acquire agreement, and to leverage that transaction into greater opportunities.

"The world is full of sales trainers who make a living teaching some of these practices. And, professional salespeople make it a quest to continually seek the best practices, and to inject them into their routines, turning them into habits.

"Here's the problem. When sales people believe that they 'have their own style of selling', they are negating the entire concept of best practices and discounting the past 70 years of development of the sales profession. It doesn't matter what anyone else says, it doesn't matter what practices the vast weight of professional judgment reinforces, it doesn't matter what behaviors research identifies as effective—the only thing that matters is 'my style.'

"How can anyone teach you anything as long as you have 'your style?'

"While I occasionally hear that in my seminars, I'm convinced that the salespeople who really believe it are the ones who don't show up at the seminars. Why bother? They have their own style.

"I suspect that, in many cases, there is something deeper going on. I suspect that those salespeople who maintain that they have their 'own style' are really hiding a more profound situation. Maintaining that you have 'your own style,' is a way of avoiding scrutiny and sliding out from under accountability. How can anyone teach you anything? How can anyone coach you? How can anyone question anything that you do? That's the issue!

"I believe that many salespeople who maintain they have their own style are really, at the heart, insecure about their performance. They may understand that they aren't really suited to selling, and they are insecure and uncomfortable with what they do. So, to avoid scrutiny, to escape being accountable for their actions, they hide under the cloud of 'their own style.' 'Their own style' is then, in many cases, the hiding place of the mediocre. Salespeople who announce it, sales managers who allow it, and sales executives who tolerate it are severely limiting the performance of their sales teams."

Source: David Kahle. "Ideas that Restrict Sales Performance: I Have My Own Style of Selling." *American Salesman*, July 2010.

When observing the actions of a person who has truly mastered the skills of his or her profession, we think the person's actions come naturally. However,

© PATRICK TUOHY/SHUTTERSTOCK

Like the skills and abilities of an athlete, the skills and abilities required for success in selling are the result of purposeful planning and many hours of practice.

closer consideration will most often reveal that these seemingly innate and natural abilities are actually the result of years of fervent and purposeful planning, combined with many hours of practice. This is true for world-class surgeons, sports stars, leading educators, top attorneys—and yes, even high-performance salespeople. Good salespeople are consciously developed, not born. Toward the objective of *developing* strong salespeople, this chapter builds on the process of self-leadership to generate a framework for developing and enhancing selling skills and abilities.

First, setting effective selling goals and objectives is discussed and integrated with methods for territory analysis and account classification. This is followed by a discussion of how the objectives and information from the territory and account analysis become inputs for generating and implementing effective multilevel sales planning. The importance of assessing performance results and level of goal attainment is also reviewed. Wrapping up the chapter is an examination of teamwork as a vehicle for expanding the capabilities of an individual salesperson, increasing customer value, and creating sustainable competitive advantage for salespeople.

LO1
Effective Self-Leadership

how often have you said or thought to yourself, "I just don't have enough time to get everything done?" In reality, most people do not need more time. Rather, they need to prioritize the time they have. There are only so many hours in a day, and highly effective salespeople know that they can never have enough quality selling time. To maximize their selling time, these high performers have developed strong self-leadership skills and treat time as a valuable, irreplaceable resource and invest it wisely where it will accomplish the most good.

Self-leadership—a critical requirement for success in any career—has been described as doing the right things and doing them well. It is not simply the amount of effort that determines an achievement, but rather how well that effort is honed and aligned with our goals. In selling, this is often restated as selling smarter rather than selling harder. That is, before expending valuable time and resources, salespeople must establish priorities in the form of objectives. Then, and only then, do they implement the strategic plan that has been specifically developed to achieve their objectives in the light of the available resources and market potential that exist within the territory. Self-leadership translates to a process of first deciding what is to be accomplished and then putting into motion the proper plan designed to achieve those objectives.

The process of self-leadership is composed of five sequential stages. First, goals and objectives must be set that properly reflect what is important and what is to be accomplished. This is followed by an analysis of the territory and classification of accounts. Next, with goals in place and accounts classified, strategic plans designed to achieve the objectives through proper allocation of resources and effort are implemented. The next stage maximizes the effectiveness of allocated resources through the process of tapping technology and automation to expand resource capabilities. Finally, assessment activities are conducted to evaluate performance and goal attainment and to assess possible changes in plans and strategies. The nature of the sequential interrelationships among these five stages is illustrated in Figure 10.1.

© BLACKRED/ISTOCKPHOTO

There are only so many hours in a day. Maximize your effective selling time by developing strong self-leadership skills.

LO2
STAGE ONE: SETTING GOALS AND OBJECTIVES

goals and objectives
The things a salesperson sets out to accomplish.

Establishing priorities by setting **goals and objectives** is the key to effective self-leadership. This first stage of self-leadership has been appropriately referred to as "beginning with the end in mind."[1] First of all, if a salesperson does not understand what is important, how does that salesperson know what to focus on? Further, if a salesperson does not understand what he or she is setting out to accomplish, how could that salesperson know where to begin, how to proceed, or even which plan is best for getting there? Finally, without clear goals, how could salespeople know when the objective has been achieved? Without clear goals and objectives, it is very natural to drift from task to task and typically focus on minor and less-productive tasks, as they are the easiest to complete. The end result of this natural drift is poor sales performance and frustration. The positive impact of planning ahead and establishing priorities is further evidenced by the experiences of Adam

FIGURE 10.1
Five Sequential Stages of Self-Leadership

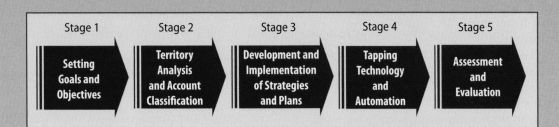

Stage 1	Stage 2	Stage 3	Stage 4	Stage 5
Setting Goals and Objectives	Territory Analysis and Account Classification	Development and Implementation of Strategies and Plans	Tapping Technology and Automation	Assessment and Evaluation

Self-leadership is a process of first deciding what is to be accomplished and then setting into motion the proper plan to achieve the desired objectives.

Spangler, an investment representative for Edward D. Jones & Co., in "Professional Selling in the 21st Century: Driving Sales through Setting Goals and Planning Sales Activities."

What Makes a Good Goal?

Although goals and objectives might best be described as desired outcomes, these two words carry specific meaning. *Desired* implies that it is something worthy of working toward and expending resources to reach. *Outcome* connotes that it is a specific result or effect resulting from certain activities or behaviours—something that can be described and pointed out. As illustrated in Exhibit 10.1, properly developed goals share three key characteristics: They are (1) realistic, yet challenging, (2) specific and quantifiable, and (3) time specific.

- *Realistic, Yet Challenging*—Goals should be realistic and reachable. When set beyond what is possible, goals cease to motivate and often become a disincentive to performance. At the same time, goals should be challenging. If goals are continually set at a level that is too easy to reach, performance tends to regress to the lower standard. Goals that are challenging tend to be more motivating than goals that are easily achieved.

MICROSOFT PRODUCT SCREEN SHOT REPRINTED WITH PERMISSION FROM MICROSOFT CORPORATION/E-VISUAL COMMUNICATIONS, INC.

Driving Sales through Setting Goals and Planning Sales Activities

Adam Spangler is a highly successful investment representative for Edward D. Jones & Co. who knows that there is much more to building a successful business than simply pulling out the local white pages and calling faceless names on a hot stock idea. Spangler emphasizes that planning, goal setting, and time management are critical to his success in managing the financial investments of his 600 customers.

Goal setting and planning are critical for success in selling. During the last week of each calendar year, we draft our performance goals and develop business plans that set the bar for goals to be accomplished during the coming year. Setting annual goals allows us to break them down further to develop quarterly, monthly, and even daily goals that can be used to assess progress and make changes in our plans.

Time management and doing the "right" work are the keys to achieving goals. To leverage available work time better, we use a contact management system to prioritize accounts and prospects by assigning a colour code of Green, Yellow, or Red based on several criteria. Our goal is to contact Green clients and prospects over the phone at least once per month and in person three times per year. Calls to Yellow clients are made only after all the Greens have been contacted in the month. Red clients are not proactively contacted because it is unlikely that they will ever become important clients. Having a planning system like this in place allows us to do the "right" work, staying in touch with those who have a need and have the resources to do something about their need. Also, since doing the "right" work leverages our time, we have more time to enjoy our personal life and the fruit of our labour.

is too easy to reach, performance tends to regress to the lower standard. Goals that are challenging tend to be more motivating than goals that are easily achieved.

- *Specific and Quantifiable*—Without specificity, goals become ambiguous and have no clear meaning. For instance, the goal of having the top territory in the district could be interpreted in many ways. Does top

EXHIBIT 10.1
Required Characteristics of Goals and Objectives

Effective Goals and Objectives Must Possess Three Fundamental Characteristics:

- Goals should be realistic yet challenging.
- Goals should be specific and quantifiable.
- Goals should be time specific.

territory translate to having the largest increase in sales, having the fewest number of customer defections, having the highest customer satisfaction scores, having the smallest number of price discounts, or possibly having the largest reduction in travel expenses? Without specificity, the goal becomes a moving target, and it is difficult to know where to apply effort. In a similar fashion, goals should be quantifiable—that is, they should be measurable. The goal of increasing sales is certainly commendable, but how might it be judged as having been accomplished? Is a 1 percent increase sufficient or is 12 percent more in line with expectations? If a 12 percent increase is the expectation, then the goal should be a 12 percent increase in sales—a quantifiable and measurable outcome that can be objectively measured and assessed.

- *Time Specific*—Stating a specific time line is the third requirement of goals and objectives. A goal of achieving a 12 percent increase in sales by December 31 is much more appealing than simply stating that the goal is to increase sales by 12 percent. Associating time lines with goals establishes a deadline for planning purposes and provides motivation by instilling a sense of urgency for taking action.

Working with Different Levels and Types of Goals

For maximum effectiveness, salespeople establish goals at four different levels: personal goals, territory goals, account goals, and sales call goals. Although each level requires different types of effort and produces different outcomes, each of the levels is interrelated and interdependent on the others. These interrelationships and dependencies are illustrated in Exhibit 10.2. A salesperson's **personal goals** might include achieving a $70,000 annual income during the current year ending December 31. If the salesperson receives a commission of 11 percent on sales, this personal goal is directly related to and dependent on achieving the **territory goal** of selling $636,364 in products across the territory in the same time period. Assuming 19 equally sized accounts compose the territory, the territory goal is dependent on achieving the **account goal** of an average of $33,493 in products sold to each account during the year. Considering that each account is called on twice every month, a **sales call goal** of $1396 in sales per call is required to achieve the account goal. As illustrated in this example, each higher level goal is ultimately dependent on the salesperson setting and achieving lower level, specific goals for each and every sales call.

personal goals A salesperson's individual desired accomplishment, such as achieving a desired annual income over a specific period.

territory goal A salesperson's desire to sell a certain amount of product within an area or territory to achieve personal goals.

account goal A salesperson's desire to sell a certain amount of product to one customer or account to achieve territory and personal goals.

sales call goal A salesperson's desire to sell a certain amount of product per each sales call to achieve account, territory, and personal goals.

EXHIBIT 10.2
Four Interdependent Levels of Salesperson Objectives

Personal goal—desired annual income	$ 70,000
Is dependent on annual territory sales goal (11% commission on sales)	$636,364
Is dependent on annual account sales goal (19 equally sized accounts)	$ 33,493
Is dependent on sales call goal (each account is called on twice a month)	$ 1,396

territory analysis The process of surveying an area to determine customers and prospects who are most likely to buy.

Although illustrative of the interdependence between different levels of goals, the previous example is admittedly simplistic in its exclusive use of goals based on sales volume. In reality, there are many different types of goals that a salesperson might effectively use. Exhibit 10.3 illustrates examples of common sales goals.

LO3
STAGE TWO: TERRITORY ANALYSIS AND ACCOUNT CLASSIFICATION

Territory analysis and classification of accounts, the second stage of self-leadership, is all about finding the customers

Territory analysis is all about finding the customers and prospects who are most likely to buy and identifying who has the purchasing authority.

© STOCKLITE/SHUTTERSTOCK

and prospects who are most likely to buy. Who are they, and where are they located? What and why do they buy? How much and how often do they purchase? Who has the authority to buy, and who can influence the purchase decision? What is the probability of selling to this account? What is the potential share of account that might be gained?

Many sources offer intelligence that will assist the salesperson in answering these questions, and the information boom on the Internet makes accessing this information easier than ever before. In addition to numerous yellow page suppliers available on the Web, commercial business information suppliers, such as *Canadian Trade Index*, Scott's Directories, *Standard & Poor's*, and *Canadian Key Business Directory*, offer easy-to-use databases that

EXHIBIT 10.3
Common Types of Sales Goals

• Financial goals	Income, financial security
• Career advancement goals	Work in chosen field, advancement
• Personal development goals	Education, training, relationships outside work
• Sales volume goals	Dollar sales, unit sales, number of orders, aggregates or by groups
• Sales call activity goals	Calls made, calls/day, calls/account, presentations made
• Sales expense goals	Total expenses, by category, percentage of sales
• Profitability goals	Gross profits, contribution margin, returns and discounts
• Market share	Total share of potential market, peer group comparisons
• Share of account	Share of customer's purchases
• Ancillary activity goals	Required reports turned in, training conducted, service calls made
• Customer retention goals	Number of accounts lost, complaints received, lost account ratios
• New account goals	Number of new accounts
• Customer service goals	Customer goodwill generation, level of satisfaction, receivables collected
• Conversion goals	Ratio of number of sales to number of calls made

are fully searchable by company, industry, and geographic location. Salespeople can also access individual company websites, trade directories, professional association membership listings, and commercial mailing list providers. Personal observation, discussions with other selling professionals, and company sales records are also excellent sources for gaining valuable information.

Much of this information can be plotted to develop detailed territory maps and pinpoint pockets of existing and potential business. In addition, understanding the territory at the individual account level provides the input required for account classification.

Account Classification

Account classification places existing customers and prospects into categories based on their sales potential and assists salespeople in prioritizing accounts for call planning and time allocation purposes. During the process of account classification, it is common for salespeople to find that 80 to 90 percent of their sales potential is generated by 10 to 20 percent of the total accounts. Consequently, the results of account classification can guide salespeople in more efficient allocation of time, effort, and resources while simultaneously enabling them to be more effective in achieving sales goals. Two commonly used methods for classifying accounts are single-factor analysis and portfolio analysis.

Single-Factor Analysis

Single-factor analysis, also referred to as ABC analysis, is the simplest and most often used method for classifying accounts. As the name suggests, accounts are analyzed on the basis of one single factor—typically the level of sales potential. On the basis of sales potential, the accounts are placed into three or four categories denoted by letters of the alphabet, A, B, C, and D. Accounts with the highest potential are traditionally sorted into category A, whereas those with medium potential go into B, and so on. All accounts in the same category receive equal selling effort. For example, A accounts may be called on every two weeks, B accounts every four to six weeks, and C accounts might receive a personal sales call once a year and be serviced by the seller's telemarketing team during the interim. Single-factor classification

schemas used by three different sales organizations are summarized in Exhibit 10.4.

The simplicity of single-factor analysis is a prime contributor to its popularity for use by field salespeople. It is straightforward and requires no statistical analysis or data manipulation. Although this lack of complexity is appealing, its ability to use only one factor for analyzing and classifying accounts is also a significant limitation. Sales potential is certainly an important input in allocating selling effort, but other factors should also be considered.

> It is common for salespeople to find 80 to 90 percent of their sales potential generated by 10 to 20 percent of their accounts.

Possible other factors of interest are the selling company's competitive strength in each account, the account's need for additional attention and effort, profitability of the account, and amount of competitive pressure on the account.

Portfolio Analysis

Also referred to as two-factor analysis, the **portfolio analysis** method attempts to overcome the weakness of single-factor analysis by allowing two factors to be considered simultaneously. Each account is examined on the basis of the two specified factors and sorted into the proper segment of a matrix. This matrix is typically divided into four cells, and accounts are placed into the proper classification cell on the basis of their individual ratings ("high" and "low" or "strong" and "weak") on each factor of interest. Cell location denotes the overall attractiveness of the different accounts and serves as a guide for the salesperson's allocation of resources

EXHIBIT 10.4

Different Single-Factor Account Analysis Schema Used by Different Companies

Class of Account	Schema One: InquisLogic Inc.	Schema Two: Web Resource Associates, LLC	Schema Three Federal Metal Products
A Accounts	Accounts with highest potential (the 20% that do or could account for 80% of sales)	Accounts with highest potential (the 20% that do or could account for 80% of sales)	High volume current customers (the 20% that currently account for 80% of sales volume)
	Annual number of calls = 24	Annual number of calls = 52	Annual number of calls = 48
B Accounts	Medium potential accounts (the 80% that account for 20% of sales volume)	Accounts with moderate sales potential but who are regular and reliable customers	Accounts with high potential but who are not current customers
	Annual number of calls = 12	Annual number of calls = 24	Annual number of calls = 12
C Accounts	Accounts with the least sales potential	Lower sales potential accounts	Medium potential accounts that are current customers
	Annual number of calls = 4	Annual number of calls = 8	Annual number of calls = 12
D Accounts	None. This schema only uses 3 classes of accounts	Accounts that cost more in time and energy than they produce in sales or profits	Accounts with medium potential but who are not current customers
		Annual number of calls = 0	Annual number of calls = 6

and effort. Typically, each account in the same cell will receive the same amount of selling effort.

Exhibit 10.5 details the account characteristics and suggested selling effort allocations for a typical portfolio analysis incorporating the factors of (1) account opportunity and (2) seller's competitive position.[2] Account opportunity takes into consideration the buyer's level of need for and ability to purchase the seller's products, along with financial stability and growth prospects. Competitive position denotes the relationship between the account and the seller and includes such variables as the seller's share of account, competitive pressure, and the key decision-maker's attitude toward the seller. Accounts sorted into Segment One are high on opportunity, exhibit strong competitive positions, and should receive the highest level of selling effort. Accounts falling into Segment Two are high on opportunity but weak on competitive position. These accounts should receive a high level of attention to strengthen the seller's competitive

position. Segment Three contains the 80 to 90 percent of accounts doing 10 to 20 percent of the seller's volume. These accounts are loyal and regular customers (high on competitive position) but offer weak opportunity.

Strategically, these accounts should receive a lower investment of selling effort designed to maintain the seller's current competitive position. Accounts sorted into Segment Four are considered unattractive and allocated minimal selling effort as they are characterized by low opportunity and weak competitive position. Within the past several years, many sellers have been successful in servicing Segment Three and Four accounts outside the personal selling channel by using alternatives, such as telemarketing, direct mail, and the Internet.

Portfolio analysis offers the advantages of enhanced flexibility and ability to incorporate multiple variables for analyzing and sorting accounts. Reflecting these strong points, the use of portfolio analysis is gaining in popularity.

STAGE THREE: DEVELOPMENT AND IMPLEMENTATION OF STRATEGIES AND PLANS

Stage One provides the salesperson with the guidelines of what is important and the goals to be accomplished at the levels of individual sales calls, accounts, and the overall territory. Stage Two identifies and establishes the priority and potential of each account in the territory, along with the relative location of each account. Top salespeople do not stop there! They use this information to develop strategies and plans that will guide them toward achieving their goals by applying their available resources in a deliberate and organized fashion that effectively cultivates and harvests the potential sales available in the territory.

Establishing and Implementing Selling Tasks and Activity Plans

When properly executed, **sales planning** results in a schedule of activities that can be used as a map for achieving objectives. First, start with the big picture—a long-term plan spanning the next 6 to 12 months. This big picture highlights commitments and deadlines and facilitates setting up the activities required to meet those commitments and deadlines. In turn, the longer range plans provide the basis for shorter time frame plans and selling activities. The salesperson planning program at Federal Metal Products (FMP) offers a good overview and prototype of effective salesperson planning.

sales planning The process of scheduling activities that can be used as a map for achieving objectives.

EXHIBIT 10.5
Portfolio/Two-Factor Account Analysis and Selling Strategies

	Competitive Position	
	Strong	**Weak**
Account Opportunity — High	**Segment One** **Level of Attractiveness** Accounts are very attractive because they offer high opportunity and the seller has a strong competitive position. **Selling Effort Strategy** Accounts should receive a heavy investment of effort and resources to take advantage of high opportunity and maintain/improve competitive position. **Exemplary Sales Call Strategy = 36 calls/yr.**	**Segment Two** **Level of Attractiveness** Accounts are potentially attractive because of high opportunity, but the seller currently has weak competitive position. **Selling Effort Strategy** Where it is possible to strengthen the seller's competitive position, a heavy investment of selling effort should be applied. **Exemplary Sales Call Strategy = 24 calls/yr.**
Account Opportunity — Low	**Segment Three** **Level of Attractiveness** Accounts are moderately attractive because of the seller having a fairly strong competitive position. However, future opportunity is low. **Selling Effort Strategy** Accounts should receive a moderately heavy level of selling effort that is sufficient to maintain current competitive position. **Exemplary Sales Call Strategy = 12 calls/yr.**	**Segment Four** **Level of Attractiveness** Accounts are very unattractive. They offer low opportunity and the seller has weak competitive position. **Selling Effort Strategy** Accounts should receive minimal personal selling effort. Alternatives such as telemarketing, direct mail, and Internet, should be explored. **Exemplary Sales Call Strategy = 6 calls/yr.**

© GERENME/ISTOCKPHOTO

> An effective plan works like a map, showing the way from where you are to where you want to go— your objective.

FMP, *a middle market supplier of metal production components, trains its salespeople to prepare and submit annual territory plans and budgets by November 15 each year. With that recurring deadline marked on their schedules, FMP salespeople work backward on their calendars to establish key checkpoints for their planning activities. This establishes a timeline to guide and assist salespeople in making the submission deadline.*

If salespeople project that it will take four weeks to assemble and draft their territory sales plan, they work back four weeks from the November 15 date and establish October 15 as the date to begin assembling their data and building their plans. How long will it take to collect the needed data properly? Six weeks? If so, their schedule should reflect beginning that activity by September 1.

Sales plans should take into consideration scheduled meetings and training sessions, holidays, trade shows, and vacation time. Plans should also contain periodic checkpoints for assessing progress toward goals. A salesperson's objective of $750,000 in sales for the year equates to a goal averaging $62,500 in sales every month. Accordingly, the long-term master plan should include monthly checkpoints to compare the schedule versus actual performance data. Is performance on course, ahead, or lagging behind? If not on schedule, the corresponding and more detailed weekly plans should be revised to

reflect salespeople's strategies for getting back on course.

Salespeople at FMP develop weekly plans from their longer term annual plan. These shorter term plans detail the selling-related activities to be accomplished that week. To create a weekly plan, first identify the priorities that must be accomplished to stay on schedule. Then, for each of these priorities, detail the associated activities and schedule the time that it will take for completion. What areas of the territory will you focus on? What accounts will be called on, and what is the objective for each call? What are the best times to call for appointments? Are there account preferences as to what days and times they work with salespeople? How much time must be allowed for travel, waiting, and working with each account? What products will be featured? What information and materials will be needed?

In turn, the priorities and activities identified in the weekly plan should become the points of focus for the daily plan. Days that end on a successful note begin with a thorough and written schedule detailing tasks and priorities for that day and the activities that must be carried out to achieve them.

The optimum schedule emphasizes tasks and activities that will make the greatest sales impact—working with customers. As illustrated by the FMP's "Daily Sales Plan Worksheet" shown in Exhibit 10.6, daily plans should detail the amount of time projected for each scheduled task and activity. To maximize the effectiveness of daily sales plans, salespeople should adhere to two guiding principles.[3]

- *Do them, and do them in writing.* Written plans are better developed and provide more motivation and commitment for salespeople to carry them through to completion. Furthermore, written plans help to ensure that priority items do not fall through the cracks because something was forgotten.

- *Keep it current and flexible.* Make a new daily plan every day. Try as we might, things do not always go as planned. Consequently, changes may be needed, and uncompleted priorities or activities from one day may have to be carried over to the next.

EXHIBIT 10.6
Example of a Typical Daily Sales Plan Worksheet

Federal Metal Products
Daily Sales Plan Worksheet

Sales person: Sujata Madari　　　　**Day:** Friday　　　**Date:** 8/29

Time	Task or Priority	Activity	People Involved	Time Needed	Goal/ Anticipated Results	Notes and Comments
8:30 a.m.	Set appointments	Phone calls	Jill Attaway Digital Systems	10 min	Appointment for next week	Requested that I come by
	" "	"	Bart Waits EnterpriseOne	10 min	"	
	" "	"	Kerri Williams Flo-Forms	10 min	"	Will be placing order in 3 weeks
9:00 a.m.	" "	"	Marilyn Henry InQuisLogic	10 min	Clarify service problem	Send info to engineering
10:30 a.m.	Demonstrate new bearing line	Sales call	Mike Humphreys ICOM	60 min	Info gathering	Currently buying from Gem Rollers
12 noon	Get order commitment	Sales call—Lunch	Jack Kessler MDQG	120 min	$12,000 order	Gem submitted proposal 8/20
3:00 p.m.	Take sample of proposed line	Sales call	Aimee Williams MOCO, Inc	60 min	$15,200 order	Ready to buy, wants to see pdct. sample
4:30 p.m.	Check on delivery	Service call	Ron Meier Web Resources	50 min	Delight the customer	First time to buy from us!
6:00 p.m.	Complete paperwork	Submit call reports		45 min		
7:00 p.m.	Prepare daily schedule	Planning		45 min		

Establishing Territory Routing Plans

Territory routing plans incorporate information developed in the territory analysis and account classification stage to minimize the encroachment of unproductive travel time on time that could be better spent working with customers. Good routing plans minimize the backtracking and crisscrossing that would otherwise occur and allow the salesperson to use time more efficiently.

Knowing how many calls can be made each day, the required call frequency for each account classification, and the relative geographic location of and distance between accounts, a salesperson can plot different routing strategies and decide on the optimal plan. Many sales professionals continue to use the traditional coloured map pins and felt-tip markers on a wall map. However, a variety of easy-to-use and affordable

FIGURE 10.2

Territory Route Patterns

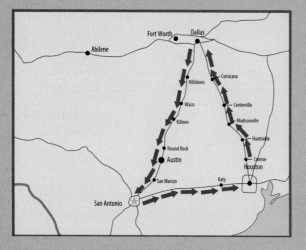

Straight-line territory routes make calls across the territory in one direction and then change direction to work back to the starting point.

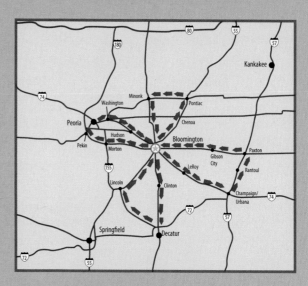

Cloverleaf territory routes work different parts of the territory in a series of circular loops.

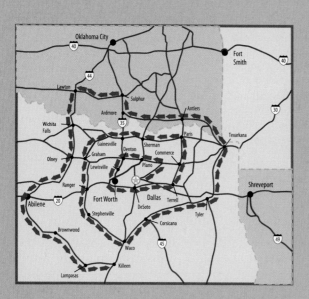

Circular territory routes cover the territory in a series of concentric circles spiralling across it.

Leapfrog territory routes work accounts clustered in one location and then jump to a different cluster of accounts.

computer applications that plot optimal routing plans are available and are growing in popularity.[4] Optimized routing plans correspond to one of five common patterns: straight line, cloverleaf, circular, leapfrog, and major city.

Straight Line Routing Plans With a **straight-line routing plan**, salespeople start from their offices and make calls in one direction until they reach the end of the territory. As illustrated in Figure 10.2, at that point they change direction and continue to make calls on a straight line following the new vector. This continues until the salesperson returns to the office location. The straight-line pattern works best when accounts are located in clusters that are some distance from one another.

Cloverleaf Routing Plans The **cloverleaf routing plan** pattern is best used when accounts are concentrated in different parts of the territory. On each trip, the salesperson works a different part of the territory and travels in a circular loop back to the starting point. An example of the cloverleaf routing plan is depicted in Figure 10.2. Each loop could take a day, a week, or longer to complete. A new loop is covered on each trip until the entire territory has been covered.

Circular Routing Plans Circular routing plans begin at the office and move in an expanding pattern of concentric circles that spiral across the territory. Figure 10.2 traces an exemplary circular routing plan working from an office in Dallas. This method works best when accounts are evenly dispersed throughout the territory.

Leapfrog Routing Plans The **leapfrog routing plan** is best applied when the territory is large and accounts are clustered into several widely dispersed groups. Beginning in one cluster, the salesperson works each of the accounts at that location and then jumps to the next cluster. As shown in Figure 10.2, this continues until the last cluster has been worked and the salesperson jumps back to the office or home. When the distance between clusters is great, the salesperson will typically make the jumps by flying.

Major City Routing Plans When the territory is composed of a major metropolitan area, the territory is split into a series of geometric shapes reflecting each one's concentration and pattern of accounts. Figure 10.3 depicts a typical **major city routing plan**. Downtown areas are typically highly concentrated with locations controlled by a grid of city blocks and streets. Consequently, the downtown segment is typically a small square or rectangular area allowing accounts to be worked in a straight-line fashion street by street. Outlying areas are placed in evenly balanced triangles or pie-shaped quadrants, with one quadrant being covered at a time in either a straight-line or cloverleaf pattern.

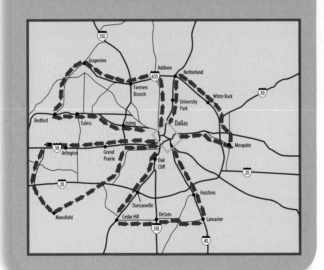

FIGURE 10.3
Major City Route Pattern

Major city territory routing patterns work downtown on a basis of street grids and work outlying areas by using a cloverleaf or straight-line pattern.

straight-line routing plan A territory routing plan in which salespeople start from their offices and make calls in one direction until they reach the end of the territory.

cloverleaf routing plan A territory routing plan in which the salesperson works a different part of the territory and travels in a circular loop back to the starting point.

circular routing plan A territory routing plan in which the salesperson begins at the office and moves in an expanding pattern of concentric circles that spiral across the territory.

leapfrog routing plan A territory routing plan in which, beginning in one cluster, the salesperson works each of the accounts at that location and then jumps to the next cluster.

major city routing plan A territory routing plan used when the territory is composed of a major metropolitan area and the territory is split into a series of geometric shapes reflecting each one's concentration and pattern of accounts.

LO4
STAGE FOUR: TAPPING TECHNOLOGY AND AUTOMATION

Selling technology and automation tools are here to stay and are being transformed from neat toys to necessary tools. Properly applied, selling technology spurs and creates creativity and innovation, streamlines all aspects of the selling process, generates new and improved selling opportunities, facilitates cross-functional teaming and intraorganizational communication, and enhances communication and follow-up with customers.[5] In summary, tapping the proper selling technologies and salesforce automation tools allows salespeople to expand their available resources for enhanced selling performance and outcomes. Experiences with improved selling efficiency and customer satisfaction are illustrated in "Professional Selling in the 21st Century: Mobile CRM Increases Salesperson Effectiveness."

selling technology and automation Tools that streamline the selling process, generate improved selling opportunities, facilitate cross-functional teaming and intraorganizational communication, and enhance communication and follow-up with customers.

PROFESSIONAL SELLING IN THE 21ST CENTURY

Mobile CRM Increases Salesperson Effectiveness

Sales cycles are growing longer, and it is increasingly difficult to break through to new prospects. In response, the Wellesley Group is using mobile CRM to help keep salespeople on task and make sure they do not drop leads. Patrick Cahill, senior associate at the Wellesley Hills Group, explains how the mobile CRM aids in automating the sales process and keeps them on schedule with follow-up calls as well as refreshing their memories as to the history and context of prior calls to a prospect.

CRM systems can retain sales notes and prospect data for years—not just your own old notes, but those of former sales employees as well. These can be mined for old-but-still-promising leads, as well as for prior customers who might be interested in buying again. Searching by location, demographics, or marketing campaign themes can net a list of new leads that is specific to your message.

We might sort through past campaigns or opportunities that we never got to proposal with or former customers. In this economy, now's the time to go back and look at past prospects. If you've had one conversation with a firm, it's more likely that you'll get to have a second conversation. So we tell people to revive those old opportunities.

Salespeople, sales managers, and customers are unanimous in their agreement that the best salespeople are those who stay up with changes and developments in technologies with selling applications. With a multitude of rapidly changing and evolving technology choices, salespeople must not only master the technology itself but must also understand when and where it can be applied most effectively. Exemplary selling technologies being used by today's salespeople include the following tools.[6]

Mobile Sales Technologies

At the centre of virtually every selling technology is the computer. Choices include desktops, notebooks, laptops, netbooks, smartphones, and personal data assistants (PDAs). With the ever-expanding availability of broadband and wireless connectivity, today's salesperson is always in touch with customers, with sales support, and with sales data and information. For immediate immersion into the high-tech side of selling, simply walk through the waiting areas of any major airport. Salespeople can be seen entering customer orders, generating reports, and submitting proposals by using standard word-processing packages and even customized online electronic forms. Others are analyzing customer accounts by using spreadsheet applications and query-based database programs that access and analyze a database according to the questions the user wants to have answered. Several will be observed reviewing and updating customer files by using one of the many mobile and highly capable contact management/CRM software applications. These user-friendly programs provide salespeople with a convenient option to catalogue, search, and access comprehensive information regarding individual customers. Looking closer, numerous salespeople will be revising and polishing graphics and presentations with software, such as PowerPoint. Still others will be checking and responding to email, submitting electronic reports, accessing online territory route maps, and using scheduling programs to set up the next day's call plans.

Salesperson Customer Relationship Management (CRM)

Effective customer relationships generate customer loyalty and the revenue increases critical for sustained performance. Toward meeting this challenge, companies of all sizes are deploying customer relationship management (CRM) applications and strategies that integrate multiple communication and customer contact channels—including the Web, email, call centres, and salespeople—to maximize customer interactions. However, detailed customer information is of little use if a salesperson cannot access it when they need it—such as during a sales call in a customer's office. Sales professionals often work outside the office and need up-to-date information while in the field. Being able to access and offer the right information to customers at the right point in the sales cycle enables salespeople to increase sales dramatically while simultaneously increasing customer satisfaction and loyalty. **Mobile salesperson CRM solutions**, such as Siebel, Salesforce.com, Microsoft Dynamics, and SalesLogix, are the key to accessing this information from the field and provide remote access to data, such as contacts, customer information, leads, reports, price lists, inventory levels, and opportunity forecasting. Mobile CRM applications use wireless broadband access to enable users instantly to view, create, and modify data on any Internet-capable device, such as smartphones, netbooks, and laptops. This handheld access to valuable account information allows a salesperson to tap into the same sales, marketing, and customer service data they have access to in the office—without having to leave the field. Mobile CRM is rapidly becoming a critical requirement for effectively competing in today's fast paced selling environment and increasing customer expectations in terms of customized levels of service.

mobile salesperson CRM solutions Wireless broadband applications that enable users to view, create, and modify data on any Internet-capable devices, such as smartphones, netbooks, and laptops.

deal analytics "Smart" salesforce automation tools that analyze data on past customer behaviour, cross-selling opportunities, and demographics to identify areas of opportunity and high customer interest.

Internet A technology tool that instantly networks the salesperson with customers, information sources, other salespeople, sales management, and others.

Deal Analytics

Deal analytics is the descriptive name given to a new set of "smart" tools in the area of salesforce automation that are proving especially useful for salespeople. These analytical tools use mobile CRM systems to access and analyze data on past customer behaviour, cross selling opportunities, and demographics to identify areas of opportunity and high interest to a customer. Salespeople also use deal analytics tools to access and compare competitive information, such as pricing and bundled offers, which can result in more effective proposals and negotiations.

The Internet, Intranets, and Extranets

Company networks have been used for many years; however, the advent of the Internet has made them much more affordable and easier to maintain.

Accessing the **Internet** instantly networks a salesperson with the world: customers, information sources, other salespeople, sales management, and others. More importantly, the Internet puts the salesperson into contact with his or her customer-community and support networks from anywhere in the world, 24 hours a day, seven days a week. Going beyond the convenience of email, many sales organizations are setting up **intranets** and **extranets**—secure and proprietary organizational websites that are protected by passwords and security authorizations. Intranets are networks within the organization that use the Internet or commercial channels to provide direct links between company units and individuals. Extranets are a special form of intranet that is still for proprietary and restricted use but links to specific suppliers and customers to allow them controlled and secure access to the organization's network to facilitate communication and exchange.

These secure websites become instant organizational intranets used for communication, training, videoconferencing, webconferencing, and secure data interchange. Using such Web-enabled intranets, Diamond Equipment Corporation's salespeople can link to the latest product information and spec sheets, obtain updated inventory and production numbers, download company information, and print customized proposals for customer presentations from anywhere in the world. CDW provides each of their major accounts with a customized extranet that gives the customer access to CDW on a 24-hour, seven-day-a-week basis. Buyers can track orders online, download product and technical specifications, access customer support technicians, check prices and availability of products, and even place orders for next-day delivery. Rather than spending time travelling to customers' offices, Windy City Wire's salespeople deliver their sales presentations by combining teleconferences and Web presentations using WebEx. The use of Internet- and intranet-based technologies shortens the sales cycle by allowing sales meetings and presentations to be created and delivered in less time than traditional

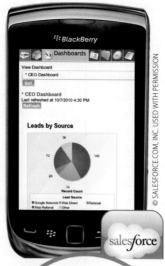

© SALESFORCE.COM, INC. USED WITH PERMISSION

Smartphones combined with mobile CRM applications enable salespeople instantly to view, create, and modify data from any location.

face-to-face processes would take. If a salesperson can save just 10 minutes a day by using Web-based presentation libraries and online product and pricing information, he or she will gain an additional week's worth of productivity over the course of a year. However, as illustrated by the situation described in "An Ethical Dilemma," the acceptance and adoption of advanced technologies are not always easy to accomplish.

High-Tech Sales Support Offices

Organizations that have salesforces widely dispersed geographically or travelling across multiple regions of the nation or world have found it advantageous to establish **high-tech sales support offices** at multiple locations. Both resident and nonresident salespeople use these offices to access a wider range of selling technology than could be easily carried on a notebook or laptop computer. These offices also provide points of access to the various networks, intranets, and extranets the organization maintains. IBM maintains such high-tech offices as these at its installations around the world. An IBM representative in Montreal might find himself working as part of a team on a project in Saint John. While in Saint John, the representative has access to the same technology and support as was available in Montreal. Full access is available to company networks, customer accounts, communication links, and software applications. Consequently, convenience and productive time are maximized for the benefit of all parties.

STAGE FIVE: ASSESSMENT OF PERFORMANCE AND GOAL ATTAINMENT

A critical, and often overlooked, stage in the process of self-leadership is the periodic assessment of progress. Although certainly important, this stage should involve more than a simple check at the end of the period to determine whether goals were achieved. Assessment checkpoints should be built into plans at progressive points in time to encourage and facilitate

intranets Secured networks within the organization that use the Internet or commercial channels to provide direct linkages between company units and individuals.

extranets A form of intranet that is still restricted but links to specific suppliers and customers to allow them controlled access to the organization's network and databases.

high-tech sales support offices Offices set up at multiple locations where salespeople can access the wider range of selling technology than could be easily carried on a notebook or laptop computer.

An Ethical Dilemma

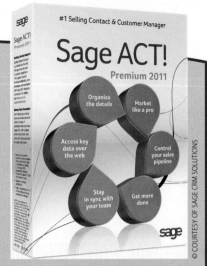

© COURTESY OF SAGE CRM SOLUTIONS

As one of the top 10 multiline insurance companies in North America, National Assurance Corporation (NAC) has an extensive network of sales agents across Canada and the United States. These salespeople operate as captive agents, meaning that they are not employed by NAC but exclusively sell NAC products and abide by NAC policies and procedures as a requirement of their agency franchise.

As part of the organization's upgrade of its sales information system to a more complete customer relationship management (CRM) system, NAC has obtained company-wide licences for ACT! (a leading contact and customer information management application). This licensing agreement allows the sales agents to obtain the latest Web-enabled version of ACT! at extremely favourable pricing. ACT! is a sophisticated customer database application that basically makes an integrated CRM available to the agents. Basic customer profiles are enriched with detailed personal and family information along with purchase details and full tracking of contact experience histories. In addition to the richer information base, customized reports can be developed and even filed automatically—an attractive feature that can greatly reduce the time that agents have traditionally had to spend every Friday to file activity reports with their district sales managers.

The rollout of the new program was going well and quickly achieved greater than 80 percent usage rate among agents. However, at last month's National Sales Meeting in Orlando, it was learned that this version of the application also allows sales supervisors and others at NAC access to their customer data files. Word quickly spread and dissension was high. Even though access to customer files is secure and requires password authentication that is controlled by NAC, sales agents are still suspicious of NAC's ability to access their customer files. The agents argue that these files are solely their property, and others (especially NAC) should not have access. Corporate, in contrast, feels that it needs the information to develop new products for the agents to sell.

The question of who owns customer account files, the salesperson or the selling organization, has been a point of contention for decades. It is nothing new. However, the advent of more advanced information technologies has brought this issue back under the spotlight. How do you feel about this issue? How might this potentially divisive issue be resolved?

the evaluation of a salesperson's progress. These frequent comparisons of actual performance with periodic checkpoints allow time to consider revisions or modifications before it is too late to make a difference. In addition to assessing progress, evaluation should also consider what is working well and what could be improved. This knowledge and understanding can be used to guide modifications in the various plans, tasks, and activities that populate the different stages of self-leadership to further enhance future success and performance.

Increasing Customer Value through Teamwork

Quality customer service is taking on a key role in competitive business strategy, and as customer expectations and needs continue to grow in complexity, selling organizations are finding

external relationships
Relationships salespeople build with customers outside the organization and working environment.

internal relationships
Relationships salespeople have with other individuals in their own company.

that they can no longer depend solely on salespeople as the exclusive arbiter of customer satisfaction. Teamwork, both inside the organization and with customers, is being emphasized as the key to customer focus and sales performance.

INTERNAL PARTNERSHIPS AND TEAMS

The practices and experiences of top-ranked selling organizations, as well as considerable sales research, support the emphasis on teamwork as a key to long-term selling success. The results from three studies of more than 200 companies that employ some 25,000 salespeople supported the belief that cooperating as a team player was critical for success in selling.[7] Similar results have been found in other studies that examine what business-to-business buyers expect from suppliers. In two studies incorporating 6708 customer evaluations of vendor performance and customer satisfaction in the financial services industry, the suppliers' performance in building internal and external partnerships was found to be the key driver of customer satisfaction.[8]

Building **external relationships** is the focal point of contemporary selling techniques and reflects the ongoing paradigm shift in today's salesforces. This emphasis on building *external* customer relationships could overshadow the critical role of building *internal*, close-working relationships with other individuals in their own company. The importance of these **internal relationships** would seem to be logical, as a salesperson's success depends on the degree of support he or she receives from others in the various functional areas of the organization. Ultimately, the salesperson owns the responsibility for customer relationships, but the strength of those customer relationships depends on the joint efforts and resources contributed by multiple individuals across the selling organization.

Account managers at Contour Plastics Corporation have full responsibility for bringing together individuals from functional departments across the organization to work as a sales team dedicated to selling and providing presale and postsale services to a specific account. As needed, team members will incorporate research chemists, application specialists, production engineers, and

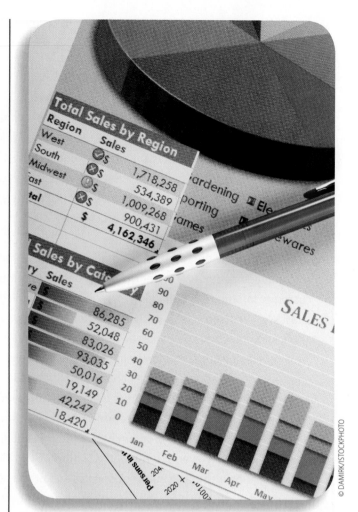

Periodic performance assessments should be built into plans so as to encourage evaluation of progress and identify where improvements might be needed in order to achieve goals.

logistics specialists. Coordinated by the salesperson, each team member contributes his or her special expertise toward maximizing the understanding of the customer's situation and needs, and then working together to create a unique, value-added solution that few, if any, competitors can equal.

Teamwork results in a synergy that produces greater outcomes and results for all parties than would be possible with multiple individuals acting independently. Consequently, it is important that salespeople also develop the ability to sell internally as they represent their customers to the selling organization and give recognition to the important role others play in winning, keeping, and growing customer accounts.

James Champy, chairman of consulting for Perot Systems, notes that customers are expecting and receiving better service and product options than ever, and he characterizes the role of the salesperson as having been transformed to that of a trusted advisor.[9]

In this adviser role, the salesperson works with customers to develop a mutual understanding of the customer's situation, needs, possibilities, and expectations. On the basis of this information, the salesperson assembles a team of individuals, experts from across the selling organization, who work together to create a product response that will deliver more unique customer value than the competitors' offerings. In delivering this unique and added value for customers, salespeople often find themselves working with other individuals in sales, marketing, design and manufacturing, administrative support, shipping, and customer service.

Sales Partnerships

Within the sales department, salespeople often team with other salespeople to gain the strengths and expertise required for a specific selling situation or customer. Partnerships with sales managers and other sales executives are also important in winning support for developing innovative responses to customer needs. XL Capital is a global leader in alternative risk transfer products, financial risk management, and surplus lines of commercial property and casualty insurance. Selling to Fortune 500 and Fortune 1000 customers, XL Capital's salespeople (customer business unit managers) specialize along customer and industry lines. It is common for XL's salespeople to work together in teams to bring together the experience and expertise required to work with customers whose businesses span a large number of different industries.

Marketing Partnerships

Teaming with individuals in the marketing department is critical for salespeople in generating integrated solutions for customers over the long term. Marketing is responsible for developing organizational marketing strategies that serve as guidelines for the salesforce. Using information gathered in the field by the salesforce, marketing also assists in the generation of new market offerings in response to changing customer needs and requests. Marketing can also be a valuable partner for salespeople in accessing information and developing sales proposals.

At Pocahontas Foods, a top-10 institutional food broker with nationwide operations, account managers regularly work with members of the marketing department to communicate changes in customer needs and

activities of competitors. This collaborative partnership allows Pocahontas to continue bringing innovative product offerings to the marketplace that are designed around the inputs from their salespeople.

Salesperson effectiveness in building internal and external partnerships is a key driver of customer satisfaction.

Design and Manufacturing Partnerships

Salespeople often find themselves selling ideas for product designs and changes in manufacturing schedules to meet the needs of customers. When individuals from design, manufacturing, and sales work as a team, performance and delivery commitments are more likely to be met and customer satisfaction further enhanced. Wallace works to maintain its industry leadership in business forms and systems by aggressively nurturing a company-wide culture emphasizing customer orientation and support. As part of their training, salespeople actually work in production facilities to understand what has to be done to meet product design and delivery requirements that the salespeople might commit to in the field. By-products of this cross-training come about in the form of one-to-one personal relationships between salespeople and production staff. In the case of complex customer needs or special delivery needs, these relationships become invaluable.

Administrative Support Partnerships

Salespeople work with others from administrative support functions, such as management, finance and credit, billing, and information systems. Like sales, each of these functional units has certain goals and objectives that translate to policies and procedures that govern their own activities and affect operations throughout the organization—including sales. Customer needs are served best when salespeople have worked to establish effective relationships within these units and all parties work together for the mutual good of the organization and customer. Jim Gavic, account manager for Cross Canada Trucking, manages a territory stretching from the industrial sector of Calgary, Alberta, east to Halifax, Nova Scotia. Gavic credits his close relationships with individuals in the company's finance and credit department for making 20 percent of his annual sales. By working together, they were able to establish special billing terms for several of his larger accounts. If finance and credit had simply enforced Cross Canada's standard terms, these customers would have been lost to a competitor with more flexible credit policies.

Shipping and Transportation Partnerships

Salespeople periodically find themselves facing an urgent customer need that requires special handling of an order. Perhaps it is an expedited shipment for immediate delivery or the processing and shipping of an interim order of less than economical size. Whatever the need, it will affect other shipments getting out on time and could even increase the department's operating costs. Curtis James, territory manager for General Electric Appliances, found sales going better than usual at a new store opening in Winnipeg. To keep the customer from being caught short, he hand-carried a fill-in order to the GE district office, walked it through credit approval, hand-delivered the shipping order to the warehouse, and helped load the truck. Teamwork enabled Curtis to accomplish in less than a day what normally would have taken 8 to 10 days. It takes a team effort to work through exceptions such as these, and it is common to find the salesperson actually helping to make it happen by pulling orders, packing boxes, and even helping to load the truck.

Customer Service Partnerships

Teamwork between sales and customer service can create a synergy that has a broad-based impact that can translate to higher customer satisfaction, higher rates of customer retention, and increased sales performance. On the one hand, customer service personnel, such as call centre operators and service technicians, often have more extensive contact with customers than the account representatives. As such, they can serve as an early warning system for salespeople and provide valuable information regarding customer complaints, problems, developing needs, and changes that they encounter through customer contacts. As a salesperson for Southwestern School Supply, Cap Williams regularly checks in and visits with the company's customer service personnel to keep abreast of contacts that they might have with any of his customers. The information he receives allows him to get ahead of any possible customer problems, provide an outstanding level of after-sale support that continues to mystify upper

Working as a team with individuals in the shipping department can provide critical relationships when a salesperson faces an urgent customer need for expedited shipment and delivery.

management, and helps to secure his receipt of Top Salesperson of the Year Award year after year. When salespeople, such as Williams, act on the information provided by customer service to further customer relationships and increase sales, customer service personnel will also be further inclined to work together to benefit the team. On the other hand, salespeople often assist customer service personnel by working directly with customers to address problems before they become complaints and provide instruction and training to assist customers in using the products sold.

LO5
BUILDING TEAMWORK SKILLS

As illustrated in "An Ethical Dilemma," effective teams do not form by default. Nor can a team be effective in producing synergistic benefits solely because it is called a team. Like customer relationships, internal relationships are built on reciprocal trust. The salesperson who arbitrarily and repeatedly asks for special production runs, extensions to customers' lines of credit, expedited shipments, or special attention from customer service is simply asking for quick fixes. These quick fixes serve the objectives of the customer and salesperson but often work against the objectives of the functional unit and the organization as a whole.

Synergistic teamwork requires a commitment on the part of all parties to look for and work for win-

win solutions. However, in the rush to take care of a customer, it is all too easy for salespeople to fall into a win-lose orientation. It is not that they want anyone to lose, but rather that they get what they want. This win orientation is most common in everyday negotiation—in which people think and act in terms of accomplishing their own goals and leave it to others to attain theirs. As illustrated in Figure 10.4, optimum solutions develop from a team orientation based on the philosophy of win-win alternatives.[10] In turn, this can happen only when there are high levels of mutual trust and communication: "Not your way, not my way, but a better way."

In his bestselling book on personal development, Stephen Covey offers six keys to developing synergistic relationships and teams.[11] These are the six **teamwork skills** that salespeople must learn and sincerely apply in their process of building internal partnerships that translate to increased sales and organizational performance.

An Ethical Dilemma

© HEMERA TECHNOLOGIES/JUPITER IMAGES

Kai Cody has been one of the top sales representatives for Altima Telecom for several years. Altima is one of the leading companies in outsourced-customer call centre services providing both outbound and inbound customer-contact services. It is not uncommon for Cody's sales numbers to lead his region, and he has received a number of significant recognitions and promotions. However, after Cody makes the sale, the nature and quality of the service program delivered is totally dependent on the service design engineers that develop the service program, the team of phone representatives that actually handle the calls, and the call-team supervisors that manage the phone representatives. Altima has been experiencing rapid growth over the past two years and has been adding additional personnel throughout the organization, especially phone teams. Many of these new hires have come from competitor organizations and the resulting level of delivered quality has become unpredictable, but consistently below the service levels promised by Cody and the other members of the salesforce. Cody has discussed these problems with his sales supervisor, but nothing seems to change. Over the past five to six months, Cody has found himself spending more and more time trying to patch over service failures by the company's phone teams and trying to win back customers that have left Altima to go with a competitor. Cody feels that his hands are tied. The quality of services delivered continues to fall below the expectations of customers and nothing is being done to correct the problems. Not only is Cody losing sales but he also believes his reputation will soon start to suffer. Last week, one of Cody's main competitors contacted him about leaving Altima and coming to work for them. What would you do if you were Cody?

- *Understanding the Other Individuals*—Fully understanding and considering the other individuals in the partnership is necessary to know what is important to them. What is important to them must also be important to the salesperson if the partnership is to grow and be effective. This means that salespeople must take time to learn the objectives of other functional areas and consider how those needs and requests might affect the salesperson's goals and objectives.

- *Attending to the Little Things*—The little kindnesses and courtesies are often small in size and great in importance. In building relationships, the little things are the big things. Properly attended to and nurtured, they enhance the interrelationships. At the same time, if they

> **teamwork skills** Skills salespeople must learn to build internal partnerships that translate into increased sales and organizational performance.

are neglected or misused, they can destroy the relationship very quickly.

- *Keeping Commitments*—We all build our hopes and plans around the promises and commitments of others. When a commitment is not kept, disappointment and problems result. As a result, credibility and trust suffer major damage that is always difficult, and often impossible, to repair. However, consistency in keeping commitments builds and solidifies trust-based relationships.

- *Clarifying Expectations*— The root cause of most relational difficulties can be found in ambiguous expectations regarding roles and goals—exactly where are we going and who is responsible for what? Investing the time up front to clarify expectations regarding goals and roles can save even more time down the road when misunderstandings become compounded and turn into goal conflicts and breakdowns in communication.

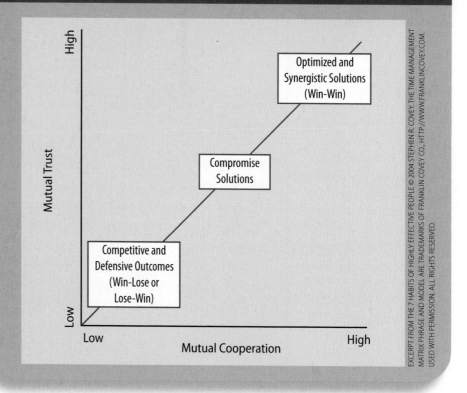

FIGURE 10.4

Relationship of Optimized Solutions, Trust, and Cooperation

Optimum buyer–seller solutions result from a team orientation and require high levels of mutual trust and cooperation.

- *Showing Personal Integrity*— Demonstrating personal integrity generates trust, whereas a lack of integrity can quickly undermine the best of teamwork orientations. People can seek to understand others, carry through on the little things, keep commitments, and clarify expectations, but still fail to build trust by being inwardly duplicitous and pursuing a personal agenda. Be honest, open, and treat everyone by the same set of principles.

- *Apologizing Sincerely When a Mistake Is Made*— It is one thing to make a mistake. It is another thing not to admit it. People forgive mistakes. What is harder to forgive are the ill intentions and motives justifying any attempt to cover up. "If you are going to bow, bow low." The apology must be perceived as sincere and not simply as automated lip-service response.

UNIVERSAL CONTROL CORP.

Background

Universal Control Corp. is a leading supplier for process control systems and equipment used in a wide variety of production and distribution applications. You have taken a sales representative job with Universal, and having just completed training, you have been given a territory of your own. Your district manager has provided you with a list of accounts as well as several boxes of notes and files that had been assembled and used by your predecessor. These are the accounts currently buying your products. You are expected to build these accounts and add new accounts to the list as you increase your territory's sales performance. You have summarized the account information into the summary set of account profiles, which follows on the next page.

Questions

1. Develop a portfolio classification of accounts and assess the allocation of sales calls your predecessor made over the past year.
2. What problems do you find with the previous allocation of calls on these accounts?
3. Based on your account classification analysis, suggest a new sales call allocation strategy that would make better use of your time in the territory.

Role Play

Situation: Read the case.

Characters: Zack Hanna, salesperson for Universal Control Corp.; Gage Waits, district sales manager and Hanna's immediate supervisor

Scene:
Location—Gage Waits's office at Universal Control Corp.
Action—Zack has just been assigned this territory and has completed an analysis of sales and customer files to profile the individual accounts and sales call allocation strategies used by the previous salesperson in the territory. Based on this information, Hanna has developed information responding to each of the three questions following the Universal Control Corp. case materials. This information includes a new sales call allocation strategy. Hanna is meeting with his sales manager to explain his new sales call allocation plan.

As Hanna, answer the three questions previously listed. Using this information, role play your interaction with your sales manager, Gage Waits, as you discuss and explain (1) your analysis of the previous salesperson's sales call allocation and (2) your new plans and how they will increase the effectiveness and efficiency of your selling efforts in this territory.

Account Name	Account Opportunity	Competitive Position	Annual Number of Sales Calls Last Year
Mueller Distribution	High	Low	30
Tri-State Specialties	Low	High	20
Birkey Paper Co.	Low	High	26
Normal Supply	Low	Low	12
Darnell Aggregate Products	Low	High	21
Reinhart Chemicals	High	High	26
ACCO Manufacturing	Low	High	23
Tri-State Manufacturing	High	Low	28
Ideal Engineering	Low	Low	11
Terracon	High	High	25
Lowry Foods	High	Low	26
SCS Industrial	High	High	27
Lowell Services	Low	High	18
Bowles and Sons	Low	High	21
American Foundry	High	Low	22
Hewitt & Associates	Low	Low	16
Bright Metals Inc.	High	High	22
Decatur Extrusions	Low	Low	14
King Chemicals	Low	High	22
Bear's Steel Corp.	Low	High	20
Hoffman Pharmaceuticals	High	Low	20
Barlow & Clark Systems	Low	High	18

After completing the role play, address the following questions:

1. How might Hanna's sales allocation plan be different if he had used single-factor analysis (ABC analysis) instead of portfolio analysis?
2. Develop a sales call allocation plan using single-factor analysis. Compare the results of Hanna's portfolio analysis with the results of your single-factor analysis. Where and how are they different?
3. How might those differences translate to increased selling effectiveness and efficiency?

Integrated Systems Inc.

Background

As a business development specialist for Integrated Systems Inc (ISI), you are responsible for acquiring new accounts and working with existing accounts to develop strong relationships so as to increase share of account and sales revenues. After you make the initial sale to an account, much of the continuing service, reordering, and account maintenance is performed by a team of three customer service representatives who work with customers through the phone and Internet. Because of a combination of rapid growth in sales and two of the customer service representatives being relatively new to the job, the resulting level of service provided by the customer service team has become unpredictable and all too often below the level you have promised to deliver to your customers.

As a result of problems with the customer service team, you are finding that you are having to spend time trying to patch over service shortcomings and working to win back accounts that have left ISI to go with a competitor. Not only are you losing business, but your reputation—and that of ISI—is beginning to suffer.

Role Play

In discussing these problems with your sales manager, it was decided that you would meet with the team of customer service representatives to discuss and address the problems.

Role play how you would approach and initiate a positive and collaborative relationship with the customer service team members that might generate positive outcomes for your customers, ISI, and everyone involved. Remember to employ the six teamwork skills discussed in this chapter.

The most successful

sales managers develop effective sales strategies
and lead salespeople to implement these strategies
and achieve desired results.

what do you think?

The best salespeople
make the best sales
managers.

1 2 3 4 5 6 7

strongly disagree   strongly agree

II

Sales Management and Sales 2.0

After completing this chapter, you should be able to

LO1 Discuss the key considerations in developing and implementing effective sales strategies.

LO2 Understand the recruitment, selection, and training processes involved in developing the salesforce.

LO3 Identify key activities in directing the salesforce by leading, managing, supervising, motivating, and rewarding salespeople.

LO4 Explain the different methods for evaluating the performance and effectiveness of sales organizations and individual salespeople.

LO5 Describe how sales organizations are using Sales 2.0 to co-create value with customers.

Introduction

a ccording to motivational speaker and super-coach Steve Chandler, your number one job as a sales leader is to increase the optimism of everyone on your team. "Managers who spend their whole sales meeting dispensing information are wasting everyone's time," says Chandler. "The only real purpose of bringing everyone together is to make sure that your salespeople leave more motivated, more encouraged, and more optimistic than they came in."

But don't get the idea that this is all about pumping 'em up and sending 'em out. Chandler, who has authored more than 20 CD courses and books, believes that external motivation is "like a drug. It's an adrenaline rush, a short-term stimulus that eventually fades, often leaving the person more down than ever. Lasting optimism is the result of changing how you think, and that happens through repetition."

Smart managers motivate not by creating wild enthusiasm at a yearly sales meeting, but rather by teaching their teams how to think optimistically on a day-to-day basis.

Most people have any number of self-limiting beliefs, many of them involving their business skills—or their perceived lack of them: "I'm not good on the phone. Cold calling scares me. I've never been able to remember names." Chandler calls these beliefs "our story."

"The funny thing about business is that it often doesn't matter what you're naturally good at," Chandler says. "You might tell yourself that you're not good at cold calling, but if you put that story aside and make the call anyway, the odds are that you'll achieve something. It's irrelevant whether or not you're good at something compared to what you can achieve if you just try."

Chandler suggests putting the brakes on your internal dialogue whenever you catch yourself telling a story, and managers should interrupt their salespeople when they begin storytelling. "You might say, 'This is hard', 'This guy is tough to close,' or 'I'm not good at this or that,'" Chandler says, "but if you drop all these stories and wander in as an innocent, as someone who doesn't have a story, you may do a great job. And you'll certainly get a lot further than if you talked yourself out of trying at all."

Chandler says managers make a big mistake when they open a sales meeting by talking about what the sales team needs to improve. "When the first item on the docket is all about what's not working," he says, "you've opened the door to a meeting of wailing and venting and excuses. Instead, start by acknowledging what is going well—people who have succeeded and opportunities that exist."

Of course, there are always problems that need to be addressed, but Chandler suggests you address them with the individual salespeople involved either before or after the meeting. "Bad news can be handled one-on-one," he says. "Spend your precious meeting time discussing where the opportunities are."

Source: Kim Wright Wiley. "Optimism Always Wins." *Selling Power.* http://www.sellingpower.com/magazine/article.php?i=1352&ia=9264

Our focus to this point has been on personal selling. The purpose of this chapter is to examine sales management. We begin by providing an overview of sales management. Then, each stage in the sales management process is presented in more detail. The chapter concludes by discussing Sales 2.0, which is the use of new and emerging technologies throughout a sales organization.

Sales Management Overview

Sales management is the managing of an organization's personal selling function. This requires attention to strategic and leadership issues by developing and executing plans. Our sales management overview examines the sales management process, different sales management positions, and best practices in sales management.[1]

SALES MANAGEMENT PROCESS

The major stages in the sales management process are presented in Figure 11.1.[2] Sales managers must have a deep understanding of the personal selling function to manage it effectively. This understanding has been provided to you in the other chapters in this book. The remaining stages of the sales management process build on this personal selling knowledge.

Defining the strategic role of the sales function addresses the strategic aspects of sales management. The development of sales strategies for individual customers or customer segments, and the integration of these sales strategies with a firm's corporate, business, and marketing strategies, are especially important. Then, an effective sales organization must be created and the deployment of salespeople and selling effort is determined.

Developing the salesforce is concerned with getting the best sales talent and providing them with the knowledge and skills to be successful. Sales managers are involved in recruiting and selecting salespeople, as well as in designing and implementing sales training programs.

Directing the salesforce focuses on efforts to encourage and help salespeople achieve personal and organizational goals. This includes effective leadership and management activities by sales managers, as well as various types of reward programs. Some companies use an incentive-driven compensation plan to get salespeople motivated. But sales managers also spend a great deal of time coaching salespeople and working closely with them to develop and implement sales plans.

Determining salesforce effectiveness and performance emphasizes an assessment of how well the sales organization and units, such as areas and districts, as well as salespeople and sales managers, are performing.

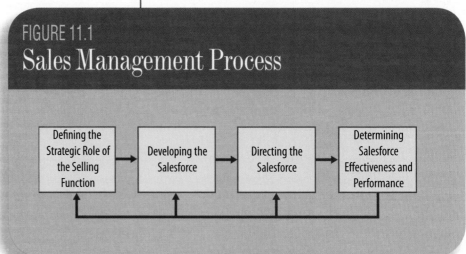

FIGURE 11.1
Sales Management Process

Defining the Strategic Role of the Selling Function → Developing the Salesforce → Directing the Salesforce → Determining Salesforce Effectiveness and Performance

The sales management process consists of understanding the personal selling function and implementing the four major stages of sales management activities.

These evaluations provide a basis for rewards, but they also generate feedback that can be used to improve all aspects of the sales management process. Companies may assess the effectiveness of their sales organization through market share and sales growth determinations and the performance of their salespeople according to achieving sales and other goals. This provides a basis for rewarding salespeople, but it also leads to improvements that reduce turnover.

SALES MANAGEMENT POSITIONS

Although there are a variety of sales management positions with different titles at different firms, most of these positions fit into three categories. Many firms have a top-level sales executive usually called a chief sales officer (CSO) or vice president of sales. This position has responsibility for the entire sales organization. Then, there are often one or more levels of sales managers who report to the top level sales executive and are responsible for sales managers below them. Typical titles are regional sales manager or area sales manager. Finally, field sales managers have direct responsibility for salespeople and report to the sales manager directly above them in the sales organization structure. These sales managers work closely with salespeople in the field and usually have titles like district sales manager or sales manager. Each of these positions is involved in the sales management process, but each usually performs different activities depending on the level of the position and the specific structure of a sales organization.

> Sales managers occupy different positions in many firms.

© ANDRES RODRIGUEZ/ALAMY

SALES MANAGEMENT BEST PRACTICES

The complex, dynamic, and competitive environment facing sales organizations has prompted sales consulting firms, such as HR Chally and Forum, and academic researchers to identify the most effective sales management practices. This research suggests that the best sales organizations[3]

1. Create a customer-driven culture throughout the sales organization and firm.

2. Recruit and hire the best sales talent.

3. Train and coach the right skill set.

4. Focus on key strategic issues by segmenting accounts in meaningful ways and providing differentiated offerings to find, win, and retain customers.

5. Implement formal sales and relationship-building processes.

6. Use information technology effectively to learn about customers.

7. Integrate sales with other business functions, especially marketing.

In essence, these research findings indicate that the best sales organizations perform all stages of the sales management process effectively.

Other research has examined the characteristics and activities of the best sales managers. Studies indicate that high-performing sales managers possess good communication and listening skills; human relations skills; organization and time management skills; industry, company, product, and general business knowledge; coaching, motivating, and leadership skills; and honest and ethical tendencies.[4] These sales managers use these skills to[5]

1. Prepare their sales team for constant change by being a role model and mentoring salespeople.

2. Earn the trust of salespeople by being dependable, competent, and exhibiting integrity.

3. Give salespeople continual feedback in a positive manner.

4. Build enthusiasm throughout the sales team.

5. Get involved by being accessible to salespeople and visible to customers.

6. Grow and develop salespeople by emphasizing continual job improvement and career development.

As you can see, sales managers occupy an important and demanding position. They need a variety of skills and must be engaged in many different activities to be successful. We will now discuss specific sales management activities in more detail.

LO1
Developing and Implementing Effective Sales Strategies

Sales managers should be aware of the key strategic decisions taking place at the corporate, business, marketing, and sales levels in their organizations. Corporate- and business-level strategic decisions typically provide guidelines within which sales managers and salespeople operate. This is typically true for firms focusing on a customer relationship management (CRM) strategy. Professional selling plays an important role in sales managers' strategic planning. Strategic decisions at the corporate, business, and marketing levels must be translated into strategies for individual accounts. Sales strategies are designed for individual accounts or groups of similar accounts. Therefore, sales managers must be continually working to identify and classify accounts into useful categories.

SALES STRATEGY

Sales managers and salespeople are generally responsible for strategic decisions at the account level. A sales strategy is designed to execute an organization's marketing strategy for individual accounts. The major purpose of a sales strategy is to develop a specific approach for selling to individual accounts within a target market. A sales strategy capitalizes on the important differences among individual accounts or groups of similar accounts. A firm's sales strategy is important for two reasons. First, it has a major impact on a firm's sales and profit performance. Second, it influences many other sales management decisions, such as recruitment, selection, training, compensation, and performance.

Sales managers must develop strategies for forming key elements of strategic decision making. A discussion on account targeting, relationship strategies, selling strategies, and channel strategies will follow.

Account Targeting Strategy

The first challenge a sales manager may face is deciding which accounts to pursue. All accounts within the target market are not created equally. Some accounts may not be good prospects because they have a solid relationship with a competitor. Even good prospects or current customers differ in how much they buy or how much they might buy in the future or how eager they are to do business with the sales organizations. Accounts may therefore require different servicing.

An **account targeting strategy** is the classification of accounts within a target market into categories for the purpose of developing strategic approaches for selling to each account or account group. The account targeting strategy provides the basis for all other elements of a sales strategy. Just as different marketing mixes are developed to serve different target markets, sales organizations need to use different relationships, selling, and sales channel strategies for different account groups.

Relationship Strategy

As discussed in previous chapters, there is a clear trend toward a relationship orientation between buyers and sellers. A **relationship strategy** is a determination of the type of relationship to develop with different account groups. The relationship strategies may range from a transaction relationship based on ease of acquisition and low price to a collaborative relationship where the buyer and seller work closely together for the benefit of both businesses. In between these extremes are intermediate types of relationships based on a lower commitment from the buyer and seller. Selling costs are increased to serve accounts with higher level relationships. Sales organizations must consider the costs associated with using different relationship strategies for different account groups. The critical task is balancing the customer's needs with the cost of serving the account.

account targeting strategy The classification of accounts within a target market into categories for the purpose of developing strategic approaches for selling to each account or account group.

relationship strategy A determination of the type of relationship to be developed with different account groups.

Selling Strategy

Successfully executing a specific relationship strategy requires a unique selling approach. A **selling strategy** is the planned selling approach for each relationship strategy. Exhibit 11.1 matches the appropriate selling strategy with the appropriate relationship strategy. As indicated, the stimulus-response and mental states approaches typically fit with transaction relationship strategy. The need satisfaction and problem-solving selling strategies are normally used with a solutions relationship strategy. The consultative approach is most effective with the partnership and collaborative relationship strategies. Sometimes, a collaborative relationship strategy requires a selling strategy that is completely customized to the specific buyer–seller situation. The important point is that achieving the desired type of relationship in a productive manner requires using different selling strategies. Matching selling strategies and relationship strategies is an important sales management task.

Sales Channel Strategy

Sales channel strategy ensures that accounts receive proper selling effort and coverage. Various methods are available to a selling organization to provide proper coverage to accounts, including a company salesforce, the Internet, distributors, independent representatives, team selling, telemarketing, and trade shows.

The Internet is quickly becoming a critical sales channel in selling to organizations. On the surface, it would appear the Internet is being used to reduce selling costs. Other applications include reordering, product information, and linkage to customer and support representatives. The Internet is being blended not only into other field selling efforts but also into other sales channels, such as industrial distributors, independent representatives, and telemarketers.

Distributors and other wholesalers provide another sales channel alternative. Distributors usually employ their own salesforce and may carry (1) the products of one manufacturer, (2) related but noncompeting products from different manufacturers, or (3) competing products from different manufacturers. Firms that employ distributors normally have a small company salesforce to serve and support the efforts of the distributors.

Companies using personal selling can choose to cover accounts with **independent representatives** or **manufacturer representatives** (sometimes referred to as reps). Reps are independent sales organizations that sell complementary, but noncompeting, products from different manufacturers. Independent representatives do not normally carry inventory or take title to the products they sell. These reps are typically compensated on a commission basis for products sold.

The use of **team selling** is increasing in many firms. This is especially true as a sales channel for a firm's most important prospects and customers. Generating the best new prospects into customers and expanding relationships with the most profitable existing customers often requires the participation of many individuals from both the buying and selling firms. This can be a very expensive sales channel approach, but prospects and customers seem to appreciate the attention they receive. The team selling strategy has helped Data Cert obtain top clients, such as UPS, Microsoft, and AT&T.[6]

Trade shows are typically industry-sponsored events in which companies use a booth

selling strategy Involves the planning of sales messages and interactions with customers. Selling strategy can be defined at three levels: for a group of customers, that is, a sales territory; for individual customers; and for specific customer encounters, referred to as sales calls.

independent representatives or manufacturer representatives Independent sales organizations that sell complementary but noncompeting products from different manufacturers; also called manufacturer's representatives or reps.

team selling The use of multiple-person sales teams in dealing with multiple-person customer buying centres.

EXHIBIT 11.1
Matching Selling and Relationship Strategies

Relationship Strategy			
Transactions	**Solutions**	**Partnership**	**Collaborative**
Stimulus response	Need satisfaction	Consultative	Consultative
Mental states	Problem solving		Customized

Source: Thomas N. Ingram, Raymond W. LaForge, Ramon A. Avila, Charles H. Schwepker, Jr., and Michael Williams, Sales Management: Analysis and Decision Making, 7th ed. (Armonk, NY: M. E. Sharpe, 2009). Copyright © 2009 by M. E. Sharpe, Inc. Used with permission.

to display products and services to potential and existing customers. Trade shows can be used to achieve both selling and nonselling objectives. Selling objectives might include testing new products and closing sales. Nonselling objectives include servicing current customers, gathering competitive information, identifying new prospects, and enhancing corporate image. Typically, trade shows are only once a year for a few days and should be viewed as a supplemental method for account coverage.

SALES STRUCTURE

Many different types of structures can be used successfully and many variations are possible within each type. Often, the resulting structure is complex and it considers specialization, centralization, span of control versus management levels, and line versus staff responsibilities.[7]

Specialization

In small organizations, each salesperson could perform all the selling tasks and the sales manager could perform all the management activities. Most organizations are too complex for this structure and require some degree of specialization. Salespeople may sell only part of the product line or call on existing accounts. Sales managers may work only with new hires or be solely involved with the training of the sales staff. Specialization allows individuals to become experts on those tasks and leads to better performance.

Managers must be prepared to manage more salespeople as organizations get flatter.

© DMITRIY SHIRONOSOV/SHUTTERSTOCK

Centralization

A centralized structure is one in which authority and responsibility are placed at higher management levels. While no organization is totally centralized or totally decentralized, most typically centralize some activities and decentralize others. When building a sales team that encourages the development of or relationships with customers, a decentralized structure facilitates such decision making in the field.

Span of Control versus Management Levels

Span of control refers to the number of individuals who report to each sales manager. The larger the span of control, the more salespeople the sales manager must manage. Management levels determine the number of different hierarchical levels of sales management within the organization.

In effect, organizations can go one of two ways. In a flat sales organization structure, there will be relatively few sales management levels, with each manager having a relatively large span of control. In a tall structure, there will be more sales management levels and smaller spans of control.

Line versus Staff Positions

Sales management positions can be differentiated as line or staff positions. Line sales managers have direct responsibility for a certain number of salespeople and report directly to management at the next highest level in the sales organization. Staff sales management positions are not in the direct chain of command in the sales organization structure. Staff managers do not directly manage people, but they are responsible for particular functions, such as training and recruiting. Staff managers are generally not responsible for sales-generating activities.

Designing the Sales Organization

There are a tremendous number of ways a sales organization might be structured. There are several traditional types to choose from and each has its advantages and disadvantages. Typical structures include geographic sales organization, product sale organization, market sales organization, and functional sales organization. We will briefly look at each type of sales organization.

Geographic Sales Organization

Probably the most widely used system for dividing responsibility is to organize the salesforce on the basis of geographic territories. This is the least specialized and the most generalized type of salesforce. Salespeople are typically assigned a geographic area and are responsible for all the selling activities to all the customers and prospects within the assigned territory. There is no attempt to specialize by market, function, or product. The greatest advantage of this structure is the low cost and few management levels. There is also no geographic or customer duplication. The greatest disadvantage of a geographic sales organization is its limited specialization.

Product Sales Organization

The type of product sold is another basis for dividing the responsibilities and activities within a sales department. Product specialization assigns a salesperson the selling responsibility for a specific product or typically a product line. The objective is for the salesperson to become an expert on the assigned product category. The major advantage of this form of organization is the specialized attention given to each product by the salesperson. There is a downside to the product sales organization: It is extremely costly. If a company carries many products, then it must hire a large salesforce to learn and sell the entire product line. It is costly to have 10–15 sales reps within a geographic territory when one or two will do.

Market Sales Organization

The focus of a market sales organization is to ensure that the salesforce understands how their customers use and purchase their products. Once this is understood, the salesforce should be able to direct their selling efforts to better satisfy customer needs. Market specialization has become an increasingly important type of specialization and is growing in use.[8] Market specialization includes selling to government, education, medical, wholesalers, retailers, military, manufacturers, and financial institutions, to name a few. The biggest advantage is getting to know the customer intimately. This in turn can help develop a better understanding of unique customer needs. Market organizational structure has disadvantages similar to a product organization in that it produces high costs and duplication of effort.

Functional Sales Organization

The final type of specialization is functional specialization. Many selling activities are required for a sales organization's success. Entry-level salespeople could be groomed to generate leads and qualify prospects, while the more experienced salespeople could concentrate on sales-generating activities. This is an example of a firm specializing by function. The major advantage of functional specialization is the efficiency in performing selling activities. Whether generating leads, qualifying prospects, or generating sales, if a salesperson has to concentrate only on one or two of these activities, he or she can progressively gain expertise. However, it has disadvantages: a great deal of geographic and customer duplication occur, requiring extensive coordination between salespeople. A review of the advantages and disadvantages of organizational structures can be found in Exhibit 11.2.

In summary, designing a sales organization is a difficult and complex task. Trends do tend to be emerging. Organizations are moving toward more specialization as salespeople are concentrating on specific types of customers. Market specialization has become an increasingly important type of specialization. As companies are doing more downsizing and eliminating middle managers, companies are becoming flatter, with larger spans of control. Restructuring in some organizations has caused a move toward decentralization, which has resulted in elimination of staff positions. This in turn has moved companies to outsource their sales-training function to sales-training firms. Decisions like these should be based on the specifics of each selling organization; different companies may take on very different strategies.

LO2
Developing the Salesforce

having determined the basic structure for personal selling efforts, sales managers must ensure the appropriate salespeople are available and have the necessary skills to function effectively and efficiently in the sales organization. This entails activities involved in planning and executing salesforce recruitment and selection activities. After the appropriate sales talent is hired, sales managers must oversee the

EXHIBIT 11.2
Sales Organization Alternatives

Organizational Structure	Advantages	Disadvantages
Geographic	• Low cost • No geographic duplication • No customer duplication • Fewer management levels	• Limited specialization • Lack of management control over product or customer emphasis
Product	• Salespeople become experts in product attributes and applications • Management control over selling effort allocated to products	• High cost • Geographic duplication • Customer duplication
Market	• Salespeople develop better understanding of unique customer needs • Management control over selling effort allocated to different markets	• High cost • Geographic duplication
Functional	• Efficiency in performing selling activities	• Geographic duplication • Customer duplication • Need for coordination

Source: Thomas N. Ingram, Raymond W. LaForge, Ramon A. Avila, Charles H. Schwepker, Jr., and Michael Williams, Sales Management: Analysis and Decision Making, 7th ed. (Armonk, NY: M. E. Sharpe, 2009). Copyright © 2009 by M. E. Sharpe, Inc. Used with permission.

training process, which may encompass both initial and ongoing training programs.

THE RECRUITMENT AND SELECTION PROCESS

Typically, principal responsibility for recruitment and selection lies with sales managers who have direct supervisory responsibilities for salespeople. This is a critical task as poor implementation can lead to supervisory problems, increased training costs, inadequate sales coverage, lack of customer follow-up, difficulty in establishing relationships, and inadequate salesforce

job analysis An examination of the tasks, duties, and responsibilities of the sales job.

job qualifications Indicate the aptitude, skills, knowledge, personal traits, and willingness to accept occupational conditions to perform the job.

performance. Figure 11.2[9] illustrates the steps in the recruitment and selection process. We will briefly examine each step.

Planning for Recruitment and Selection

When planning for recruitment and selection, it is important to understand the position for which candidates are sought. This can be accomplished by conducting a **job analysis**, which involves examining the tasks, duties, and responsibilities of the sales job. Once we understand what the job involves, we need to determine the qualifications necessary to execute the job. Thus, **job qualifications** indicate the aptitude, skills, knowledge, personal traits, and willingness to accept occupational conditions to perform the job. Typical job qualifications address communication skills, relationship management skills, problem-solving skills, education level, sales experience, willingness to travel and relocate, attitude, enthusiasm, empathy, integrity, and self-motivation, among others. The company's

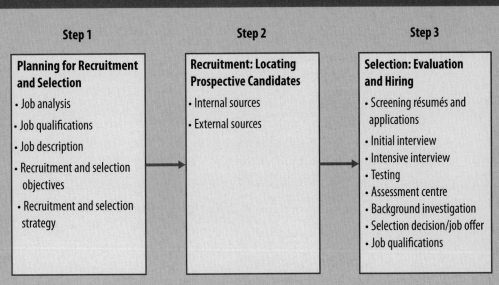

FIGURE 11.2
Recruiting and Selecting Sales Talent

Step 1

Planning for Recruitment and Selection

- Job analysis
- Job qualifications
- Job description
- Recruitment and selection objectives
- Recruitment and selection strategy

Step 2

Recruitment: Locating Prospective Candidates

- Internal sources
- External sources

Step 3

Selection: Evaluation and Hiring

- Screening résumés and applications
- Initial interview
- Intensive interview
- Testing
- Assessment centre
- Background investigation
- Selection decision/job offer
- Job qualifications

The recruitment and selection process involves planning, recruiting, and selecting sales talent.

sales manager or human resource manager uses the job analysis and job qualifications to write a written summary of the job, the **job description**. This document provides candidates a picture of what the job involves and the characteristics they must possess to be successful. It is important that the planning stage lay out the recruitment and selection objectives (e.g., increasing the number of qualified applicants at a speci-

The career fair hosted by the National Collegiate Sales Competition provides participating companies with an excellent source of sales candidates.

fied cost) and strategy. While the objectives determine what is to be achieved, the strategy includes the scope and timing of recruitment activities, such as how the job will be portrayed, when the process will occur, the best sources for qualified candidates, who will do the recruiting and selecting, and the amount of time given to a candidate to accept an offer.

Locating Prospective Candidates

The second major step in the recruitment and selection process is to locate prospective job candidates. Both internal and external sources can be helpful in locating sales talent. A very popular internal source is the employee referral program. Having employees refer sales candidates can be a very effective means of locating quality salespeople. In one study, 47 percent of sales managers surveyed indicated they found their best salespeople through referrals.[10] Other internal sources include using company newsletters, the company intranet, bulletin boards, meetings, or memos to announce sales job openings. External sources are varied. For instance, companies may advertise job openings in newspapers (print or online), online through the company's website, or in job banks, such as Monster.com,

job description A written summary of the job.

© COURTESY OF NATIONAL COLLEGIATE SALES COMPETITION

careerbuilder.com, salesjobs.com, and salestheladders.com. Online recruiting and résumé-search services offered by companies, such as wonderlic.com and cirssearch.com are also useful. Private employment agencies will help locate candidates for a fee, typically 15–25 percent of the first year's earnings of the employee hired. Companies often recruit on college and university campuses or attend career fairs, in which employers are brought together in one location (even in the virtual world) for recruiting. Sales managers who belong to professional organizations, such as Sales & Marketing Executives International or the American Marketing Association, use these organizations to network and identify potential job candidates.

Evaluation and Hiring

The final step in the recruitment and selection process is evaluation and hiring. Various tools are used to evaluate job candidates' qualifications to find the best talent. Having gathered many potential candidates in the recruitment phase, the first step is to narrow the list by screening candidates' résumés and job applications. While résumés provide useful insight, a job application can ensure essential information and exclude unnecessary information. When the pool is large, screening software provided by companies such as taleo.com or authoria.com can help identify the candidates who best match the company's job qualifications. After narrowing the pool of candidates, it is important to get a more comprehensive look at the candidate. An initial interview that is typically an hour or less allows the recruiter to clarify any questions about the candidate's job qualifications and make an initial judgment. This is typically followed by a more intensive interview that may encompass several hours or days and may include meetings with several individuals from the employing firm. Candidates may also be subjected to tests designed to assess intelligence, aptitude, personality, or other interpersonal factors. Depending on the job, a physical exam and drug testing may be required. Some companies utilize an

assessment centre, in which several assessment tools, such as presentations, role-playing exercises, group discussion, and business game simulations, are used to identify candidate strengths and weaknesses relative to job qualifications. Candidates who make it through these screening processes may be subjected to a background investigation in which references and others are contacted to verify information reported by the job candidate. Finally, the sales manager chooses the sales talent that best fits the job qualifications and makes the job offer, or decides to search further. When making the job offer, the sales manager should enthusiastically pursue the job candidate while being mindful to accurately portray the job. The job offer should be written but can initially be given orally.

SALES TRAINING

Having hired new talent, the next step in developing them is sales training. An extensive review of sales management research suggests that although who the company recruits is important, it is likely to be less important than what the sales manager does to and with the recruits that determines salesforce performance.[11] Research indicates that U.S. companies spend around $15 billion a year on sales training, averaging $2000 per year in training expenditures per salesperson,[12] all in an attempt to maintain or improve the performance of the salesforce. Some research suggests that when well designed and executed, sales training has the fastest return on investment that a company can make.[13]

Sales managers play an important role in both planning and implementing sales training. Figure 11.3[14] outlines the sales training process, which, if executed properly, should produce a more effective salesforce. We will now briefly look at each of these steps.

Assess Sales Training Needs

The first step is to conduct a **needs assessment** to determine the extent to which the salesforce possesses the skills, attitudes, perceptions, and behaviours required to be successful. A variety of methods can be used to determine training needs. In some cases, performance testing can determine the proficiency of salespeople in a particular area, such as product knowledge. In some cases, by simply observing the salesforce, sales managers can identify training needs. Some firms will poll their salesforce to determine where they believe they need training. Similarly, a customer survey might be conducted to ask customers where they believe salespeople are deficient

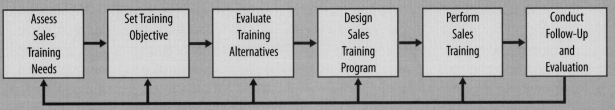

FIGURE 11.3
Sales Training Process

| Assess Sales Training Needs | Set Training Objective | Evaluate Training Alternatives | Design Sales Training Program | Perform Sales Training | Conduct Follow-Up and Evaluation |

These are the steps involved in the training process. Future training may be altered as a result of feedback obtained during follow-up and evaluation.

in serving their needs. Finally, the job analysis discussed earlier can be used to provide insights regarding training needs. While any number of training needs might be identified, typical needs include sales techniques, time and territory management skills, and knowledge regarding products, customers, and competitors. To explore a scenario that suggests the need for additional training, read "An Ethical Dilemma."

Set Training Objectives

After determining the areas in which training is needed, training objectives should be set. The objectives will vary by training need, but all should be specific, measurable, and obtainable to maximize their effectiveness. General objectives might include, for example, increasing sales or profits by a certain amount, teaching salespeople relationship-building skills, or improving the ethical decision making of salespeople. Setting objectives helps sales managers to determine training expectations and avoids training simply for training's sake.

Evaluate Training Alternatives

In the third step of the sales training process, the sales manager evaluates various options for achieving the training objectives. Criteria including cost and time constraints, training location, flexibility of training materials, and opportunity for reinforcement training should be established for evaluating the alternatives. In this step of the process, the sales manager must decide who will

do the training, where it will be conducted, and what methods and media will be used. Typically, sales training is done by company personnel, such as sales managers, senior salespeople, or company sales trainers. However, sometimes companies find it more effective and efficient to hire an outside sales training company. Although some organizations use central training facilities or off-site locations, the sales organization's home, regional, or field sales offices are typically where the training is conducted. When it comes to training methods, there are a variety from which to choose that can be broken down into four categories. One method involves a trainer providing lectures, demonstrations, and class discussion in a classroom or conference setting. This might be used for teaching product knowledge or legal and ethical issues, among other topics.

> Some companies use sales training software that allows salespeople to interact with a buyer in a simulated sales call.

© KLAUS TIEDGE/PHOTOLIBRARY

An Ethical Dilemma

You are the sales manager for the XYZ company, and your salespeople have been reaching or exceeding your sales goals for the year. Your region is on pace to have one of the best years on record, putting you in line for a big bonus. Your boss, always vigilant in her quest to improve the salesforce, has asked you to closely observe the salesforce with the intent of identifying areas in which to improve through sales training. You believe that you are on top of things when it comes to your salespeople (although you have not had an opportunity to do a lot of close observation of them over the past several months) and the results of your sales team to date speak for itself. However, given the request of your boss, coupled with your own desire to lead your sales team to new heights, you decide to ride along with several of your salespeople to observe their behaviours. To your surprise, you notice many of your salespeople "stretching the truth" to make the sale. Some might call this exaggerating; others, lying. In particular, you notice that some of your salespeople are overselling their customers. In other words, they are selling customers the more expensive product (that *more* than meets their needs) when a similar, less expensive version of the product is exactly what they need. This is typically done by exaggerating the seriousness of the customer's problem. Having discovered these behaviours, what would you do?

(a) Do nothing. After all, my salespeople are exceeding their sales goals and my region is on pace for its best year on record, which will result in significant bonuses.

(b) Have a meeting of the full sales team to congratulate them on their record-setting performance in the field. Then provide them with advanced sales training on customer-oriented selling and its importance in developing customer satisfaction and long-term customer relationships.

(c) Coach each salesperson individually. Help them realize the extent to which they are overselling customer and endangering long-term customer relationships and the continued sales revenue those relationships will produce in favour of short-term gains.

A second method, on-the-job training, involves salespeople learning while doing the job, often with the help of a supportive mentor or sales manager. Behavioural simulations, whereby learning occurs through a simulated experience through the use of business games, simulations, and role play, offer yet another training method. Games and simulations offer a means for salespeople to practise skills or decision making in a contrived but relevant environment by playing games or interacting with a computer to address simulated real-world selling scenarios. Role playing is extremely popular and generally involves one trainee playing the salesperson and the other the buyer as they interact in a simulated sales presentation. Finally, absorption training involves providing trainees or salespeople with materials that they can study on their own, such as product manuals or sales bulletins. The media used to deliver the training message must also be chosen. While personal or written media have been long used, advances in technology allow for providing training materials via the Internet or a company's intranet, desktop personal computer, video Web conferencing, online chat rooms, satellite television feeds, sales training software, and email, among others.

Design the Sales Training Program

Step four in the sales training process involves committing resources to the training so that inputs from the first three steps can be used to design the actual training program. Budget approval may have to be obtained. The responses to *what, how, where,* and *when* are finalized as the ideas from the first three steps materialize.

Perform Sales Training

The fifth step involves actually conducting the training as planned. During this stage, the sales manager should monitor the progress of trainees and ensure that training topics are being adequately covered. At the beginning of training, it is important to make sure that trainees understand how the training will benefit them as this is likely to improve their motivation to learn.

Conduct Follow-Up and Evaluation

The final step in the training process is to determine the effectiveness of the sales training. This can be done in a variety of ways, including trainee feedback, exams, sales manager observations of trainees back in the field, customer feedback, new business and sales volume growth, and return on investment, among others. It is also important to do training reinforcement that is integrated with the salesperson's current work to enhance behaviour change, as one study of more than 6000 sales professionals found that training participants remember only half of what they learned within five weeks of the training.[15]

LO3
Directing the Salesforce

directing the salesforce includes two broad dimensions: leadership, managerial, and supervisory functions; and motivation and reward system management. In more progressive sales organizations, the leadership, managerial, and supervisory functions are not entirely a collection of top-down processes in which higher-ups dictate what subordinates must do. Rather, these functions are shared responsibilities in which senior sales leaders, field sales managers, and salespeople play an active role in leadership, management, and supervision. **Sales leadership** includes activities that influence others to achieve shared goals to advance the organization. **Sales management** focuses on planning, implementation, and control of

the sales management process. **Sales supervision** involves working with subordinates on an ongoing basis. As illustrated in Exhibit 11.3,[16] senior sales leaders, sales managers, and salespeople are frequently engaged in sales leadership, sales management, and sales supervision activities. Since this chapter deals with sales management, we will use the sales manager as the key person in our discussion of directing the salesforce. In this discussion, we are thinking primarily of sales managers who have salespeople reporting directly to them and who spend a considerable amount of time working with salespeople in their respective territories. These types of sales managers are frequently referred to as **field sales managers.**

Directing the salesforce also includes motivating salespeople and managing the reward system. The most commonly used definitions of **motivation** have three dimensions: intensity, persistence, and direction.[17] Intensity is the amount of mental and physical effort salespeople expend. Persistence is the salesperson's ongoing choice to expend effort, especially when faced with adversity. Direction recognizes that salespeople may make choices about how they spend their time on the job. To be fully motivated, salespeople must expend enough effort on the right job activities and be capable of pursuing goals even when they do not have immediate success.

Reward system management involves the selection and administration of organizational rewards to encourage salespeople to achieve organizational objectives. Rewards include compensation, such as salaries, bonuses, and commissions, and noncompensation rewards, such as recognition and opportunities for growth and development.

sales leadership Activities that influence others to achieve shared goals to advance the organization.

sales management Managing an organization's personal selling function to include planning, implementing, and controlling the sales management process.

sales supervision Sales managers working with subordinates, including salespeople and sales staff, on an ongoing basis.

field sales managers Sales managers who have salespeople reporting directly to them and who spend a considerable amount of time working with salespeople in their respective territories.

motivation Comprising three dimensions: intensity, persistence, and direction. Intensity is the amount of effort expended, persistence is the ongoing choice to expend effort, and direction refers to how salespeople spend their time on the job.

reward system management Selection and administration of organizational rewards to encourage salespeople to achieve organizational objectives.

EXHIBIT 11.3
Multilevel Leadership, Management, and Supervision

	Leadership	Management	Supervision
Senior sales leadership	Influencing the entire sales organization or a large subunit by creating a vision, values, culture, direction, alignment, and change, and by energizing action	Planning, implementation, and control of sales management process for entire sales organization or large subunit	Working with sales administrative personnel on a day-to-day basis
Field sales managers	Influencing assigned salespeople by creating a climate that inspires salespeople	Planning, implementation, and control of sales management process within assigned sales unit	Working with salespeople on a day-to-day basis
Salespeople	Influencing customers, sales team members, others in the company, and channel partners	Planning, implementation, and control of sales activities within assigned territory	Working with sales assistants on a day-to-day basis

SALES LEADERSHIP APPROACHES

One way to view sales leadership is in terms of **leadership style**, which is a general orientation applied to leadership activities. Among many alternative leadership styles, two have received the most attention in sales management. A transactional leadership style relies heavily on the use of rewards and punishment, which are administered according to subordinates' job performance.[18] A transformational leadership style is quite different in that it concentrates on inspiring employees to engage in certain behaviours and to perform at high levels. Important dimensions of transformational leadership include articulating a vision, leading as a role model, encouraging acceptance of group goals, giving individual support, and providing intellectual stimulation.[19] There are many variations of these two basic leadership styles, and current research indicates that the most effective leaders use multiple leadership styles, depending on the situation. Thus, in some cases, effective leadership could call for the use of rewards and punishment in a transactional mode, while other leadership challenges are best addressed through one or more dimensions of transformational leadership. The importance of different leadership approaches is presented in "Sales Management in the 21st Century: Leading the Salesforce."

Another way to view sales leadership is to focus on the relationships between the sales manager and each salesperson within the work unit. This is referred to as the leader-member exchange (LMX) model. Studies of the LMX model indicate that when sales managers and salespeople establish mutual trust, it has positive effects on salespeople's job satisfaction, perceived job climate, willingness to change, goal commitment, and performance.[20]

Given the emphasis on establishing trust-based relationships with customers, it seems highly appropriate that sales organizations would embrace trust-building among sales leaders, sales managers, salespeople, and other key people within the organization. In the intensely competitive, ever-changing business environment facing many sales organizations, the need to move quickly is essential. In such situations, it is advantageous to have interpersonal trust between the key players. As is true in the sales process, trust between sales managers and salespeople can be built through demonstrated expertise, dependability,

leadership style A general orientation applied to leadership activities. Transactional and transformational leadership styles are two well-known leadership styles.

candour, compatibility and likability, and being responsive to the needs of the other party. With these thoughts in mind, we will now discuss several key areas that should be considered when directing a salesforce.

THE ROLE OF POWER

As people work together, they routinely exercise various forms of power to influence the actions of others. According to the pioneering work of social psychologists French and Raven,[21] individuals in the workplace may establish power by virtue of their position, for example sales managers have the right of power to direct salespeople simply because they are higher up on the organizational chart. Sales managers also have the power to reward and punish salespeople based on job performance and job behaviour. Both salespeople and sales managers have power related to their job knowledge and expertise. In some cases, highly knowledgeable, top-performing salespeople hold a great deal of power in their dealings with sales managers. Salespeople and sales managers also have power based on their interpersonal skills and their ability to work well with others.

The use of power in leadership, management, and supervision is essential, but it is wise to use it judiciously. For example, sales managers who overuse the power of their position in a "my way or the highway" approach will most likely have difficulty in motivating and retaining top salespeople. The same is true for sales managers who overrely on punishment as a coercive tool in directing salespeople. To use power effectively, sales managers should

PROFESSIONAL SELLING IN THE 21ST CENTURY

Leading the Salesforce

Jeff LeClaire, district marketing manager for Federated Mutual Insurance, discusses his leadership approach:

I have found over time that leadership requires a unique and positive approach to each team member. Early in my career, I thought it best to treat everyone equally, that is, one leadership style fits all. As I matured as a manager, I determined that one leadership style fits one.

I have to tailor my approach to each individual salesperson's motivation. Some of my reps appreciate a pat on the back and a good word. Others look to me for direction and a firm hand. Sure, money motivates every one of my sales reps to a degree, but it is my job to determine what gets them out of bed each morning to go above and beyond company expectations. Once I learn this, I can constantly look for ways to nurture their motivators for extraordinary performance.

It is not easy, but it is well worth it in the long run.

- Not be reluctant to use any form of power if the situation warrants it. Punishment is sometimes necessary, such as terminating a poor performer who will not respond to corrective action.

- Be careful not to overuse the power of the position or punishment in directing the salesforce. The most talented salespeople are typically less tolerant of managers who are inflexible or lead by intimidation, and turnover can become a problem.

- Not fall into the trap of rewarding all desired job outcomes or behaviours. Some things just have to be done and cannot be immediately rewarded. Consistent good performance and desired job behaviours can and should be rewarded.

- Enhance their power and therefore effectiveness by increasing their knowledge and expertise and by establishing a good working relationship with subordinates.

SALESFORCE COMMUNICATIONS

Most sales organizations are spread across a large geographic area in which salespeople work in a fast-moving, ever-changing environment. Sales managers must communicate effectively not only with their salespeople but also with key customers and others within their companies. To maintain effective communications, sales managers should

- Use coaching as a primary communications and developmental tool.
- Seek feedback from salespeople, customers, and other important parties on a regular basis.
- Use persuasion and promises far more frequently than threats to influence others.

The most successful sales managers spend a lot of time on coaching activities to help their salespeople develop and improve.

Successful sales managers rely heavily on **coaching**, which focuses on the continual development of salespeople by providing job feedback and serving as a role model to salespeople. When giving salespeople feedback, it is important to provide insights into job outcomes; that is, whether or not salespeople accomplish the desired result. It is also important to provide insights into why and how salespeople should pursue job outcomes. More talented employees appreciate the opportunity to learn on the job and become more effective at their work. To be effective coaches, sales managers should

- Establish a team approach that focuses on collaboration and learning from other members of the salesforce and others in the organization.
- Encourage salespeople to evaluate themselves and take appropriate corrective action.

coaching Sales managers focus on continual development of salespeople through provision of feedback and serving as a role model.

- Ensure that salespeople diagnose successes, not just failures, in an attempt to improve overall sales performance.

- Document corrective actions expected of salespeople, and have salespeople confirm that the corrective actions have been taken.
- Recognize that salespeople are individuals and attempt to communicate with each salesperson in a manner suited to that person.
- Follow up coaching sessions with structured training when necessary.
- Serve as a role model to demonstrate desired behaviours to salespeople.

Giving feedback is an important part of sales management, and it is also important that sales managers receive reliable feedback. One of the best ways for sales managers to seek feedback is to work with salespeople in the field. Customer feedback, when coupled with salespeople's opinions, provides sales managers with extremely valuable information. When calling on customers, sales managers can assess sales support and customer service, product performance, and customer satisfaction. In addition, as they accompany salespeople in the field, sales managers can solicit feedback from those salespeople about what is working and what is not. To supplement feedback gained in the field, sales managers can establish customer advisory boards and use feedback from proven salespeople to assist in decision making and strategy development. Another option is to have salespeople submit call reports and weekly summaries that identify major accomplishments, problems, competitive activity, and support needed from sales management.

In communicating with the salesforce, it is advisable to use persuasion and promises rather than threats to gain compliance. Certainly, there are times when a straightforward directive is appropriate and persuasion is unnecessary. When major changes are on the horizon, however, it is wise to get salesforce buy-in before implementing the changes. For example, if a company is changing its salesforce compensation plan to redirect salespeople's efforts to new strategic priorities, it is wise to gain the enthusiastic support of the salesforce in advance of the changes.

MOTIVATION AND REWARD SYSTEMS

Salespeople may be motivated in part because they find their job to be interesting and challenging, and thus

An Ethical Dilemma

As sales manager for the ABC company, you decided it would be a good idea to hold a sales contest to motivate your salespeople during the fourth quarter of the year. As the quarter neared its close, the competition among salespeople for the top prize was very tight. The day before the competition was scheduled to end, one of your sales reps, Vanessa Pran, came to visit you. She said that she had information concerning the sales contest. She had learned that fellow sales rep Mike Madoff was asking some of his customers to purchase and take delivery of their next scheduled order early. Moreover, it was her understanding that Madoff was even offering some customers special incentives if they agreed to order more product than usual. Pran and Madoff just happened to be neck-and-neck for the contest's grand prize, a trip to the Bahamas. Madoff has worked for ABC company for four years. He is not only a star salesperson (he had the highest sales in the company the past three years), but he has an impeccable reputation with customers and the company alike. Pran is fairly new with ABC. However, she was an outstanding salesperson with a competing company before joining ABC. When hiring Pran, you believed her to be a person of integrity, and up to this point she has been. You are concerned that confronting Madoff regarding Pran's accusations could push your star to look for employment elsewhere. What would you do?

(a) Schedule an individual meeting with Mike and confront him with Kelly's accusations.

(b) Work with your direct supervisor, the company's chief sales officer, to set up two grand prizes: one for Mike and the other for Kelly. After all, they are running neck-and-neck and this would be a positive recognition of both salespeople's hard work and top selling performance.

(c) Investigate Kelly's accusation of special incentives given for ordering more product than usual. If you find that Mike did grant incentives that are out of line with company policy, those can be the topic of discussion for a meeting with Mike rather than any linkages to Kelly's accusations. Inform Mike that such behaviour will not be tolerated.

inherently rewarding. Salespeople are also typically motivated by rewards provided by the sales organization, such as pay and formal recognition programs. Sales managers may have the opportunity to completely develop a reward system, while in other cases, they can modify reward systems to balance the needs of the sales organization, salespeople, and customers. The reward system should help attract and retain productive salespeople who want a competitive pay package, some stability of future earnings, and performance-based incentive pay. Salespeople also expect that their pay levels to be equitable, that is, fair when compared with others in the sales organization who are achieving comparable job results. Reward systems should also be consistent with the employer's financial objectives and strategic priorities. For a challenging situation in managing the reward system, read "An Ethical Dilemma."

Some sales organizations pay their salespeople on a straight salary basis, and others choose commission-based plans in which sales commissions are paid on sales volume or a percentage of profit. Most sales organizations use combination pay plans with a salary component plus some form of commission and/or bonus. These combination plans are popular because they offer salespeople a component of earnings stability with the upside potential to earn more based on performance. Further, sales organizations can direct salespeople's efforts not only by virtue of the salary component but also through

sales organization effectiveness An overall assessment of how well the sales organization achieved its goals and objectives.

salesperson performance How well salespeople perform the activities necessary to carry out their sales responsibilities, as well as their results and contributions to organizational objectives.

variable pay components, such as commissions, bonuses, and sales contests.

It takes more than a decent reward system to motivate salespeople fully. Sales managers should recruit salespeople whose personal motives match job requirements and rewards. It is important to ensure that salespeople understand how they should proceed on the job and that they are properly equipped through coaching and training. When possible, sales managers may be able to enrich the sales job by adding new duties and responsibilities for selected salespeople. It is important to build the confidence and job-related self-esteem of salespeople to maximize salesforce motivation. Finally, sales managers should actively seek out sources of motivational problems and take action as early as possible to maximize motivation and the overall morale of the salesforce.

LO4
Determining Salesforce Effectiveness and Performance

s depicted in the four-stage sales management process model shown earlier in Figure 11.1, effective sales management requires that sales managers continually monitor the salesforce to determine

The objective of evaluating sales organization effectiveness and salesperson performance is to improve the performance of individual salespeople and the overall operations of the sales organization.

current performance. The information from this evaluation process provides critical inputs for future sales strategy and salesforce development decisions, as well as diagnosing problems and developing solutions to positively affect future sales performance. Determining salesforce effectiveness and performance is not an easy task, as it requires evaluations to be made at multiple levels: (1) evaluation of the effectiveness of sales units within the organization and (2) evaluation of the performance of individual salespeople.

Sales organization effectiveness is an overall assessment of how well the sales organization achieved its goals and objectives. **Salesperson performance** evaluates how well salespeople perform the activities necessary to carry out their sales responsibilities, as well as their results and contributions to organizational objectives.[22] As illustrated by these definitions, salesperson performance contributes to, but it is not the sole determinant of, sales organization effectiveness. Additional factors, such as sales organization structure, selling strategies, deployment, sales management, and uncontrollable environmental influences, also affect sales organization effectiveness.[23]

EVALUATING SALES ORGANIZATION EFFECTIVENESS

Performance evaluation at the sales organization level focuses on evaluating the effectiveness of the various selling units that compose the overall sales organization. The focus is typically on results, such as total sales volume, market share, costs, profit contribution, return on assets, and other relevant outcomes. These indicators of effectiveness might refer to the entire sales organization or to subdivisions, such as regions, districts, territories, and even zones. The results from these organizational evaluations provide important managerial feedback regarding the effectiveness of plans and quality of execution, which serve as inputs for strategic decision making and corrective actions. There is no one best method for evaluating sales organization effectiveness, and the preferred approach and methodologies used will vary from company to company. In practice, typical evaluation methods include the more comprehensive sales organization audit as well as a variety of more focused analyses designed to assess sales, costs, and profitability. Each of these methods is discussed in turn here.

Sales Organization Audit

The **sales organization audit** is a comprehensive, systematic approach for evaluating sales organization effectiveness and provides management with diagnostic and prescriptive information.[24] Accordingly, audits such as this are undertaken for the purpose of identifying existing or potential problems, determining their causes, and facilitating the needed corrective actions. Sales organization audits analyze four major areas: sales organization environment, sales management evaluation, sales organization planning system, and sales management functions. Important factors in the business environment include competition, technology, customer perceptions, the level of support and integration of sales and other functions within the company, and economic trends. Sales management is evaluated in terms of adequacy of sales managers and management practices. The sales organization planning system is examined in light of its objectives and strategies. Finally, sales management functions, such as recruiting, training, motivation, supervision, and budgeting are analyzed.

To better ensure objective and unbiased evaluations, audits are best conducted by individuals outside the sales organization with sales managers and salespeople serving an active role and providing most of the information for the audit. Reflecting the comprehensive nature of this approach, it can become an expensive and time intensive process. Nevertheless, this approach is widely used as the benefits realized from analysis significantly exceed the costs incurred. Exemplary benefits resulting from sales organization audits include increased productivity as well as enhanced sales and profits because of the improvements in sales operations and management.

sales organization audit A comprehensive, systematic approach for evaluating sales organization effectiveness, which provides management with diagnostic as well as prescriptive information.

sales analysis Examines the sales organization's past, current, and future sales performance in comparison with projections, competition, and industry sales.

Sales Analysis

With the basic function of a sales organization being the generation of sales, **sales analysis** is obviously an important element in evaluating sales organization effectiveness and examines the sales organization's past, current, and future sales performance in comparison with projections, competition, and industry sales. Figure 11.4 illustrates the many different types and combinations

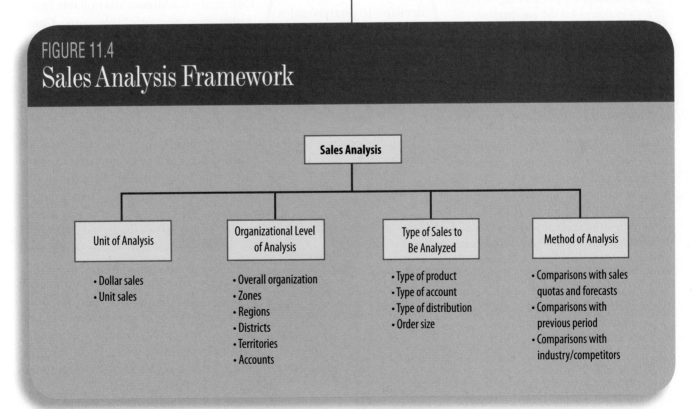

FIGURE 11.4
Sales Analysis Framework

Sales Analysis

Unit of Analysis
- Dollar sales
- Unit sales

Organizational Level of Analysis
- Overall organization
- Zones
- Regions
- Districts
- Territories
- Accounts

Type of Sales to Be Analyzed
- Type of product
- Type of account
- Type of distribution
- Order size

Method of Analysis
- Comparisons with sales quotas and forecasts
- Comparisons with previous period
- Comparisons with industry/competitors

Sales analysis can be conducted using different combinations of unit of analysis, level within the organization, type of sale, and analysis methods.

of sales analyses that can be performed across four key decision areas: (1) unit of analysis, (2) organizational level of analysis, (3) type of sales to be included, and (4) method of analysis to be used.

- *Unit of Analysis*— Sales can be analyzed in dollar or in unit terms. The decision as to which unit is appropriate is important and can affect the results of the analysis. For instance, in a period of rising prices, it is possible for dollar sales to increase even while unit sales decrease.

- *Organizational Level of Analysis*—Sales analysis should be performed at each level that is relevant to the subject organization. Managers at each level of the organization need the results from sales analysis at their level and the levels immediately under them if they are to carry out their managerial responsibilities effectively. For example, a district sales manager needs sales analysis for all districts as well as for all territories within his or her district. This makes it possible for the manager to assess the effectiveness of the region in comparison with other regions and also to determine the comparative sales contribution of each territory within his or her responsibility.

- *Type of Sales*—Examining sales at the aggregate level of total sales can obscure useful details that might be occurring within different areas or categories of sales, such as product or account type, distribution method used, or size of order placed. Disaggregating sales data for analyses by relevant types of sales can solve this problem. For example, Central Equipment Corporation (CEC) manufactures hydraulic control equipment and sells through its own company salesforce as well as independent distributors. A recent sales analysis documented that overall sales for the year had increased by 14 percent over the previous period. Further analysis by type of sale revealed that sales through the CEC salesforce had increased by 21 percent while sales through independent distributors were actually down by 16 percent. This led to changes in sales strategies and policies relevant

Are we counting apples or oranges? The decision to analyze sales in either dollar or unit terms can yield very different results.

© PHOTOS.COM

to the independent distributors to address the problems identified from the sales analysis. Had aggregate sales analysis been the sole focus, the differences across types of distribution would not have been identified.

- *Method of Analysis*—Actual dollar and/or unit sales results for the different organizational levels and types of sales certainly provide important information for management. The information content resulting from these analyses can be further enhanced by methods of analysis allowing comparisons of actual sales with benchmarks, such as sales forecasts and quotas, previous periods, and industry or competitor sales. Continuing with the Central Equipment Corporation sales analysis example, their 14 percent increase in overall sales became more meaningful to management when it was compared against the industry's growth figure of only 6 percent for the same period.

Cost and Profitability Analysis

In **cost analysis**, the focus is on assessing costs the sales organization incurs in the process of generating sales. The more typical approach to cost analysis compares incurred costs with the planned costs as reflected in sales budgets. Cost analysis addresses controllable costs rather than uncontrollable costs. Controllable costs are those that are directly controlled by sales organization management, such as salaries and commissions, bonuses, travel expenses, recruiting, training and development, meetings, and sales administrative costs.

The purpose of incurring selling costs within the sales organization is to generate sales. Consequently, it should be noted that the purpose of cost analysis is *not* to minimize selling cost. The purpose of cost analysis is to ensure that the selling plan's budgeted relationships between sales and selling costs are maintained. In accomplishing this objective, costs analysis examines variances between actual costs and budgeted costs. For units or types of sales in which large variances are found, especially when actual costs exceed budgeted costs, further analysis can be undertaken to determine the reasons for the variations.

Assessing the results from combining sales and cost data is the essence of **profitability analysis**.

As with sales and cost analyses, profitability analysis can be done at different levels of the organization and different types of sales. Profitability analysis routinely includes a detailed evaluation of the income statement, commonly called the profit-and-loss statement. Additional profitability analysis may calculate the return on assets managed, which goes beyond income statement analysis by including the asset investment that is required to produce sales outcomes.

EVALUATING SALESPERSON PERFORMANCE

This level of analysis focuses on the performance and effectiveness of salespeople relative to how well they perform the activities necessary to carry out their responsibilities and contribute to organizational objectives. Salesperson performance analysis pertains to individual salespeople, not the sales organization. While the analysis of sales organization effectiveness is most often focused on strategic issues and decisions, the results of salesperson performance evaluations tend to be more tactical in nature. That is, they provide information leading sales managers to take specific actions to improve the performance of an individual salesperson.

In practice, performance appraisal continues to be primarily a top-down approach in which each manager evaluates each of the people directly reporting to them. However, with the growing complexity and strategic importance of the selling function, the trend is toward more comprehensive and broader-based assessment methods. One such assessment method is **360-degree feedback**. As the name describes, 360-degree feedback involves performance assessments from multiple sources having a relationship with the salesperson. These raters might include sales managers, internal and external customers, sales team members, and even salespeople themselves. Reflecting the multiple input sources, results from 360-degree feedback help managers better understand customer needs, assess training and development needs, detect barriers to success, increase job involvement, reduce assessment bias, and improve salesperson performance.

360-degree feedback involves performance evaluations from the full circle of sources having relationships with the salesperson.

Another evaluation approach gaining favour over the traditional top-down method is referred to as **performance management**. This approach involves sales managers and individual salespeople working together on setting goals, giving feedback, reviewing, and rewarding. Under this evaluation approach, salespeople participate in setting realistic quotas and budgets, create their own development plans, and assume responsibility for their careers. Rather than an autocratic supervisor, the sales manager is a partner in this process and provides timely feedback focused on what is within the salesperson's control to change.

Regardless of the specific approach used, performance evaluation typically incorporates four distinct stages. In stage one, the sales manager and salesperson discuss the salesperson's evaluation. This evaluation might come from the traditional manager's appraisal of the salesperson, a 360-degree feedback methodology, or the performance management approach. In stage two, the sales manager rates the salesperson according to predetermined criteria or performance standards to determine whether the salesperson is above or below expectations. Stage three reviews the salesperson's performance relative to his or her previous performance evaluation to determine accomplishments in areas noted as needing improvement in the previous appraisal. Effective evaluations focus on both the good and the bad to assist the salesperson in identifying and understanding what he or she can do to further improve his or her performance. The final stage focuses on the future. In this stage, mutual agreements are reached regarding sales objectives, action plans for improvement, as well as the resources, structure, and training that are needed to support the objectives and plans. When properly integrated into a systemic evaluation, these four stages identify the salesperson's current level of activity and performance, develop relevant comparisons to expected performance standards and previous

360-degree feedback Performance assessments of a salesperson from multiple sources having a relationship with the salesperson.

performance management A performance evaluation approach that involves sales managers and individual salespeople working together on setting goals, giving feedback, reviewing, and rewarding.

performance appraisals, and construct a thoughtful plan for performance improvement in the upcoming period.

Criteria for Evaluating Salesperson Performance

Sales jobs are multidimensional, involving numerous products sold to a diverse set of customers and requiring a variety of selling and nonselling activities. As a result, any valid and comprehensive evaluation of performance must include multiple criteria. These criteria are most often grouped into two types: the behavioural perspective and the results or outcome perspective. The behaviour-based perspective incorporates assessments—often subjective—of salesperson characteristics and behaviours with considerable monitoring and directing of salesperson behaviour by sales managers. In contrast, the outcome-based perspective focuses on objective measures of selling results with minimal monitoring or directing by sales managers.[25] The importance of using multiple criteria is presented in "Professional Selling in the 21st Century: Salesperson Performance Evaluation Criteria."

Considerable support from sales management practice and research supports the conclusion that sales organizations should use both outcome-based and behaviour-based evaluations when assessing salesperson performance. Hybrid approaches incorporating

PROFESSIONAL SELLING IN THE 21ST CENTURY

Salesperson Performance Evaluation Criteria

Steve Randazzo, vice president of sales for KV Pharmaceutical (ETHEX Division), discusses how he uses different criteria for salesperson performance evaluation:

Our salespeople are evaluated on several criteria: industry/product knowledge, promotion of specified and new products, relationship development skills, territory management/work habits, and sales and profitability. While achieving sales and profitability goals are important, it is equally important for our salespeople to be able to develop customer relationships, be creative, and think "outside the box." Good sales numbers might be achieved because we launched a new product, or offered a very competitive price. However, we want to establish relationships with customers that will enable us to withstand turbulent times in the market. For instance, salespeople are evaluated on their ability to get customers to implement promotional programs developed by our marketing department that are designed to help customers move products. Customers who use these programs are more likely to see us as a partner. Therefore, we evaluate salespeople's ability to build relationships just as seriously as we do their ability to achieve sales and profits. Territory management and work habits are also extremely important to being a successful salesperson. My top producers are always the ones who understand how to work with the corporate office to meet customer needs and work equally hard for the customer and close for the business.

both types of measures place considerable emphasis on supervision, evaluation of attitude, effort, and quantitative results, and complex, accurate paperwork. Regardless of the mix between the two types of sales management controls, research also documents that greater levels of control lead to higher levels of salesperson job satisfaction, organizational commitment, and job performance while reducing the level of job stress.[26]

Outcome-Based Evaluations

Outcome-based evaluations focus on actual results salespeople achieve. This immediate and direct connection to the purpose of the selling function has resulted in its attractiveness and logical choice as a component of the salesperson evaluation process. Sales outcomes frequently evaluated include total sales volume, current year sales compared with last year's sales, sales versus quota, percentage increase in sales volume, sales volume by product line, and sales volume per customer.

While sales outcomes are extremely important in evaluating salesperson performance, they present several challenges in use. One such challenge is that measures of sales outcomes by themselves do not reflect the differing territory situations faced by individual salespeople in the organization. The salesperson having the highest sales productivity may have the best territory and may not be the best performer in generating sales. When salespeople perceive performance criteria as arbitrary and without consideration for situational differences in accounts and territories, there can be a negative effect on performance and job satisfaction. Sales managers address this potential problem by comparing actual sales outcomes with standards designed to reflect unique territory situations faced by each salesperson. These territory standards are typically referred to as sales quotas—a sales objective for a specific sales unit, such as a territory, region, district, or zone.

Behaviour-Based Evaluations

Behaviour-based evaluations consist of criteria related to the activities salespeople perform. These criteria include activities directly related to the generation of sales, as well as nonselling activities necessary for assuring customer satisfaction, self-development, and providing accurate information to the sales organization. The most common sales behaviours considered in evaluations include number of sales calls, number of sales calls per day, and the completion of administrative requirements, such as submitting reports in a timely manner.

Performance Evaluation Methods

Sales managers have a number of different methods available for evaluating salesperson performance. For example, a graphic rating or checklist could be used or salespeople could be ranked against other salespeople on various performance dimensions. In some cases, salespeople are evaluated against written objectives. If

behaviour is to be evaluated instead of or in addition to sales outcomes, a **behaviourally anchored rating scale (BARS)** could be used. BARS instruments are developed with input from sales managers and salespeople, and the idea is to define the desired behaviour, which will lead to desired sales outcomes. Whichever method, or combination of methods, is used, the evaluation methods should have these characteristics:

- *Reliability:* The measures should be stable over time and exhibit internal consistency.
- *Validity:* The measures should provide accurate assessments of the criteria they are intended to measure.
- *Standardization:* The measurement instruments and evaluation process should be similar throughout the sales organization.
- *Practicality:* Sales managers and salespeople should understand the entire performance appraisal process and should be able to implement it in a reasonable amount of time.
- *Comparability:* The results of the performance evaluation process should make it possible to compare the performance of individual salespeople directly.
- *Discriminability:* The evaluative methods must be capable of detecting differences in the performance of individual salespeople.
- *Usefulness:* The information provided by the performance evaluation must be valuable to sales managers in making various decisions.

Developing evaluation methods possessing all these characteristics is a complex, essential task. It is a crucial task, however, as evaluating sales performance and effectiveness provides important information to sales management. The critical sales management task is to use this information to improve the performance of individual salespeople and the over all operations of the sales organization. This requires that sales managers have a detailed understanding of the personal selling and sales management processes so they can determine the causes of performance problems

outcome-based evaluations Evaluation of the actual sales results salespeople achieve.

behaviour-based evaluations Evaluation of the activities salespeople perform in the generation of sales and in completing nonselling responsibilities.

behaviourally anchored rating scales (BARS) A performance evaluation method with the ability to link salesperson behaviours with specific outcomes and allow managers to indicate the level of behaviour a specific salesperson has achieved.

and identify appropriate strategies, plans, and managerial actions to solve the problems.

LO5
Sales 2.0

© SALESFORCE.COM, INC. USED WITH PERMISSION

a major focus of this chapter is on the need for sales organizations to develop and execute strategies and processes to guide personal selling and sales management activities. Our attention now turns to technology. The basic role of technology is to help salespeople and sales managers implement these strategies and processes effectively. Strategies and processes should drive sales organizations with the appropriate technologies employed to facilitate successful execution.

The use of technology in sales has evolved in several phases.[27] Contact management software was used initially to organize basic information about prospects and customers. This was expanded into salesforce automation products to keep track of leads and the basic stages in the sales process for account planning and forecasting purposes. Then, customer relationship management (CRM) systems were introduced to collect and manage extensive information about customers and relationships with access available to individuals in different business functions. These technologies have been useful in providing information to help salespeople communicate more effectively to prospects and customers. However, the orientation has been internal with an emphasis on one-way communication.

Now, new Web-based technologies, often called Web 2.0, are being used to help sales organizations change to an external orientation based on two-way communication and collaboration with customers. **Sales 2.0** is the use of customer-driven processes enabled by the latest Web 2.0 technologies to co-create value with customers. The focus is on interaction between buyer and seller, and the

Web-based CRM products with mobile versions are useful to salespeople.

Sales 2.0 The use of customer-driven processes enabled by the latest Web technology to co-create value with customers.

alignment of strategy, people, process, and technology to enhance the art and science of sales.[28] These technologies engage customers in an ongoing dialogue and can be used throughout the sales and sales management processes presented in this book. We will discuss key trends in CRM systems and specific Web 2.0 products that salespeople and sales managers are using to implement a Sales 2.0 approach.

CUSTOMER RELATIONSHIP MANAGEMENT (CRM)

CRM software is being used by many sales organizations. One study found that more than 67 percent of sales organizations employ a CRM system, with the major benefits being improved sales communication, improved forecast accuracy, and reduced sales administrative burden. However, only about 52 percent of users were satisfied with the benefits received from their CRM system.[29]

Recent trends indicate that CRM systems are becoming more valuable to users. First, CRM product offerings have evolved from large software installations at individual firms to Web-based products that use a software-as-a-service model. NetSuite and Salesforce.com are examples. These firms maintain and update the software regularly, with companies paying a monthly fee for each user. The software-as-a-service model makes CRM systems available to sales organizations of all sizes. Another important trend is the commercial open-source model for CRM systems. For example, SugarCRM is based on a modular architecture and provides access to its source code so that users can customize the software to meet their specific needs by making changes, adding applications, or fixing problems and publishing these fixes online for others to use. This lowers the operating costs for SugarCRM, which generates a lower price and a more adaptable product for users.[30] Third, more CRM vendors are providing wireless access for salespeople and sales managers from smart phones. This gives salespeople and sales managers access to "real time" CRM in the field. Finally, new Web 2.0 products are continually being introduced. A few years ago, there were fewer than 100 Sales 2.0 applications, now there are more than 1000.[31] More and more of these products are designed to collaborate with or be integrated into CRM systems.

WEB 2.0 PRODUCTS

One increasingly important category of Web 2.0 products is social networking services. **Social networking** is the ability to create, access, and interact with networks of contacts electronically. The use of Facebook for personal social networking has exploded in recent years. And, business applications of Facebook are increasing. Web-based social networking is also growing rapidly in the B2C marketplace. Now, new social networking products, such as LinkedIn, Jigsaw, Orkut, Xeequa, and Tweeter, are being used more by salespeople and sales managers in B2B situations.[32]

Although each product has somewhat different features, all provide an opportunity to develop a profile and list of contacts, and to access the networks and profile information of those in an individual's contact list. LinkedIn is one of the most popular sites for salespeople and sales managers. Salespeople can use it to identify key decision makers at prospect companies, learn about them from their profiles, and get access to them through someone in their network. Sales managers find LinkedIn helpful in identifying, learning about, and accessing potential hires for various sales positions.

A list and brief application description of other Web 2.0 products useful to salespeople and sales managers is presented in Exhibit 11.4. The table provides a sample of the various ways that Web-based products can be used to improve different aspects of the sales and sales management process.

The rapid pace of Web-based technology development continues. An interesting trend is cloud computing. **Cloud computing** is combining applications, communications, and content into one digital cloud that can be easily accessed from many different devices. For example, Siri has introduced an artificial intelligence system that can be used as a virtual assistant. A salesperson could ask this virtual assistant to pull together all the needed information to make the best sales presentation to a specific customer. The virtual assistant draws from a variety of sources to assemble what the salesperson requests.[33] The most successful sales organizations are likely to be those that create effective personal selling and sales management processes and use the emerging technologies to co-create value for their salespeople and customers.

social networking The ability to create, access, and interact with networks of contacts electronically.

cloud computing Combining applications, communications, and content into one digital cloud that can be easily accessed from many different devices.

EXHIBIT 11.4
Selected Web 2.0 Applications for Sales 2.0

Sales Process Applications

Genius increases collaboration between marketing and sales as emails from marketing are sent to salespeople when a prospect indicates interest in a firm's product.

Hoover's improves prospecting and sales dialogue planning by providing detailed information about a prospect's business.

Landslide guides salespeople through the best sales process for specific types of buyers.

Brainshark helps salespeople develop customized, multimedia sales presentations for specific buyers.

EchoSign assists salespeople in gaining commitment through an automated contract and approval management system.

Sales Management Process Applications

SAVO is a knowledge management system that facilitates the sharing of information and knowledge by everyone in a sales organization.

TerrAlign is an automated system that helps sales managers optimize sales territory design.

Synygy helps sales managers plan, implement, and manage sales compensation and incentive programs.

Lucidera provides analytics to help sales managers improve sales forecasts.

Sales ScoreBoard helps sales managers evaluate salesperson performance and identify problems that need to be addressed.

ALLIANCE ADHESIVES & PLASTICS, INC.

Background

As one of three regional sales managers for Alliance Adhesives and Plastics, Inc., you have just received summary details from a study of the company's national field salesforce. The study was done at the request of the vice president for sales and marketing and used a variety of assessment tools to identify the strengths and weaknesses of the company's 97 salespeople located across Canada. Based on these results, the vice president for sales and marketing has assigned you and your three-person regional managers team the task of developing a step-by-step program that will move the company forward toward a revitalized and more effective salesforce.

In response to the company's new marketing strategy designed to "get close to the customer," the salesforce was completely reorganized a little over four years ago, moving from a strictly geographic-based territory system to a specialized selling force organized around the different served markets. As the result of the reorganization and transformation of the company's salespeople into a salesforce specialized around served markets, definite improvements were realized in account penetration and customer retention. Nevertheless, spot checks randomly made across various customers indicate that there is still much room for improvement. Customer satisfaction levels are still low, and the company has some difficulty keeping good accounts.

Current Situation

Customers give Alliance salespeople strong marks for product knowledge—probably a reflection of the existing training program, which has intensive initial and recurrent training on the wide variety of products offered. Surprisingly, while customers rate the salespeople high for their product knowledge, they also indicate that Alliance salespeople appear somewhat arrogant and self-centred. Many of the responses show that, overall, the salesforce does not care about the customer and does not attempt or even take the time to fully explore and understand problems or new applications requiring novel solutions. Instead, the salesforce always seems to have some fixed response and attempt to pressure and persuade buyers rather than offering creative or customized product solutions.

Questions

1. Based on the information given, what are the major problems facing the sales organization?
2. What changes in the recruiting and selection of salespeople would you suggest? Why?
3. What changes in sales training would you suggest? Why?
4. What changes in sales management leadership would you suggest? Why?

Role Play

Situation: Read the case.

Characters: The four regional sales managers

Scene:
The four regional sales managers are meeting in a conference room to identify ideas to improve the company's sales organization. The ideas generated will be presented to the vice president of sales and marketing next week.

Role play the meeting among the four regional sales managers to determine the plan that will be presented to the vice president of sales and marketing next week.

After completing the role play, answer the following questions:

1. Discuss the advantages and disadvantages of the ideas discussed during this meeting.
2. Present the details of what was agreed to during this meeting.
3. Describe the process used to determine the plan that will be recommended.

Improving Sales Training

Background

Daniel Roche, national sales manager at The Widget Company, is concerned about his company's sales training program. The Widget Company is based in Hamilton, but operates throughout Canada with 100 salespeople. Sales and profit growth has slowed in recent quarters. Some of this is due to the tough economic climate, but company studies indicate that customer satisfaction and retention rates have been declining. A sales organization audit identified potential problems with the current sales training program.

The audit indicated that current training costs are about 23 percent higher than those of other companies in the industry. The costs of bringing all salespeople to Hamilton for face-to-face, centralized training, conducted by members of the corporate Training and Development Division, was particularly high. However, the centralized training seemed to produce strong camaraderie and commitment among the members of the salesforce. In addition, most of the current training focused on the technical attributes of the products. So, it was also convenient to have training in Hamilton, where the main development and testing labs and technicians are located. There are clear benefits to centralized training, but the costs associated with this approach are increasing rapidly.

The results from the audit also suggested that The Widget Company was overemphasizing product and technical training, and shortchanging business knowledge and consultative sales skills. There was not enough training emphasis on questioning and listening skills, presentation skills, and relationship-building skills. Many salespeople were dissatisfied with the sales training being offered and indicated that the lack of training in these areas put them at a disadvantage against salespeople from competing firms.

Current Situation

Daniel Roche has decided to bring a regional sales manager, field sales manager, and salesperson to meet with him in Hamilton to determine the best ways to improve the company's sales training program. Each stage in the sales training process will be discussed at this meeting. The objective of the meeting is to develop a basic sales training improvement plan.

Role Play

Situation: Read the role play

Characters: National sales manager, regional sales manager, field sales manager, and salesperson

Scene: The meeting takes place in the national sales manager's office in Hamilton

Role play this meeting by discussing each stage of the sales training process from the perspective of the national sales manager, regional sales manager, field sales manager, and salesperson.

After completing the role play, address the following questions:

1. What ideas were generated for each stage of the sales training process?
2. How did the perspectives of the national sales manager, regional sales manager, field sales manager, and salesperson differ during this meeting?
3. What ideas for improving the sales training program were agreed to during the meeting? Why?

71% The percentage of students who go online to study for a class.

LOG IN!

SELL was designed for students just like you: busy people who want choices, flexibility, and multiple learning options.

SELL delivers concise, electronic resources, such as role-play videos, crossword puzzles, flashcards, interactive quizzing, PowerPoint notes, and more!

At **www.sell.nelson.com**, you'll find electronic resources, such as **flashcards, PowerPoint notes, games, interactive quizzing,** and **role-play videos** to test your knowledge of key concepts. These resources will help supplement your understanding of core **sales** concepts in a format that fits your busy lifestyle.

"I really like how you use students' opinions on how to study and made a website that encompasses everything we find useful. Seeing this website makes me excited to study!"

—Abby Boston, Fanshawe College

Visit **www.sell.nelson.com** to find the resources you need today!

ENDNOTES

Chapter 1

1 Marjorie J. Caballero, Roger A. Dickinson, and Dabney Townsend, "Aristotle and Personal Selling," *Journal of Personal Selling & Sales Management* 4 (May 1984): 13.

2 William T. Kelley, "The Development of Early Thought in Marketing," in *Salesmanship: Selected Readings*, ed. John M. Rathell (Homewood, IL: Irwin, 1969): 3.

3 Thomas L. Powers, Warren S. Martin, Hugh Rushing, and Scott Daniels, "Selling Before 1900: A Historical Perspective," *Journal of Personal Selling & Sales Management* 7 (November 1987): 1–7.

4 Stanley Hollander, "Anti-Salesman Ordinances of the Mid-19th Century," in *Salesmanship: Selected Readings*, ed. John M. Rathmell (Homewood, IL: Irwin, 1969): 9.

5 Jon M. Hawes, "Leaders in Selling and Sales Management," *Journal of Personal Selling & Sales Management* 5 (November 1985): 60.

6 Thomas Wotruba, "The Evolution of Selling," *Journal of Personal Selling & Sales Management* (Summer 1991): 1–12; Jon M. Hawes, Anne K. Rich, and Scott Widmier, "Assessing the Development of the Sales Profession," *Journal of Personal Selling & Sales Management* 24 (Winter 2004): 27–38; Synthesized from Eli Jones, Steven P. Brown, Andris A. Zoltners, and Barton A. Weitz, "The Changing Environment of Selling and Sales Management," *Journal of Personal Selling & Sales Management* 25 (Spring 2005): 105–111; William C. Moncrief and Greg W. Marshall, "The Evolution of the Seven Steps of Selling," *Industrial Marketing Management* 34 (January 2005): 13–22; Raymond W. LaForge, Thomas N. Ingram, and David W. Cravens, "Strategic Alignment for Sales Organization Transformation," *Journal of Strategic Marketing* (June–August 2009): 199–219; Jagdish N. Sheth and Arun Sharma, "The Impact of the Product to Service Shift in Industrial Markets and the Evolution of the Sales Organization," *Industrial Marketing Management* 37 (May 2008): 260–269.

7 "America's 500 Largest Sales Forces," *Selling Power* (October 2009): 43–60.

8 Robert A. Willett, "Transforming to a Customer Centric Enterprise," Presentation February 14, 2008, http://www.slideshare.net/nasscom/transforming-to-a-customer-centric-enterpriserobert-a-willett-chief-executive-officer-best-buy-international, accessed April 1, 2009; Laura Heller, "Customer-Centric Model Future Focus at Best Buy," *DSN Retailing Today* (April 25, 2005): 22.

9 To learn more about what customers expect from salespeople, see Tom Atkinson and Ron Koprowski, "Sales Reps' Biggest Mistakes," *Harvard Business Review* 84 (July–August 2006): 20; Philip Kreindler and Gopal Raj guru, "What B2B Customers Really Expect," *Harvard Business Review* 84 (July–August 2006): 22–24.

10 Robert F. Gwinner, "Base Theory in the Formulation of Sales Strategy," *MSU Business Topics* (Autumn 1968): 37.

11 Adapted from D. Forbes Ley, *The Best Seller* (Newport Beach, CA: Sales Success Press, 1986).

12 Marji McClure, "What's the Problem?" *Selling Power* (May 2008): 64–67.

13 This section on consultative selling is based on Kevin J. Corcoran, Laura K. Petersen, Daniel B. Baitch, and Mark F. Barrett, *High Performance Sales Organizations* (Chicago: Irwin, 1995): 44; Marvin A Jolson, "Broadening the Scope of Relationship Selling," *Journal of Personal Selling & sales Management* (Fall 1997): 77; Keith M. Eades, *The New Solutions Selling* (New York: McGraw-Hill, 2004): ix–x.

14 Yellow Pages. *Yellow Pages Group, 2010*, http://www.ypg.com/en/, January 3, 2010; Mark Marone and Seleste Lunsford, *Strategies That Win Sales* (Chicago, IL: Dearborn Trade Publishing, 2005): 83.

15 E. Robert Dwyer, Paul Schurr, and Sejo Oh, "Developing Buyer–Seller Relationships," *Journal of Marketing* (April 1987): 11–27; Jon M. Hawes, Kenneth E. Mast, and John E. Swan, "Trust Earning Perceptions of Sellers and Buyers," *Journal of Personal Selling & Sales Management* 9 (Spring 1989): 1; Gary K. Hunter and William D. Perreault, "Making Sales Technology Effective," *Journal of Marketing* 71 (January 2007): 16–34.

Appendix Chapter 1

1 Thomas N. Ingram and Charles H. Schwepker, Jr., "Perceptions of Salespeople: Implications for Sales Managers and Sales Trainers," *Journal of Marketing Management* 2 (Fall/Winter 1992–1993): 1–8.

2 Katherine B. Hartman, "Television and Movie Representations of Salespeople: Beyond Willie Loman," *Journal of Personal Selling & Sales Management* 26 (Summer 2006): 283–292.

3 Thomas N. Ingram, "Relationship Selling: Moving from Rhetoric to Reality," *Mid-American Journal of Business* 11 (Spring 1996): 5–12.

4 Emin Babakus, David W. Cravens, Ken Grant, Thomas N. Ingram, and Raymond W. LaForge, "Removing Salesforce Performance Hurdles," *Journal of Business and Industrial Marketing* 9, no. 3 (1994): 19–29.

5 See Herbert M. Greenberg and Jeanne Greenberg, *What It Takes to Succeed in Sales* (Homewood, IL: Dow-Jones Irwin, 1990).

6 James M. Comer and Alan J. Dubinsky, *Managing the Successful Sales Force* (Lexington, MA: D.C. Heath and Co., 1985): 5; Steven P. Brown, Thomas W. Leigh, and J. Martin Haygood, "Salesperson Performance and Job Attitudes," in *The Marketing Manager's Handbook*, 3rd ed., eds. Sidney J. Levy, George R. Frerichs, and Howard L. Gordon (Chicago: The Dartnell Corporation, 1994): 107.

7 Babakus et al., "Removing Salesforce Performance Hurdles," 19; Greg W. Marshall, Daniel J. Goebel, and William C. Moncrief, "Hiring for Success at the Buyer–Seller Interface," *Journal of Business Research* 56 (April 2003): 247–255.

8 Rosann L. Spiro and Barton A. Weitz, "Adaptive Selling: Conceptualization, Measurement, and No mological Validity," *Journal of Marketing Research* 27 (February 1990): 61.

9 Marshall et al., "Hiring for Success," 251.

10 Kevin J. Corcoran, Laura K Petersen, Daniel B. Baitch, and Mark F. Barrett, *High Performance Sales Organizations* (Chicago: Irwin Professional Publishing, 1995): 77.

11 Marshall et al., "Hiring for Success," 251.

12 Arun Sharma and Rajnandini Pillai, "Customers' Decision-Making Styles and Their Preference for Sales Strategies: Conceptual Examination and an Empirical Study," *Journal of Personal Selling & Sales Management* 16 (Winter 1996): 21.

13 Victoria D. Bush, Gregory M. Rose, Faye Gilbert, and Thomas N. Ingram, "Managing Culturally Diverse Buyer–Seller Relationships: The Role of Intercultural Disposition and Adaptive Selling Behavior in Developing Intercultural Communication Competence," *Journal of the Academy of Marketing Science* 29, no. 4 (Fall 2001): 391–404.

14 Gabriel R. Gonzalez, K. Douglas Hoffman, and Thomas N. Ingram, "Improving Relationship Selling Through Failure Analysis and Recovery Efforts: A Framework and Call to Action," *Journal of Personal Selling & Sales Management* 25 (Winter 2005): 57–66.

Chapter 2

1 Sherry Kilgus, "Building Trust into High Level Alliances," *NAMA Journal* 34 (Winter 1998).

2 John Andy Wood, James S. Bales, Wesley Johnston, and Danny Bellinger, "Buyers' Trust of the Salesperson: An Item-Level Meta Analysis," *JPSSM* 28, no. 3 (Summer 2008): 263–283.

3   Michael Ahearne, Ron Jelinck, and Eli Jones, "Examining the Effect of Salesperson Service Behavior in a Competitive Context," *Journal of Academy of Marketing Science* 35 (2007): 603–616.

4   *Ibid.*

5   John E. Swan and Johannah Jones Nolan, "Gaining Customer Trust: A Conceptual Guide for the Salesperson," *Journal of Personal Selling & Sales Management* 5, no. 2 (November 1985): 39.

6   Robert F. Dwyer, Paul H. Schurr, and Sejo Oh, "Developing Buyer–Seller Relationships," *Journal of Marketing* 51 (April 1987): 11.

7   Lubomira Radoilska, "Trustfulness and Business," *Journal of Business Ethics* 79 (2008): 21–28.

8   This was the concluding point of the symposium on trust held by the National Account Management Association at Wake Forest University, September 24–26, 1997.

9   Kevin Bradford and Barton Weitz, "Salespersons' Management of Conflicts in Buyer–Seller Relationships," *JPSSM* 29, no. 1 (Winter 2009): 25–42.

10 Interview with Missy Rust, GlaxoSmithKline, February 13, 2000.

11 Robert Petersen, "Consultative Selling: A Qualitative Look at the Salesperson Credibility Requirements," *AMA Educator Proceeding Enhancing Knowledge Development in Marketing* 8 (1997): 224.

12 *Ibid.*

13 From "Balancing Act: By Learning How to Balance Two Basic Drives—The Need to Close with the Need to Develop Relationships—Every Salesperson Can Become a Star," by L. B. Gschwandtner and Gerhard Gschwandtner from *Selling Power* (June 1996): 24. Reprinted with permission from *Selling Power* magazine.

14 American Marketing Association's Code of Ethics. Reprinted by permission of American Marketing Association.

15 Sergio Roman and Salvador Ruiz, "Relationship Outcomes of Perceived Ethical Sales Behavior: The Customer's Perspective," *Journal of Business Research* 58 (2005): 439–445; Douglas B. Grisaffe and Fernando Jaramillo, "Toward Higher Levels of Ethics: Preliminary Evidence of Positive Outcomes," *Journal of Personal Selling & Sales Management* 27, no. 4 (2007): 355–371.

16 Reprinted by permission of Sales & Marketing Executives International, Inc. (http://www.smei. org). "SMEI Certified Professional Salesperson" and "SCPS" are registered trademarks of Sales & Marketing Executives International, Inc.

17 *Ibid.*

18 Thomas Ingram, Scott Inks, and Lee Mabie, *Sales and Marketing Executive Certification Study Guide* (Memphis, TN: Marketing Executive International, 1994).

19 Nigel F. Piercy and Nikala Lane, "Ethical and Moral Dilemmas Associated with Strategic Relationships between Business-to-Business Buyers and Sellers," *Journal of Business Ethics* 72 (2007): 87–102; Thomas N. Ingram, Raymond W. LaForge, and Charles H. Schwepker, Jr. "Salesperson Ethical Decision Making: The Impact of Sales Leadership and Sales Management Control Strategies," *Journal of Personal Selling & Sales Management* 27, no. 4 (2007): 301–324.

20 Interview with John Huff, Shering-Plough, November 15, 2004.

Chapter 3

1   Mark Bishop, "Actions Speak Louder Than Words in B2B Sales," *Sales & Marketing Management* 161 (November 2009): 43.

2   Adapted from Jagdish N. Sheth, Bahwari Mittal, and Bruce I. Newman, *Customer Behavior: Consumer Behavior and Beyond* (Fort Worth, TX: The Dryden Press, 1999); Jagdish N. Sheth, Bruce I. Newman, and Barbara L. Gross, *Consumption Values and Market Choice: Theory and Application* (Cincinnati, OH: South-Western Publishing Co., 1991).

3   Bixby Cooper, Cornelia Drodge, and Patricia Daughtery, "How Buyers and Operations Personnel Evaluate Service," *Industrial Marketing Management* (February 1991): 81–85.

4   Adapted from Michael A. Humphreys and Michael R. Williams, "Exploring the Relative Effects of Salesperson Interpersonal Process Attributes and Technical Product Attributes on Customer Satisfaction," *Journal of Personal Selling & Sales Management* 16 (Summer 1996): 47–58; Michael A. Humphreys, Michael R. Williams, and Ronald L. Meier, "Leveraging the Total Market

Offering in the Agile Enterprise," *ASQ Quality Management Journal* 5 (1997): 60–74.

5   D. W. Merrill and R. H. Reid, *Personal Styles and Effective Performance* (Radnor, PA: Chilton Book Company, 1981).

6   Reprinted by permission of Growmark, Inc.

7   Wesley J. Johnston and Thomas V. Bonoma, "The Buying Center: Structure and Interaction Patterns," *Journal of Marketing* (Summer 1981): 143–156.

8   Geoffrey James, "How to Make Technology Productive," Selling Power, June 2007, 65–68.

9   Jakki Mohr and John R. Nevin, "Communication Strategies in Marketing Channels: A Theoretical Perspective," *Journal of Marketing* (October 1990): 36–51.

10 Jessica, Rivchin, "Staying Productive in a Mobile World," *Mobile Enterprise,* July 19, 2006, http://www.mobileenterprisemag.com/mobilizer/071906 leadsfory.shtml, accessed July 19, 2006. Business Link, "Mobile Technology," http://www.businesslink.gov.uk/bdotg/action/detail?itemId=1074298219&type=RESOURCES accessed July 25, 2011.

Chapter 4

1   Jeff Thull, *Exceptional Selling* (Hoboken, NJ: John Wiley and Sons, 2006).

2   S. D. Morgan, *Selling with Integrity: Reinventing Sales Through Collaboration, Respect, and Serving* (San Francisco, CA: Berrett-Koehler Publishers, Inc., 1997).

3   R. L. Jolles, *Customer Centered Selling* (New York: The Free Press, 1998).

4   *Ibid.*

5   Neil Rackham, *Spin Selling* (New York: McGraw Hill, 1998).

6   Thomas Ingram, Tubs Scott, and Lee Mabie, *Certification Study Guide* (New York: Sales and Marketing Executives International, 1994): 44–46.

7   Jerry Acuff and Wally Wood, *The Relationship Edge in Business* (Hoboken, NJ: John Wiley & Sons, Inc., 2004): 149–150; Geoffrey James, "How to Build Customer Relationships—An Interview with Jerry Acuff," *Selling Power* (March 2006): 43–46.

8   T. N. Ingram, C. Schwepker, Jr., and D. Huston, "Why Salespeople Fail," *Industrial Marketing Management* 21 (1992): 225–230.

9   R. P. Ramsey and R. S. Sohi, "Listening to Your Customers: The Impact of Perceived Salesperson Listening Behavior on Relationship Outcomes," *Journal of the Academy of Marketing Science* 25 (Spring 1997): 127–137.

10 L. Barker, *Listening Behavior* (Englewood Cliffs, NJ: Prentice Hall, 1971): 30–32.

11 Lucette Comer and Tanya Drollinger, "Active Empathetic Listening and Selling Success: A Conceptual Framework," *Journal of Personal Selling & Sales Management* 9 (Winter 1999): 15–29; Stephen B. Castleberry and C. David Shepherd, "Effective Interpersonal Listening and Personal Selling," *Journal of Marketing Theory and Practice* 7, no. 1 (Winter 1999): 30–39.

12 From *Effective Listening: Key to Your Success* by L. K. Steil, L. L. Barker, and K. W. Watson: 21. Reprinted by permission of The McGraw-Hill Companies.

13 *Ibid.*; Ramsey and Sohi, "Listening to Your Customers."

14 *Ibid.,* 72–73.

15 J. C. Mowen and M. Minor, *Consumer Behavior* (New York: Macmillan Publishing Co., 1997).

16 Julia Chang, "Selling in Action," *Sales & Marketing Management* 156 (May 2004): 22; G. P. Thomas, "The Influence of Processing Conversational Information on Inference, Argument Elaboration, and Memory," *Journal of Consumer Research* 19 (June 1992): 83–92.

17 R. A. Avila, T. N. Ingram, R. W. LaForge, and M. R. Williams, *The Professional Selling Skills Workbook* (Fort Worth, TX: The Dryden Press, 1996): 83.

18 Joann Peck and Jennifer Wiggins, "It Just Feels Good: Customers' Affective Response to Touch and Its Influence on Persuasion," *Journal of Marketing* 70, no. 4 (October 2006): 56–69; R. A. Peterson, M. P. Cannito, and S. P. Brown, "An Exploratory

Investigation of Voice Characteristics and Selling Effectiveness," *Journal of Personal Selling & Sales Management* 15 (Winter 1995): 1–15.

19 *Ibid.*

20 Adapted from R. M. Rozelle, D. Druckman, and J. C. Baxter, "Nonverbal Communication," in *A Handbook of Communication Skills,* ed. O. Hargie (London: Croom and Helm, 1986): 59–94; T. Alessandra and R. Barrera, *Collaborative Selling* (New York: John Wiley & Sons, Inc., 1993): 121–122.

Chapter 5

1 Lain Chroust Ehmann, "Sales Up! Why Reports Selling Is a Dying Profession Are Widely Exaggerated," *Selling Power* (January/February 2011): 40–44.

2 *Ibid.*

Chapter 6

1 Geoffrey James, "Tom Sant Demystifies the Mystery of Effective Proposals," *Selling Power* (June 2004): 27–30.

2 Bob Kantin, *Sales Professionals Guide to Writing Winning Proposals* (Minneapolis, MN: Bascom Hill Publishing Company, 2007): 31–38.

3 From "Quality Selling through Quality Proposals, A Guide to Writing Winning Sales Proposals," by R. F. Kantin and M. W. Hardwick. Copyright © 1994. Reprinted with permission of South-Western, a division of Thomson Learning: http://www.thomsonrights.com.

4 For more discussion of customer value propositions, see James C. Anderson, James A. Narus, and Wouter van Rossum, "Customer Value Propositions in Business Markets," *Harvard Business Review* (March 2006): 91–99.

5 Thomas N. Ingram, Michael D. Hartline, and Charles H. Schwepker Jr., "Gatekeeper Perceptions: Implications for Improving Sales Ethics and Professionalism," *Proceedings of the Academy of Marketing Science* (1992): 328.

Chapter 7

1 Adapted from Brian Tracy, *Advanced Selling Strategies* (New York: Simon & Schuster, 1995): 302.

2 Author interview with Jamie Howard, August 1, 2004.

3 Jeffrey Jacobi, "Voice Power," *Selling Power* (October 2000): 66.

4 Author interview with David Jacoby.

5 Adapted from Mary Ann Oberhaus, Sharon Ratliffe, and Vernon Stauble, *Professional Selling: A Relationship Approach* (Fort Worth, TX: The Dryden Press, 1995): 410–412.

Chapter 8

1 Marc Diener, "Don't Know When to Cut Your Losses and Leave the Negotiating Table? Look for These Telltale Signs," *Entrepreneur Magazine,* August 2003, http://www.entrepreneur.com/magazine/entrepreneur/2003/august/63334.html, accessed July 26, 2011.

2 Brad Huisken, "Saving the Sale: Objections, Rejections and Getting to Yes," *JCK* (January 2003): 62–63.

3 Tom Reilly, "Why Do You Cut Prices?" *Industrial Distribution* (June 2003): 72.

4 Robert Menard, "'Cost' Is About More Than the Price," *Selling* (July 2003): 9.

5 Kim Sydow Campbell and Lenita Davis, "The Sociolinguistic Basis of Managing Rapport when Overcoming Buying Objections," *Journal of Business Communication* (January 2006): 43–66.

6 Salespeople can forestall known concerns, but they should not bring up issues that are not even a problem with a particular prospect. Thus, the need for good precall information gathering becomes obvious. See "Think Like a Consumer to Make Buying from a Cinch," *Selling* (November 2004): 8.

7 Mark Borkowski, "How to Succeed in Closing Deals, without Closing," *Canadian Electronics* 19 (May 2004): 6.

8 Neil Rackham, *Spin Selling* (New York: McGraw-Hill, 1988): 19–51.

9 Joan Leotta, "Effortless Closing," *Selling Power* (October 2001): 28–31.

10 Susan Del Vecchio, James Zemanek, Roger McIntyre, and Reid Claxton, "Updating the Adaptive Selling Behaviors: Tactics to Keep and Tactics to Discard," *Journal of Marketing Management* 20 (2004): 859–875.

Chapter 9

1 Howard Stevens and Theodore Kinni, *Achieve Sales Excellence* (Avon, MA: Platinum Press, 2007).

2 Robert W. Palmatier, Srinath Gopalakrishna, and Mark B. Houston, "Returns on Business-to-Business Relationship Marketing Investments: Strategies for Leveraging Profits," *Marketing Science* 25 (September-October 2006): 477–493.

3 Strativity Group, "2009 Customer Experience Management Benchmark Study," http://www.strativity.com/pdf/2009CEMStudyExecSummary-final.pdf, accessed January 12, 2011.

4 John Tashek, "How to Avoid a CRM Failure," *eWeek* 18, no. 40 (October 15, 2001): 31.

5 Michael Ahearne, Ronald Jelinek and Eli Jones, "Examining the Effect of Salesperson Service Behavior in a Competitive Context," *Journal of the Academy of Marketing Science,* 35 (Winter 2007): 603–616.

6 Strativity Group, "Recent Customer Experience Management Benchmark Study," http://www.strativity.com/products/Experience-Management-Benchmark-Study.aspx, accessed January 12, 2011.

7 Interview with John Haack, Saint-Gobain Containers, April 19, 2000.

8 Ontario Systems.

9 Christine Galea, "What Customers Really Want," *Sales & Marketing Management* 158 (May 2006): 11.

10 Kelley Robertson, "Inadequate Salesmen," *Sales & Service Excellence* 9 (January 2009): 14.

11 "Advance CRM Solutions," *Personal Selling Power* (January/February 2007): 96–99.

12 Michael W. Michelson, "Fielding Customer Complaints," *American Salesman* 50 (December 2005): 22–25.

13 The Forum Corporation, "Why Do Customers Stop Buying?" *Sales & Marketing Management* (January 1998): 14; Eileen McDargh, "Provide Great Service," *Sales & Service Excellence,* 10 (June 2010): 10.

14 Chris Taylor, "The Art of the Winback," *Sales & Marketing Management* 157 (April 2005): 30–34.

15 Sandra Rothenberger, Dhruv Grewal, and Gopalkrishnan R. Iyer, "Understanding the Role of Complaint Handling on Customer Loyalty in Service Relationships," *Journal of Relationship Marketing,* 7, no. 4 (2008): 359–376.

16 Chia-Chi Chang, "When Service Fails: The Role of the Salesperson and the Customer," *Psychology & Marketing* 23 (March 2006): 203–224.

17 "Consistent Success in an Inconsistent World: Solid Customer Relationships Are the Key," *Selling Power* (May 1996): 28; Robert D. Ramsey, "How to Handle Customer Complaints," *American Salesman,* 55 (June 2010): 25–30.

18 "At Your Customer's Service: The True Test of a Salesperson's Value Comes after the Sale," *Selling Power* (May 1996): 58.

19 Howard Stevens and Theodore Kinni, *Achieve Sales Excellence* (Avon, MA: Platinum Press, 2007).

20 *Ibid.*

Chapter 10

1 S. R. Covey, *The 7 Habits of Highly Effective People* (New York: Simon & Schuster, 2004).

2 T. Ingram, R. W. LaForge, R Avila, C. H. Schwepker Jr., and M. Williams, *Sales Management: Analysis and Decision Making,* 7th ed. (Armonk, NY: M.E. Sharpe, 2009).

3   B. Kimball, *AMA Handbook for Successful Selling* (Chicago: American Marketing Association 1994).

4   W. Ferguson, "A New Method for Routing Salespersons," *Industrial Marketing Management* (April 1980): 171–178; "Planning a Road Trip?" *An Executive Guide to Sales and Marketing Technology,* a supplement to *Sales & Marketing Management* (June 1996): 39; E. Strout, "Charting a Course," *Sales & Marketing Management* (August 1999): 46–53.

5   For a good discussion of selling technology, see D. Peppers and M. Rogers, "Marketing's New Direction: How Campaigns Are Becoming Faster and More Precise through Automation," *Sales & Marketing Management* (March 1999): 48–54; Peppers and Rogers Group and Microsoft Business Solutions, *Striking the CRM Balance: Greater Productivity, Lower Costs, Tight Integration,* http://www.knightent.com/Striking%20the%20CRM%20Balance.pdf, 2003, accessed July 25, 2011; Sue Hildreth, "Six Smart CRM Strategies for Meeting Sales Quotas in a Down Economy," http://searchcrm.techtarget.com/news/1353734/Six-smart-CRM-strategies-for-meeting-sales-quotas-in-a-down-economy, April 14, 2009, accessed on July 26, 2011.

6   For a guide to sales and marketing automation systems, technology, and software, see http://www.salesandmarketing.com/article/implementing-integrated-sales-management-process.

7   E. Babakus, D. W. Cravens, K. Grant, T. N. Ingram, and R W. LaForge, "Removing Salesforce Performance Hurdles," *Journal of Business and Industrial Marketing 9,* no. 3 (1994): 19–29.

8   J. Attaway, M. Williams, and M. Griffin, *The Rims-QIC Quality Scorecard* (Nashville, TN: The Quality Insurance Congress, 1998, 1999).

9   James Champy, "Selling to Tomorrow's Customer," *Sales & Marketing Management* (March 1999): 28.

10 Excerpt from *The 7 Habits of Highly Effective People,* © 2004 Stephen R. Covey. The Time Management Matrix phrase and model are trademarks of Franklin Covey Co., http://www.franklincovey.com. Used with permission. All rights reserved.

11 Covey, *The 7 Habits of Highly Effective People.*

Chapter II

1   The sales management portion of this chapter borrows heavily from Thomas N. Ingram, Raymond W. LaForge, Ramon A. Avila, Charles H. Schwepker, Jr., and Michael R. Williams, *Sales Management: Analysis and Decision Making* (Armonk, New York: M.E. Sharpe, 2009).

2   This figure is adapted from Ingram et al., *Sales Management: Analysis and Decision Making,* 5.

3   This section is synthesized from The HR Chally Group, *The Chally World Class Sales Excellence Research Report,* 2007, http://www.salesleader.com/images/World_Class_Sales_Research_Overview.pdf, accessed July 26, 2011; and Forum Corporation, *How Sales Forces Sustain Competitive Advantage: Research Report,* http://www.forum.com/_assets/download/4f928d21-072a-485f-b757-90e7fb884d13.pdf, 2008, accessed July 26, 2011.

4   Dawn R. Deeter-Schmelz, Karen Norman Kennedy, and Daniel J. Goebel, "Understanding Sales Manager Effectiveness: Linking Attributes to Sales Force Values," *Industrial Marketing Management* (2002): 617–626; Dawn Deeter-Schmelz, Daniel J. Goebel, and Karen Norman Kennedy, "What Are the Characteristics of an Effective Sales Manager? An Exploratory Study Comparing Salesperson and Sales Manager Perspectives," *Journal of Personal Selling and Sales Management* (Winter 2008): 7–20.

5   Maryann Hammers and Gerhard Gschwandtner, "Tap Into the 7 Qualities of the Best Sales Managers," *Selling Power* (May 2004): 60–65; Deeter-Schmelz et al., "What Are the Characteristics of an Effective Sales Manager? An Exploratory Study Comparing Salesperson and Sales Manager Perspectives," 7–20.

6   Adapted from John F. Tanner, Jr., Michael Ahearne, Thomas W. Leigh, Charlotte H. Mason, and William C. Moncrief, "CRM in Sales-Intensive Organizations: A Review and Future Directions," *Journal of Personal Selling & Sales Management* (Spring 2005): 169–170.

7   See Robert W. Ruekert, Orville C. Walker, Jr., and Kenneth J. Roering, "The Organization of Marketing Activities: A Contingency Theory of Structure and Performance," *Journal of Marketing* (Winter 1985): 13, for a more complete presentation of structural characteristics and relationships. The discussion in this section borrows heavily from this article.

8   Christian Homburg, John P. Workman, Jr., and Ove Jensen, "Fundamental Changes in Marketing Organization: The Movement toward a Customer-Focused Organizational Structure," *Journal of the Academy of Marketing Science* (Fall 2000): 459–478.

9   Thomas N. Ingram, Raymond W. LaForge, Ramon Avila, Charles H. Schwepker, Jr., and Michael R. Williams, *Sales Management: Analysis and Decision Making,* 7th ed. (Armonk, NY: M.E. Sharpe, Inc., 2009).

10 James A Breaugh, Leslie A. Greising, James W. Taggart, and Helen Chen, "The Relationship of Recruiting Sources and Pre-Hire Outcomes: Examination of Yield Rations and Application Quality," *Journal of Applied Social Psychology* 33 (November 2003): 2257–2287.

11 Gilbert A. Churchill, Jr., Neil M. Ford, Steven W. Hartley, and Orville C. Walker, Jr., "The Determinants of Salesperson Performance: A Meta-Analysis," *Journal of Marketing Research* 22 (May 1985): 117.

12 Jennifer J. Salopek, "The Power of the Pyramid," *T & D* 63 (May 2009): 70–75.

13 Geoffrey James, "Budget Your Investment Wisely," *Selling Power* (March 2006): 86–89.

14 Thomas et al., *Sales Management: Analysis and Decision Making,* 7th ed.

15 Julia Chang, "What Worked," *Sales & Marketing Management* 155 (July 2003): 29.

16 This exhibit is adapted from Thomas N. Ingram, Raymond W. LaForge, William B. Locander, Scott B. MacKenzie, and Philip M. Podsakoff, "New Directions for Sales Leadership Research," *Journal of Personal Selling & Sales Management* (Spring 2005): 137–154.

17 Orville C. Walker, Jr., Gilbert A. Churchill, Jr., and Neil M. Ford, "Where Do We Go from Here? Selected Conceptual and Empirical Issues Concerning Motivation and Performance of the Industrial Salesforce," in *Critical Issues in Sales Management: State-of-the-Art and Future Research Needs,* eds. Gerald Albaum and Gilbert A. Churchill, Jr. (Eugene, OR: Division of Research, College of Business Administration, University of Oregon, 1979): 25.

18 Bernard M. Bass, *Leadership and Performance Beyond Expectations* (New York: Free Press, 1985).

19 Philip M. Podsakoff, Scott B. MacKenzie, Robert H. Moorman, and Richard Fetter, "Transformational Leader Behaviors and Their Effects on Follower's Trust in Leader, Satisfaction, and Organizational Citizenship Behaviors," *Leadership Quarterly* (1990): 107–142.

20 Karen E. Flaherty and James M. Pappas, "The Role of Trust in Sales Organizations," *Journal of Personal Selling & Sales Management* (Fall 2000): 271–278.

21 John French, Jr., and Bertram Raven, "The Bases of Social Power," in *Studies in Social Power,* ed. D. Cartwright (Ann Arbor, MI: The University of Michigan Press, 1959).

22 Artur Baldauf and David W. Cravens, "The Effect of Moderators on the Salesperson Behavior Performance and Salesperson Outcome Performance and Sales Organization Effectiveness Relationships," *European Journal of Marketing* 36, no. 11/12 (2002): 1367.

23 David W. Cravens, Thomas N. Ingram, Raymond W. LaForge, and Clifford E. Young, "Hallmarks of Effective Sales Organizations," *Marketing Management* 1 (March 1992): 56; Thomas et al., *Sales Management: Analysis and Decision Making,* 7th ed.

24 Thomas et al., *Sales Management: Analysis and Decision Making,* 7th ed.

25 Erin Anderson and Richard L. Oliver, "Perspectives on Behavior-based versus Outcome-based Salesforce Control Systems," *Journal of Marketing* 51 (October 1987): 76.

26 Artur Balauf, David W. Cravens, and Ken Grant, "Consequences of Sales Management Control in Field Sales Organizations: A

Cross-National Perspective," *International Business Review* 11 (October 2002): 577–609; David W. Cravens, Greg W. Marshall, Felicia G. Lassk, and George S. Low, "The Control Factor," *Marketing Management* 13 (January/February 2004): 39–44.

27 Julia Chang, "Sales 2.0," *Sales & Marketing Management* (April 2007): 31–34.

28 "How Will Sales 2.0 Increase Your Sales?" *Selling Power* (May 2009): 19–25 and Anneke Seley and Brent Holloway, *Sales 2.0: Improve Business Results Using Innovative Sales Practices and Technology* (Hoboken, NJ: John Wiley & Sons, 2009): 5–9.

29 Chang, "Sales 2.0," 34; Geoffrey James, "The Process of CRM," *Selling Power* (May 2007): 100–104.

30 Kim Wright Wiley, "How Sweet It Is," *Selling Power* (April 2009): 44–47.

31 "Sales 2.0 Innovation Leads to Sales Acceleration," *Selling Power* (March 2009): 73.

32 Marshall Lager, "Sales and Social Media: No One's Social (Yet)," *Customer Relationship Management* (June 2009): 29–33.

33 Steve Hamm, "Cloud Computing's Big Bang for Business," *Business Week* (June 15, 2009): 42–48.

A

B

Chapter Summary

LO1 **Define personal selling and describe its unique characteristics as a marketing communications tool.** Personal selling, an important part of marketing, relies heavily on interpersonal interactions between buyers and sellers to initiate, develop, and enhance customer relationships. The interpersonal communications dimension sets personal selling apart from other marketing communications, such as advertising and sales promotion. Personal selling is also distinguished from direct marketing and electronic marketing in that salespeople are talking with buyers before, during, and after the sale. This allows a high degree of immediate customer feedback, which becomes a strong advantage of personal selling over most other forms of marketing communications.

LO2 **Distinguish between transaction-focused traditional selling and trust-based relationship selling, with the latter focusing on customer value and sales dialogue.** As summarized in Exhibit 1.2, trust-based selling focuses more on the customer than does transaction-focused selling. The salesperson will act as a consultant to the customer in trust-based selling, whereas in transaction-based selling the salesperson concentrates more on making sales calls and on closing sales. There is far more emphasis on postsales follow-up with relationship selling than with transaction selling, and salespeople must have a broader range of skills to practise relationship selling. Rather than pitching products to customers, trust-based selling focuses on establishing sales dialogue with customers, and salespeople not only communicate customer value but also help create and deliver customer value.

LO3 **Describe the evolution of personal selling from ancient times to the modern era.** The history of personal selling can be traced as far back as ancient Greece. The Industrial Revolution enhanced the importance of salespeople, and personal selling as we know it today had its roots in the early twentieth century. The current era of sales professionalism represents a further evolution.

LO4 **Explain the contributions of personal selling to society, business firms, and customers.** Salespeople contribute to society by acting as stimuli in the economic process and by assisting in the diffusion of innovation. They contribute to their employers by producing revenue, performing research and feedback activities, and composing a pool of future managers. They contribute to customers by providing timely knowledge to assist in solving problems.

LO5 **Discuss five alternative approaches to personal selling.** Alternative approaches to personal selling include stimulus-response, mental states, need satisfaction, problem solving, and the consultative approach. Stimulus-response selling often uses the same sales presentation for all customers. The mental states approach prescribes that the salesperson leads the buyer through stages in the buying process. Need satisfaction selling focuses on relating benefits of the seller's products or services to the buyer's particular situation. Problem-solving selling extends need satisfaction by concentrating on various alternatives available to the buyer. Consultative selling focuses on helping customers achieve strategic goals, not just meeting needs or solving problems.

Glossary Terms

adaptive selling The ability of salespeople to alter their sales messages and behaviours during a sales presentation or as they encounter different sales situations and different customers.

AIDA An acronym for the various mental states salespeople must lead their customers through when using mental states selling: attention, interest, desire, and action.

business consultant A role the salesperson plays in consultative selling in which he or she uses internal and external (outside the sales organization) sources to become an expert on the customer's business. This role also involves educating customers on the sales firm's products and how these products compare with competitive offerings.

canned sales presentation Sales presentations that include scripted sales calls, memorized presentations, and automated presentations.

combination sales job A sales job in which the salesperson performs multiple types of sales jobs within the framework of a single position.

consultative selling The process of helping customers reach their strategic goals by using the products, services, and expertise of the sales organization.

continued affirmation An example of stimulus-response selling in which a series of questions or statements furnished by the salesperson is designed to condition the prospective buyer to answering "yes" time after time until, it is hoped, he or she will be inclined to say "yes" to the entire sales proposition.

customer value The customers' perception of what they get for what they have to give up, for example, benefits from buying a product in exchange for money paid.

detailer A salesperson in the pharmaceutical industry working at the physician level to furnish valuable information regarding the capabilities and limitations of medications in an attempt to get the physician to prescribe the product.

diffusion of innovation The process whereby new products, services, and ideas are distributed to the members of society.

economic stimuli Something that stimulates or incites activity in the economy.

ego drive An indication of the degree of determination a person has to achieve goals and overcome obstacles in striving for success.

ego strength The degree to which a person is able to achieve an approximation of inner drives.

empathy The ability to see things as others would see them; salespeople with empathy are better able to adapt to various sales situations and adjust to customer feedback.

enthusiasm A strong excitement of feeling. Salespeople should have an enthusiastic attitude in a general sense and a specific enthusiasm for selling.

inside sales Nonretail salespeople who remain in their employer's place of business while dealing with customers.

interpersonal communication skills Skills that include listening and questioning.

long-term ally A role the salesperson plays in consultative selling in which he or she supports the customer, even when an immediate sale is not expected.

mental states selling An approach to personal selling that assumes that the buying process for most buyers is essentially identical and that buyers can be led through certain mental states, or steps, in the buying process; also called the formula approach.

missionary salespeople Salespeople who usually work for a manufacturer but may also be found working for brokers and manufacturing representatives. Sales missionaries are expected to "spread the word" to convert noncustomers to customers.

need satisfaction selling An approach to selling based on the notion that the customer is buying to satisfy a particular need or set of needs.

order-getters Salespeople who actively seek orders, usually in a highly competitive environment.

order-takers Salespeople who specialize in maintaining existing business.

personal selling An important part of marketing that relies heavily on interpersonal interactions between buyers and sellers to initiate, develop, and enhance customer relationships.

pioneers Salespeople who are constantly involved with either new products, new customers, or both. Their task requires creative selling and the ability to counter the resistance to change that will likely be present in prospective customers.

problem-solving selling An extension of need satisfaction selling that goes beyond identifying needs to developing alternative solutions for satisfying these needs.

revenue producers A role fulfilled by salespeople that brings in revenue or income to a firm or company.

sales dialogue Business conversations between buyers and sellers that occur as salespeople attempt to initiate, develop, and enhance customer relationships. Sales dialogue should be customer focused and have a clear purpose.

LO6 **Understand the sales process as a series of interrelated steps.** As presented in the figure below, the sales process involves initiating, developing, and enhancing customer relationships. Salespeople must possess certain attributes to earn the trust of their customers and be able to adapt their selling strategies to different situations. Throughout the sales process, salespeople should focus on customer value, first by understanding what customer value is to the customer and then by working to create, communicate, and continually increase that value. Salespeople initiate customer relationships through strategic prospecting, assessing the prospect's situation, planning value-based sales dialogue, and activating the buying process. Relationships are then further developed through engaging prospects in a true dialogue to earn commitment from those prospects. Salespeople enhance customer relationships by following up after the sale, taking a leadership role, and sometimes working as part of a team to increase constantly the value received by the customer. The details of the sales process are covered in Chapters 5–10 in this book.

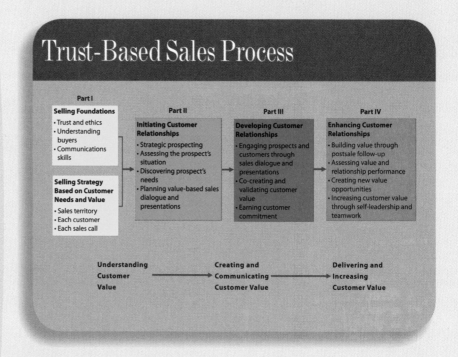

sales process A series of interrelated steps beginning with locating qualified prospective customers. From there, the salesperson plans the sales presentation, makes an appointment to see the customer, completes the sale, and performs postsale activities.

sales professionalism A customer-oriented approach that uses truthful, nonmanipulative tactics to satisfy the long-term needs of both the customer and the selling firm.

sales support personnel A firm's personnel whose primary responsibility is dissemination of information and performance of other activities designed to stimulate sales.

self-efficacy The strong belief that success will occur on the job.

service motivation A strong desire to provide service to the customer. Service motivation comes from desiring the approval of others.

stimulus-response selling An approach to selling in which the key idea is that various stimuli can elicit predictable responses from customers. Salespeople furnish the stimuli from a repertoire of words and actions designed to produce the desired response.

strategic orchestrator A role the salesperson plays in consultative selling in which he or she arranges the use of the sales organization's resources in an effort to satisfy the customer.

technical support salespeople Technical specialist who may assist in design and specification processes, installation of equipment, training of the customer's employees, and follow-up service of a technical nature.

trust-based relationship selling (a form of personal selling) A form of personal selling that requires that salespeople earn customer trust and that their selling strategy meets customer needs and contributes to the creation, communication, and delivery of customer value.

Chapter Summary

LO1 Explain what trust is, explain why it is important, and understand how to earn trust. Trust occurs when a buyer believes that he or she can rely on what the salesperson says or promises to do in a situation where the buyer is dependent on the salesperson's honesty and reliability. One of the keys to a long-term relationship with any client is to create a basis of trust between the sales representative and the client organization.

The *trust* described here goes beyond the typical transaction-oriented trust schema. Many issues—Will the product arrive as promised? Will the right product actually be in stock and be shipped on time? Will the invoice contain the agreed-on price? Can the salesperson be found if something goes wrong?—are only preliminary concerns. In relationship selling, trust is based on a larger set of factors because of the expanded intimacy and longer term nature of the relationship. The intimacy of this relationship will result in both parties sharing information that could be damaging if leaked or used against the other partner.

In today's increasingly competitive marketplace, buyers typically find themselves inundated with choices regarding both products and suppliers. Buyers are demanding unique solutions to their problems, which are customized on the basis of their specific needs. This shift toward relationship selling has altered both the roles played by salespeople and the activities and skills they exercise in carrying out these roles—the selling process itself. Today's more contemporary selling process is embedded within the relationship marketing paradigm. As such, it emphasizes the initiation and nurturing of long-term buyer-seller relationships based on mutual trust and value-added benefits. The level of problem-solving activity common to relationship selling requires deliberate and purposeful collaboration between both parties. These joint efforts are directed at creating unique solutions based on an enhanced knowledge and understanding of the customer's needs and the supplier's capabilities so that both parties derive mutual benefits.

Buyers are constantly asking themselves whether the salesperson truly cares about them. Salespeople can answer this question for the buyer through trust-building activities. Trust can be earned by demonstrating expertise, dependability, candour, customer orientation, competence, and compatibility.

LO2 Know how knowledge bases help build trust and relationships. Salespeople do not have much time to make a first impression. If a salesperson can demonstrate competitive knowledge and expertise in the buyer's industry, company, marketplace, and so on, then the buyer will more likely be willing to listen. The salesperson must bring valued experience to the buyer.

LO3 Understand the importance of sales ethics and its legal implications. Salespeople are constantly involved with ethical issues. A sales manager might encourage his or her salesforce to pad their expense account in lieu of a raise. A salesperson might sell a product or service to a customer that the buyer does not need. A salesperson might exaggerate the benefits of a product to get a sale. The list goes on and on. How a salesperson handles these situations will go a long way in determining the salesperson's credibility. One wrong decision can end a salesperson's career.

Glossary Terms

bait and switch selling Firms or individuals advertise products at bargain prices that they do not have available in reasonable quantities and try to sell more expensive products instead.

basis of the bargain A term used when a buyer relied on the seller's statements in making a purchase decision.

bid rigging An agreement in which competitors agree in advance who will win a bid based on the tenders submitted.

candour Honesty of the spoken word.

competitor knowledge Knowledge of a competitor's strengths and weaknesses in the market.

compatibility and likeability A salesperson's commonalities with other individuals.

confidentiality A salesperson is entrusted with information from a buyer that cannot be shared.

contributions Something given to better a situation or state for a buyer.

customer knowledge Information about customers that is gathered over time and from very different sources that helps the salesperson determine what needs those customers have to better serve them.

customer orientation The act of salespeople placing as much emphasis on the customer's interests as on their own.

dependability The predictability of a person's actions.

ethics The right and wrong conduct of individuals and institutions of which they are a part.

expertise The ability, knowledge, and resources to meet customer expectations.

express warranty A way a salesperson can create product liabilities by giving a product warranty or guarantee that obligates the selling organization even if the salesperson does not intend to give the warranty.

fairness Impartiality and honesty.

honesty Fairness and straightforward conduct.

market knowledge A knowledge tool salespeople must have if larger companies break their customers into distinct markets; salespeople must be familiar with these markets to tailor their sales presentations.

misrepresentation A way a salesperson can create product liabilities by making a false claim about a product.

negligence A way a salesperson can create product liability by making a claim about a product without exercising reasonable care to see that this claim is accurate.

openness Completely free from concealment; exposed to general view or knowledge.

predictability A salesperson's behaviour that can be foretold on the basis of observation or experience by a buyer.

predatory pricing A firm or an individual deliberately sets prices to incur losses for a long time to eliminate a competitor or inhibit competition in the expectation that the firm or individual will later be able to recoup its losses by charging prices above competitive levels.

price discrimination Knowingly and systematically selling the same goods or services at different prices to buyers.

price fixing Agreements between sellers to prevent or unduly lessen competition or to unreasonably enhance the price of a product.

price knowledge A knowledge tool sales-people must have about pricing policies to quote prices and offer discounts on products.

product knowledge Detailed information on the manufacture of a product and knowing whether the company has up-to-date produc-tion methods.

promotion knowledge A knowledge tool salespeople must have to explain promotional programs their firms have.

pyramid selling Fees or commissions paid not on the basis of product sales but on the recruitment of others to make sales.

reliability Consistency over time of doing what is right

security The quality of being free from danger.

service issues Concerns of the buyer that the salesperson should address.

technology knowledge A knowledge tool salespeople must have about the latest technology.

trust The extent of the buyer's confidence that he or she can rely on the salesperson's integrity.

Three of the more popular areas of unethical behaviour are deceptive practices, illegal activities, and noncustomer-oriented behaviour.

- Deceptive practices: Salespeople giving answers they do not know to be right, exaggerating product benefits, and withholding information may appear only to shade the truth, but when it causes harm to the buyer, the salesperson has jeopardized future dealings with the buyer.

- Illegal activities: Misuse of company assets has been a long-standing problem for many sales organizations. Using the company car for personal use, charging expenses that did not occur, and selling samples for income are examples of misusing company assets. Some of these violations discovered by company probing also constitute violations of Canada Revenue Agency (CRA) law and are offences that could lead to jail time or heavy fines.

- Noncustomer-oriented behaviour: Most buyers will not buy from salespeople who are pushy and practise the hard sell. Too much is at stake to fall for the fast-talking, high-pressure salesperson.

Chapter Summary

LO1 **Categorize the primary types of buyers, and discuss the distinguishing characteristics of business markets.** Buyers are classified according to the unique buying situations that influence their needs, motivations, and buying behaviour. The most common categorization splits buyers into either consumer markets or business markets. Consumers purchase goods and services for their own use or consumption whereas members of the business market acquire goods and services to use as inputs into manufacturing, for use in doing business, or for resale. Business markets are further divided into firms, institutions, and governments.

Among the more common distinguishing characteristics of business markets are consolidation, which has resulted in buyers being fewer in number but larger in size; demand that is derived from the sale of consumer goods; more volatile demand levels; professional buyers; multiple buying influences from a team of buyers; and increased interdependence and relationships between buyers and sellers.

LO2 **List the steps in the business-to-business buying process.** This process involves (1) recognition of the problem or need, (2) determination of the characteristics of the item and the quantity needed, (3) description of the characteristics of the item and quantity needed, (4) search for and qualification of potential sources, (5) acquisition and analysis of proposals, (6) evaluation of proposals and selection of suppliers, (7) selection of an order routine, and (8) giving of performance feedback and evaluation.

LO3 **Discuss the different types of buyer needs.** Salespeople are better able to generate and demonstrate value-added solutions by understanding different types of buyer needs. The five general types of buyer needs are described as follows:

Situational needs: Needs that are related to, or possibly the result of, the buyer's specific environment, time, and place.

Functional needs: The need for a specific core task or function to be performed—the need for a sales offering to do what it is supposed to do.

Social needs: The need for acceptance from and association with others; a desire to belong to some reference group.

Psychological needs: The desire for feelings of assurance and risk reduction, as well as positive emotions and feelings, such as success, joy, excitement, and stimulation.

Knowledge needs: The desire for personal development and need for information and knowledge to increase thought and understanding as to how and why things happen.

LO4 **Describe how buyers evaluate suppliers and alternative sales offerings by using the multiattribute model of evaluation.** Using the multiattribute model, buyers establish the attributes they perceive as important and evaluate the degree to which each of the specified attributes is present (or how well each performs) in a proposed solution. Each evaluation is then multiplied by the attribute's relative level of importance to calculate a weighted average for each attribute. These weighted averages are then totalled to derive an overall score for each supplier or product being compared. The product or supplier having the highest score is favoured for the purchase.

LO5 **Explain the two-factor model that buyers use to evaluate the performance of sales offerings and develop satisfaction.** The two-factor model is a special type of multiattribute model in which further analysis of the multiple characteristics results in two primary groupings of factors: functional attributes and psychological attributes.

Glossary Terms

acceleration principle When demand increases (or decreases) in the consumer market, the business market reacts by accelerating the buildup (or reduction) of inventories and increasing (or decreasing) plant capacity.

actual states A buyer's actual state of being.

amiables Individuals who are high on responsiveness, are low on assertiveness, prefer to belong to groups, and are interested in others.

analyticals Individuals who are low on responsiveness and assertiveness, and are analytical, meticulous, and disciplined in everything they do.

assertiveness The degree to which a person holds opinions about issues and attempts to dominate or control situations by directing the thoughts and actions of others.

business markets A market composed of firms, institutions, and governments that acquire goods and services to use as inputs into their own manufacturing process, for use in their day-to-day operations, or for resale to their own customers.

buying teams Teams of individuals in organizations that use the expertise and multiple buying influences of people from different departments throughout the organization.

competitive depositioning Providing information to create a more accurate picture of a competitor's attributes or qualities.

consumer markets A market in which consumers purchase goods and services for their use or consumption.

deciders Individuals within an organization who have the ultimate responsibility of determining which product or service will be purchased.

delighter attributes Augmented features included in the total market offering that go beyond buyer expectations and have a significant positive impact on customer satisfaction.

derived demand Demand in business markets that is closely associated with the demand for consumer goods.

desired states A state of being based on what the buyer desires.

drivers Individuals who are low on responsiveness, high on assertiveness, and detached from relationships.

electronic data interchange Transfer of data electronically between two computer systems.

expressives Individuals who are high on both responsiveness and assertiveness, are animated and communicative, and value building close relationships with others.

functional attributes The features and characteristics that are related to what the product actually does or is expected to do.

functional needs The need for a specific core task or function to be performed.

gatekeepers Members of an organization who are in a position to control the flow of information to and between vendors and other buying centre members.

influencers Individuals within an organization who guide the decision process by making recommendations and expressing preferences.

initiators Individuals within an organization who identify a need.

knowledge needs The desire for personal development, information, and knowledge to increase thought and understanding as to how and why things happen.

modified rebuy decision A purchase decision that occurs when a buyer has experience in purchasing a product in the past but is interested in acquiring additional information regarding alternative products and suppliers.

multiattribute model A procedure for evaluating suppliers and products that incorporates weighted averages across desired characteristics.

must-have attributes Features of the core product that the customer takes for granted.

needs gap A perceived difference between a buyer's desired and actual state of being.

new task decision A purchase decision that occurs when a buyer is purchasing a product or service for the first time.

outsourcing The process of giving to a supplier certain activities that the buying organization previously performed.

psychological attributes The augmented features and characteristics included in the total market offering that go beyond buyer expectations and have a significant positive impact on customer satisfaction.

psychological needs The desire for feelings of assurance and risk reduction, as well as positive emotions and feelings, such as success, joy, excitement, and stimulation.

purchasers Organizational members who negotiate final terms of the purchase and execute the actual purchase.

requests for proposals (RFPs) A form created by firms and distributed to qualified potential suppliers that helps suppliers develop and submit proposals to provide products as specified by the firm.

responsiveness The level of feelings and sociability an individual openly displays.

situational needs The needs that are contingent on, and often a result of, conditions related to the specific environment, time, and place.

social needs The need for acceptance from and association with others.

straight rebuy decision A purchase decision resulting from an ongoing purchasing relationship with a supplier.

supply chain management The strategic coordination and integration of purchasing with other functions within the buying organization as well as external organizations.

target price The price buyers determine for their final products through information gathered from researching the marketplace.

two-factor model of evaluation A postpurchase evaluation process buyers use that evaluates a product purchase by using functional and psychological attributes.

users Individuals within an organization who will actually use the product being purchased.

Functional attributes are the more tangible characteristics of a market offering whereas the psychological attributes are primarily composed of the interpersonal behaviours and activities between the buyer and seller. The psychological attributes have been repeatedly found to have higher levels of influence than functional attributes on customer satisfaction and repeat purchase.

LO6 Explain the different types of purchasing decisions. The three types of purchasing decisions are described as follows:

Straight Rebuy—Comparable with a routine repurchase in which nothing has changed, the straight rebuy is often the result of past experience and satisfaction, with buyers purchasing the same products from the same sources. Needs have been predetermined, with specifications already established. Buyers allocate little, if any, time or resources to this form of purchase decision, and the primary emphasis is on continued satisfactory performance.

Modified Rebuy—The buyer has some level of experience with the product but is interested in acquiring additional information regarding alternative products and suppliers. The modified rebuy typically occurs as the result of changing conditions or needs. Perhaps the buyer wants to consider new suppliers for current purchase needs or new products offered by existing suppliers.

New Task—New task decisions occur when a buyer is purchasing a product or service for the first time. With no experience or knowledge on which to rely, buyers undertake an extensive purchase decision and search for information designed to identify and compare alternative solutions. Reflecting the extensive nature of this type of purchase decision, multiple members of the buying centre or group are usually involved. As a result, the salesperson often works with several different individuals rather than a single buyer.

LO7 Describe the four communication styles and how salespeople must adapt their own styles to maximize communication. Based on high and low levels of two personal traits, assertiveness and responsiveness, communication styles can be categorized into four primary types:

- Amiables are high on responsiveness and low on assertiveness.
- Expressives are defined as high on both responsiveness and assertiveness.
- Drivers are low on responsiveness but high on assertiveness.
- Analyticals are characterized as low on assertiveness as well as responsiveness.

Mismatched styles between a seller and a buyer can be dysfunctional in terms of effective collaboration and present significant barriers for information exchange and relationship building. Differences in styles manifest themselves in the form of differences in preferred priorities (relationships versus task orientation) and favoured pace (fast versus slow) of information exchange, socialization, and decision making. To minimize potential communication difficulties stemming from mismatched styles, salespeople should adapt their personal styles to better fit the preferred priorities and pace of the buyer.

LO8 Explain the concept of buying teams and specify the different member roles. In the more complex modified rebuy and new task purchasing situations, purchase decisions typically involve the joint decisions of multiple participants working together as a buying team. Team members bring the expertise and knowledge from different functional departments within the buying organization. Team members may also change as the purchase decision changes. Team members are described by their roles within the team: initiators, influencers, users, deciders, purchasers, and gatekeepers.

Several key developments are shaping the face of purchasing today, including the increasing use of information technology, an emphasis on building cooperative and collaborative relationships, the increasing use of supply chain management, the expanded use of outsourcing by buying organizations, more emphasis on establishing target prices by buyers, and greater dependence on salespeople to provide buying organizations with creative solutions to unique customer problems.

Chapter Summary

LO1 **Explain the importance of collaborative, two-way communication in trust-based selling.** The two-way exchange inherent in collaborative communication facilitates accurate and mutual understanding of the objectives, problems, needs, and capabilities of each of the parties. As a result, solutions can be generated that provide mutual benefits to all participants. This would not be possible without collaboration, and one party would benefit at the expense of the other. Although this might be good for the winning party, the disadvantaged party would be less inclined to continue doing business and would seek out other business partners.

LO2 **Explain the primary types of questions and how they are applied in selling.** Questions can be typed into two categories according to (1) the amount of information and specificity desired and (2) the strategic purpose of the question.

- Questions typed by the amount of information and specificity desired include open-end questions, closed-end questions, and dichotomous questions. *Open-end questions* encourage the customer to respond freely and provide more expansive information. They are used to probe for descriptive information. *Closed-end questions* limit responses to one or two words and are used to confirm or clarify information. *Dichotomous questions* request the buyer to choose between specified alternatives.

- Questions typed by their strategic purpose include questions for (1) probing, (2) evaluative, (3) tactical, and (4) reactive purposes. *Probing questions* penetrate beneath surface information to provide useful details. *Evaluative questions* uncover how the buyer feels about something. *Tactical questions* are used to shift the topic of discussion. *Reactive questions* respond to information provided by the other party and ask for additional details about that information.

LO3 **Illustrate the diverse roles and uses of strategic questioning in trust-based selling.** Questions are used to elicit detailed information about a buyer's situation, needs, and expectations while also providing a logical guide promoting sequential thought. Effective questioning facilitates both the buyer's and the seller's understanding of a problem and proposed solutions. Questioning can also test the buyer's interest and increase his or her cognitive involvement and participation in the selling process. Questions can also be used to redirect, regain, or hold the buyer's attention subtly and strategically.

LO4 **Identify and describe the SPIN and ADAPT systems for effective questioning in a sales dialogue.** The four steps of SPIN are situation questions, problem questions, implication questions, and need-payoff questions.

- *Situation questions* are used early in the sales call to provide salespeople with leads to develop the buyer's needs and expectations fully.
- *Problem questions* are used to further probe for specific difficulties, developing problems, and areas of dissatisfaction that might be positively addressed by the salesperson's proposed sales offering.
- *Implication questions* are used to assist the buyer in thinking about the potential consequences of the problem and to understand the urgency of resolving the problem in a way that motivates him or her to seek a solution
- *Need-payoff* questions are based on the implications of a problem; they are used to propose a solution and develop commitment from the buyer.

Glossary Terms

activation questions One of the five stages of questions in the ADAPT questioning system used to "activate" the customer's interest in solving discovered problems by helping him or her gain insight into the true ramifications of the problem and to realize that what may initially seem to be of little consequence is, in fact, of significant consequence.

active listening The cognitive process of actively sensing interpreting, evaluating, and responding to the verbal and nonverbal messages of present or potential customers.

ADAPT A questioning system that uses a logic-based funnelling sequence of questions, beginning with broad and generalized inquiries designed to identify and assess the buyer's situation.

assessment questions One of the five stages of questions in the ADAPT questioning system that do not seek conclusions but rather address the buyer's company and operations, goals and objectives, market trends and customers, current suppliers, and even the buyer as an individual.

closed-end questions Questions designed to limit the customer's responses to one or two words.

dichotomous questions A directive form of questioning; these questions ask the customer to choose from two or more options.

discovery questions One of the five stages of questions in the ADAPT questioning system that follows up on the assessment questions; they should drill down and probe for further details needed to develop, clarify, and understand the nature of the buyer's problems fully.

evaluative questions Questions that use the open- and closed-end question formats to gain confirmation and to uncover attitudes, opinions, and preferences the prospect holds.

implication questions One of the four types of questions in the SPIN questioning system that follows and is related to the information flowing from problem questions; they are used to assist the buyer in thinking about the potential consequences of the problem and understanding the urgency of resolving the problem in a way that motivates him or her to seek a solution.

need-payoff questions One of the four types of questions in the SPIN questioning system that is based on the implications of a problem; they are used to propose a solution and develop commitment from the buyer.

nonverbal clusters Groups of related nonverbal expressions, gestures, and movements that can be interpreted to better understand the true message being communicated.

nonverbal communication The conscious and unconscious reactions, movements, and utterances that people use in addition to the words and symbols associated with language.

open-end questions Questions designed to let the customer respond freely; the customer is not limited to one- or two-word answers but is encouraged to disclose personal and business information.

probing questions Questions designed to penetrate below generalized or superficial information to elicit more articulate and precise details for use in needs discovery and solution identification.

problem questions One of the four types of questions in the SPIN questioning system that follows the more general situation questions to further probe for specific difficulties, developing problems, and areas of dissatisfaction that might be positively addressed by the salesperson's proposed sales offering.

projection questions One of the five stages of questions in the ADAPT questioning system used to encourage and facilitate the buyer in "projecting" what it would be like without the problems that have been previously "discovered" and "activated."

proxemics The personal distance that individuals prefer to keep between themselves and other individuals; an important element of nonverbal communication.

reactive questions Questions that refer to or directly result from information the other party previously provided.

serious listening A form of listening that is associated with events or topics in which it is important to sort through, interpret, understand, and respond to received messages.

SIER A model that depicts active listening as a hierarchical, four-step sequence of sensing, interpreting, evaluating, and responding.

situation questions One of the four types of questions in the SPIN questioning system used early in the sales call that provides salespeople with leads to develop the buyer's needs and expectations fully.

social listening An informal mode of listening that can be associated with day-to-day conversation and entertainment.

SPIN A questioning system that sequences four types of questions designed to uncover a buyer's current situation and inherent problems, enhance the buyer's understanding of the consequences and implications of those problems, and lead to the proposed solution.

tactical questions Questions used to shift or redirect the topic of discussion when the discussion gets off course or when a line of questioning proves to be of little interest or value.

transition questions One of the five stages of questions in the ADAPT questioning system used to smooth the transition from needs discovery into the presentation and demonstration of the proposed solution's features, advantages, and benefits.

trust-based sales communication Talking *with* rather than *at* the customer. A collaborative and two-way form of communication that allows buyers and sellers to develop a better understanding of the need situation and work together to co-create the best response for resolving the customer's needs.

The five steps of ADAPT are assessment questions, discovery questions, activation questions, projection questions, and transition questions.

- *Assessment questions* are broad, general, nonthreatening questions designed to spark conversation. Assessment questions elicit factual information about the customer's current situation that can provide a basis for further exploration and probing.

- *Discovery questions* probe for details needed to identify and understand a buyer's problems and needs. The buyer's interpretations, perceptions, feelings, and opinions are sought in regard to his or her needs, wants, dissatisfactions, and expectations.

- *Activation questions* help the customer evaluate the negative impact of an implied need. The objective is to activate interest in solving discovered problems by helping the customer gain insight into the true consequences of the problem.

- *Projection questions* encourage the buyer's decision making by projecting what it would be like if the problems or needs did not exist. They switch the focus from problems to benefits—the payoff for taking action and investing in a solution—and allow the buyer to establish the perceived value of solving the problem or need.

- *Transition questions* smooth the transition to a subsequent phase in the selling process. They are typically closed end and evaluative in format and strive to confirm the buyer's desire to seek a solution and move forward with the buying/selling process.

LO 5 Discuss the four sequential steps for effective active listening.

- *Sensing* is the first activity in active listening and involves receiving the message. Sensing is more than just hearing the message and requires concentration and practice.

- *Interpreting*. After sensing the message, it must be interpreted in terms of what the sender actually meant. In addition to meanings of words and symbols, the experiences, knowledge, and attitudes of the sender should also be considered.

- *Evaluating*. Effective communication requires the receiver to decide whether or not he or she agrees with the sender's message. This requires evaluating the results from the interpretation stage to sort fact from opinion and emotion.

- *Responding*. Collaborative communication requires listeners to provide feedback to the other party. Responses take the form of paraphrasing the sender's message, answering questions, or asking questions to gain additional details and clarification.

LO 6 Describe and interpret the different forms of verbal and nonverbal communication.
Verbal communication refers to statements of fact, opinion, and attitude that are encoded in the form of words, pictures, and numbers in such a way that they convey meaning to a receiver. However, many words and symbols mean different things to different people. Different industries, different cultures, and different types of training or work experience can result in the same word or phrase having multiple interpretations. Nonverbal behaviours are made up of the various movements and utterances that people use. These can be conscious or unconscious and include eye movement and facial expressions; placement and movements of hands, arms, head, and legs, as well as body orientation; the amount of space maintained between individuals; and variations in vocal characteristics. Sensing and interpreting groups or clusters of nonverbal cues can provide a reliable indicator of the underlying message and intent. Evidence shows that nonverbal behaviours carry 50 percent or more of the meaning conveyed in the process of interpersonal communication.

Chapter Summary

LO1 Discuss why prospecting is an important and challenging task for salespeople. Prospecting is important because market changes could cause current customers to buy less, customers could go out of business or be acquired by other firms, or business could be lost to competitors. Salespeople often fear rejection, and prospective buyers may be difficult to contact because they have never heard of a salesperson's firm, do not have the time with all potential new suppliers, and are somewhat shielded by gatekeepers trained to limit access.

LO2 Explain strategic prospecting and each stage in the strategic prospecting process. Strategic prospecting is a process for identifying the best sales opportunities. The strategic prospecting process consists of generating sales leads, determining sales prospects, prioritizing sales prospects, and preparing for sales dialogue.

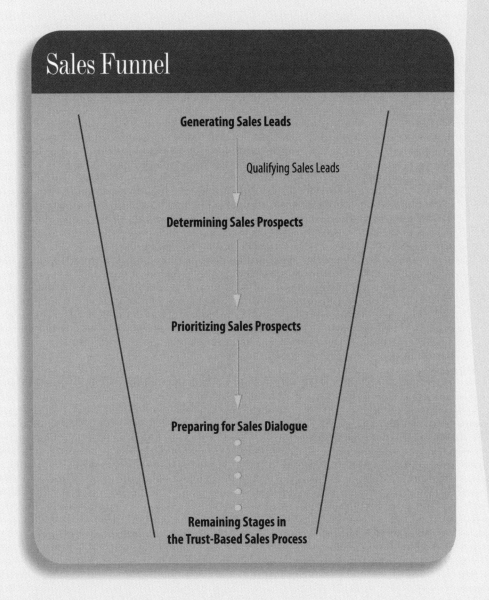

Sales Funnel

Generating Sales Leads

Qualifying Sales Leads

Determining Sales Prospects

Prioritizing Sales Prospects

Preparing for Sales Dialogue

Remaining Stages in the Trust-Based Sales Process

Glossary Terms

advertising inquiries Sales leads generated from company advertising efforts.

centres of influence Well-known and influential people who can help a salesperson prospect and gain leads.

cold calling Contacting a sales lead unannounced and with little or no information about the lead.

commercial lead lists Lists that focus on virtually any type of business or individual; they range from simple listings of names, addresses, and phone numbers to more detailed listings with a full profile of the different entries included in the list.

company records Information about customers in a company database.

directories Electronic or print sources that provide contact and other information about many different companies or individuals.

electronic networking Using websites designed to help salespeople identify and gather information about prospects.

ideal customer profile The characteristics of a firm's best customers or the perfect customer.

inbound telemarketing A way to locate prospects in which the prospect calls the company to get information.

introduction A variation of a referral in which, in addition to requesting the names of prospects, the salesperson asks the prospect or customer to prepare a note or letter of introduction that can be sent to the potential customer.

noncompeting salespeople Salespeople selling noncompeting products.

outbound telemarketing A way to locate prospects in which the salesperson contacts the prospect by telephone.

qualifying sales leads The salesperson's act of searching out, collecting, and analyzing information to determine the likelihood of the lead being a good candidate for making a sale.

referral A name of a company or person given to the salesperson as a lead by a customer or even a prospect who did not buy at this time.

sales funnel or **pipeline** A representation of the trust-based sales process and strategic sales prospecting process in the form of a funnel.

sales leads or **suspects** Organizations or individuals who might possibly purchase the product or service a salesperson offers.

sales prospect An individual or organization that has a need for the product or service, has the budget or financial resources to purchase the product or service, and has the authority to make the purchase decision.

seminars A presentation salespeople give to generate leads and provide information to prospective customers who are invited to the seminar by direct mail, word of mouth, or advertising on local television or radio.

strategic prospecting A process designed to identify, qualify, and prioritize sales opportunities, whether they represent potential new customers or opportunities to generate additional business from existing customers.

strategic prospecting plan A salesperson's plan for gathering qualified prospects.

tracking system Part of the strategic prospecting plan that records comprehensive information about the prospect, traces the prospecting methods used, and chronologically archives outcomes from any contacts with the prospect.

trade shows Events at which companies purchase space and set up booths that clearly identify each company and its offerings and that are staffed with salespeople who demonstrate the products and answer questions.

LO3 **Describe the major prospecting methods and give examples of each method.** Salespeople should use different prospecting methods. The major prospecting methods are cold canvassing (cold calling, referrals, and introductions), networking (centres of influence, noncompeting salespeople, and electronic networking), company sources (company records, advertising inquiries, telephone inquiries, trade shows, and seminars), and published sources (directories and commercial lead lists).

LO4 **Explain the important components of a strategic prospecting plan.** A strategic prospecting plan consists of setting specific goals for the numbers of prospects to be identified, a regular schedule for prospecting activities, a tracking system to keep records of prospecting activities, an evaluation system to assess prospecting progress, and a positive and confident attitude.

LO5 **Discuss the types of information salespeople need to prepare for sales dialogue.** Salespeople must gather information about the prospect that will be used to help formulate the sales presentation. Buyer's needs, buyer's motives, and details about the buyer's situation should be determined. The more a salesperson knows about the buyer, the better chance he or she will have to meet the buyer's needs and eventually earn the commitment.

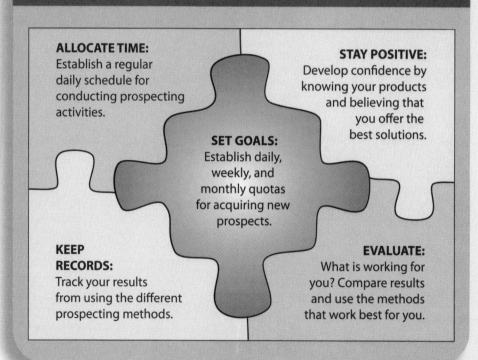

Prospecting Plans Are the Foundation for Effective Prospecting

ALLOCATE TIME: Establish a regular daily schedule for conducting prospecting activities.

STAY POSITIVE: Develop confidence by knowing your products and believing that you offer the best solutions.

SET GOALS: Establish daily, weekly, and monthly quotas for acquiring new prospects.

KEEP RECORDS: Track your results from using the different prospecting methods.

EVALUATE: What is working for you? Compare results and use the methods that work best for you.

Chapter Summary

LO1 **Explain why it is essential to focus on the customer when planning sales calls.** Buyers are well informed and have little time to waste on unproductive conversations with salespeople. To optimize the time spent on sale calls, salespeople should focus on customer needs and how the customer defines value. Customers differ in how they define value, and salespeople must understand each customer's concept of value so that they can establish sales dialogues that are clear, credible, and interesting.

LO2 **Understand alternative ways of communicating with prospects and customers through canned sales presentations, written sales proposals, and organized sales dialogues or an organized sales presentation.** Canned sales presentations include scripted sales calls, memorized presentations, and automated presentations. Effective canned presentations have usually been tested with real customers before an entire salesforce uses them. Canned sales presentations can be complete and logically structured. Objections are anticipated in advance, and appropriate responses can be formulated as part of the presentation. A written sales proposal is a complete, self-contained sales presentation. A sales proposal should be prepared after the salesperson has made a thorough assessment of the buyer's situation as it relates to the seller's offering. An organized sales dialogue, which could include a comprehensive sales presentation, is tailored to the prospect's particular situation and needs. It is a flexible format that allows for maximum input and feedback from the prospect. Sales dialogues and organized sales presentations (sometimes referred to as sales conversations) can take place over multiple sales calls before a purchase decision is made.

LO3 **Discuss the nine components of the sales dialogue template that can be used for planning an organized sales dialogues or presentations.** The sales dialogue template consists of nine sections: (1) prospect information; (2) customer value proposition; (3) sales call objective; (4) situation and needs analysis—linking buying motives, benefits, support information, and other reinforcement methods; (5) competitive situation; (6) beginning the sales dialogue; (7) anticipating questions and objections; (8) earning prospect commitment; and (9) building value through follow-up action. This template should not be used to develop a rigid script for a sales call. It is properly used to help the salespeople ensure that they are prepared to discuss all pertinent content with the customer.

LO4 **Explain how to write a customer value proposition statement.** A customer value statement should be simple so that it provides a clear direction for upcoming sales dialogues. Salespeople should not attempt to include all their benefits in a value proposition statement—rather, they should choose the key benefits that are likely to be most important to the specific customer. The value proposition should be as specific as possible, on listing tangible outcomes, such as revenue improvement, cost containment or reduction gain in market share, process speed and efficiency, or the enhancement of a customer's strategic priority. Value proposition statements should promise only what can be consistently delivered. Strictly speaking, a customer value proposition in the planning stage is not a guarantee; it is a belief based on the salesperson's knowledge and best judgment. As the sales process moves along, appropriate guarantees can be made.

Glossary Terms

benefits The added value or favourable outcome derived from features of the product or service the seller offers.

buying motives A need-activated drive to search for and acquire a solution to resolve a need or problem; the most important factors from the customer's perspective in making a purchase decision.

canned sales presentation Sales presentations that include scripted sales calls, memorized presentations, and automated presentations.

customer value proposition A statement of how the sales offering will add value to the prospect's business by meeting a need or providing an opportunity.

emotional buying motives Includes such motives as security, status, and the need to be liked; sometimes difficult for salespeople to uncover these motives.

features Qualities or characteristics of a product or service that are designed to provide value to a buyer.

organized sales dialogue Also known as the organized sales presentation. Unlike a canned sales presentation, an organized sales dialogue has a high level of customer involvement.

organized sales presentation A sales presentation that allows a salesperson to implement appropriate sales strategies and tactics based on customer research or information gathered during previous sales calls. Organized sales presentations feature a high-level two-way dialogue with the customer.

rational buying motives Typically relate to the economics of the situation, including cost, profitability, quality, services offered, and the total value of the seller's offering as perceived by the customer.

sales call An in-person meeting between a salesperson or sales team and one or more buyers to discuss business.

sales dialogue Business conversations between buyers and sellers that occur as salespeople attempt to initiate, develop, and enhance customer relationships. Sales dialogue should be customer focused and have a clear purpose.

sales dialogue template A flexible planning tool that assists the salesperson in assembling pertinent information to be covered with the prospect.

sales presentations Comprehensive communications that convey multiple points designed to persuade the customer to make a purchase.

written sales proposals A complete self-contained sales presentation on paper, often accompanied by other verbal sales presentations before or after the proposal is delivered.

LO5 **Link buying motives to benefits of the seller's offering, support claims made for benefits, and reinforce verbal claims made.** Organized sales dialogues and organized sales presentations should focus on the most important motives for a given buyer. Benefits must be linked to both rational and emotional motives, and supporting information must be given for each claim made about a benefit. In some cases, the claim needs support beyond the spoken word (e.g., through audio-visual content, printed collateral material, third-party research studies, or testimonials from satisfied customers).

LO6 **Engage the customer by setting appointments.** Salespeople customarily set an appointment, at least for their initial sales calls on new prospects. Appointments may be arranged by telephone, email, or a combination of phone and mail and should include a request for a specific time and date, as well as the amount of time being requested for the sales call. Salespeople have a better chance of securing an appointment if they are prepared to give the customer a good reason for spending time with them.

Chapter Summary

LO1 Describe the key characteristics of effective sales dialogue. The most effective sales dialogues are planned and practised by salespeople, encourage buyer feedback, focus on creating value for the buyer, present value in an interesting and understandable manner, engage and involve the buyer, and support customer value through objective claims.

Salespeople must diagnose customer problems before prescribing solutions.

© YURI ARCURS/SHUTTERSTOCK

LO2 Describe the differences among features, potential benefits, and confirmed benefits, and describe the role they play in benefits selling. Salespeople can generate feedback from buyers by paying attention to nonverbal cues from the buyer and using check-backs or response checks to get the buyer to respond to what the salesperson has said throughout the sales dialogue.

LO3 Describe how verbal support can be used to communicate value in an interesting and understandable manner. Salespeople need to communicate value in an interesting and understandable manner. This can be accomplished by varying the pitch and speed of speech, using examples and anecdotes, and including comparisons and analogies.

LO4 Discuss how sales aids can engage and involve buyers. Sales aids are various tools salespeople can use to engage and involve buyers, generate interest and attention, and be more persuasive. Visual materials, electronic materials, and product demonstrations are the major categories of sales aids. It is important for salespeople to select the appropriate sales aids, but also to use them effectively. The SPES sequence of stating the selling point and introducing the sales aid, presenting the sales aid, explaining the sales aid, and summarizing can help salespeople use sales aids successfully.

Glossary Terms

analogy A special and useful form of comparison that explains one thing in terms of another.

anecdote A type of example that is provided in the form of a story describing a specific incident or occurrence.

case histories A testimonial in story or anecdotal form used as a proof provider.

check-backs or **response checks** Questions salespeople use throughout a sales dialogue to generate feedback from the buyer.

comparison A statement that points out and illustrates the similarities between two points.

confirmed benefits The benefits the buyer indicates are important and represent value.

electronic materials Sales aids in electronic format, such as slides, videos, or multimedia presentations.

example A brief description of a specific instance used to illustrate features and benefits of a product or service.

FAB A form of selling that focuses on the features, advantages, and benefits of a product.

features Qualities or characteristics of a product or service that are designed to provide value to a buyer.

potential benefits A general form of value that is assumed by the salesperson to be of importance but is not yet acknowledged as such by the buyer.

preselling Salespeople present their product or service to individual buyers before a major sales dialogue with a group of buyers.

proof providers The use of statistics, testimonials, or case histories to support product claims.

sales aids The use of printed materials, electronic materials, and product demonstrations to engage and involve buyers.

statistics Facts that lend believability to product claims and are used as proof providers.

testimonials Proof providers that are in the form of statements from satisfied users of the selling organization's products and services.

verbal support The use of voice characteristics, examples and anecdotes, and comparisons and analogies to make sales dialogue interesting and understandable.

visual materials Printed materials, photographs and illustrations, and charts and graphs used as sales aids.

voice characteristics The pitch and speed of speech, which salespeople should vary to emphasize key points.

LO5 **Explain how salespeople can support product claims.** Salespeople need to be able to support the claims they make concerning their products. Proof providers, such as statistics, testimonials, and case histories, represent the major approaches for supporting product claims.

LO6 **Discuss the special considerations involved in sales dialogue with groups.** Sales dialogues with individual buyers and with groups have many similarities and several important differences. Salespeople interacting with a group of buyers need to address their arrival tactics, how to handle questions, the proper use of eye contact, and how to communicate most effectively to the group and to individuals within the group.

Chapter Summary

LO1 **Explain why it is important to anticipate and overcome buyer concerns and resistance.** During the early years of selling, salespeople looked at sales resistance as a negative that was a likely indication that their buyer was not going to buy. This notion has changed over the years, and now objections are viewed as opportunities to sell. Salespeople should be grateful for objections and always treat them as indications that the prospect needs more information; if the salesperson provides the correct information, he or she is moving closer to gaining the sale.

LO2 **Understand why prospects raise objections.** Some prospects are happy with their present suppliers and want to avoid the sales interview. In other instances, the salesperson has failed to qualify the prospect properly. A prospect who has recently purchased a product is probably not in the market for another. Sometimes, prospects simply lack information on the salesperson's product category, and they are uncomfortable making a decision.

© IMAGE SOURCE/JUPITER IMAGES

Secretaries, assistants, receptionists, and even voice mail can block your access to your prospect; they can be the gatekeepers.

Glossary Terms

alternative or legitimate choice A selling technique in which the salesperson asks the prospect to select from two or more choices during a sales presentation.

assumptive close A sales closing technique in which the salesperson assumes that an agreement has been reached, places the order form in front of the buyer, and hands him or her a pen.

commitment signals Favourable statements a buyer makes during a sales presentation that signal buyer commitment.

company or **source objection** Resistance to a product or service that results when a buyer has never heard of or is not familiar with the product's company.

compensation A response to buyer objections in which the salesperson counterbalances the objection with an offsetting benefit.

continuous yes close A sales closing technique that uses the principle that saying yes gets to be a habit; the salesperson asks a number of questions formulated so that the prospect answers yes.

direct commitment A selling technique in which the salesperson asks the customer directly to buy.

direct denial A response to buyer objections in which the salesperson tells the customer that he or she is wrong.

fear or emotional close A sales closing technique in which the salesperson tells a story of something bad happening if the purchase is not made.

forestalling A response to buyer objections in which the salesperson answers the objection during the presentation before the buyer has a chance to ask it.

indirect denial A response to buyer objections in which the salesperson takes a softer, more tactful approach when correcting a prospect or customer's information.

LAARC An acronym for listen, acknowledge, assess, respond, and confirm that describes an effective process for salespeople to follow to overcome sales resistance.

minor-points close A sales closing technique in which the salesperson seeks agreement on relatively minor issues associated with the full order.

need objection Resistance to a product or service in which a buyer says that he or she does not need the product or service.

price objection Resistance to a product or service based on the price of the product being too high for the buyer.

product or **service objection** Resistance to a product or service in which a buyer does not like the way the product or service looks or feels.

questioning or **assessing** A response to buyer objections in which the salesperson asks the buyer assessment questions to gain a better understanding of what the buyer is objecting to.

sales resistance Buyer's objections to a product or service during a sales presentation.

standing-room only close A sales closing technique in which the salesperson puts a time limit on the client in an attempt to hurry the decision to close.

success story commitment A selling technique in which a salesperson relates how one of his or her customers had a problem similar to the prospect's and solved it by using the salesperson's product.

summary commitment A selling technique in which the salesperson summarizes all the major benefits the buyer has confirmed during the sales calls.

T-account or **balance sheet commitment** A selling technique in which a salesperson asks the prospect to brainstorm reasons on paper of why to buy and why not to buy.

third-party reinforcement A response to buyer objections in which the salesperson uses the opinion or data from a third-party source to help overcome the objection and reinforce the salesperson's points.

time objection Resistance to a product or service in which a buyer puts off the decision to buy until a later date.

translation or **boomerang** A response to buyer objections in which the salesperson converts the objection into a reason the prospect should buy.

LO3 Describe the five major types of sales resistance. Typically, objections include the following: "I don't need your product," "Your product is not a good fit," "I don't know your company," "Your price is too high," and "This is a bad time to buy."

EXHIBIT 8.2
Types of Objections

No Need	Buyer has recently purchased or does not see a need for the product category. "I am not interested at this time.
Product or service objection	Buyer may be afraid of product reliability. "I am not sure the quality of your product meets our needs." Buyer may be afraid of late deliveries, slow repairs, etc. "I am happy with my present supplier's service.
Company objection	Buyer is intensely loyal to the present supplier. "I am happy with my present supplier."
Price is too high	Buyer has a limited budget. "We have been buying from another supplier that meets our budget constraints.
Time or delay	Buyer needs time to think it over. "Get back with me in a couple of weeks."

LO4 Explain how the LAARC method can be used to overcome buyer resistance. LAARC allows the salesperson to listen carefully to what the buyer is saying. It allows the salesperson to better understand the buyer's objections. After this careful analysis, the salesperson can then respond. The buyer feels that the salesperson is responding to his or her specific concern rather than giving a prepared answer.

LO5 Describe the recommended approaches for responding to buyer objections. Salespeople have a number of traditional techniques at their disposal for handling resistance. Some of the more popular techniques include forestalling, or answering the objection before the prospect brings it up; direct denial; indirect denial, which softens the answer; translation or boomerang, which means to turn a reason not to buy into a reason to buy; compensation, or offsetting the objection with superior benefits; questions, which are used to uncover the buyer's concerns; and third-party reinforcements, which use the opinion or research of others to substantiate claims.

LO6 List and explain the techniques for earning commitment that secure commitment and closing. Many techniques can be used to earn commitment. Most are gimmicky in nature and reinforce the notion of traditional selling. Successful relationship-building techniques include the summary commitment, the success story commitment, and the direct commitment or ask for the order.

Chapter Summary

LO1 **Explain how to follow up to assess and take action to ensure customer satisfaction by using the latest technology.** When assessing customer satisfaction, salespeople cannot be afraid to ask their customers, "How are we doing?" Periodic follow-up is critical to long-term sales success. New customers generally feel special because they have received a lot of attention from the salesperson. Long-standing customers may feel neglected because the sales rep has many new customers and cannot be as attentive as he or she was previously. Routine follow-up to assess "How are we doing?" can go a long way in letting a customer know that the salesperson cares and is willing to make sure that he or she is satisfied.

To ensure customer satisfaction, salespeople must follow up by performing specific relationship-enhancement activities, such as the following:

- Providing useful information to their customers
- Expediting orders and monitoring an installation for success
- Training customer personnel
- Correcting billing errors
- Remembering the customer after the sale
- Resolving complaints in a timely manner

Salespeople can use technology to enhance follow-up and buyer–seller relationships. Effective follow-up should include specific components designed to help salespeople interact, connect, know, and relate with their customers:

- *Interact*: The salesperson maximizes the number of critical encounters with buyers to encourage effective dialogue and involvement between the salesperson and the buyer.
- *Connect*: The salesperson maintains contact with multiple individuals in the buying organization who influence purchase decisions and manages the various touch points the customer has in the selling organization to ensure consistency in communication.
- *Know*: The salesperson coordinates and interprets the information gathered through buyer–seller contact and collaboration to develop insight regarding the buyer's changing situation, needs, and expectations.
- *Relate*: The salesperson applies relevant understanding and insight to create value-added interactions and develop relationships between the salesperson and buyer.

Salespeople can use a variety of technology-based salesforce automation tools to better track increasingly complex buyer–seller interactions and to manage the exchange, interpretation, and storage of diverse types of information. Among the more popular salesforce automation tools are the many competing versions of PC- and Internet-based software applications designed to record and manage customer contact information. PC-based software applications, such as Maximizer, Goldmine, and ACT!, and Internet-based applications, such as Netsuite and Salesforce.com, enable salespeople to collect, file, and access comprehensive databases detailing information about individual buyers and buying organizations.

Glossary Terms

adding value The process of improving a product or service for the customer.

building goodwill The process of converting new customers into lifetime customers by continually adding value to the product.

collaborative involvement A way to build on buyer–salesperson relationships in which the buyer's organization and the salesperson's organization join together to improve an offering.

communication A two-way flow of information between the salesperson and the customer.

connect The salesperson maintains contact with the multiple individuals in the buying organization who influence purchase decisions and manages the various touch points the customer has in the selling organization to ensure consistency in communication.

customer relationship management (CRM) system A system that dynamically links buyers and sellers into a rich communication network to establish and reinforce long-term, profitable relationships.

critical encounters Meetings in which the salesperson encourages the buyer to discuss tough issues, especially in areas in which the salesperson's organization is providing less than satisfactory performance.

extranet Proprietary computer networks created by an organization for use by the organization's customers or suppliers and linked to the organization's internal systems, informational databases, and intranet.

interact The salesperson acts to maximize the number of critical encounters with buyers to encourage effective dialogue and involvement between the salesperson and buyer.

intranet An organization's dedicated and proprietary computer network that offers password-controlled access to people within and outside the organization (e.g., customers and suppliers).

know The salesperson coordinates and interprets the information gathered through buyer–seller contact and collaboration to develop insight regarding the buyer's changing situation, needs, and expectations.

relate The salesperson applies relevant understanding and insight to create value-added interactions and generate relationships between the salesperson and buyer.

resilience The ability of a salesperson to listen to a customer's complaint and always answer with a smile.

service motivation The desire of a salesperson to service customers each day.

service quality Meeting and or exceeding customer service expectations.

service strategy A plan in which a salesperson identifies his or her business and customers and what the customers want and what is important to them.

LO2 Discuss how to expand collaborative involvement. The easiest way to expand collaborative involvement is to get more people involved in the relationship from both the buyer's and the seller's firms.

LO3 Explain how to add value and enhance mutual opportunities. The salesperson can enhance mutual opportunities by reducing risk for the buyer through repeated displays of outstanding customer service. The salesperson can also demonstrate a willingness to serve the customer over extended periods of time. The buyer needs to experience a readiness on the seller's part to go to bat for the buyer when things get tough.

LO1 Explain the five sequential steps of self-leadership. As a process, self-leadership is composed of five sequential stages. First, goals and objectives must be set that properly reflect what is important and what is to be accomplished. In turn, an analysis of the territory and classification of accounts is conducted to better understand the territory potential and prioritize accounts according to revenue-producing possibilities. With goals in place and accounts prioritized, the third step develops corresponding strategic plans designed to achieve sales goals through proper allocation of resources and effort. The next stage maximizes the effectiveness of allocated resources by incorporating technology and salesforce automation to expand salesperson resource capabilities. Finally, assessment activities are conducted to evaluate performance and goal attainment and to assess possible changes in plans and strategies.

LO2 Identify the four levels of sales goals and explain their interrelationships. There are four different levels of goals that salespeople must establish to maximize sales effectiveness:

(a) Personal goals: what the seller wants to accomplish for himself or herself

(b) Sales call goals: the priorities to be accomplished during a specific call

(c) Account goals: the objectives for each individual account

(d) Territory goals: what is to be accomplished for the overall territory

Each level requires different types of effort and produces different outcomes, and each of the levels is interrelated with and interdependent on the others. Ultimately, each higher level goal is dependent on the salesperson setting and achieving the specific goals for each lower level.

LO3 Describe two techniques for account classification. There are two basic methods of classifying accounts. In ascending order of complexity, these methods are single-factor analysis and portfolio analysis (also referred to as two-factor analysis).

- *Single-factor analysis:* Also referred to as ABC analysis, this is the simplest and most often-used method for classifying accounts. Accounts are analyzed on the basis of one single factor—typically the level of sales potential—and placed into either three or four categories denoted by letters of the alphabet: A, B, C, and D. All accounts in the same category receive equal selling effort.

- *Portfolio analysis (two-factor analysis):* This classification method allows two factors to be considered simultaneously. Each account is examined on the basis of the two factors selected for analysis and sorted into the proper segment of a matrix. This matrix is typically divided into four cells, with accounts placed into the proper classification cell on the basis of their individual ratings (high and low or strong and weak) on each of the two factors. Accounts in the same cell share a common level of attractiveness as a customer and will receive the same amount of selling effort.

LO4 Interpret the usefulness of different types of selling technology and automation. Properly applied, selling technology spurs creativity and innovation, streamlines the selling process, generates new selling opportunities, facilitates communication, and enhances customer follow-up. Salespeople must not only master the technology itself but they must also understand when and where it can be applied most effectively. A wide selection of different-sized computers is at the centre of most selling technologies. They

Glossary Terms

account classification The process of placing existing customers and prospects into categories based on their sales potential.

account goal A salesperson's desire to sell a certain amount of product to one customer or account to achieve territory and personal goals.

circular routing plan A territory routing plan in which the salesperson begins at the office and moves in an expanding pattern of concentric circles that spiral across the territory.

cloverleaf routing plan A territory routing plan in which the salesperson works a different part of the territory and travels in a circular loop back to the starting point.

deal analytics "Smart" salesforce automation tools that analyze data on past customer behaviour, cross-selling opportunities, and demographics to identify areas of opportunity and high customer interest.

external relationships Relationships salespeople build with customers outside the organization and working environment.

extranets A form of intranet that is still restricted but links to specific suppliers and customers to allow them controlled access to the organization's network and databases.

goals and objectives The things a salesperson sets out to accomplish.

high-tech sales support offices Offices set up at multiple locations where salespeople can access the wider range of selling technology than could be easily carried on a notebook or laptop computer.

internal relationships Relationships salespeople have with other individuals in their own company.

Internet A technology tool that instantly networks the salesperson with customers, information sources, other salespeople, sales management, and others.

intranets Secured networks within the organization that use the Internet or commercial channels to provide direct linkages between company units and individuals.

leapfrog routing plan A territory routing plan in which, beginning in one cluster, the salesperson works each of the accounts at that location and then jumps to the next cluster.

major city routing plan A territory routing plan used when the territory is composed of a major metropolitan area and the territory is split into a series of geometric shapes reflecting each one's concentration and pattern of accounts.

mobile salesperson CRM solutions Wireless broadband applications that enable users to view, create, and modify data on any Internet-capable devices, such as smartphones, netbooks, and laptops.

personal goals A salesperson's individual desired accomplishment, such as achieving a desired annual income over a specific period.

portfolio analysis A method for analyzing accounts that allows two factors to be considered simultaneously. Also called two-factor analysis.

sales call goal A salesperson's desire to sell a certain amount of product per each sales call to achieve account, territory, and personal goals.

sales planning The process of scheduling activities that can be used as a map for achieving objectives.

self-leadership The process of doing the right things and doing them well.

selling technology and automation Tools that streamline the selling process, generate improved selling opportunities, facilitate cross-functional teaming and intraorganizational communication, and enhance communication and follow-up with customers.

single-factor analysis A method for analyzing accounts that is based on one single factor, typically the level of sales potential. Also called ABC analysis.

straight-line routing plan A territory routing plan in which salespeople start from their offices and make calls in one direction until they reach the end of the territory.

teamwork skills Skills salespeople must learn to build internal partnerships that translate into increased sales and organizational performance.

territory analysis The process of surveying an area to determine customers and prospects who are most likely to buy.

territory goal A salesperson's desire to sell a certain amount of product within an area or territory to achieve personal goals.

provide the production tools for generating reports, proposals, and graphic-enhanced presentations. Spreadsheet applications and database applications facilitate the analysis of customer accounts and searching for information needed by customers. Contact management software enables the salesperson to gather and organize account information and schedule calls. Access to the Internet and World Wide Web provide salespeople with access to an assortment of public and corporate networks that enable them to communicate, research, and access company information and training from anywhere in the world. Using pagers and cell phones puts salespeople in touch with customers, the home office, and even family while travelling cross-country or just walking across the parking lot to make a customer call. Voice mail voids the previous restrictions of time and place that accompanied the requirement to make personal contact. Messages can now be left and received 24 hours a day and seven days a week. High-tech sales support offices provide geographically dispersed salespeople with a common standard of computing technology, access to software applications, and portals to organizational networks at offices around the world. Wherever they may be working, salespeople have the tools and capabilities identical to those available to them in their home offices.

LO5 Delineate six skills for building internal relationships and teams.

(a) *Understanding other individuals:* Fully understanding and considering the other individuals in the partnership is necessary for knowing what is important to them. What is important to them must also be important to the salesperson if the partnership is to grow and be effective.

(b) *Attending to the little things:* Little kindnesses and courtesies are small in size but great in importance. Properly attended to and nurtured, they enhance the interrelationships. However, when neglected or misused, they can destroy the relationship very quickly.

(c) *Keeping commitments:* We build hopes and plans around the promises and commitments made to us by others. When a commitment is not kept, disappointment and problems result and credibility and trust suffer major damage that will be difficult or impossible to repair.

(d) *Clarifying expectations:* The root cause of most relational difficulties can be found in ambiguous expectations regarding roles and goals. By clarifying goals and priorities, as well as who is responsible for different activities up front, the hurt feelings, disappointments, and lost time resulting from misunderstandings and conflict can be prevented.

(e) *Showing personal integrity:* Demonstrating personal integrity generates trust. Be honest, open, and treat everyone by the same set of principles.

(f) *Apologizing sincerely when a mistake is made:* It is one thing to make a mistake. It is another thing not to admit it. People forgive mistakes, but ill intentions and cover-ups can destroy trust.

Chapter Summary

LO1 Discuss the key considerations in developing and implementing effective sales strategies.
A sales organization must look closely at blending the following basic concepts in designing an effective sales organization structure: specialization, centralization, span of control versus management levels, and line versus staff positions. Different decisions in any of these areas produce different sales organization structures. There is no one right sales structure. A good sales manager will look at the specific characteristics of a given selling situation to determine the appropriate structure. Sales managers and salespeople are generally responsible for strategic decisions at the account level. A sales strategy is designed to execute an organization's marketing strategy for individual accounts. The major purpose of a sales strategy is to develop a specific approach for selling to individual accounts within a target market. A sales strategy capitalizes on the important differences among individual accounts or groups of similar accounts. A firm's sales strategy is important for two reasons. First, it has a major impact on a firm's sales and profit performance. Second, it influences many other sales management decisions, such as recruitment, selection, training, compensation, and performance.

LO2 Understand the recruitment, selection, and training processes involved in developing the salesforce.
Developing the salesforce involves recruiting and selecting sales talent, as well as training both new hires and those already on the salesforce. Recruitment and selection is a three-step process that involves planning for recruitment and selection, locating prospective candidates, and evaluating and hiring. After talent has been acquired, they must be properly trained. The training process involves six interrelated steps: (1) assessing sales training needs, (2) setting training objectives, (3) evaluating training alternatives, (4) designing the sales training program, (5) performing sales training, and (6) conducting follow-up and evaluation.

LO3 Identify key activities in directing the salesforce by leading, managing, supervising, motivating, and rewarding salespeople.
Sales leadership includes activities that influence others to achieve shared goals to advance the organization. As shown in Exhibit 11.3, sales executives, sales managers, and salespeople can all be involved in sales leadership. Sales management focuses on planning, implementation, and control of the sales management process. Sales supervision involves working with subordinates on an ongoing basis. Sales managers may use one or more leadership styles, including transactional, transformational, and leader-member exchange (LMX) to direct the salesforce. In directing the salesforce, sales leaders should use power judiciously and rely on coaching as a primary communications and development tool.

LO4 Explain the different methods for evaluating the performance and effectiveness of sales organizations and individual salespeople.
Sales organization effectiveness is a summary evaluation of the overall sales organization's success in meeting its performance goals and objectives in total and at different organizational levels. In contrast, salesperson performance is an evaluation of individual salesperson performance in individual situations. Evaluations of sales organization effectiveness provide important information for managers to use in strategic decision making and policy development. At the sales organization level, the most comprehensive type of performance evaluation is a sales organization audit, which is a systematic assessment of all aspects of a sales organization: the sales organization environment, sales management, planning system, and sales management functions. The performance and effectiveness of sales organizations are also assessed through more focused analysis methods, such as sales analysis, cost analysis, and profitability analysis, where comparisons are made to forecasts, quotas, previous time periods, and competitors.

Glossary Terms

360-degree feedback Performance assessments of a salesperson from multiple sources having a relationship with the salesperson.

account targeting strategy The classification of accounts within a target market into categories for the purpose of developing strategic approaches for selling to each account or account group.

assessment centre Systematic use of several assessment tools, such as presentations, role-playing exercises, group discussion, and business game simulations, to identify candidate strengths and weaknesses relative to job qualifications or for employee development.

background investigation References and others are contacted to verify information reported by the job candidate.

behaviourally anchored rating scales (BARS) A performance evaluation method with the ability to link salesperson behaviours with specific outcomes and allow managers to indicate the level of behaviour a specific salesperson has achieved.

behaviour-based evaluations Evaluation of the activities salespeople perform in the generation of sales and in completing nonselling responsibilities.

cloud computing Combining applications, communications, and content into one digital cloud that can be easily accessed from many different devices.

coaching Sales managers focus on continual development of salespeople through provision of feedback and serving as a role model.

cost analysis Assesses costs the sales organization incurs in the process of generating sales by comparing incurred costs with the planned costs in sales budgets.

field sales managers Sales managers who have salespeople reporting directly to them and who spend a considerable amount of time working with salespeople in their respective territories.

independent representatives or manufacturer representatives Independent sales organizations that sell complementary but noncompeting products from different manufacturers; also called manufacturer's representatives or reps.

job analysis An examination of the tasks, duties, and responsibilities of the sales job.

job description A written summary of the job.

job qualifications Indicate the aptitude, skills, knowledge, personal traits, and willingness to accept occupational conditions to perform the job.

leadership style A general orientation applied to leadership activities. Transactional and transformational leadership styles are two well-known leadership styles.

motivation Comprising three dimensions: intensity, persistence, and direction. Intensity is the amount of effort expended, persistence is the ongoing choice to expend effort, and direction refers to how salespeople spend their time on the job.

needs assessment Activities undertaken to determine the extent to which the members of the salesforce possess the skills, attitudes, perceptions, and behaviours required to be successful.

outcome-based evaluations Evaluation of the actual sales results salespeople achieve.

performance management A performance evaluation approach that involves sales managers and individual salespeople working together on setting goals, giving feedback, reviewing, and rewarding.

profitability analysis Evaluates the results from combining sales and cost data to identify and assess sales organization profitability.

relationship strategy A determination of the type of relationship to be developed with different account groups.

reward system management Selection and administration of organizational rewards to encourage salespeople to achieve organizational objectives.

Sales 2.0 The use of customer-driven processes enabled by the latest Web technology to co-create value with customers.

sales analysis Examines the sales organization's past, current, and future sales performance in comparison with projections, competition, and industry sales.

sales leadership Activities that influence others to achieve shared goals to advance the organization.

sales management Managing an organization's personal selling function to include planning, implementing, and controlling the sales management process.

sales organization audit A comprehensive, systematic approach for evaluating sales organization effectiveness, which provides management with diagnostic as well as prescriptive information.

sales organization effectiveness An overall assessment of how well the sales organization achieved its goals and objectives.

sales supervision Sales managers working with subordinates, including salespeople and sales staff, on an ongoing basis.

salesperson performance How well salespeople perform the activities necessary to carry out their sales responsibilities, as well as their results and contributions to organizational objectives.

selling strategy Involves the planning of sales messages and interactions with customers. Selling strategy can be defined at three levels: for a group of customers, that is, a sales territory; for individual customers; and for specific customer encounters, referred to as sales calls.

social networking The ability to create, access, and interact with networks of contacts electronically.

span of control The number of individuals who report to each sales manager.

team selling The use of multiple-person sales teams in dealing with multiple-person customer buying centres.

Salesperson evaluations are more tactical in nature and provide inputs in compensation, promotion, training, and motivation decisions designed to support and improve performance. Salesperson performance is commonly evaluated in terms of both outcome-based and behaviour based assessments. Outcome-based appraisals examine the actual results achieved by a salesperson. Behaviour based evaluations focus on the activities salespeople use in generating the sales outcomes. Sales managers use different methods to evaluate salesperson performance, including graphic ratings/checklists, rankings, objective-based methods, and behaviourally anchored rating scales (BARS). These methods allow for reliable and valid comparisons of salespeople across territories, selling units, and product types for the purpose of identifying problems, determining their causes, and suggesting sales management actions to solve them.

LO5 Describe how sales organizations are using Sales 2.0 to co-create value with customers.
Sales 2.0 is the use of customer-driven processes enabled by the latest Web 2.0 technologies to co-create value with customers. The focus is on two-way, interactive communication between buyer and seller and the alignment of strategy, people, process, and technology. New Web 2.0 technologies are being introduced and employed by sales organizations to improve personal selling and sales management processes. Customer relationship management (CRM) and social networking technologies are being integrated and used in a variety of ways by sales organizations. The Sales 2.0 trend is growing and likely to expand in the future as new technologies are developed and applied by sales organizations.

Introduction

The National Copier Company (NCC) sells a variety of copiers to small and medium-sized businesses. NCC has been in business for five years and has been growing at a steady pace. NCC differentiates itself from other copier companies by customizing its products to meet the specific needs of each customer and by providing excellent customer service. The company's salesforce plays a key role in creating value and managing customer relationships.

Brenda Smith has been a NCC salesperson for the past three years. She has steadily improved her sales performance during her time with NCC, and now she is in the top 25 percent of all NCC sales representatives as measured by two key metrics: overall sales volume and customer satisfaction. Brenda has been especially successful with small professional firms, such as attorneys, architects, accountants, and medical professionals. She is excited to begin her fourth year with NCC and has established challenging goals to increase sales from existing customers and to generate new customers.

Brenda recently met with Jin Tan, her sales manager and was quite excited about the upcoming year. Jin had told Brenda that she was progressing toward a possible promotion into sales training if she had another good year in her sales position. In addition, Jin gave Brenda this feedback: "Brenda, I think you are doing a fine job with your customers, but I would like to see you become more of a consultative salesperson in the coming year. I would also like for you to sharpen your group communications skills, as that will be important if you are promoted into sales training. We will talk about the specifics more as the year goes along. Meanwhile, thanks for your results to date and good luck with the upcoming year."

Questions

1. Brenda had been thinking about Jin Tan's feedback that directed her to become more of a consultative salesperson. In thinking about her own selling approaches, she knew that she had been concentrating on the needs satisfaction and problem-solving approaches. What must Brenda do to become a more consultative salesperson?

2. Three months later, Brenda was having mixed results with the consultative selling approach. She was finding that some of her customers just wanted the convenience of having a copier in their offices and did not seem eager to discuss their strategic goals. She was beginning to wonder about the consultative selling model, thinking it was not such a good idea after all. What recommendations do you have for Brenda?

3. A month before the annual meeting for all NCC sales representatives, Jin Tan told Brenda, "For the upcoming meeting, I want you to prepare a 10-minute presentation about the pros and cons of the basic selling approaches that we use at NCC compared with our competitors." NCC's sales training program advocated the use of needs satisfaction, problem-solving, and consultative selling. Many of NCC's key competitors used the same approaches. However some of the toughest competitors used stimulus-response and mental states (AIDA) approaches. This latter category of competitors often stressed lower prices and used telemarketing instead of field sales representatives in selling their products. Put yourself in Brenda's role and prepare the presentation requested by Jin Tan.

4. Early in the year, Jin Tan told Brenda that her efforts were needed to gain more exposure for NCC's university recruiting program: "Brenda, I want you to be part of a two-person team to help with recruiting on two university campuses in your territory. The other team member will be an experienced recruiter who had sales experience before moving into recruiting. The two of you should seek out opportunities as guest speakers for classes and student organizations. Your role will be to talk about how sales can be a great place to start a career and for some, a great career path. Think about the future of selling and what it takes to be

successful and share your thoughts with students." Acting as Brenda, make note of ten key points you would like to make about the future of professional selling and what it takes to be successful. (Hint: be sure you read the Appendix to Chapter 1 along with Chapter 1 before you undertake this task.)

Notes

_____

_____

_____

_____

_____

_____

_____

_____

_____

_____

_____

_____

_____

_____

_____

_____

_____

_____

_____

_____

Building Trust

Because the National Copier Company (NCC) has been in business for only five years, Brenda Smith is concerned that most of her competitors are older than she is. The prospective customers she has been calling on state they know they can count on her competitors, because they have a long track record. As NCC expands into new markets some of her prospects are not familiar with her company. One prospective customer, who works for one of the most prestigious and largest medical offices (30 doctors) in the area, told her he has been buying copiers from the same company for more than 25 years. He also told her his sales representative for the company has been calling on him for more than seven years, and he knows that when he calls on his copier supplier for advice, he can count on him for a solid recommendation. Brenda realizes these are going to be tough accounts to crack.

Brenda does have an advantage because of the high quality of NCC products. In a recent trade publication, NCC's copiers tied for first in the industry on ratings of copier quality and dependability. NCC was also given a high rating for service. Brenda has had this information for two weeks now and has brought it up in conversations with her prospective customers without much success. To make matters worse, one of her competitors must have started rumours about NCC. In the past month, she has heard the following rumours:

"NCC is going out of business because of financial troubles."

"NCC has missed several delivery deadlines with customers."

"NCC's copiers have a software glitch that cannot be corrected."

"NCC has cut its service staff."

Brenda knows these rumours are not true, but prospects might believe them. At a recent sales meeting, Brenda's manager suggested that their competitors must be getting nervous about NCC's success, causing them to tell those lies.

Brenda is sitting at her desk trying to figure out what to do next and she is not exactly sure how to proceed.

Questions

1. What would you recommend Brenda do to handle the challenges she faces?
2. Brenda appears to have an advantage with her products and services. Develop a plan for Brenda to build trust in NCC with prospective customers.
3. What do you recommend Brenda do to compete effectively against competitors that have a long and successful track record?
4. How should Brenda go about handling the rumour mill?

Understanding Tom Penders

It was Monday afternoon and Brenda Smith was very excited. She had just got off the phone with Tom Penders, the administrator in charge of a large medical office in her territory. After an introductory letter and several follow-up phone calls, Tom Penders had finally agreed to meet with Brenda next Friday to discuss the possibility of replacing his organization's old copiers, as well as adding new copiers to keep pace with his organization's rapid growth. The primary purpose of the meeting was for Tom to learn more about the National Copier Company (NCC) and its products and for Brenda to learn more about Tom's company and its specific needs.

When Brenda arrived about 10 minutes early for her meeting with Tom Penders at the medical offices on Friday, she was greeted by a receptionist who asked her to be seated. Ten minutes passed and Brenda was promptly shown to Tom's office. Brenda couldn't help but notice how organized Tom's office was. It appeared to Brenda that Tom was a man of detail. First, Tom explained that the medical offices housed more than 30 doctors specializing in a variety of fields. They occupied two floors and were planning to expand to the vacant third floor in the near future. Currently, they were organized into five divisions with an office professional assigned to approximately six doctors for each division. Each division ran its own office with a separate copier and administrative facilities. Tom also had an assistant and a copier. After giving his overview, Tom provided Brenda with an opportunity to ask questions. After that, Tom systematically went down a list of questions he had about NCC, its products, and Brenda herself. Following this, Tom had his assistant take Brenda on a tour of the facility so she could overview their processes. Before leaving, Tom agreed to meet with Brenda in two weeks.

Based on her conversation with Tom, Brenda did not find Tom to be a particularly personable individual. In fact, she found him to be somewhat cool and aloof, deliberate both in his communication and his actions. Yet Tom was willing to learn how NCC could help his medical office. Although Brenda preferred communicating with someone more personable and open, such as herself, she was determined to find a way to win Tom's business.

Questions

1. What type of communication style do you believe that Tom exhibits? What are the characteristics of this communication style?
2. Based on your understanding of Tom's communication style, outline a plan for selling to Tom Penders.
3. Identify other members of Tom Penders' organization that may play a role in the buying decision and explain the role they might play. How should Brenda handle these individuals?
4. Explain the types of buyer needs that will be most important in this selling situation.

Sharpening the Selling Tools

Brenda Smith is working in the office this morning preparing for tomorrow's sales call with Gage Waits, managing partner, and Tanisha Autry, operations manager, at Energy-Based Funds LLC. Energy-Based Funds is a major investment banking organization specializing in managing and marketing a variety of energy-based mutual funds. The company operates throughout Canada and employs 175 people, with offices occupying the top three floors of a major office building in the heart of the financial district. For the past several years, Energy-Based Funds has been leasing and purchasing office equipment from Altima Systems, one of Brenda's biggest competitors. Brenda has been working her network to get a chance to begin a sales dialogue with Energy-Based Funds and she finally has an appointment with the main players on the purchasing team: Gage and Tanisha.

Brenda knows that planning is a key part of success in selling and is diligently working on her strategy and plans in preparation for tomorrow's sales call with Gage and Tanisha at Energy-Based Funds. According to the sales call plan that Brenda is developing, the purpose of this initial meeting is twofold: (1) to discover more about Energy-Based Funds' current operations, their future plans, and the nature of their use of and needs for copiers; (2) to begin acquainting Gage and Tanisha with NCC and the value they can provide Energy-Based Funds. At this point in her sales call plan, Brenda is considering the different pieces of information she needs to get from the dialogue and what questions she might use to elicit that information from Gage and Tanisha.

Questions

1. Based on the purpose of probing questions explained in your text, explain how Brenda should use probing types of questions in her initial sales dialogue with Gage and Tanisha at Energy-Based Funds. Consider the types of information Brenda needs and develop several illustrative examples of probing questions Brenda might use.
2. Evaluative questions are also effective in sales conversations. Explain the purpose of evaluative questions and how Brenda might effectively use them in this initial sales call. Provide several illustrative examples of evaluative questions Brenda could use.
3. The ADAPT questioning system is a logic-based sequence of questions designed for effective fact-finding and gaining information about a buyer's situation. Develop a series of ADAPT questions that Brenda might use in her sales call to develop the information she needs regarding Energy-Based Funds, their operations, and their needs for copiers.
4. What recommendations would you give Brenda regarding nonverbal communication and how she might use it for more effective communication in this sales call?

Fishing for New Customers

Brenda Smith has been very successful at getting existing customers to upgrade or purchase new copiers during the past two months. She is, however, disappointed in her efforts to get new customers. To add more new customers, Brenda has been spending a great deal of time prospecting. These efforts have produced a large number of leads. Once she generates a lead, she contacts the firm and tries to set up an appointment. Unfortunately, most of these leads are not interested in talking about copiers and are not willing to schedule a meeting with her. This has been so frustrating that she decided to make several cold calls this week to see if this would be a good way to get to meet with prospective customers. The cold calls were also not very successful and were extremely time consuming. Brenda did finally get a few leads to agree to meet with her, but these appointments were not very productive. The leads were typically satisfied with the copiers they were using and were not interested in learning about NCC copiers.

Jin Tan, her sales manager, accompanied her on a recent sales call to a lead. After the sales call, Jin expressed his disappointment that they had really wasted their time with this meeting. Jin then asked Brenda about her prospecting process, because it was clear that she was not identifying and spending her time with the best sales opportunities. Her approach was not working well and was taking a lot of time. If she continued doing the same things, Brenda was not likely to generate many new customers and might lose some existing customers, because she was spending too much of her time prospecting.

Brenda realizes that she must improve her prospecting process, but she is not sure exactly how to proceed.

Questions

1. What is Brenda doing wrong? What would you recommend Brenda do to improve her prospecting efforts?
2. Explain the strategic prospecting process to Brenda and discuss how she can implement it.
3. What secondary lead sources would you recommend Brenda use to identify the best attorneys, architects, accountants, and medical professionals as prospects?
4. What specific types of information should Brenda obtain before contacting a qualified prospect?

Custom Product, Custom Presentation

During the past three months, Brenda has improved her prospecting process. She is identifying more prospects that represent better sales opportunities. Brenda knows that it is important to plan her sales calls in advance to maximize the time she spends in face-to-face selling. In this selling environment, most customers are not interested in all the features of Brenda's products. Brenda has to determine what was important to each customer and customize her presentations accordingly. Further, she has to clearly communicate the benefits of her products and not overwhelm potential buyers with too much technical language. Assume that Brenda has an appointment with EFP, a nonprofit organization that raises money to promote environmentally friendly practices, such as recycling. The organization uses email, Web-based communications, and direct mail campaigns to reach potential donors. EFP currently uses an older-generation analog copier. Brenda hopes to sell EFP a modern digital copier that offers several advantages over the analog copier currently in use.

Questions

1. Using an Internet search engine, such as Google, find the general benefits of digital copiers over analog copiers. You might enter "benefits of digital copiers" in the search engine, or examine data from copier providers, such as Ricoh, Canon, or Xerox, to find these benefits. List six to eight potential benefits of a digital copier to EFP.
2. From the listing developed in question 1, select four benefits. For each benefit, write a sentence or two that Brenda might use to communicate these benefits during her sales call with EFP.
3. For the four benefits identified in question 2, describe what information Brenda should have on hand when she makes the sales call on the EFP buyer. Also describe how this information would be best communicated, that is, what support materials will Brenda need to enhance her verbal communications?
4. Assume that the buyer acknowledges interest in at least two of benefits identified in question 2. Write a realistic buyer–seller dialogue of Brenda's interaction with the EFP buyer concerning these benefits.

Up for the Challenge

Brenda has a meeting today with the office manager at the law firm Arseneau and Wilson (A&L). A&L is a local law firm with five attorneys and one main office. During her initial telephone conversation, the office manager indicated that the firm was reasonably satisfied with their current copiers but that he was always looking for ways to increase office productivity. He also mentioned that he was a little concerned that the firm was paying for many copier features that were not really used. The law firm needed to make a lot of legal-sized copies and be able to collate and staple them. There was little need for other "bells and whistles." It was also important that a copier was dependable, because the law firm made many copies each day. When the copier did break down, fast service was needed to get it repaired as soon as possible.

The office manager had some familiarity with NCC products and was eager to talk to Brenda. However, he made it clear that any decision to switch to NCC copiers would require that Brenda also meet with the attorneys and office personnel to get their approval. If Brenda convinced him that NCC copiers would increase office productivity at the law firm, he would be glad to set up a meeting for her with the attorneys and office personnel.

Brenda is excited about this opportunity. She knows that NCC copiers are very dependable and that NCC provides exceptional service. She can also offer the law firm a copier with the specific features A&L needs.

Questions

1. Prepare the sales dialogue Brenda might employ use and an anecdote to communicate the dependability of NCC copiers to the office manager.
2. Brenda will not be able to demonstrate a copier during this sales call. Describe the types of sales aids she should use to show the buyer an NCC copier with the exact features needs.
3. How can Brenda best use statistics and testimonials to support the excellent service provided by NCC?
4. Brenda did a terrific job in her sales call with the office manager. He is interested in NCC copiers and has scheduled a meeting for Brenda with the five attorneys and the office personnel. Discuss the major things Brenda should do during her sales call to this group.

Handling Sales Resistance

Brenda recently returned from a two-week training session that focused on how to handle sales resistance and how to earn commitment. Brenda has become quite familiar with the ADAPT questioning system and knows she must use assessment questions to allow the buyer to describe their present situation. She has also developed a pretty good set of discovery questions that helps her identify the buyer's needs and problems. Her challenge has been what to do with this information. Whenever Brenda attempts to use features and benefits to make her case, she encounters myriad objections. Brenda knows she has great products and service, but she has not been able to communicate this effectively to her prospects.

The objection she hears most often is, "I've never heard of your company. How long have you been in business?" If that is not bad enough, she heard the following objections in just one morning:

"I'm not sure I am ready to buy at this time. I'll need to think it over."

"Your company is pretty new. How do I know you'll be around to take care of me in the future?"

"Your price is a little higher than I thought it would be."

"Your company was recently in the news. Are you having problems?"

"I think your company is too small to meet our needs."

Brenda hears most of these objections right after she attempts to earn a commitment. She is now getting a little reluctant about asking her prospects for the order.

Brenda is sitting at her desk trying to figure out what to do next. She is not sure how to proceed.

Questions

1. What would you recommend Brenda do to handle the challenges she faces?
2. Brenda appears to have an advantage with her products and services. Develop a plan for Brenda to overcome the sales resistance she is receiving.
3. Use the LAARC process to develop a suggested dialogue Brenda can use to address one of the major types of resistance she is receiving.
4. What can Brenda do in the future to encounter less sales resistance when she asks for the order?

The Disgruntled Customer

It was 8:30 a.m. Friday morning when Brenda received the voice mail. It was Susan Swanson, owner of a small architecture firm, who Brenda had acquired as a customer nearly three months ago. "I'm finished with you all," she barked. "Come get my copier. I want my money back! This blasted machine you sold me keeps jamming. I was billed for extra toner that I never received. You promised me training, and I have yet to see any. And this machine is much slower than I thought it would be. I don't see how your company stays in business. I knew I should have gone with Xerox!"

It's true, Brenda had told Susan that she would provide training on how to use some of the advanced features of the copier. She had neglected to get back to Susan and since she had not heard from Susan she assumed Susan no longer desired the training. As for the paper jams, Brenda found this to be unusual. NCC carried high-quality copiers and she could not imagine what might be wrong. She was sure she had told Susan the specific type of paper to use for her application. However, using the wrong paper could lead to more frequent paper jams. But why hadn't Susan said anything to her about this sooner? As for the extra toner, Brenda recalls that Susan did order it and later contacted her to let her know that she had not received it. Brenda then contacted NCC's shipping department who said they would ship Susan the product. Brenda just assumed that it had been shipped. As for the speed of the machine, Brenda was certain its output was per specifications as equipment at NCC must pass strict quality control measures. Perhaps Susan simply misunderstood the machine's capabilities. *Wow,* Brenda thought, *now what am I going to do?*

Questions

1. How should Brenda handle this complaint?
2. What could Brenda have done to avoid this incident?
3. What steps can Brenda take to do a better job of maintaining open, two-way communication with Susan?
4. Assuming that Brenda can retain Susan as a customer, how can she add value to her relationship with Susan's firm?

Managing and Classifying Accounts

Brenda's planning and extra effort in servicing and developing her accounts continue to produce increasing levels of profitable business for NCC. Her methodical approach to identifying new prospects and building repeat business within her existing accounts has been observed by her sales manager as well as the regional vice president of sales. As a result of Brenda's consistent performance, she has been given the opportunity to expand her current list of accounts by taking over part of the account list of a retiring salesperson and integrating them into an expanded territory. Brenda is working through the account information files for each of these added accounts and has summarized the information into the following table.

Account Name	Account Opportunity	Competitive Position	Annual Number of Sales Calls (Last Year)
Maggie Mae Foods	Low	High	23
C³ Industries	High	Low	28
Trinity Engineering	High	High	28
Britecon Animations	High	High	22
Lost Lake Foods	High	Low	26
Attaway Global Consulting	High	High	24
Waits and Sons	Low	High	21
Reidell Business Services	High	High	26
Ferrell & Associates	Low	Low	16
Biale Beverage Corp	High	High	18
Captain Charlie's Travel	High	Low	23
Cole Pharmaceuticals	High	Low	20
PuddleJumper Aviation	Low	High	18
Tri-Power Investment Services	Low	Low	18
Ballou Resin & Plastics	Low	Low	14
Tri-Chem Customer Products	Low	High	20
Guardian Products	High	High	25
Bartlesville Specialties	Low	High	26

Questions

1. Develop a portfolio classification of Brenda's 18 new accounts. What is your assessment of the allocation of sales calls made by Brenda's predecessor over the previous year?
2. What specific suggestions would you make in terms of sales call allocation strategy for Brenda to make better use of available selling time in calling on these new accounts?
3. Develop a classification of these 18 accounts by using the single-factor analysis method. How do these results differ from the results from the portfolio analysis?
4. How might the differences between the single-factor analysis and the portfolio classification translate to increased selling effectiveness and efficiency for Brenda?

The Finish Line

It is two weeks before the end of the fiscal year for NCC. Brenda has already achieved her annual sales quota and is pleased with her performance this year. She knows that she has improved her sales skills and is doing a good job in each stage of the sales process. Her sales manager, Jin Tan, will be working with her in the field this week and then will be conducting her annual performance review and discussing it with her within the next month.

Jin Tan and Brenda have just completed a sales call together. Although Brenda did not get the sale, she thought she did a good job and thinks the prospect might contact her in the future about NCC copiers. Jin Tan, however, is disappointed that Brenda did not move the sales process forward. Although the prospect was not necessarily expected to buy during this presentation, Jin thought Brenda missed an opportunity to get the prospect to visit the NCC office for a copier demonstration. This would have moved the sales process forward.

Jin was also thinking about the annual performance reviews next month. This is always a tense time. Jin is generally satisfied with Brenda's performance last year and with her development as a salesperson. But, as indicated in the recent sales call, she needs to improve her skills in gaining commitment. Brenda could also be more productive if she became more proficient in using some of the new sales 2.0 technologies, especially LinkedIn. These are two areas Jin will address during the annual performance review meeting with Brenda.

Questions

1. Jin and Brenda have just finished the joint sales call and are meeting for a coaching session. Present an example of the dialogue that should take place during this meeting.
2. Develop a sales training program Jin might use to improve Brenda's skills in gaining commitment from prospects.
3. Explain to Brenda how she might use LinkedIn to increase her sales productivity.
4. Jin and Brenda are getting ready to have their annual performance meeting. How should Jin conduct this meeting to motivate Brenda to increase her performance next year?

Notes

Notes

Notes

Notes

Notes

Notes